KD2

DUNKIRK

Also by Sean Longden

To the Victor the Spoils
Hitler's British Slaves

DUNKIRK
The Men They Left Behind

SEAN LONGDEN

CONSTABLE • LONDON

Constable & Robinson Ltd
3 The Lanchesters
162 Fulham Palace Road
London W6 9ER
www.constablerobinson.com

First published in the UK by Constable,
an imprint of Constable & Robinson Ltd, 2008

ISBN 978-1-84529-520-2

Printed and bound in the EU

Dedicated to all those who were left behind forever.

Contents

Illustrations

A pre-war soldier of the Territorial Army displaying his kit,1939. Courtesy of Norman Barnett.

The retreat through Belgium and France. Imperial War Museum F4495.

A British medical officer attending a wounded soldier at St Maxent, May 1940. Imperial War Museum 4640.

Solider destroying petrol store. Imperial War Museum F4756.

Soldiers of the 51st Highland Division defending the line of the River Bresle, 7 June 1940. Imperial War Museum F4745.

Burning houses on the waterfront at St-Valery-en-Caux. Imperial War Museum RML 358.

British and French prisoners of war being marched from the cliff tops to the west of St-Valery-en-Caux. Imperial War Museum RML 399.

A mixed group of British and French prisoners of war are marched into captivity by the victorious Germans. Imperial War Museum RML 141.

British POWs near Calais, June 1940. Imperial War Museum AP 7271.

Letter in French to Jim Charters' parents. Courtesy of Jim Charters.

Official letter to Jim Charters' parents. Courtesy of Jim Charters.

Forged identification card. Imperial War Museum SJO/DOC2.

British evaders are picked up off the coast of North Africa by HMS *Kelvin*. Imperial War Museum 2430.

Repatriation of wounded soldiers. Imperial War Museum PL.13867.D.

Group shot at Stalag 21D, 1941. Courtesy of Eric Reeves.

British POWs photographed following their liberation by American troops, May 1945. Imperial War Museum AP 10772.F

Acknowledgements

The idea for *Dunkirk: The Men They Left Behind* emerged during the research for my previous book, *Hitler's British Slaves*. In conversation with former POWs, I realized that so much of the story about what had happened in 1940 had never been revealed to the public. Les Allan, one of the interviewees for my earlier book, stressed that he thought the story should be told and offered much help and advice with this project. He supplied me with the names of numerous other veterans who agreed to be interviewed for this book. My thanks go to the following: Eric Reeves, Bill Holmes, Fred Coster, Fred Goddard, Fred Gilbert, David Mowatt, Jim Reed, Jim Pearce, Dick Taylor, Jim Charters, Ernie Grainger, Graham King, Bob Davies, Cyril Holness, Norman Barnett and Major Peter Wagstaff. Sadly Fred Gilbert, Cyril Holness and Bob Davies passed away between their interviews and the publication of this book.

Two other veteran POWs, Gordon 'Nobby' Barber and Ken Willats, who I interviewed for my previous book, again helped by revealing the details of their experiences of capture in France in 1940.

Other veterans helped out with background on the situation in 1940, including Ken Dampier, Ron Burch, Sid Seal, Tony Hibbert and Noel Matthews. My thanks also go to Sylvie Norman, who telephoned from Canada to talk about the experiences of her husband Frank. Kerry McQueeney of the Croydon *Guardian* put me in touch with Cyril Holness and Norman Barnett – my thanks to her. I must also thank Fred Kennington, who kindly sent me a copy of his book *No Cheese After*

Dinner and helped me make contacts among veterans of the 51st Highland Division, including Mrs Arnott who kindly sent me a copy of her late husband Tommy's memoirs *A Long Walk to the Garden*.

In addition, my thanks go to staff at the National Archives who have constantly provided the files I need, when I need them. My thanks also go to the staff and trustees of the Imperial War Museum, in particular those in the Department of Documents whose help was, as ever, invaluable. I must thank the copyright holders for the following collections held at the Imperial War Museum for allowing me to reproduce quotations from their memoirs. Thanks to Jean Bolton for permission to quote from the papers of her brother, Walter Kite. Also to Margaret Foster for allowing me to quote her late husband Fred's poem in the introduction to this book. To Michael Watt for granting permission to quote his father Hugh Watt. To David Evans for allowing me to quote from the memoirs of his late father R. P. Evans. To Richard Wilson for permission to quote his late father. To Lorraine and Jeannette for granting permission to quote from the memoirs of their late father, William Simpson. To Betty Barclay for permission to quote her late husband, R. L. Barclay. To Frank Sweeney for permission to include his father's memoris of the sinking of the *Lancastria*. To Carolyn Christie for granting permission to quote from the memoirs of her late grandfather, John Christie. To Peter Trew for permission to quote from the memoirs of his late uncle, Harold Houthakker. To Cynthia Jones for permission to quote from the memoirs of her late father, E. Vernon Mathias. To the family of Bill Bampton for permission to quote from his memoirs. To Mrs Shorrock for granting permission for me to quote from the memoirs of her late husband Leslie. To Joan, who granted permission to quote from the papers of her late uncle, W. Hewitt. In the case of the papers of C. Raybould, V. Tattan and Major G. S. Lowden, I was unable to trace the copyright holders. Anyone having information should contact the Department of Documents at the Imperial War Museum.

I must also give thanks to my agent Andrew Lownie, my editor Leo Hollis, Geoff and Victoria at Arris for giving me my first break as a writer and to Beth and Bethan at MGA for their hard work on my earlier books. Finally, I must thank my wife Claire for all the advice she has offered and – in particular – her proof reading skills.

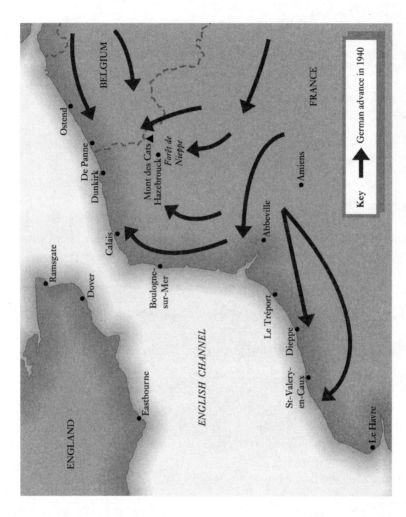

The German advance and encirclement of the British Expeditionary Force (BEF), May–June 1940.

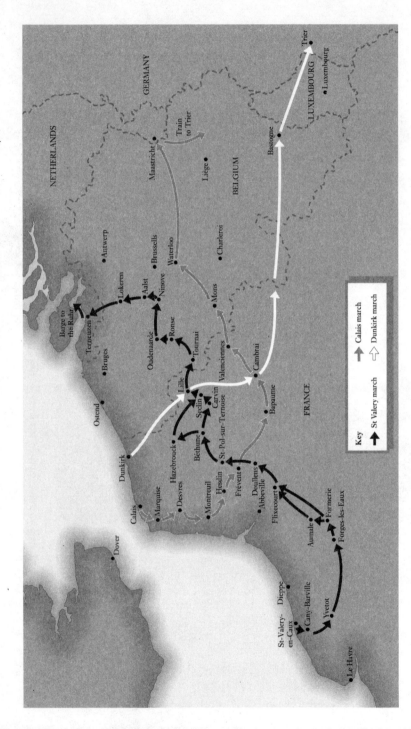

Some of the routes taken by British prisoners on the so-called 'Hell March', May–June 1940.

Prologue

'*Is anyone there? Is anyone there?*'[1] With these words General Harold Alexander signalled the end of the drama of Dunkirk. Searching along the quayside within the port and patrolling the waters beside the beach, the general held firmly onto his megaphone, calling out for any stragglers still waiting for evacuation. It was 2 a.m. on the morning of 3 June 1940. For six long, arduous days the beleaguered British Expeditionary Force (BEF) had been slowly but surely evacuated from the harbour and beaches of Dunkirk. For some, the story had seemed miraculous – somehow, with the enemy just miles away and their planes dominating the skies above the beaches, 338,226 soldiers had been embarked on ships and sent home to Britain. With their evacuation completed it was time for Operation Dynamo to end. As the last of the Royal Navy destroyers slipped safely away into the waters of the English Channel, there was nothing to do but draw the proceedings to a close.

When Alexander had allowed himself a final search of the perimeter, calling out to any who might yet remain on shore and receiving no reply, he returned to the harbour and boarded a waiting destroyer. Satisfied that the evacuation was complete, the order to set sail was given and the ship cast off, zig-zagging its way across the night waters towards Dover. As his ship tied up alongside the quay next morning, and the general disembarked to make his way to the War Office, the story of Dunkirk came to an end. Now it was time for the legend to grow.

However despite the ominous silence that had greeted Alexander as he scoured Dunkirk and its beaches for waiting troops, some men were still out there. Somewhere in the darkness were over 68,000 British soldiers who had never reached safety. On the beaches and sand dunes of Dunkirk, in the fields of Flanders, besides the roads and amidst the ruins, lay the corpses of hundreds who had not reached the boats. They had paid the ultimate price during the fighting retreat. They were not alone in their defeat. Elsewhere were hospitals full of the sick and wounded who had been left behind to receive treatment from the enemy's doctors. And further afield – still fighting hard alongside its French allies – was the entire 51st Highland Division, and a myriad of other units, some large and some small, whose war had not finished as the last boats slipped away from the port of Dunkirk.

Also scattered across the countryside were hundreds of lost and lonely soldiers. These were the 'evaders' who had missed the boats and evaded capture and were now desperately trying to make their own circutous ways home independently, whether by walking across France or rowing across the Channel. All that mattered was that they were heading home, no matter how long it took or how far their journey would take them.

But for the majority left behind, now prisoners of war, the journey was not to freedom. Hour upon hour, mile upon mile, day after day, they walked. The feet of the dejected and defeated men shuffled over the cobblestones of the seemingly endless roads. Shoulders hunched, staring at the ground in front of them, they moved ever onward. Beneath the searing summer sun the starving rabble continued their journey into the unknown. Like the remnants of some pitiful ancient tribe sold into slavery, they shuffled forwards. Stomachs shrunken and throats parched, they hardly dared think of the food and water that might bring salvation.

Some were half-carrying, half-dragging their sick and exhausted friends. Others, too weak to help the sick, were forced to abandon their mates at the roadside. Yet most simply trudged on in silence – men like twenty-one-year-old Ken Willats who just five months earlier had been a chef in a London restaurant. Now, not having seen food for days, he was too weak even to raise a hand to wipe a squashed fly from his forehead.

Desperate men summoned up their last vestiges of energy and fought for scraps of food. They dropped to their knees in ditches just to drink from the dirty brown water. At night they collapsed by the roadside, often deep in sleep before their heads touched the bare earth. Then, just a few short hours later, they dragged themselves to their feet again to continue their journey.

As they walked they listened to the shouts of their guards – screaming at them to hurry up – and to the cries of their comrades as blows rained down on those who hesitated. Whips, sticks, truncheons and rifle-butts beat the offenders back into line. For some the end to their misery came quickly, as the marching men listened for the tell-tale rifle crack that meant someone had finally given up and been executed by the roadside.

At last, after two weeks of painful marching across the country-side and through the villages of France, Belgium and Germany, the column of starving men arrived in the once great city of Trier, once the northern capital of the Roman Empire, one of the foremost cities in the ancient world. Yet the marching men, their empty bellies aching and bodies weakened, had not reached civilization. Instead they were paraded through the streets to the taunts and jeers of the inhabitants. Under a hail of spittle, the desperate men kept their heads down and marched onwards. Where once slaves had left Germany destined for Rome, now a vast new slave army was heading eastwards into the heart of Europe's newest empire, the Third Reich.

These forgotten men had fought the rearguard in northern France and paid the price of enabling their comrades to escape. These were not the legendary men who crossed the English

Channel in the 'little ships' ready to fight again. Destined for captivity, they would not see freedom for five long years.

These dreadful days were never forgotten by those who endured them. Yet somehow their sufferings never became part of the folklore of Second World War. They had fought the battles to ensure the successful evacuation of over 300,000 fellow soldiers at Dunkirk. Their sacrifice had brought the salvation of the British nation. Yet they had been forgotten whilst those who escaped to safety and made their way back home were hailed as heroes. It was an indignity that long remained in the minds of that defeated army.

Who could forget that ordeal? Certainly not Les Allan. Sixty years on he surveyed the rows of veterans parading through the streets of Dunkirk. Heads held high, chests swollen with pride and festooned with medals, the ageing veterans had gathered once more to commemorate the anniversary of the miraculous rescue of a defeated army from the beaches of Dunkirk. These were the men whose escape from under the noses of the advancing Germans had become so famous. None among them doubted the achievement of rescuing the forlorn force from the beaches of France, nor would any underestimate their sacrifices in the years that followed. Yet some among them, Les Allan included, had their own, very different, memories of the aftermath of Dunkirk – memories that were once more stirred up at the sight of the parading men.

Though many years had passed since 1940, the gallant veterans still marched in step as they approached the grandstand. Amidst the dignitaries Allan – former stretcher-bearer, BEF veteran, and prisoner of war – who had been granted his place as the founder of the National Ex-Prisoner of War Association, found his thoughts were immediately consumed by his own memories of suffering and sacrifice. As the parade came to a halt he leaned forward and called out to one of the men standing near him.

'Hey, mate, which POW camp were you in?'

'Twenty A,' came the reply. 'What about you?'

'Twenty B at Marienburg.'

After a brief conversation, the parade moved on. Perplexed, a veteran officer seated beside him turned to ask how he knew this man, amongst all the assembled ranks, was a fellow POW. Allan allowed himself a smile and replied.

'It's simple. Look at his chest. The blokes with the least medals are always the old POWs.'

He was right. There hadn't even been a campaign medal for those who fought in France in 1940. The Dunkirk POWs – the soldiers that were left behind – were men who had shared all the horrors of war but none of the glory.

Victory or Defeat?

Those men, the ones we left behind,
   Those beaches would not see,
Those men to whom fate was unkind,
   Had set their comrades free.
Those other men who would not see
   The safety of our shores,
For five more years would not be free,
   But prisoners of war.

Frederick Foster,
Royal West Kent Regiment[1]

Surely it was a miracle. Under the very eyes of the mighty German Army the beleaguered British Army had somehow returned home. Day after day, night after night, the evacuation had continued. Their decks crowded with the exhausted remnants of a battered and bloody army, the ships slipped quietly back across the dark waters of the Channel. Even if the waters had parted, like the Red Sea before Moses, to allow the soldiers to walk home, the watching world could hardly have been more surprised.

It was an exodus that seemed impossible, yet it had happened. All across Britain people celebrated – from the soldiers who reached the sanctuary of home, to the mothers, wives and lovers who awaited their safe return. As a nation rejoiced, the reality of what had happened was obscured. A disastrous defeat was somehow turned into a great victory. Yet as in all victories, it had come at a price – the surrender of the truth to a myth that has survived longer than most of the soldiers involved.

At first the evacuation had remained a secret. Newspapers were quite simply forbidden from reporting the events in France. Although the BEF had suffered a crushing defeat, the British people were not to be told of its humiliation. The fact that the BEF had been routed on the battlefield and driven back to the coast was not for public consumption. There was no choice but for the army to withdraw to England to lick its wounds. What followed was indeed a miracle. For an entire week the Royal Navy, and latterly the legendary 'little ships', transported 338,226 British, French and Belgian soldiers back across twenty miles of sea.

As the troopships, destroyers, barges, trawlers, ferries and plea-sure boats disgorged the vanquished army it soon became clear that the defeat could be concealed no longer. So the news was released and the story turned upside down, with the humiliation of defeat reported as a victorious escape. Even three days in, on 31 May, the first BBC report on the evacuation stressed that the British Army was returning home 'undefeated'. This was far from the truth, but the public knew no different. Indeed no one – not the journalists, politicians nor generals – wanted them to know different. The news was bleak, but for the people of an increasingly isolated nation this was something to celebrate – their sons had come home.

Whilst wounded, sick and dejected troops were hidden from sight, the British press heralded the men who had returned with a smile on their faces. Those who came home waving from train carriages, clutching their souvenirs, giving the thumbs-up and kissing the women who handed out tea and buns at railway stations became a thing of legend.

News spread across the world that Britain stood alone yet defiant. A haven for the soldiers, sailors, airmen and royal families of Europe's defeated nations, Great Britain used the escape from

Dunkirk as a clarion call for the fight against tyranny. In the skilful hands of Britain's new prime minister, Winston Churchill, the BEF's return became a propaganda triumph. As he told the world: 'The battle of France is over, the Battle of Britain is about to begin.'

Churchill's belligerent spirit helped raise the nation. Britain had not folded like its European allies, instead the army had come home. The nation had rallied and was ready to fight another day. Germany's inability to crush the British forces on the sands of Dunkirk was a turning point in their fortunes. A failure to extract those troops from the beaches would have left Britain defenceless. With no army left to fight, Britain would have been forced to sue for peace or have been an easy target for a Nazi invasion.

Yet this never happened. They had lived to fight another day and Dunkirk had become the springboard to victory. Although, there would be no quick win – the battle in France may have been lost but one battle does not make a war – from Dunkirk grew the legend of the plucky British Army, outclassed on the battlefield, withdrawing against all the odds but sailing home across the Channel. It was the classic tale of the British underdog. The 'little ships' that ferried the soldiers home grew to symbolize a spirit of improvisation. The Nazis may have created a powerful modern, mechanized army but even all the iron and steel of its war machine could not crush the spirit of the British nation.

The emerging legend was perfectly suited to the mood of defiance that swept the country that summer. 1940 was Winston Churchill's year – the year of Dunkirk; the rush to volunteer for the Home Guard; the glamour and excitement of the legendary 'Few' who defended the skies during the Battle of Britain and the enduring Blitz spirit. This was the year that Churchill and the British people raised two defiant fingers to their enemies across the Channel. In the nation's moment of peril there was no time to dwell on defeat – or on the defeated.

Yet hidden beneath this tale was an untold story. As time passed, historians revisited the Dunkirk story many times but the public had not yet learnt how the army had been unceremoniously defeated. They did not hear of the failure of BEF officers at all levels. Nor did they the read the details of drunken soldiers who refused calls to leave the cellars of Dunkirk and proceed for embarkation. In the mythology there was no room for tales of the failure of a poorly trained army, nor for stories of men scrambling to board boats being shot or forced away at gunpoint. Nor was the full story revealed of how the figures for the miraculous Dunkirk evacuation only talked of men who escaped via one port. Forgotten were more than 100,000 men whose escape to the UK came via a host of other coastal towns, from Normandy to the Bay of Biscay.

It would be many years before the real story of the evacuation even began to be told. Richard Collier's 1961 book *The Sands of Dunkirk* was one of the first to reveal much of the chaos, indiscipline and terror that had been obscured by the myth. Later works like Walter Lord's *The Miracle of Dunkirk* and Nicholas Harman's *Dunkirk – The Necessary Myth* further helped to balance the story.

However, even in all these works one detail has remained missing. These stories ended with the final evacuations from the beaches of Dunkirk, drawing a veil over the desperate fate of those left behind.

As the boats sailed off they had abandoned 2,472 guns, nearly 65,000 vehicles and 20,000 motorcycles. In the chaos of retreat they had also left behind 416,000 tons of stores, over 75,000 tons of much-needed ammunition and 162,000 tons of petrol.

More shocking than all this, however, was a single chilling statistic – 68,111 men of the BEF did not return home across the Channel at all. Thousands were the dead, wounded or missing but almost 40,000 British soldiers were alive and already being marched off into a captivity that would last for five long years.

However, back at home in Britain, rather than mourning for the defeated or lost, people felt they had something to celebrate. There was a genuine outpouring of excitement and relief that the majority of the army had come home safely and were ready to defend Britain's shores from its enemies. In homes the length and breadth of Great Britain families rejoiced when they heard the news that their sons had returned. The war may not have been over but their loved ones had survived to fight another day. For the moment, that was enough.

At the Reeves family home in Reigate, a mother, father and siblings celebrated the safe return of their eldest son, Les, from France. For them, the nation's collective relief had been a very personal one – their boy had survived. The joyous mood in the house continued for a few days until a lone voice cut through the celebrations. It was Ivy, the soldier's sister. She had been thinking and had suddenly realized something was missing. Finally she asked the question that had been troubling her: 'But hang on a minute, didn't our Eric go to France as well? Where's he?'

In all the excitement their younger son had been forgotten. As they spoke, nineteen-year-old Eric Reeves was trudging forlornly along the roads of northern France, destined for a German prisoner of war camp. It would be five years before he would return home to tell his story. Like almost 40,000 of his comrades, he was one of Dunkirk's forgotten heroes – one of the men they left behind.

CHAPTER ONE

Missing the Boat

The truth of the last day will never be published.

Major R.L. Barclay, 44th Division
RASC, writing to his wife in June 1940
following his return from France[1]

Looming high above the fields of Flanders, this seemed to be an obvious vantage point. Like some wooded island crowned with a medieval monastery, the Mont des Cats gave its occupiers a vast and unrivalled panorama both eastwards into Belgium and westwards across the landscape of France. But as the month of May 1940 drew to a close there was only one view that really mattered. Twenty miles to the north-east plumes of smoke were rolling skywards – rising above the flames of Dunkirk.

A few days previously this had been a depot for the British Army, a dump for vehicles and stores. But with the spearpoint of the German blitzkrieg plunging through Belgium, pushing back the Allied armies ever westwards, the Mont des Cats was no longer a rear echelon sanctuary. Instead it had become a hastily improvised strongpoint. With his troops forced back into France, Major-General Edmund Archibald Osborne, commanding officer of the 44th Infantry Division, had assembled them on the only available high ground. Originally an officer in the Royal Engineers,

who had served with honour in the fields of Flanders during the
Great War, Osborne was the very picture of the old-fashioned
British general. With his service dress, riding breeches and boots,
grey hair and clipped military moustache he seemed to epitomize
just how out of date the British Army had become. In the era of
blitzkrieg, of air support, carrier-borne infantry, paratroopers and
tanks, Osborne seemed to reflect the days of the static trench
warfare of his first conflict.

To the senior officers of the British Expeditionary Force, men
like Major-General Osborne, this was the textbook defensive
position. It had everything they needed, a commanding view of
the lands around, plenty of cover for the troops and, most
importantly, it sat immediately in the face of the enemy advance.

For others that was exactly the problem. Footsore and weary
after days of fighting and retreating in the face of the advancing
'lightening war', the men of the 4th Battalion Royal Sussex
Regiment were less impressed by the sight. Certainly this was a
fine defensive position – any fool could see that – but there was
something far more important to them. Sitting high upon the only
hill for miles around, they were conspicuous – they were a target.
For twenty-two-year-old Private Bill Holmes it was a relief not to
be marching, but war had entered his life swiftly and viciously and
it was about to get worse. As he would later describe it, with the
deliberate understatement so common to the British infantryman:
'We really had a dose there. The British Army really did some silly
things – for one thing, we were right on the top of the hill. So the
Germans just kept bombing it! It was the most stupid thing they
could have planned.'

These were strong words for such an inexperienced soldier. Just
nine months earlier Holmes had been working on his father's farm in
East Sussex. His had been a simple life, one so common in the
countryside of pre-war Britain. There were few luxuries, he worked
hard from dawn till dusk, tending the animals and maintaining the
orchards that provided the family with its income. But along with
the hard work came a slow pace of life that made the long hours

tolerable. In many ways it was an idyllic existence, one which none in the village had realized would soon be over. In these final days before war, horses still worked the land, many homes were still without electricity or relied on pumped water. Through the spring and summer of 1939, as war had approached, the young men inhabiting this world were slowly caught up in political machinations that seemed so far removed from their own world. When Holmes and his mates went to the cinema in nearby Haywards Heath, they saw newsreels revealing what was going on in Europe, but still it all seemed so distant. What did the Sudentenland, the Munich crisis or Hitler's insistent sabre rattling mean to them?

Then in summer 1939, with war seemingly inevitable, the outside world finally took a grasp of the towns and villages of Britain. The government's announcement that it was to form a militia from more than 200,000 men, aged twenty and twenty-one, was a firm declaration of intent. It may not have been a full-scale mobilization, but it was one more step on the road to war. Each man called up to the militia was told he would serve just six months and then be released back into civilian life as a trained infantryman, ready to be called up in the event of war. Like all his mates, Bill Holmes had registered for the militia in July. Now he was certain war would come. This knowledge could not help but affect their lives: 'I had a summer of freedom, but in the back of my mind I knew what was going to happen.' It was the calm before the storm.

When his call-up papers had arrived, falling ominously onto the doormat of the family cottage, Holmes' father had made him a stark offer. He could apply for his son to be excused service, to register as an essential worker, since farming could be classed as a reserved occupation. The youngster had considered the offer but realized he could never accept. Quite simply, he knew that to remain at home would seem like a betrayal of his mates, all of whom would themselves be going to war. It was a decision that would trouble him many times in the five long years that followed.

Sitting atop the Mont des Cats, with shells bursting around him and machine-gun fire raking the hillside, it was easy for these thoughts to return to his mind. Just eight months before, he had said goodbye to his mates and headed off to the barracks at Chichester. Life in the army was a shock to most of the new recruits, but for those from quiet villages it made all the more impact upon their lives. 'Suddenly nothing was private anymore – like showering with other people. That took a bit of getting used to, but in the end you were as bad as everyone else. The others were nearly all London lads – a rough old bunch, but a good bunch. You couldn't be a weakling among them.'

These new soldiers may have learned to live together but they had still not learned all the skills of the infantryman. Compared to the well-trained forces heading towards them the British soldiers were, in the most part, mere novices. That said, they were not fools.

In the world of the tacticians and military theorist, of the generals and staff officers with their grandiose plans and years of experience, the views of novice soldiers like Bill Holmes were ridiculously simple. Such men did not understand the art of war. And yet he was right when he pondered the wisdom of their positions on the Mont des Cats. Every German gunner could range his shells onto the hill. Every Luftwaffe pilot could spot the monastery or the windmill and unload his deadly cargo with hardly a chance of missing. And every soldier of the Wehrmacht, from the lowliest private to the mightiest general, knew the British Army would occupy the hill.

As Holmes and his comrades in the 44th Division awaited the German assault on their positions, they had a brief moment to look back on all that had happened in the previous weeks. The British Army had been engaged in a valiant attempt to stall the German advance. They had held hideously exposed positions on the riverbanks and canalsides that crisscrossed the low-lying fields of Belgium and northern France. As a review of the campaign commissioned by the War Office later revealed, defensive positions on canals and rivers caused immense problems for the defenders: they could not patrol, did not hold the high ground, were unable to camouflage their positions competently and could not counterattack. All they could do was dig trenches, blow bridges, fortify houses and pray they might hold off the rampaging force that had launched itself across the Low Countries.

Britain's almost total lack of preparedness seemed reflected in the situation experienced at the Mont des Cats. Just a few short months earlier, this vast new army of regular soldiers, reservists, Territorials, new recruits and conscripts to the British Army had laughed at their situation. Following the declaration of war, thousands of new soldiers had arrived at barrack rooms and drill halls across Britain only to be issued with uniforms, weapons and equipment that seemed like museum pieces. Many had started their military careers in uniforms little changed since the last great conflict: boots that had been date-stamped '1920' and packed in grease for nearly twenty years; rifles that had last seen service in their fathers' hands back in the Great War; 'pisspot' helmets; cloth puttees – all relics of some long forgotten era of warfare. As they stumbled across the parade grounds and agonized over polishing brasses, boots and buttons, they had taken some comfort in the constant claims that war would last no more than a few months. All could laugh at ill-fitting uniforms and the caps that seemed to litter the parade ground every time the drill-sergeants shouted instructions.

Yet there was a sober fact behind this comic spectacle. Following the Great War the British Army had been allowed to run down to a state in which it was hardly equipped for modern warfare. Only in 1932, after more than ten years of neglect, had the government admitted that something needed to be done. Even so, it took two further years of talking before any real changes began to be made. As the British government discussed rearmament, its potential enemies had pushed forward with modernizing their fighting forces. Even after rapid expansion and investment in the armies following the Munich crisis, the British Army had still been left lagging far behind its enemies. As Lord Gort, the commander of the BEF, wrote in a report about the territorial units under his command: 'The standard of training is low and in my opinion, against a first-class enemy they are as yet fit only for static warfare.'

He was blunt in his assessment that they 'possessed little more than token equipment.'[2]

Gort's assessment was spot-on: one officer in an anti-aircraft unit recalled that after four years in the Territorial Army he had learned no more than basic drill and knot-tying. In one tank unit the crews were only allowed to attend lectures on tank warfare after they had perfected sword drill. A War Office report of early 1939 had given a stark indication of the problems faced by the army:

> The instruction is incompetent. The instructors almost without exception, lack general intelligence; they have learnt the lessons parrot fashion and can only teach in that fashion; they cannot answer questions which are not in the drill book, and finally their method and speed of instruction is entirely ill-suited to their audience. They take in fact an hour to teach what their hearers can all fully grasp in five minutes . . . the system of training throughout the TA seems to have been designed to suit the stupidest class of recruits i.e. the rural ploughman.[3]

There had been no more than a few short months of vigorous training to realign the mentality of the pre-war army and mould the expanding force into something fit for the modern battlefield. Despite the rigorous efforts that had taken place during 1939 – doubling the size of the Territorial Army, introducing new weapons and equipment and the induction of 200,000 men into the militia – it was easy for the men of this new army to realize that the nation was unprepared for war. Every man among them had watched in awe as the weekly newsreels displayed the might of the German war machine – modern aircraft, column after column of vicious-looking tanks, row upon row of field artillery, deadly machine-guns, tracked troop-carrying vehicles and unflinching belief in both the might and right of their cause – everything an army could need to guarantee victory.

Despite the visible might of the German Army there remained a dogged self-belief within Britain's armed forces. After all, by the end of April 1940 there were 394,165 British soldiers in France, with more still on their way. More than 235,000 were in the main fighting force, over 17,000 were training in France to join the main force and nearly 80,000 were performing duties in the lines of communication. In addition there were also 9,000 men on their way to join their units, over 2,500 unallocated soldiers and over 23,000 serving at various HQs. On paper, though small compared to the French Army, this seemed a formidable fighting force.

For almost a year the media had fed the public a diet of propaganda about how their troops would 'Hang out the washing on the Siegfried Line' and myths about how the tanks they had seen on the German newsreels were actually made of cardboard. Such stories had boosted public confidence, but by 1940 their light-hearted tone was no longer appropriate. Almost from the very moment the Germans had launched their assault on 10 May, the smile had been wiped from the collective face of the British Army. As one NCO noted in his diary, his company went to war with just fifty rounds of ammunition per man, one box of hand grenades and only seven rounds for their Boyes anti-tank rifle. There was no longer anything humorous about being part of an army that had gone to war in requisitioned delivery lorries and butchers' vans that had been hastily repainted as machines of warfare.

Awaiting the assault at the Mont des Cats, Bill Holmes realized war was no longer a joke. Like all his comrades he had heard the tales of cardboard tanks and aircraft – he'd even listened to lectures on them back at his barracks – but now he knew the truth. They were real, made of steel and very, very dangerous.

Among the thousands of men who gathered on the Mont des Cats, or streamed back towards Dunkirk, there were few that had not shared a vicious introduction to war. At daybreak on 10 May the long-awaited German offensive had begun, with the Luftwaffe striking at Allied airbases across northern France. At a quarter to six that morning the BEF received the official *alerte* from the French High Command and then half an hour later the British Head-quarters issued the immediate order to advance. The so-called Dyle

Plan entailed a sixty-mile advance through Belgium to take up positions along a seventeen-mile section of the River Dyle between Wavre and Louvain. To their left the Belgian Army were to hold the line and to their right it was the responsibility of the French. This was the moment of truth, the point at which they discovered whether all the propaganda had been no more than myth and whether their hurried training had been worthwhile. They were about to learn the harsh truth behind the prophetic words of a report written by Lord Gort exactly one month before: 'The clash, when it comes, will be violent.'[4]

Despite the violence sweeping the Low Countries, morale had remained high. Such confidence was openly expressed on 16 May when Lt.-Colonel Chitty of the 4th Battalion Royal West Kent Regiment, like Bill Holmes' regiment a part of the 44th Home Counties Division, had issued the following message to his men: 'We are now on the eve of one of the great moments in the history of our Empire. The struggle will be hard and long but we can be confident of final victory.'[5] Yet for all the confident predictions expressed publicly by some officers, there were plenty among them who were less certain of what the future might bring. Second-Lieutenant Peter Wagstaff, a young officer also serving in the 44th Division, as a platoon commander in the 1/6th Battalion of the Queen's Regiment, was certain Britain was not ready for war. He felt there was a smug complacency about Britain's belief it could wage war against the Germans. As a twenty-year-old Supplementary Reserve officer serving in a Territorial Army battalion, of whose officers only two were regular soldiers, he recognized the lack of awareness of modern warfare displayed by so many in the British Army:

Our defensive position was dug on the same zig-zag lines of the First World War – I still remember the specifications that the parapets had to be so high – it was chaos. Do you realise I had a Lewis gun from First World War in my platoon, instead of a Bren Gun? I think I'm right in saying we had two wireless sets in the battalion. One to brigade HQ and brigade had two, one to battalion and one to division. For messages I was given a message book. If I wanted to communicate with the platoon, or company, next door I wrote it down, gave it to my runner and said 'Off you go'. Poor little bugger goes off and, if he didn't get shot on the way, the message would arrive. It was incredible! There was a horrible foreboding. We didn't know what was going to hit us.

He later summed up the uncertainty of the period following the opening of the German offensive, when he wrote of 'a great fear engulfing me and the realisation of what exactly I had to face . . . I passed through an hour of complete dread and the realisation of the responsibility entailed by those lives under my command and not knowing whether I would come through or not.'[6] He was not alone in expressing anxiety for the future. On the same day that Lt.-Colonel Chitty had told his men of his optimism for the outcome of the battles ahead, the French commander in chief was admitting to Churchill that his armies had no reserves and that, effectively, all was lost.

Despite the depth of such feeling, in the days immediately following the opening of the German offensive there was little reason for the optimists to be doubted. As they had crossed the Belgian frontier on 12 May, the men of the 44th Division could not fail to notice the enthusiastic flag-waving hordes that emerged to welcome them. Despite the welcome, there was a darker side to the experience, something that was noted by few but the officers whose job it was to make contact with the Belgian authorities. It seemed they were not gripped by the same sense of defiance displayed by their people. Maybe they just knew too much about the reality of the situation, or maybe they were simply drained by the notion that their lands would once again become the battleground of Europe's great powers. Whatever their reason, one British intelligence officer noted how they were 'singularly uncooperative or caught completely with their trousers down'.[7] As one unit approached the border they were stopped by frontier guards who refused to allow them passage. The situation was resolved when a British lorry charged the barrier and the advance continued.

For the troops advancing through France and into Belgium, this scarred landscape offered a constant reminder of the vicious impact of war. The names of the places they passed through were chillingly familiar to them all: Ypres, Cambrai, the Somme valley, Vimy, Mons – all locations infamous for their connection with the Great War. The ruins of homes and signs of hasty repairs had been a constant sight on their travels. Most ominously, they marched past the innumerable cemeteries, shrines and memorials that had sprung up in the aftermath of war. As the men of 1940 slogged their way through the morning mist they appeared like ghosts of that earlier generation who had fallen in battle. When they looked at the names of the dead and missing, few did not feel an eerie sense of disquiet. These were the fallen comrades of the own fathers. These were the names of young men who, just like themselves, had been called to the colours to fight the Germans.

Yet unlike their forebears, the new BEF would not halt the advancing enemy. It soon became clear the Dyle Plan had exposed the weakness of Allied planning. French thinking was submerged deep in the bunkers and tunnels of the Maginot Line. Whatever Germany did the French believed the strength of their defences would prove sufficient. Such singular faith in static defence strangled any hope of innovation. With France's obstinate belief in the infallibility of the Maginot Line, and Lord Gort's British Expeditionary Force placed under command of the French, the British role, along with French and Belgian units, was to hold firm on the French flank.

The Allies had been further hampered by the Belgian government and its belief the Germans would respect its neutrality. As a result, Belgium had initially refused the British and French Armies permission to cross its frontiers to take up positions along the German border. Their naïve hopes had been cruelly dashed when the Germans punched across the frontier. Even with the British and French Armies coming to their aid, the Belgian forces had little hope of holding out. All their major defensive positions were soon redundant as the Germans advanced. As a result, the British found themselves occupying not carefully considered and fortified positions, but hastily dug trenches. The Dyle Plan had envisaged the Belgians holding out for long enough for them to fortify the line, something that had soon proved impossible. By the time most of the British units approached their intended positions the Belgian Army was already in retreat.

Furthermore, the River Dyle did not offer the ideal defensive position since it was little more than a wide stream, with heavily wooded banks, within a valley between 500 and 1,500 yards (450–1,370 metres) wide. Added to that, the Germans advanced to occupy the eastern banks, thus holding the high ridge that gave them a commanding view of the British positions. The folly of those who had planned the move into Belgium was not lost on the men of the BEF. They had laboured for months to build comfortable dugouts and well-fortified positions across northern France. Yet these were abandoned to do battle in hastily scraped-out holes in the fields and canalsides of Belgium.

Despite the clear deficiencies in the plan, the morale in the British Army remained high. There was a self-belief that even in defeat seemed hard to extinguish. Bill Holmes and his comrades in the Sussex Regiment were no different. As twenty-year-old Sid Seal, a pre-war Territorial and one of Holmes's mates, explained: 'It was all a big adventure. It was our first time out of England. We were all in it together – all mates together. I knew all the boys in the regiment. We were all enjoying it.'

At first the situation for them and the rest of the 44th Division had been relatively safe, as they held reserve positions behind the intended front line. They had even found comfortable billets in a flax factory where the footsore infantrymen bedded down for the night in the soft flax. In the days that followed the crossing of the Belgian border they had a gradual introduction to war. There had been patrols to carry out, trenches to dig and strong-points to fortify. Yet there were soon ominous signs of the reality of the situation on the Belgian front. Just four days after the opening of the German assault, patrols of the 4th Sussex encountered Belgian troops who had withdrawn from around Brussels. Three days later the same men found themselves sent out to control the tide of refugees who had begun to crowd the roads, all desperate not to be caught up in the battles. It was not until eleven days after the opening of the offensive that they finally faced the reality of war. On 21 May they met troops from the Royal West Kent Regiment who had been forced back from positions along the River Escaut. Attempts were also made to reconnoitre positions to the north but word came that the front ahead of them had collapsed, rendering the planned reconnaissance futile. At 5 p.m. that day the battalion moved to the village of Anseghem where they came under artillery fire. The battalion's first fatal casualties were Captain Watson and Private Hemmings. They may have been the first, but they were certainly not the last. As the evening progressed no one bothered to keep any further record of where and when casualties were inflicted.

The refugees encountered by the troops soon became a constant reminder of the terrifying disruption and dislocation caused by war. Military Police who attempted to control the first waves, noted how the first they encountered were wealthy Belgian and Dutch refugees. These appeared with their cars, carrying mattresses, blankets, pillows and eiderdowns tied firmly to the roofs. Atop of the bedding were tied bicycles, prams and even children's scooters. There was something resolutely bourgeois about the people within, as they sat there dressed in their Sunday best with the car windows firmly shut despite the summer heat.

The following day they watched as more refugees arrived. First came the young people who had cycled ahead of the Germans, desperate to reach safety. Next came the most forlorn of all those who had left their homes. There were weary pensioners pushing handcarts, and mothers pushing prams loaded with both babies and family heirlooms. The roads were clogged with farm carts pulled by broad Flemish horses, all loaded high with household goods. There were ancient buses, crammed with refugees and their luggage, whose engines wheezed as they struggled to transport their loads. In the town of Avesnes British soldiers were shocked when the strangest of all refugee vehicles appeared. It was the lumbering hulk of a steamroller. Pulled behind it were two large farm carts carrying around thirty people. Behind that were two cows, tied to the wagons by rope.

In some towns and villages the soldiers watched as the pitiful columns arrived. As they passed through, their numbers were swelled by locals who decided they too should join the rush to escape to safety. Once the columns had departed, the local trades-men finally shut up shop and joined the exodus.

Although many of the refugees came from rural communities, there were few animals among them. There were the ever-present horses pulling carts, and a few dogs trotting faithfully beside their masters, but little else. Some families had birdcages tied to the top of their possessions but most pets had been left behind. Every-where, farm animals stood dejectedly in their pens, as if expecting to be let out into the fields. Livestock seemed to stare at the retreating soldiers, their eyes pleading for the feed their owners had neglected to leave for them. Dogs barked desperately for food, as they strained at the chains that restricted their movements and prevented their joining the hordes fleeing the front. The most wretched among the animals were executed by retreating soldiers unable to endure the miserable sight of the abandoned creatures starving to death.

For the refugees, there was a sense of hopelessness and confusion. They had left their homes far behind them but had no idea when they might reach safety. Exhausted people collapsed at the road-sides and burst into tears. Babies screamed, children cried and mothers wept — but everyone kept moving westwards. When asked where they were going, the people simply shrugged their shoulders and kept shuffling aimlessly towards the horizon.

The true nature of warfare was most brutally exposed, not by the sad sight of civilians trudging away from the front lines, but by the carnage inflicted upon them by the Luftwaffe. The sight of German fighters and bombers sweeping down to attack refugee columns became a regular feature of the retreat. Many soldiers avoided any contact with the slow-moving columns that were such an easy target. Instead they hurried past them or took detours across fields. Some among the troops experienced a strange sense of calm as they sheltered beneath trees and watched as the exposed refugees were attacked by German warplanes.

For Bill Holmes, his introduction to war came when the enemy bombed a bridge across the Albert Canal:

> The noise was terrifying. It was hell. The Stukas came right down at us. It was the first time I was really shaken. The planes blew up the bridge along with all the refugees who were on it. That horrified me, it was a terrible thing to see. There were women pushing prams along and they were all blown up. We saw bits and pieces of bodies everywhere. It really takes a toll on you. Especially when it's the bodies of little kiddies. It was something you can't forget – people really are worse than animals.

For all the horrors and hardship he endured in the days, then years, that followed, this one image haunted Holmes for the rest of his life.

Despite the horrors, the soldiers had no choice but to keep moving. One observer attempted to explain why he was able to watch the slaughter of civilians without being troubled by the scenes: 'It was not that we were callous, we were not horrified nor indignant, it simply was we were disinterested . . . Did we feel it and know it. We could not. We were living in a continuous present and our consciousness was not registering.'

Amidst the crowds fleeing westwards were gangs of French, Belgian and Dutch soldiers. Some were disciplined, still fully armed and carrying their kit. Dutch soldiers on bicycles weaved in and out of the marching throng. Belgian recruits – called up when their homeland was invaded and who had been issued nothing more than a scarlet army blanket – appeared in the confusion, uncertain of where they should go or what their role was supposed to be. One gang of Belgian recruits told British MPs they had been ordered to cycle to the French town of Albert to report, little knowing the town would be in German hands long before they arrived. Whilst they pedalled away, eager to receive arms and uniforms ready to defend their homeland, others simply sat around in town squares as if waiting for someone – anyone – to tell them what to do. At Boulogne 1,800 unarmed sixteen-year-old Belgian Army recruits turned up and requested they be immediately shipped to England to be trained. When one British NCO watched as his men passed a gang of dispirited French soldiers, he decided to demonstrate that his own men were not yet beaten. The French-men were leaderless, unshaven and had abandoned their weapons. With a precision born of years on the parade ground, the NCO called his men to fall in and march in step, showing their Allies how soldiers should behave.

Yet such displays were futile. No amount of parade-ground precision could stop the rout. Such was the clamour to flee the advancing Germans that families upped and left their homes at a moment's notice. British soldiers found themselves entering aban-doned houses, with the tables laid for breakfast and the food still warm. It was as if the population of whole villages had become invisible. Yet the truth was simpler – they had joined the flight westwards without pausing to think of what might happen. One group of retreating soldiers were asked by some Belgian women to show them how to drive the family car – their brother was the only one with experience of driving but he had left to join the army. After a few brief moments of instruction the women drove away, the gears straining as they endeavoured to flee as fast as possible.

The story was the same across the front. The British attempted to hold their positions but could do little to stem the advance of the enemy. At Audenarde on 19 May, the 4th Battalion of the Royal West Kent Regiment had been ordered to make a stand, something they had done with great success. For two days they held out against an enemy assault that had begun with thirty bombs dropped on their positions, inflicting twenty casualties. In the action that had followed, the West Kents stunned the enemy with a perfectly coordinated counterattack. First the British mortars had struck the enemy positions, then swift attacks had come in from Bren carriers, pouring fire at the German flanks, targeting troops who had fled the mortaring. After each attack the carriers swiftly withdrew then struck again at a different position. By the time the enemy replied with mortar fire the carriers were long gone, their crews already drinking beer outside a cafe to celebrate their bluff. Despite the valiant efforts of units such as the West Kents, there was little they could do to stem the advance and they eventually withdrew, joining in the retreat with a twenty-mile overnight march.

There were plenty of heroic encounters that brought the Germans to a halt, but these were not enough to prevent collapse across the whole front. Hundreds of men were sacrificed in engagements that became futile when officers discovered that neighbouring units had retreated, leaving their flanks exposed. When the troops saw their allies, the Belgians or the French, withdrawing in such a manner it was the source of immense distrust. The growing sense of disharmony between the Allies would continue in the weeks that followed, with all sides accusing each other of betrayal.

Unknown to the soldiers fighting in the north, theirs was not the only battle being fought. The advance to the River Dyle was further revealed as a folly as the Germans had surged through the Ardennes and punched through the French positions. By 13 May advanced parties had crossed the River Meuse near Sedan. The next day a full attack went in along the Meuse, preceded by a vicious aerial assault on the French defenders. This was the move that determined the entire campaign. With the British only making initial contact with the enemy at the Dyle, they were already threatened from the rear. Led by General von Rundstedt's Army

Group A, the German forces swung northwards, along the Somme valley and towards the Channel, thus potentially trapping the British and French Armies with their backs to the sea.

The unfolding chaos of the drama facing the British became clear to one Royal Artillery officer, Lieutenant Tony Hibbert, as he moved his battery into a hillside position ready to face the enemy outside Armentières, where he expected an attack from the north-east:

> It was pure chaos. I went to the top of the hill and found a battery of guns on the other slope of the hill facing the other way. I knew the chap, I'd trained at Woolwich with him. I pointed north-east and said 'Nice to see you, but just in case it has slipped your attention but the Boche are that way.' He replied 'I know, but just in case it has slipped your attention, if you happen to look through your binoculars in the other direction you'll see a column of dust.' It was a lovely clear day and I could see it about three or four miles away. He said 'That is the head of an armoured column that is zapping along this road and will soon be in range.' He asked for my help and I offered the assistance of my guns, which were ack–ack guns that were able to fire anti tank rounds. He replied 'My dear boy, The very thing! Do come and join us.'

But by the time Hibbert had returned to his guns the order had already come through to retreat to form the perimeter at Dunkirk, where his guns continued to engage the enemy until their ammunition was exhausted.

Caught between the twin pincers of the blitzkrieg, and trapped amidst the crowds of refugees, the British had little choice but to fall back into an ever-shrinking pocket. At first the fall back through Belgium had been intended to strengthen the line, hoping that by ensuring a balance between the British, French and Belgian forces their defences could hold. Yet, as each day passed, it became more obvious that something had to be done to prevent the enemy reaching the sea and trapping the BEF.

Day by day the troops fought vicious engagements, falling back by night to occupy the next defensive line. Each day the British withdrew proud in the knowledge that at no point had the enemy broken the British line. Thus the troops, unaware of the danger of being cut off by the enemy's advance to the south, were uncertain why they were falling back. Between 16 and 19 May the BEF withdrew, first from the Dyle to the Senne, then to the River Dendre, then to the Escaut Line. At every canal and riverbank the troops fought rearguard actions to give the engineers long enough to demolish bridges; at Audenarde just six pioneers were ordered to hold a one-mile front. Many among the retreating men noticed how every bridge they seemed to cross had a representative of the Royal Engineers standing at the roadside awaiting the opportunity to blow the bridge once the majority of the Allied forces had crossed.

Surrounded by their exhausted comrades, the troops faced an almost constant struggle to keep moving. In the dark days of the retreat, physical strength, and indeed the mental will to keep marching, had an impact upon so many among them. Each step strained their last reserves of energy. Men stumbled from the roads and collapsed into ditches. Sleeping men somehow managed to summon up enough strength to remain upright and kept dragging one foot in front of the other. Like automatons, they keep shuffling along the roads to an unknown destination. All that mattered was that they were still alive – the lack of water assaulted their throats, the desire for hot food aggravated their bellies – but every step westwards was a step nearer home and safety.

If marching taxed their dwindling reserves of energy, then to halt and have to prepare defensive positions only deepened their misery. The experiences of the 2nd Battalion of the Gloucestershire Regiment reflected the experiences of thousands of retreating soldiers. In one day they marched thirty miles, much of the time wearing gas masks, the result of unfounded rumours about im-minent chemical attacks. Despite the heat of the summer sun they had marched onwards, the sweat collecting inside the rubber of their masks. The dust they kicked up from the roads as they marched further heightened their sense of despondency when the battalion's exhausted anti-tank gunners mistakenly shot-up two British tanks. As the battalion's adjutant later wrote, the men were 'drunk from lack of sleep.'[8] But if the Gloucesters were exhausted, the effects of the weather, constant marching, lack of hot food and shortage of sleep had an even greater effect on their officers whose responsibilities prevented them taking proper rest: 'To stop moving: to sit down was to sleep at once. To obey an order was simple, to have to give one was torture to the brain. The desire for sleep predominated all others.'[9] At one briefing of three officers it was found that none had been awake all the time. Eventually the meeting was abandoned when the adjutant had fallen asleep for the fourth time. At another briefing officers arrived, saluted the CO, then immediately sank to the floor and fell asleep. Once all the officers were slumbering, a liaison officer was forced to wake them. Eventually the RSM placed an upturned bayonet into his belt. His logic was simple, if he fell asleep, his head would slump forward, then the bayonet would prick him and cause him to awake.

Despite such deprivations, the BEF had slogged onwards, seldom more than one step ahead of the enemy. As they retreated, the troops were struck by the contrast between their advance into Belgium to meet the enemy and the disarray that now surrounded them. One unit had engaged the enemy for a total of thirty-six hours and then marched for twenty-seven hours, covering forty miles. The men of another battalion recalled stopping during the march into Belgium to change their socks and have their feet powdered. As they fell back there was no time for such niceties. Instead they had to scrounge socks and towels from a nearby convent and slumped down to sleep on grass verges as they waited for the endless columns of refugees to pass. Such was their exhaustion that their commanding officer was rendered speechless by exhaustion before finally collapsing. Weighed down by their weapons and equipment, some dumped their arms in the battalion carriers alongside the carcasses of pigs and chicken that had been taken from abandoned farms. Failing to carry their weapons was against all orders, they should always have remained ready to fight, but these were men approaching the limit of their physical endurance.

Nature itself seemed to be working against them. In the mornings they awoke to the sun rising in the east, obscuring the day's first movements by the enemy. For the rest of the day the summer sun scorched them, soaking their already dirty and stinking uniforms with sweat, while the heat assaulted throats parched by the clouds of dust kicked up from beneath their weary feet. On days when the sun failed to shine, the heavens opened and rain soaked the marching men. Their blistered feet squelched in sodden boots and the musty aroma of dirty, sodden clothes arose to suppress the stench of unwashed bodies. At the end of each day nature taunted the men marching westwards. As they looked towards the horizon they could see the sun setting far in the distance, mocking them as it signalled the seeming impossibility of ever reaching the end of their journey.

This interaction with nature was experienced by many among the troops. There were brief interludes where the beauty of the early summer landscape was heightened by the juxtaposition between war and nature. Living in hedgerows and on riverbanks, the soldiers were drawn briefly into the natural world. Peter Wagstaff, of the 1/6th Battalion Queen's Regiment, later wrote of a night awaiting the inevitable enemy assault: 'Over the river hung a thin pall of mist which had spread over the meadows in front of our battle positions, there the cattle waded almost belly deep, as if in some stream. There must have been half a dozen nightingales, all singing their heads off, oblivious to the rattle of machine gun and small arms fire. What a fantastic world it was – nature could not have been lovelier and the face of man more brutal.'[10]

Yet such scenes were soon eclipsed by the reality of their situation. It was not just the vast columns of refugees and retreating infantrymen that clogged the roads. Thousands of military vehicles also joined the retreat. With few Military Police to organize the columns, units became mixed up in the traffic jams. As drivers became increasingly exhausted, the usual convoy discipline was abandoned. All that mattered was to keep moving. Crowds of tired soldiers seemed to hang from anything with wheels and an engine. Alongside the overcrowded vans, trucks and lorries, moved soldiers pushing their kit in wheelbarrows. Every village seemed to have hastily constructed roadblocks that were little more than farm carts and barrels piled in the roads, then abandoned. If they could be dismantled by an exhausted army in retreat, they would surely prove no barrier to headlong advance of the German Army.

As lorries carrying men of the Gloucestershire Regiment became bunched up in a traffic jam, they were the ideal target for enemy fighters roaming the skies in search of prey. As the weary troops slumbered under the canvas of the trucks, nine Messerschmitt fighters swooped upon them: 'Approaching from the rear in threes, they first bombed then machine gunned the column. Wheeling, they repeated the attack without bombing, once from the front and once from the rear, flying very low in each attack.' Stunned by the speed of the attack, numbed and sleep-sodden, the troops struggled to dismount and find cover. The tarpaulins covering the trucks made escape difficult, trapping some unfortunate souls within. Nothing could be done to save the wounded trapped within the burning lorries. Of the five that received direct hits, two were carrying troops, one was carrying the cook's equipment and one contained stores. The final vehicle was loaded with the battalion's spare ammunition. As the ordnance ignited it became too danger-ous to approach the flaming vehicles, sealing the fate of those trapped within. Once the fighters had flown off in search of more prey, the Gloucesters assessed the human cost of the tragedy. Around one in seven of the battalion's total strength – 104 soldiers – were killed, wounded or missing.

The impact of aerial attacks was obvious to the retreating British Army, nor was the lesson lost on the Royal Air Force. In a desperate attempt to stall the enemy advance, the RAF threw its bombers into action. They targeted bridges and railways across northern Germany and the Low Countries, hoping the damage they inflicted might win a breathing space for the hard pressed army. Their valiant efforts cost the lives of many of the crews. In one afternoon the RAF sent seventy-one bombers against enemy targets, just forty returned to their bases – a loss of 56 per cent.

If the dive bombing of the clogged roads was not enough, the Allied forces had to contend with the constant attention of the highly mobile enemy reconnaissance units whose motorcycle patrols often followed just in the wake of the retreating forces, and who engaged the British with terrifying mortar attacks and deadly sniper fire almost as soon as they attempted to form defensive positions. The Allies also had to contend with 'fifth columnists'. These were the German agents and spies whose job was to help sow confusion across the Allied front and in the rear areas. Long hours were wasted on fruitless sweeps through woodland, searching for non-existent spies and firing nervously into the shadows. At Boulogne officers reported how the rumours of fifth columnists created an atmosphere of distrust and tension.

Despite the impact these rumours had on morale, the real significance of the fifth columnists was in the front lines. During the siege of Calais there were numerous reports of snipers infiltrating into the town. One officer even reported a priest working as an artillery spotter from a church tower. Bob Davies recalled the fears: 'There were eight of us put on a roadblock to check out the refugees. But how in the hell do you check out hundreds and hundreds of people, all pushing wheelbarrows and handcarts piled up with their belongings? For all we knew there could have been Germans among them.' Without doubt some Germans did find their way through the roadblocks, as Davies later found out: 'We realised we were being shot at from this row of old houses 50 yards away. We looked back and saw three or four French soldiers. They went into one of the houses and pulled a woman out. She had been hiding in the roof and firing at us. They belted the living daylights out of her and then carted her off.'

In similar incidents, soldiers of the 48th Division even reported 'refugees' pulling out weapons and attacking their positions. Although these were very real examples of the fifth columnists attacking Allied troops, there were plenty of other incidents where the truth was uncertain. Rumours had spread that the spies and saboteurs might be dressed as priests or nuns, resulting in many innocents being interrogated to determine their true identity. For those suspected of being spies, justice was rapid. When the Tyneside Scottish captured a German spy he was interrogated. Then, with no need for an investigation or trial, he was swiftly executed by a Sergeant Chambers.

The scenes of death and destruction were not entirely the work of the enemy and their agents. As British units withdrew they were forced to destroy anything they could not carry. Broken down tanks and lorries had to be rendered unusable; petrol dumps were blown up; ammunition was dumped into rivers; assault boats were smashed by axe-wielding soldiers; even sandbags were set alight – anything that could be of use to the enemy was destroyed. At headquarters throughout northern France maps, plans, reports, stationery, official documents, and even unit diaries fed the bonfires that marked the retreat. When one regiment was forced to abandon their supply dump a total of 20,000 cigarettes were quickly divided up amongst the willing soldiers.

Yet amidst the chaos not every unit continued the journey directly towards the coast. There were plenty among them who were given firm orders to stop and prepare defensive positions. If an entire army was going to escape from the beaches of France they would need someone to hold back the enemy. The units chosen to be the rearguard had little choice but to muster whatever weapons and ammunition they could find. The experiences of these units provided a fitting reflection of the chaos of the campaign as it would be remembered in the minds of the defeated army. When one unit of the RASC were pulled into the line to the east of the Dunkirk perimeter, they were taken off their previous duties, guarding a dump of redundant shells for howitzers that the BEF did not even possess. A company of the Gloucesters equipped itself with a French anti-tank gun. The problem was they had only practice shells for it. These were useless since they did not explode when they hit the target. The HQ staff of the same battalion found themselves unable to return enemy fire since they did not even have any rifles. When the War Office attempted to evaluate the performance of weapons in the aftermath of the defeat they were unable to report on the 2-inch mortar. Quite simply, too few high explosive bombs had been supplied to be able to report on their effectiveness. Nor did the increasing chaos have any respect for rank. There were officers who had been separated from their men and who were adopted by other units, like the commander of an anti-aircraft battery who spent a week fighting as an infantryman.

For all those men detailed to hold off the enemy there was a sense of dread. Ever since the retreat had started, the troops had faced the realization that the enemy was far stronger and better organized than the Allied forces. Yet every day some unit – somewhere across the front lines – was thrown into battle to halt the enemy advance. Like King Canute, it seemed to the troops, they were being asked do the impossible and hold off the tide. But unlike Canute, the troops of the rearguard were soon washed away.

Bill Holmes and the men of the Royal Sussex Regiment were among those forming the rearguard. On 22 May, at Anseghem, Holmes watched through the clear morning skies as German planes above them directed shellfire into their positions. From 4 a.m. onwards the battalion found themselves under fire. In the early afternoon they watched as their own 2nd Battalion withdrew through their lines, a sure sign the battle was not going well. Then, in the early evening, the Sussex infantrymen made contact with the enemy. This was the moment the volunteers among them had signed up for. For all among them it was a life-changing moment, the time when they first opened fire on a real, live enemy. Sid Seal, defending the battalion HQ recalled: 'It was a big step for us all. People have often asked me if I killed anyone. I don't know. You are just firing at people in the distance. We were all firing. But when they go down you don't know if it is you or the man next to you who killed them. You just think "Get him before he gets you." The survival instinct takes over.'

For Bill Holmes it was something he had never expected, never wanted and yet could not avoid:

> You don't aim as if you are shooting pigeons. You just lay in hedgerows and watch and wait making yourself scarce. I was on the Bren gun – I didn't have trouble shooting at people, but you do feel guilty. But you can't do anything about it. It's awkward. When you get to war, every day you knew another of your mates would be dead. It was terrible but you got used to it – because you've got your mates with you. You'd go through hell for each other. We laughed about things. You had to have a sense of humour – we'd see the funny side of things, like somebody having their clothes blown off, or being shot. It seems awful but we lived with it every day.

His views were reflected by a soldier who was seen sitting on a wall reading a text in Latin. When asked why he was reading it he replied with a grim humour that Latin was useful because it was a dead language and he liked to be prepared.

That evening, following their first contact with enemy infantry, the Sussex withdrew to the River Lys. Unlike their experiences earlier in the day, the move went well and they retreated without difficulty, enjoying an uneventful march towards Courtrai. By the 25th the Sussex found themselves at Caestre, a position they held for the next three days. Having established themselves, the infantry came under fire throughout the 26th. For Bill Holmes, it was another of the violent introductions to man's hideous appetite for destruction:

> We were tired from marching. That night our food was a long time coming. We were in dugouts – two per trench. The time came to get our food. My mate asked me should he go or would

I? You had to run, crawl and jump to reach the food. So I went. When I got back to the trench he was dead, hit by a shell. I thought how lucky I was, 'cause it was him or me. You can't describe the sight – it was a charred, disfigured body still holding his rifle.

The horrors continued the next day when the battalion HQ came under artillery fire and then at midday around twenty enemy tanks approached. Sid Seal remembered the attacks on the HQ:

We soon realised there was a war on! It was pretty terrible. You were seeing chaps alongside you getting killed and you just thought 'God. Is it my turn next?' It was a horrible thing to see chaps you'd known all your life get shot and killed or blown to pieces. I thought 'What the devil's happening?' Fear just takes hold. All these silly buggers who say they were never afraid – well, they were! Everyone was. It was natural. It affects you terribly but after a time you get used to seeing dead people around you.

Thanks to the heroic efforts of soldiers manning the much maligned Boyes anti-tank rifle – a weapon that was already obsolete since it was only effective against the enemy's most lightly armoured tanks – six tanks were put out of action and the rest withdrew to harass the Sussex with machine-gun fire for the rest of the day. During the early afternoon a heavy rain began to fall, bringing further misery to the troops. So heavy was the rainfall that the flares they fired to call for supporting artillery fire could not be seen.

That evening, as the rain cleared, Bill Holmes and his comrades looked up to see enemy bombers in the skies above Caestre. It was an ominous sight. They slowly circled the village without opening fire. With each turn the watching infantrymen felt their mouths go dry with fear as they became certain the end had come. But for the moment they had been granted a reprieve. Like vultures circling their prey, the German pilots decided this was not a suitable target and flew off, ready to unleash their destruction on some other poor target.

As the infantrymen of the Sussex Regiment held off the enemy in Caestre, they were unaware of the total chaos across the Allied front. It was clear the battle was not going well in their sector, but the position elsewhere was unclear. Even many officers were uncertain of the scale of the defeat being inflicted by the Germans. The progress of the enemy towards the Channel via the Somme valley was unknown to most. The fall of Calais and Boulogne had not been made known to them, nor the momentous decision to withdraw the army from the beaches at Dunkirk.

The fateful decision to withdraw to the coast and embark the army at Dunkirk had been brewing in the minds of the generals for some days. As early as the 19th Lord Gort had realized that unless the gap between the British and French Armies was closed the consequences would be dire. So he began to consider falling back as far as the River Somme or withdrawing to the coast. It seemed, with Army Group A facing a virtually unchallenged run towards the coast, that the retreat to the coast was the only logical option. Gort had telephoned the War Office to discuss the matter. It was the beginning of the process that saw the evacuation finally ordered on 26 May.

Oblivious of these orders, the infantrymen of the Sussex Regiment continued in their duty to fight as part of the rearguard. Meanwhile, their divisional commander, Major-General Osborne, was embroiled in his own battle. His enemy was not the German Army. Instead he was facing an indignant Frenchman. Osborne had been called to a conference in the town of Steenvoorde, to meet with General Prioux under whose command his division had been placed. Both men knew the British were withdrawing to Dunkirk but Prioux was pessimistic about the chances of escaping. He was convinced they would be slaughtered and maintained they should surrender to avoid further bloodshed. Furthermore, he insisted that evacuation was impossible and that it would cause bad feeling

between the Allies. Osborne argued against the Frenchman's
defeatism, telling him that attemping to escape would be worthwhile if he could ensure the escape of French troops ready to
continue the war from Britain. The Englishman told Prioux that
nothing was impossible and that if he broke out 'the whole world
would acclaim his feat'.[11] Osborne's optimism was well placed – in
the weeks that followed, the world was indeed astounded by the
miraculous escape from Dunkirk.

It was a strange situation for Osborne. Some of the French
officers openly supported the idea of fighting back to the coast.
Others were gloomy, obediently siding with their defeatist commander. With no final decision made, Osborne left the French and
returned to his HQ. When he returned to Prioux that evening the
Frenchman was even more subdued. Osborne found him sitting
with a pair of his staff officers in a room lit by just two candles. The
gloom of the scene was a fitting situation for what followed. Prioux
told the general he had made his final decision. He informed
Osborne that he was preparing for the surrender of his forces and
that the Englishman was at liberty to make his own decision over
the future of the 44th Division.

It was decided that the positions would be held until midday on
the 29th, when the 44th Division would withdraw towards the sea.
However, Major-General Osborne was then given another shock
at the headquarters of the British 3 Corps. He discovered his corps
commander had decided not to wait for the time agreed with
General Prioux. Instead the corps was going to commence the
withdrawal at 11 p.m. that evening. The shock decision left
Osborne with a dilemma – his men were fully engaged with
the enemy, and could not simply disengage and head northwards.
Indeed, as they spoke, the Sussex Regiment were engaging German tanks. Yet, with the rest of 3 Corps about to depart and with a
French Army beside him about to surrender, Osborne had no
choice but to order a withdrawal. And so at 10.30 that evening he
ordered all units of the division to retreat north. There was an eerie
sense of finality for the officers who received the orders. Not only

were they told to destroy all excess transport but they were also instructed to destroy all secret papers. And so, the division withdrew to the nearest high ground, the Mont des Cats.

At 3 a.m. on 29 May the first troops of the 4th Sussex arrived on the hill. It marked the battalion's final hours as a cohesive unit. Approaching the hill in the faint morning light, Bill Holmes and his comrades could see the outline of the monastery's gothic stone walls. Beneath them, the steep road leading to the summit mocked the soldiers, who gasped for breath as they made their weary way past the queues of lorries all heading for the doubtful sanctuary of the monastery, with its boarded up restaurant and shuttered souvenir shop. The lines of transport, nose to tail, wheezed just as desperately as the troops as they inched their way up the forbidding slope. Above them, the hilltop was crowded with troops all awaiting an assault they knew must come. They were not wrong.

In the words of Lieutenant Hodgins, an officer at the 131 Brigade HQ: 'There was very little chance of any cover and the situation was the most unpleasant as the whole of the Mont des Cats was covered with troops.'[12] His words hardly did justice to their situation. Once atop the hill the troops were subject to the most terrifying assault they had so far experienced. At 8.30 a.m., just as Bill Holmes and his mates reached the summit, the first artillery fire of the day commenced. Not waiting for the inevitable toll of casualties, they moved straight down to positions in the relative safety of the wooded hillside. Then, one hour later, twenty German warplanes arrived overhead, bombing and machine-gunning the troops clustered around the hilltop. Bill Holmes watched in awe as tanks fired flaming tracer rounds towards them to guide the aircraft circling in the skies. Their attack lasted a full thirty minutes. Once the planes departed, German mortars and tank guns opened fire on the infantrymen as they scrambled for whatever cover they could find. Again Holmes watched men dropping dead before his eyes as shell splinters and piercing shards of tree bark filled the air. From his position he could see the town

of Cassel burning atop a nearby hill. Closer still, he could make out
the ominous grey-clad figures of German soldiers in the fields
around. Discarded uniforms and helmets littered the ground. Arms
and ammunition were scattered everywhere. There was little the
soldiers could do. If they stayed where they were they would surely
die. Yet death seemed just as certain for any man who ran away.
Indeed, where could they run?

It was little wonder the hillsides were so covered with troops.
This one small area was crowded with soldiers: the 2nd, 4th and 5th
Battalions of the Royal Sussex Regiment, three battalions of the
Queen's Regiment, two battalions of West Kents and one of men
from the East Kents. The commanding officer of the 1/5th
Queen's Regiment ordered his men to move to positions clear
of the hilltop to help stem the ever-increasing toll of casualties
being inflicted on them. As the casualties mounted, their padre,
Reverend Brode, moved out into the open to help them. Dis-
regarding his personal safety, he tended the wounded and dying
men. As a fellow officer of the battalion later described it, his
'fearless example was a great encouragement to everyone'.[13]

At 10.30 a.m., with the death toll mounting and their situation
hopeless, the order was finally issued for the entire division to
abandon the hill. Sid Seal was at the 4th Sussex HQ when the signal
came through: 'We got the order "All troops withdraw from Mont
des Cats to Dunkirk via Poperinghe. No transport to be taken.
Travel in parties. Scatter if enemy tanks approach".'

The withdrawal commenced at 11 a.m. The orders for the
retreat towards Dunkirk made no reference to the wounded. For
Sid Seal this could mean only one thing: 'We were soon aware of
how bad things were. The officer told us we were to leave the
wounded where they were and that anyone wounded on the way
back would be left behind. What we had to do was save ourselves.
It was a real blow. Several of our chaps were left there. One of
them was a good friend of mine, Bill Stone. We'd been in the
Territorials together before the war. He'd had his leg smashed and I
had to leave him there. He lost his leg.'

Whilst some of the wounded were left behind to be taken prisoner, others were fortunate enough to escape towards the coast. It was all a matter of timing. Among them was Noel Matthews, a signaller from the Queen's Regiment: 'I was blown up twice. One shell landed slap-bang right beside the trench. I was half-buried. I struggled out of that and got myself into a shed. Then another shell came down and demolished the shed on top of me. It must have had bags of grain upstairs because it all collapsed on me. I was pinned against the wall. I thought this was like a film. The fact that I had almost been killed didn't enter my mind.' Dragged to safety, he was taken to the battalion aid post. Although seriously shaken, he was unwounded and later the same day was put on a truck. Rather than being deposited at the Mont des Cats, the truck he was in continued north towards Dunkirk. Had he been sent to the monastery for treatment his fate would have been very different: 'I missed the bombing of the hill. Instead I reached De Panne in safety.'

Whilst some units were able to move from their positions in relative safety, others were not so fortunate. Bill Holmes and the rest of D Company were among the latter. As he descended the hill, Holmes turned back to watch as the monastery was hit by incoming artillery fire. Doing their best to ignore the slaughter of their mates and the dedicated doctors and orderlies, the men of D Company moved around the south-east edge of the hill, beneath a canopy of trees, but failed to reach the assembly point chosen by Lt.-Colonel Whistler. The fate of the wounded was not their concern. As they escaped, shells burst around them, a stark reminder that they could not linger on the hill.

As they withdrew, the troops were forced to scatter as a French convoy came under attack by low-flying enemy aircraft. With the battalion no longer operating as a cohesive unit, the remaining troops began to divide into small groups who made their way northwards without either interference or guidance from their officers. Sid Seal watched as his platoon split into two groups, one on each side of a hedge. He later discovered the other party were all taken prisoner before they reached Dunkirk.

In the chaos troops were found wandering around on the hill, uncertain of their orders. Officers who attempted to round up these stragglers found themselves left behind in the rush to escape the hail of incoming fire. Every soldier at the Mont des Cats shared fears and uncertainties familiar to soldiers throughout history. For most of them – teenage Territorials, barely trained militiamen, ageing reservists hastily recalled to the colours and the old sweats of the regular battalions – the only thing that had made military life bearable was standing shoulder to shoulder with their comrades. Even the most reluctant recruits had found a camaraderie they had seldom known in civvy street, realizing military service could be tolerable if they shared the burdens of life in uniform with their new mates. Yet, as the withdrawal commenced, this too was denied them.

In the days that followed, life became a lottery as the men streamed back towards Dunkirk. The first of the parties of Sussex infantrymen embarked from the beaches of Dunkirk the very same day they had left the Mont des Cats. For others the journey took days – meaning it would be years before they once more headed home across the English Channel.

There was a finality in the order given to Bill Holmes after they left the Mont des Cats. The sergeant had uttered the words that every soldier dreaded: 'Every man for himself.' All they knew was that they should head towards the plumes of smoke reeling into the sky above Dunkirk. As some of his comrades tried to escape across country in vehicles that had survived the bombing, Bill Holmes decided it safest to remain on foot. He soon found himself separated from the main body of troops as he headed across fields to avoid the roads he knew would be full of Germans:

I was with three lads. We walked away from the hill. As we were walking off we were talking. And all of a sudden a shell took my mate. It covered him – buried him underground. If we could've got him out straight away he would've lived. But we couldn't, because we were being bombed and machine-gunned. I ended up hiding under a clamp of rotting mangels. There were two German planes firing at us, peppering the ground. I could feel the bullets hitting around me. How I escaped, I'll never know.

In the chaos all that counted was survival. As Sid Seal headed towards Dunkirk his mind was filled with dread that he might be left behind. Having already been forced to leave some of his mates behind, he dreaded sharing their fate:

On the way to the coast we came under fire and I got hit by a piece of shrapnel. It cut my hand and split my lip open. The front of my battledress was covered in blood. Oh God, I thought my time was up. Luckily it wasn't a bad wound, but it bled a lot. But at first I didn't know. I was relieved. I didn't wait to get it dressed. I kept going. I could remember what the officer had said about leaving the wounded behind. But my one thought was that I would not be left there.

Every man who left the Mont des Cats that morning shared certain experiences. There were soldiers of all regiments and all nationalities mixed up in the retreat. By day they walked with their heads turned skywards in a desperate search for enemy aircraft. By night they walked in the eerie light of German flares, fired to illuminate the retreating troops. Scenes of chaos and confusion seemed to symbolize the entire retreat – corpses, burning vehicles, abandoned equipment, men who remained resolute and men who had abandoned hope. Everywhere they looked they saw ruined churches, their steeples destroyed to prevent their use as observation posts. All among them felt the quickening of the heart and dryness of throat provoked by fear. And all knew they would be lucky to survive.

Each soldier who made the march towards the coast had his own memories, sights he would carry like snapshots of through his life. There were plenty of the surreal scenes. Small trucks hung from the branches of trees, where they had been blasted. There was the vision of a drunken British soldier riding around on a carthorse, laughing as he waved his hat at the men he passed. Elsewhere troops watched as a traumatized horse swam up and down a canal, unable to escape the water, until it was put out of its misery by a soldier appalled by its plight. In the chaos one infantry officer found himself hitching a lift on an artillery gun tractor. He soon found the driver had little idea of his destination and appeared to be going around in circles.

Bill Holmes and his mates shared all these horrors as they marched silently past a column of burning trucks. The convoy had been bombed just minutes before, but no one had come to its assistance. As the marching soldiers turned to look, they could see the charred figure of a driver within each truck. Their desperate situation was reinforced as Holmes turned back to watch sappers blowing up a canal bridge they had just crossed. Now he was certain – they must surely be the last of the rearguard to reach Dunkirk.

In those final days thousands of men like Sid Seal and Bill Holmes finally reached the dubious safety of the Dunkirk perimeter. Once there, whether they slipped safely across the Channel in the reassuring hands of the Royal Navy, were mown down on the beaches by marauding German warplanes, were wounded or left behind to be taken prisoner – it was all a lottery.

As the men of the rearguard arrived in Dunkirk they entered a surreal world. Burnt out trucks littered the verges on the outskirts. The entire town was surrounded by the wreckage of vehicles. It seemed bizarre to the arriving soldiers that drivers, who had so lovingly tended these vehicles, should now be destroying them. Soldiers stood in front of trucks smashing windscreens with rifle-butts, as others removed vital engine parts and threw them into ditches and canals. Lorries stood with their bonnets open, tangled wires, holed sumps spilling oil onto the road. Everywhere were cars with smashed windscreens and slashed tyres. Motorcycles, their petrol tanks cracked open by axe blows, lay in heaps alongside twisted bicycles. The ground was littered with the remains of smashed car batteries, abandoned on the roadsides along with the sledgehammers that had destroyed them. One soldier saw an officer seated upon a packing crate. The forlorn man was holding his head in his hands, unable to watch the destruction. The soldier realized it was his own brigade commander. Utterly dejected, the brigadier could not watch as his driver battered his staff car with a pick-axe. Vehicles were not the only victims of this destruction. Like hideous metal trees, the ruptured barrels of wrecked artillery pieces pointed skywards, as if taunting the natural world with man's ability to wreak havoc.

Once within the town the soldiers were faced with mounting horrors. Dunkirk assaulted their senses. Burning buildings lined the roadsides and a dark pall of smoke and dust hung over the entire town, whilst at night a deep red glow filled the skies. The crackle of flames, the crash of collapsing buildings and the vicious pinging of exploding ammunition joined the hideous drone of aircraft and the shrieking of incoming shells to lay siege to their ears. The radiant heat seared the skin of the men walking these streets. They could smell nothing but the heavy smoke. Indeed, the retreating soldiers could taste the very air around them as they advanced through a rain of burning embers towards the port and its waiting ships. By contrast, burst water mains sent water pouring into the streets. It mattered little that the water mains had been shattered, there was no one left to put out the fires.

In scenes that had become chillingly familiar throughout the retreat, the corpses of men and animals lay unattended where they had fallen. No one troubled to cover the dead or record their names. The swollen forms of the horses that had pulled French gun carriages into Dunkirk lay beside the wreckage of their weapons. Taking no notice of the stench of death, the soldiers marched onwards, stepping over the corpses. As he looked around, in streets lit only by the fires, with tangled trolley wires above his head and twisted corpses beneath his feet, Bill Holmes couldn't help but compare the scene to Old Testament tales of the wrath of God. It seemed that Dunkirk must be facing the vengeful wrath of its maker.

Yet this was a human tragedy, not divine intervention. This was the work of the Luftwaffe and the German gunners. On every corner, in every street, the evidence of their ferocious assault could be found. The rubble of fallen buildings filled the streets. Glass crunched under every footfall of the weary soldiers and clouds of hot dust were kicked up from beneath their boots. Amidst scenes worthy of Armageddon, drunken soldiers roamed the streets, their boots crushing the shop contents strewn across the cobblestones. Leaderless and uncertain of what they should do, drunken looters raided shops, carrying away radios, clothing, food and drink. In the chaos, small groups of men sat around eating whatever they could find – one group who had not eaten for days, gorged themselves on a combination of bananas and tinned beetroot.

In the last days before the fall of Dunkirk, anarchy reigned. Officers took little notice of drunks or looters. When terrified soldiers refused to leave their basement shelters and make their way to the port, officers simply ignored them. Instead they devoted their energies to those men who wanted to be saved.

Territorial anti-aircraft gunner and former City of London office worker Leslie Shorrock was one of the thousands whose fate was determined on the beaches. Since having been given the order to destroy his vehicle and head to the coast, he had trudged across ploughed fields, clambered through hedgerows, stumbled in and out of ditches and crossed canals on makeshift wooden bridges. All the time he had walked in virtual silence, hardly passing a word with the men around him. It was as if each of them had been consumed by their own personal drama.

Upon arriving at the coast, Shorrock saw thousands of soldiers filling the beaches that spread eastwards towards the flames of Dunkirk. He later wrote of the scene:

A vast queue of men, three or four abreast, stretched from the top of the beach down to the sea, a distance of hundreds of yards.

it was a very warm sunny day, with a clear blue sky, the sea appeared very calm and immediately in front of me, approximately one quarter of a mile from the beach, a large ship was slowly sinking bow first . . . As I stepped onto the beach at the top I saw immediately in front of me, lying on his back in the sand, a dead British soldier, partly covered with a gas cape and on top of his chest his army pay book, with his name written thus, Driver Barraud RASC.[14]

In the hours that followed he watched as officers were forced to draw their weapons to control crowds of soldiers all intent on rushing to gain a place on the departing boats. The scenes of chaos and desperation convinced him there was little future in the operation. Subsequently he fell asleep and lost contact with his mates. What followed would influence the course of the next five years of his life.

Fate had also brought Noel Matthews to the evacuation beaches. Unlike the other wounded who had been left to face the shelling of the monastery at the Mont des Cats, his ambulance had taken him the thirty miles towards safety. Still shaken by his experiences on the battlefield, Matthews trudged over the dunes, little knowing what to expect: 'I got there late afternoon to be greeted by the sight of hundreds of chaps shooting at aeroplanes in the sky. I was with these two chaps and we moved along towards an empty ambulance. We kipped down there for the night. Next day I went around the back of the sanatorium and asked a French soldier for food. We hadn't eaten for three days. He filled my mess tin with wine and gave me bread.' With De Panne under fire, Matthews walked towards Dunkirk: 'After a day of waiting a bloke came along yelling out for any blokes from the Queen's Regiment, because the colonel was collecting men. There were about 20 of us there. He gathered us together and said "Wait here while I get us a boat." That was the last we saw of him. So we just dispersed.'

He waited another day on the beaches, uncertain whether he would ever get away. At times it hardly seemed worthwhile attempting to find a boat: 'You saw these chaps standing all day waist deep in the water, waiting for boats. Plus the German planes were trying to knock the boats out. So all the time you were on land you were safer. I decided I wasn't going to swim out into the sea unless I saw the Jerries coming over the dunes.' Eventually, after hanging around the beaches, Matthews made his way to the quay and took a running jump onto a ship. His fears about aerial attack were justified when the ship was dive-bombed three times on the passage to Dover.

Also experiencing the hell of Dunkirk and the beaches was Bill Holmes. Whilst some among his comrades had arrived in Dunkirk within a day or so of leaving the Mont des Cats, Holmes and his pals had been wandering through fields and lanes for three or four days, surviving on eating raw vegetables they dug from the fields. When they finally arrived within the Dunkirk perimeter they had little idea of what might happen next. Such was the ferocity of the German assault that it seemed there could be little hope of survival: 'It was so fierce you didn't know what was going on – there seemed to be a constant drone of aircraft above us. One of the saddest things was seeing the blokes who got on boats and then the boats got bombed. It was mass murder. It made me feel lucky. At Dunkirk there was nothing else but bodies.'

Whilst Bill Holmes took four days to reach the fiery wasteland of Dunkirk, not all his comrades were so unfortunate. Despite his wounded face, Sid Seal reached the coast just one day after leaving the Mont des Cats. As luck would have it he arrived in the Belgian seaside town of De Panne. At the far eastern end of the evacuation beaches, the scenes in De Panne were not like those in Dunkirk. For a start there were fewer soldiers awaiting evacuation and, more importantly, there were fewer German planes overhead:

It was the 30th of May when we got there and we could already see Dunkirk in flames. We could see crowds of troops at Bray Dunes, there was plenty of panic there, thousands of men were on the beach. But where we were wasn't so busy. We were just fortunate. On the night of the 31st we found a rowing boat. It had probably come off one of the ships that had been bombed. The Germans were shelling and bombing De Panne, so it was get into the boat or stay in the town and get blown to pieces. So seven or eight of us – just one of them was a chap from my battalion – got in and rowed out into the channel, just hoping we were going in the right direction. Fortunately we were. A fishing boat picked us up and took us back to Ramsgate.

In contrast to the situation at De Panne, the apocalyptic scenes in Dunkirk left Bill Holmes utterly despondent. There were still vast crowds of soldiers desperate to be rescued. Some were still fully armed and equipped, others had nothing more than the clothes they stood up in. There were wounded men everywhere, all hoping they might be able to get on board a ship to safety. Terrified horses seemed to be running everywhere, through the town and across the sand dunes. He even watched as half-buried corpses of soldiers were dragged from their sandy resting places by starving dogs. Waiting on the beach, it seemed there was nowhere to go. As the evacuation drew to a close there were fewer and fewer boats arriving on the French coast to evacuate the troops. Those men waiting on the dunes no longer found lines of men snaking out into the water. There was no longer a constant ferry service of small boats running in to the beaches. For the stragglers who had fought the rearguard battles, allowing their comrades to make their way to safety, escape to England was a lottery.

Sid Seal was fortunate to make good his escape:

Oh God, it was amazing to see those white cliffs. What a relief! We were going home. I slept on a hatch and when we reached Ramsgate they woke me up. I was stuck to the tar on the hatch! So I had blood all down my front and tar all over my back. I must have looked a picture. Some kind lady came up to me and threw an army blanket over my shoulders. I still had my haversack and rifle and as soon as we got off the boat they took them off us.

Then we got on a train and they gave us a cup of tea – it was better than champagne. It was a great feeling of relief. It was a defeat, but we didn't think about it. We were just glad to be home.

On the train journey northwards, he passed through his home village, but missed it since he was in a deep sleep. However, he was one of the lucky ones. As the train moved through Sussex it passed the homes of many soldiers who would not see England for many years.

Bill Holmes was one of those to whom fate was unkind. He had arrived in Dunkirk too late to join the queues of men who were safely transported home. Instead he joined the forlorn crowds of men for whom the story of Dunkirk was far different from the one celebrated in newspapers around the world. This was not a victory but a terrible defeat that condemned them to five years of captivity.

When the end came it was a shock, but Holmes and his comrades no longer had the energy or the will to resist the enemy:

I hadn't dreamt I'd ever be taken prisoner. I thought I might be killed, but never once did I think I'd be a POW. Then before we knew what was happening, several of these German motorcycle combinations arrived. They fired tracer bullets at us, so we had no choice. You either gave up or died. I never thought I'd ever be a prisoner. I thought I might be killed. But one thing was I thought if I'm going to die I'd like to die at home. I didn't mind being shot but I didn't want to die out there. I was a long way from home.

For Holmes, and the others who were rounded up that morning, the story of Dunkirk had come to an end. Their story had not ended in salvation but in fear, chaos and confusion. The conclusion did not come in the safe hands of the Royal Navy, but standing on the beach at Dunkirk staring down the barrel of a machine-gun. Now was not the time to pray for escape. All that mattered was survival. For Holmes one thing was certain. General Alexander's fabled tour of the beaches, standing on the deck of a launch, calling out for the stragglers to come forward, was not his experience of that day: 'I never heard any calls for that final evacuation.' Put quite simply, Bill Holmes and the men around him had 'missed the boat'. For those abandoned on the beaches of Dunkirk it was a phrase that would forever have a new and poignant meaning.

CHAPTER TWO

The Round Up

Tommy, for you the war is over, but your troubles have just begun.

German soldier to Private John Lawrence,
France, May 1940[1]

It is impossible for any non-POW to understand what the effect of capture is. There is fear, being unarmed, surrounded by armed, vicious, filthy looking men . . . Exhaustion, physical and neural, hunger after several days without food, thirst, and no hope of going home soon, perhaps never, caused severe mental depression.

Corporal Graham King, Royal Army Medical Corps

The frantic actions of those final days seemed long past as the exhausted remnants of the BEF faced up to the reality of their situation. The desperate efforts to snatch hundreds of thousands of men to safety were over. The Royal Navy was no longer the dominant power on the beaches of northern France. Instead, they had been withdrawn across the Channel to prepare for what surely would be the next step in this already vicious war – the invasion of Great Britain.

Men like Bill Holmes, who had watched and waited for boats that never came, had been sacrificed for the greater good. Quite simply, the Royal Navy needed its vessels to protect Britain's shores and shipping routes. The fate of those who had arrived too late to escape and were still stranded in France was nothing compared to the fate of the entire nation. Now, as the men who waited for boats that never came discovered, the beaches of France belonged to the Germans: 'Everybody was trying to get away but it was impossible. I was lucky, I was unwounded, but there were men there with broken legs and all kinds of wounds. I was frightened because I thought we were going to die. I expected to be lined up against a wall and shot. Most of us thought the same. We knew the Germans didn't care about what they were doing. It played hell with your nerves.' Tired, dirty and weak, Bill Holmes was too exhausted to fully comprehend what was happening. Like so many around him all he could think about were sleep and food. Once the German motorcyclists had come into view every emotion was submerged beneath one basic instinct, as he remembered: 'I just hoped to survive.'

As the troops remaining in Dunkirk were rounded up by machine-gun-wielding German soldiers, they were sharing the same emotional turmoil thousands of soldiers throughout Belgium and France had already experienced. The dreadful realization that they were now prisoners was not confined to those unfortunates who had 'missed the boats'. It was shared by thousands of soldiers of the BEF. Men of every rank and every background went 'into the bag'. In the weeks ahead even a major-general joined the ranks of men destined to spend five long years in captivity. At the other end of the scale, there were also raw recruits, like the former merchant seaman, who had been in the army just twenty-four hours. He had signed on in England and been sent immediately to France, still without a uniform. He arrived in France and was taken prisoner before he could reach his regiment.

The circumstances of each man's capture was something intensely personal. Every prisoner had his own thoughts and memories of what defeat and capture meant. Yet amidst these varying circumstances were certain themes that emerged time and time again. There were the soldiers who, lost and alone, stumbled into the hands of the enemy. There were others who had fought desperate last-ditch battles to hold back the advancing Germans before finally surrendering. For every man who made the conscious decision to lay down his rifle and raise his arms in surrender there was another who was simply dragged, dazed and confused, from the ruins of a defensive position, hardly realizing the battle was over.

In the days leading up to the end of the evacuation, and the Wehrmacht's triumphal entry into Dunkirk, in an almost constant stream of battles, frightened and exhausted British soldiers became prisoners of war. The rearguard battle at the Mont des Cats, from which Bill Holmes had barely escaped with his life, was just one of many vicious encounters. From the opening defeats in Belgium that had shaken the entire western world, to the bloody battles for vital Channel ports like Boulogne and Calais, or the desperate defence of towns like Cassel and Hazebrouck, British soldiers had found themselves rounded up and herded into captivity.

For the soldiers of the BEF the thought of being a prisoner of war had not entered their minds. Surely, they were far better men than their enemies? The sense of confidence with which they had gone to war meant the sudden discovery they were not invincible had a profound emotional and psychological impact upon them. Graham King, a corporal in the Royal Army Medical Corps, summed up the emotions shared by the prisoners of 1940: 'My world had collapsed around me.'

As the defeated remnants of the BEF went into captivity all shared this sense of hopelessness. In the brief but bloody battles that raged through May, the troops had rapidly learnt the realities of war. Death had become a close companion to all, taking the lives of their friends whilst fate spared them – for the moment at least. The sickening sight of suffering, the screams of the wounded, the pitiful expressions on the faces of their friends as they realized they were dying, and the sheer exhaustion of war, had soon made the youths, who had spent the phoney war in optimistic expectation, face up to the truth. Just to survive the battle was a bonus. If that meant being torn by bullets but still being able to walk, that too was a blessing.

Such fortune was encapsulated in the memories Fred Gilbert, a pre-war trainee commercial artist. In the lead up to battle he had not felt particularly scared, but soon learned the truth. In his very first action he had found his section pinned down in a trench. Raising his helmet above the parapet on the butt of his rifle, it was swiftly struck by two bullets from a sniper hiding in the trees around them. After some time he was instructed to pull his section back to the company HQ. As they retreated bullets smacked into the ground and whistled through the air all around them. Soon they reached an open road: 'I was waiting for bullets to go by, to tell one man to run. Get up, get out, get down – one at a time. The first one looked at me as if to say "What do you know about it?" He stood up and – bang! – down he went with a bullet straight through him. I couldn't do anything, he was a goner. Going up that strip of road, the same thing happened to all my section, because they didn't go when I told them to go.'

Gilbert himself reached company HQ in safety. Finding some other members of the company still in action – including a captain who was standing up desperately trying to clear his jammed revolver – Fred Gilbert rejoined the battle, firing his rifle at the advancing enemy, until he had exhausted all his rounds. At that moment he realized he was helpless, unable to defend himself, yet unable to rise from the ground for fear of being shot, all he could do was remain in position until fate intervened. He didn't have to wait long, for the Germans had worked their way behind their position: 'I was hit by three bullets, from behind. I got one in the side, one went through my arm and one went through my ear – I saw that bullet hit the ground in front of me. I just lay still. I knew I couldn't do anything. My arm couldn't move. But I was lucky, the bullet in my arm hadn't hit an artery.' After a few minutes he raised himself from the ground, still holding a now useless rifle, that he couldn't fire since his left arm was similarly useless, only to see the captain still fiddling with his revolver. As he watched, a German officer and three other soldiers approached. The officer waved his pistol towards Gilbert and told him to walk back down the road along which his ill-fated comrades had retreated.

The wound in his arm was not bleeding too heavily and his senses had been dulled enough to take the edge off the pain of his wounds, however what Fred Gilbert saw in the minutes that followed brought home just how fortunate he had been:

I went down the road and could see the ditch we had been sheltering in. And in the road I could see my six men who I had tried to tell when to run and when to lay down. They hadn't done as they were told and now they were corpses in the ditch. That was very sad. I knew them well, they were all men I'd known for some time. I couldn't do anything for them now, they were just bodies laying on the ground. Also, as I walked, there were fully armed German soldiers walking up the road. I couldn't go and see the others to see if they were alive because the Germans had told me to go straight down the road. I'd already been hit by three bullets – no thank you, that's enough! I didn't want to risk another one. I was all on my own as I walked down to the village. It was hopeless.

This dreadful sense of hopelessness was shared by all the men who survived to make the long journey into captivity that summer, whatever the circumstances of their capture.

As the British Army fought to hold the line of the Escaut Canal, there were large numbers of soldiers who were trapped within the jaws of the German advance. Peter Wagstaff was one of those captured by the advancing Germans. As the Germans broke through the battalions on either side of his positions, Wagstaff and his men continued to fight hard. He tried to explain the feelings of an officer, barely out of his teens, as he received his introduction to the confusion of war:

We were not aware of the attack coming in. There was too much noise, so we didn't have the faintest idea. I could hear

firing to the right and firing to the left. I could also hear firing to
the rear and I remember thinking 'I hope that's being mopped
up by somebody else.' It's ominous to hear firing behind you but
you have enough to do just holding the front. You are bemused,
you are not conscious of anything apart from what is immediately in front of you. You haven't got time to think and you
haven't got time to analyse. And you haven't got time to be
afraid of anything. You are just swept along on the tide of war.

The pressures faced by Wagstaff and his men were immense as
they came under increasing enemy fire:

The gunner on the Boyes anti-tank rifle had his arm shot off next
to me. But you got on with the job. Your 'automatic pilot' takes
over. I do remember our cook went off his head completely – he
was absolutely hysterical. I remember he said 'I can't face it, sir. I
can't face it at all.' He almost fell in the fire. I thought to myself
'What do you do in a case like this?' In the First World War it
would be a case of 'The hero dragged out his revolver and shot
him'. I remember that crossing my mind for a fleeting, idiotic
second. But what do you do? I left him, but God knows what
happened to him after that.

Eventually, orders came through that Wagstaff should pull his
men back. In the chaos every second counted. Unfortunately for
Wagstaff, vital moments were lost as he waited for his forward section
to pull back from the canal. He could not withdraw without his men,
but their delay was to prove costly: 'By the time they joined us I had
about 12 wounded with me. We ran up this roadway with a high
bank on our left and a wall on the right. We ran right into them.
There were 12 of us facing three German machine guns. There was
nothing we could do. I couldn't go to the right or the left. The 12
wounded men had about two rifles between them.'

As it became clear they were prisoners of war, Second Lieutenant Wagstaff reacted in an unexpected manner:

I let out a short burst of laughter. I remember vividly thinking, 'Of all the things that could happen to me it wasn't this!' It was fear, the build up – it is just hysterics really. I think I was laughing at my own misfortune. Your mind is so muddled that the obvious answer is ridicule. My Corporal – Corporal Thomas – said to me 'Take off your badges of rank, Sir!' He later told me I said 'I will not. I am a British officer and I will die a British officer.' But I don't remember saying it.

Though the battle was over, the suffering was not at an end, as he soon discovered: 'The German took me to the other side of the road. There was this poor little bugger there. He'd had a hole blown out of his back. He was breathing heavily, except that the air was coming through the torn remnants of his battledress and the back of his lung. Myself and Corporal Thomas stayed with him until he died.'

Despite the last-ditch battles fought through France and Belgium, there were some whose capture seemed to be just the result of bad luck. Typical of those whose capture was almost farcial was Lance-Corporal Eric Reeves of the 2/5th Battalion, Queen's Regiment. Just nineteen years old, he was typical of the young volunteers that swelled the ranks of the British Army in the late 1930s. Enthused by the notion of being a soldier, he had joined the Territorial Army at sixteen, taking the rank of 'boy'. He had only been accepted for service after a wily old recruiting sergeant, a veteran of the retreat from Mons, gave him a pair of oversized, double-thick soled boots to put on at his medical. Without the boots, he would never have reached the necessary height. As the sergeant told him, 'Look at that my lad, 5ft 2 and a half inches, just the minimum height for an infantryman.'

Undeterred, he had trained hard and thought himself ready for war when his unit was mobilized on 1 September 1939. Despite his enthusiasm, he had little idea of what he would soon be facing:

I was a plumber's mate. I was at work when I heard we were being mobilised. I was delighted – excited – I couldn't wait. My thought was 'Let's get at 'em'. All the volunteers were like me. We'd have been very disappointed if war hadn't come. Well, ignorance is bliss! We'd read books at the library about the First World War. We looked at the pictures, we thought it was great. Of course, it didn't show the horrors of it. Even the guys down at the British Legion never talked about it. We looked at it like 'Cowboys and Indians' – all we knew was what we'd learnt down at the pictures. We thought we were invincible, we were the young lions. They couldn't beat us.

Fired up by such unrealistic notions, Reeves was still filled with enthusiasm for war when his battalion arrived in France in April 1940. He had his mates by his side and felt no fear as they moved towards Abbeville to meet the enemy as their forces advanced up the Somme valley. When he finally faced the enemy he discovered war held little of the glamour he had expected. On 20 May they watched as Abbeville was bombed by Junkers bombers that circled the skies above the town. Next, it was to be their turn to face the forces of the blitzkrieg: 'At about half four we could hear the war coming towards us – small arms fire and the bang, bang, bang of tanks. Their tanks were firing at us from the flanks. We couldn't move our section to face them. There was tracer going over our heads. I could hear the noise of bullets above my head – like whipcracks – we were lucky but a section behind us copped it.' As darkness fell they were ordered to withdraw along a sunken lane to a hilltop wood. So ended an ignominious first day of war for Eric Reeves: 'I'd never even opened fire. We hadn't see anything to fire at apart from tanks. One or two blokes had "pooped off" at tanks, but all they did was draw their fire. The rounds from the Boyes anti-tank rifle were just bouncing off them. So we'd just lay there and taken it.'

Along with two men from his section, Reeves was sent to a listening post where he spent the hours of darkness watching German flares float down through the air, illuminating the fields around with a sickly red and green light. Even more ominous was the noise of the tanks whose engines could be heard rumbling through the night air. What happened next was a fitting reflection of the chaos faced across the Allied front. As dawn broke, a sergeant appeared and asked Reeves what he was doing. Reeves replied that they were D Company's standing patrol. What he heard next shocked him: 'The sergeant said "They left three hours ago! They went in small parties, they're making for the Somme river. But I got lost in the dark, like these blokes." He pointed to the men he had with him. So we teamed up and headed off together.'

The lost soldiers began to make their way across country, hoping to catch up with the rest of the battalion. With the Germans seemingly having departed, the fields seemed curiously quiet. In the dull morning light they could just make out the corpses of cows that had been caught up in the previous day's battles. When they finally met a French civilian he reassured them the Germans had moved on. Emboldened, the soldiers moved onto the road and continued their march, hoping to make better time. Once again, Reeves and his new comrades were in for a surprise:

After about half an hour we reached a roadblock – it was a hay cart and all sorts of other stuff. There was a bank on one side of the road and a field of clover on the other. Then we heard a voice. In perfect English it called out 'Gentlemen of The Queens, where have you been? We have been expecting you.' And the sergeant said, 'That's a bit of luck, it's our blokes!' Then the owner of the voice showed himself. He had a long green coat on, a 'coalscuttle' helmet with a skull and crossbones badge and was holding a machine gun.

For a brief moment there was a stand-off between the lone German and the dozen or so British soldiers. Unconcerned, the British sergeant called out: 'Hang on a minute, mate, there are more of us than there are of you.' Remaining calm, the SS officer told the men not to be foolish. At that moment the carts of the roadblock were pulled apart and the British soldiers marched through, to be met by the sight of two Mark II Panzer tanks with their guns trained on them. The German then explained how he had been able to confuse them with his accent: 'Mummy is English and Daddy is in the German army. And I owe it to my father to support him. I came down from Oxford and joined the German army. So here I am.'

Showing concern for his prisoners, the English-speaking officer told them his men would bring them food and quickly arranged treatment for the wounded. Despite this, Eric Reeves was hit by the realization of his situation:

> You didn't expect to be taken prisoner. It went through your mind that you might be killed or you might be wounded. But being captured never came into the equation. The first thing that went through your mind was fear – we'd all heard about the SS. All the time you're thinking 'What's going to happen next?' Then next I felt humiliated, I thought 'What a waste of time!' I'd not even fired a shot. I was ashamed. I felt indignation – somebody had let me down or I'd let someone down. You don't know what's what. What made it worse was we'd gone out there thinking we were invincible.

For so many of the troops their deflation was compounded by the realization of how well equipped the Germans were. The British had discarded their First World War vintage rifles and surrendered to an enemy carrying modern automatic weapons. Some among the prisoners approached German tanks and banged on their hulls. After all, the propagandists had assured them many of the German tanks were made of wood or cardboard. Furthermore, the Germans seemed to have vast amounts of transport for their infantry – with motorcycle combinations and armoured half-tracks appearing everywhere on the battlefield – whilst the British had been transported in requisitioned and hastily repainted civilian delivery lorries.

Sharing the field with Reeves were others of his battalion who had also been captured in the fighting around Abbeville. Not all among them had been as enthusiastic as Reeves. There were plenty of young conscripts and militiamen who had been less than eager to play their part in the war. Indeed, the 2/5th Battalion of the Queen's Regiment had been formed the previous year when the army underwent massive expansion. When the 1/5th Battalion, the best of the regiment or 'the creamy boys', as Eric Reeves referred to them, travelled to France, Reeves himself had been left behind since he was still too young to serve abroad. In the weeks that followed, the new battalion had absorbed men who seemed far less enthusiastic than his pre-war colleagues. Among them were recruits from Somerset, including Jim Lee, a Romany Gypsy who had rapidly become one of Reeves' mates and who happily admitted his pre-war employment had been as a poacher. This was typical of the experiences of regiments throughout the army. When war came the regular soldiers and Territorials were eager to 'have a crack at the Hun'. They were followed into uniform by a wave of patriotic recruits, equally eager to do their bit. By late 1940 the army began to absorb conscripts who were less than enthused about the idea of war.

Typical of this breed was twenty-one-year-old Ken Willats. A former chef from South London, Willats had no aspirations to military glory. He had not been caught up in the wave of patriotism that had sent so many others his age to the recruiting offices. He was blunt in his appraisal of his military aptitude: 'I had no ambition to be a soldier. I didn't volunteer, I wasn't the military type. Like thousands of others I went because I was told to go.' Despite this, he accepted his fate and reported to Crawley, where he was sent to join his battalion. He was not over concerned. As Willats remembered: 'I didn't realise the importance of the declaration of war. I thought it would be over by Christmas. Then we ended up saying the same thing every year. Eventually we were right – but it took six years.'

Once he found himself in Guildford, training to be an infantry-man, Willats soon realized the army was less than ready for him and his new comrades. They had uniforms but no barrack rooms and were forced to sleep on the floors of private billets. Parading each morning at a Territorial Army drill hall, they were marched to receive their meals in the town's cattle market. It was an inauspicious start to what would be a brief war for Willats.

In keeping with the desperate need to get infantry battalions to France, the Queen's received just ten weeks' training before they were sent to France in April 1940, as Ken Willats remembered:

> Things were going beserk at that time. It was frantic. You can't learn much about being a soldier in ten weeks. We drilled, did route marches, went on the rifle range, had kit inspections – lots of squarebashing. It was just getting us into the ways of the army. I wasn't particularly enthusiastic. I just went along with things. Basic training couldn't have been more basic. No one had great patriotism or enthusiasm. We were mostly 21 year old working class boys. None of had a military bias. All the enthusiasts had already volunteered. They were really scraping the bottom of the barrel and we were the scrapings!

What made matters worse was that, just before the Germans launched their attack on France, Willats had been told he was going to be sent back to England to be posted to the School of Army Cookery as an instructor – a better use of his talents than being a cook in a front-line battalion. But his orders had never come through and as the Germans reached Abbeville he had found himself in a farmhouse holding a rifle rather than a wooden spoon. For all the good his rifle did in the next few hours, the wooden spoon might have been just as effective.

Although Willats knew the Germans were advancing towards Abbeville, the realization of how close they were was a tremendous shock:

> We looked out of the back of the farmhouse and saw tracer bullets being fired towards us. There were about 20 or 30 of the

crack tank regiments of Hitler's panzers in front of us on the
heath. We had a rifle and five rounds of ammunition each. We
fired – not knowing who or what we were firing at, I think we
probably never killed any Germans, we just fired blindly in the
direction of the tanks. When you'd used those five rounds, you
went back to Colour Sergeant Davey and asked 'Can I have five
more rounds please?' It was ridiculous. But I don't remember
being frightened. I just did what I was told.

What Willats didn't know was that these tanks were from the
German 2nd Armoured Division, the spearhead of von Rundstedt's
Army Group A. This was the force that had punched through the
Ardennes, crossed the River Meuse, then headed north to endanger
the BEF from the rear. Such strategic considerations, and the
implications for the BEF, were far from Willats' mind as the battle
for Abbeville continued: 'The Sergeant Major sent me to help a
chap manning a Boyes anti-tank rifle. I went out fetch him because
he'd been wounded. It was strange. The road was as quiet as a tomb.
I found him. He was wandering about, very badly wounded. His
eye was out hanging out on his cheek. So I led him back to the
farm.' Safely back, Willats continued to fire at the tanks but soon
realized the situation was hopeless when they heard the sound of
German vehicles entering the farmyard: 'About 30 Germans appeared, led by an SS man. We knew there was no hope so we came
out. That was the end of my military career, it was all over in a flash.'
    Uncertain of their fate, Willats and his four comrades were
marched away to a barbed wire enclosure that had been hastily
erected in a nearby field. What happened next was the natural
reaction for men who had been on the move for days: 'The first
thing I did was to fall asleep. I'd been awake for two nights and
sleep was the biggest enemy of the soldier. The body can only go so
far without rest. I was completely exhausted. It was uncontrollable.
I just went to sleep.'
    For the men within this enclosure, surrounded for the first time
with barbed wire, there was a terrible feeling of emptiness. It was

the same for all the men taken prisoner in the battles across France and Belgium. They were physically, and often mentally, exhausted. Many had not eaten for days, or washed and shaved – but it was not a time for NCOs to start berating men for being unshaven. Some had mates around them, others had seen their mates die and were left along among unfamiliar faces. Each of them began to learn the skills that would help them survive through all the trials that lay ahead. Some tried desperately to find someone they knew. Others retreated into a state where the mind focused entirely on self-preservation. Fighting for a comfortable place to sleep became as much a part of their lives as showing discipline or defiance of the enemy. It was the beginning of the dog-eat-dog existence that would follow them through their lives within Germany's prisoner of war camps.

Those taken prisoner around Abbeville were marched from their makeshift enclosure. Their journey took them northwards, spending the first night in the grounds of a local gendarmerie. Once again they dropped to the cold, bare earth and slept where they lay. Those still with blankets blessed their good fortune. Those without were too exhausted to care, since there was hardly a man among them who would not have swapped a blanket for a hot meal.

In the final days of May and the early days of June, groups of prisoners were collected all over the battlefields. The battered and bloodied survivors of the defeat and the rearguard actions were slowly herded together, ready to begin the long march into Germany. In twos and threes, men stumbled out with their arms raised and were marched to large pens with hundreds of others. Then the crowds joined up with other crowds until thousands were bundled together into vast khaki-clad hordes. It was not long before the men captured at Abbeville were joined by similarly dazed and desperate survivors from one of the most vicious encounters of the entire campaign.

Of all the battles leading up to the Dunkirk evacuation none was more significant than the siege of Calais. What made it so important was that the soldiers sent to the port only arrived in France on 23

May. With the BEF already retreating, the 1st Battalion, the Rifle Brigade, the 60th Rifles (officially known as the 2nd Battalion, the King's Royal Rifle Corps), the Queen Victoria Rifles and the 3rd Royal Tank Regiment were sent to Calais to help secure the route back to Dunkirk. However, when they arrived it was soon clear there was little they could do to help the BEF. Instead it would be a miracle for them to survive.

One of those who did survive was Bob Davies, a former Harrods clerk and pre-war Territorial. He was so typical of many young Territorials who had joined, not out of a sense of patriotism but because it was like a club. In his case, he loved motorcycles and had joined the TA's only motorcycle battalion, the Queen Victoria Rifles. The irony was they arrived in France without their transport that had been left languishing in Kent: 'When we unloaded all we had was our rifles and the ammunition we carried – bugger all else. We just had Bren guns and no heavy machine-guns. That's all we needed. What can you do with a rifle against a tank?' When he first reached the front line Davies found himself firing at every opportunity: 'Every time I saw a bird fly I thought it was a German and fired at it.' He was soon able to calm himself, finding that his training had worked and military discipline meant he was able to follow orders without question.

For four days the battle raged through the town. Stukas rained down their screaming high explosives. Artillery fire poured down into the British and French positions. German Panzers advanced and blew apart the buildings held by the desperate defenders. Like its northerly neighbour Dunkirk, Calais was pounded to prevent its use. However, unlike Dunkirk, no ships came to rescue the soldiers. Instead they were to fight on, holding up the advance on Dunkirk.

Valiant British tank crews attempted to advance from the town, only to be destroyed by the far superior enemy armour. All manner of makeshift units, including anti-aircraft units and searchlight crews, found themselves, rifle in hand, manning strong-points and trenches. The lightly armed infantrymen did their utmost to hold off the enemy advances, slowly pulling back towards the port. Every hour brought fresh casualties who made their way back to the safety of the sixteenth-century citadel, where they sheltered in deep, vaulted cellars, listening to the rumbling of gunfire above them. The citadel, with its formidably thick walls, along with later bastions added to protect the port from attack from the sea, were Calais' main defences. Fortunately, there was also a series of canals and basins protecting the port area. As the defenders were forced back, these played an increasingly important role in holding off the German advance.

The pounding of Calais took its toll on the defenders. From his position on the eastern edge of town – with little enemy activity in front of them – Bob Davies counted his blessings. He could see the flames rising above the town and could hear the constant roar of explosions, knowing that plenty of his mates were fighting and dying. As the Germans took control of large parts of Calais, they occupied the imposing Hôtel de Ville, from where their snipers were able to cover vast swathes of the port area. As the battle raged above them, desperate doctors did their best to treat the wounded, despite a shortage of equipment. In order to amputate limbs, the doctors attempted to use knives until a rusty hacksaw was found in the corridors of the citadel cellars. This was soon sterilized and put to work.

For four days the defenders hung on. Short of food, water and, above all, ammunition, their position became desperate. By 26 May there was no longer a cohesive defence of the town, rather pockets of men were still fighting. Determined young officers and the remnants of their men fought on, some even attempting to counterattack the enemy, until their ammunition was exhausted. Extraordinary acts of heroism were performed by men whose actions were never rewarded since there were no witnesses to report their deeds. Stretcher-bearers defied machine-gun fire to run out into the open to rescue the wounded. In desperate hand-to-hand encounters, the defenders used fixed bayonets to prevent the enemy overrunning their positions. Throughout the shrinking perimeter, machine-guns were fired to the very last round, mortars fired until they were out of ammunition – and then it was hopeless. With the bastion surrounded there was no point in fighting on. Any further resistance would only endanger the wounded men sheltering underground. And so with a heavy heart, the British commander, Brigadier Nicholson, finally surrendered Calais.

At the end of the four-day battle, Bob Davies found himself walking about in a dream:

> About six of us went down to a boat and rowed across to this flat, marshy area that went out to the sea. We just headed for the sea. I don't know why, I suppose we thought that was the direction of home. We found an old cargo boat washed up on the beach. We thought there might be food on it, so we climbed up onto the deck. There were the dead bodies of the crew everywhere. We searched everywhere – through the cabins and the wheel-house – looking for food. It was a real mess. Then all of a sudden we heard a yell, turned and saw a Jerry at the top of the ladder.

Then Davies heard the of words dreaded by soldiers: 'For you the war is over.' Looking over the side of the boat, they could see a tank with its gun pointed towards them. Worried they might be shot, Davies and his comrades descended to the beach. They were immediately marched to a field where they gathered with other survivors of the battle. There was little chance to think about what was happening, as Davies admitted: 'I don't know what my feelings were. Everything had happened so quick. One day we were tucked away in a hop farm in Kent, then we were in Calais with no hope of getting home again. But it didn't sink in. Maybe if we'd been older and more worldly wise we would have understood it better. It was like dream gone wrong.'

The sense of utter mental confusion suffered by Davies was also illustrated by the experience of another man captured on the same beach. Vernon Mathias, like Bob Davies, a London shopworker, was shot in the arm whilst patrolling the sand dunes outside Calais.

Weak and confused from the loss of blood, blacking out as he walked, with his fingers numb where the tourniquet was cutting off circulation, Mathias headed for the same boat that had run aground. As he approached the boat he asked a man he assumed to be a Belgian soldier if he had any food. The man nodded and passed him a tin of blood sausage. Then Mathias spotted a group of his comrades and approached them. One called to him: 'Hello Taff. How does it feel to be a prisoner of war?' Only then did he realize the Belgian soldier had in fact been a German.

Around 60 per cent of the defenders of Calais were killed or wounded in the course of the four days' fighting. Approximately 500 wounded men were left in the cellars of the citadel. As the exhausted defenders began the long march into captivity, they surveyed the scene. The blackened wrecks of army trucks and civilian vehicles of all descriptions littered the streets. The hulks of tanks sat amidst the ruins, abandoned in the rubble alongside machine-guns, ammunition and equipment. Five of the tanks had actually been destroyed by their crews who, expecting to be evacuated by sea, had not wanted them to fall into enemy hands.

Yet it was not just the destruction of the town that appalled the survivors. One group of prisoners marched past truckloads of dead French soldiers whose vehicles had been spotted and dive bombed by the Luftwaffe. Alongside the numerous corpses of those who had fallen in the battle for Calais lay the seriously wounded. Their pitiful cries seared into the minds of the prisoners as they marched past. The begging of the wounded for water went unheeded as the victorious Germans refused to let the prisoners break ranks to offer assistance.

However, some of the prisoners who went into captivity at Calais showed quite different emotions from the men captured in some of the other battles. Since they had been surrounded, and had fought virtually to the last round, they did not feel their own role in the battle for France had been so pathetic. Unlike Eric Reeves, who had been captured before he had been able to fire his weapon, they had upheld the proud traditions of the British Army. They had fought against the odds, had held the enemy off for days and – even as the town collapsed into flames around them – they had continued to stall the enemy advance. Captain Munby, one of the officers taken prisoner when the defenders of Fort Neuilly finally surrendered, later explained why he felt no shame in having been captured: 'I must confess that I was secretly relieved at the decision being taken out of my hands – a resolve to make a last stand would only have resulted in the sacrifice of some forty lives and would have merely delayed the enemy advance a few more minutes. This will be seen as unheroic to those not on the spot.'[2]

As the night skies closed in, the prisoners were herded into a churchyard where they lay down upon the cobblestones. They were so tightly packed there was little room to move. One soldier tripped over a wounded man. He bent down to help the man, only for him to die in his arms. South African-born Sergeant Stephen Houthakker recalled how he 'slept the sleep of one who was completely oblivious to his surroundings. What pleasure was that sleep! Dreams of pleasant days that seemed centuries ago. Thus ended my first day of captivity, but the dawn of horrors was only just starting. Little did we know what fate had in store for us.'[3]

That valiant band of Calais' defenders who marched into captivity had fought hard, known fear, endured hardship and then finally surrendered. Yet they had one thing that helped them through the days of hardship ahead. They were captured alongside their comrades. As Sergeant Houthakker marched out of the port he had his commanding officer beside him. He later watched with pride as the colonel offered eggs to his famished men. For the regular soldiers among them, the men marching beside them were men who had shared barrack rooms and drill squares for years. Even the Territorials went into captivity with friends around them. All had lost plenty of good mates in the battles, but all had those who remained to help sustain them in the trials that awaited them.

Yet for others the moment of capture was one of great loneliness. It seemed their world had collapsed as they were left alone amidst the chaos of defeat. One of those who experienced this

sense of isolation was Les Allan, a young Territorial in the Buckinghamshire Battalion of the Oxfordshire and Buckinghamshire
Light Infantry. Allan had never wanted to be an infantryman, but
fate had determined he would relinquish any notion of joining the
artillery. Back in 1938, he and a mate had made the decision to join
the Territorial Army: 'We were always hearing about Hitler on the
radio and like everyone else we thought this chap needed to be
taught a lesson. We were young, naïve and patriotic.' However,
when they attempted to sign on as gunners in their home town of
Slough: 'we couldn't find the office for the artillery so Pete went to
ask the infantry recruiting sergeant. That was it. The RSM
wouldn't let him go. It turned out the artillery recruitment centre
was six miles away and we had no way of getting there. So we
joined the Territorial Army as infantrymen.'

Fate again took charge of Allan's destiny when it was decided he
would not go to war armed with a rifle but with a stretcher. There
were not enough bearers in one company and, since the colonel
knew Allan had some experience of first aid from his days with the
St John Ambulance, he was chosen to fill the vacant position. This
was why, on 27 May 1940, Les Allan was not manning a slit trench
or sniping from the window of some battered house. Instead he was
deep within the cellars of a convent, in an aid post filling up with
the battered and bloodied victims of battle.

But this was not some rear-echelon hospital, well marked with
Red Cross flags and fed by streams of ambulances. Instead it was in
the town of Hazebrouck, some twenty-five miles south of Dunkirk
and directly in the line of the German advance. If that was not
enough, the supposed sanctuary of the aid post was directly beneath
the headquarters of a battalion whose commanding officer had
received the stark order: 'Hold at all costs.'[4] In the final day of
fighting at Hazebrouck, Les Allan and his comrades would discover
the price of such words – the orders that meant the majority of the
BEF would be able to escape. As Les Allan later remarked: 'We
were waiting for reinforcements, but the reinforcements were busy
being evacuated from the beaches of Dunkirk.'

Throughout the day, the full fury of war descended on the defenders of Hazebrouck. All day the enemy bombarded the town. From their fortified houses the Ox and Bucks did their best to fend off the attacks but with just four field guns and two anti-tank guns there was little they could do. Light tanks and infantry probed their defences, artillery fire and mortar bombs rained down in the streets and on the houses, planes circled overhead bombing and machine-gunning the men below. These aerial attacks made a great impression on Les Allan as he ran around the town trying to bring in casualties for treatment: 'The Germans were very infuriated that they were being held back. They were anxious to push past us. So the bombing was terrific. They say that Stukas were no good – maybe that's true, they may have been no good in a dogfight against a Spitfire – but they were deadly when against men armed with just rifles and bayonets.'

In the forward positions some of the men put their weapons to good use. One platoon found itself overlooking an open stretch of road being used by enemy traffic. With impunity they were able to pick off anyone trying to use the road: 'We found that motorcyclists didn't have a chance to survive, that nearly all tanks passed safely . . . and that troop carrying vehicles presented an easy target. We even had the pleasure of blowing an idle traffic controller to pieces with the anti-tank rifle.'[5]

With casualties growing, Les Allan had no choice but to keep working, which meant being outdoors, in full view of the enemy. At least the riflemen were supposed to keep their heads down. The medics and bearers just had one armband and a haversack with Red Cross on it. Those he could help were taken to the cellars where the medics tried desperately to patch them up. Unfortunately for the wounded there were no doctors to help them. The medical officer had already been evacuated to find a safer position for the wounded. So many bodies were filling the floor that movement through the cellar became difficult: 'As I entered I saw a man laying there in the entrance. It was a chap called Johnson, he had awful head wounds. His face was all torn open. There was blood everywhere. His jaw and skull were bashed in. I just kicked him out of the way. You soon realise you have to help those who can be saved, not those who are virtually dead.' Many years later, at a battalion reunion, Les Allan came face-to-face with Private Johnson again. Amazingly, he had survived the destruction of the convent and his wounds had slowly recovered. As they chatted, Allan noted Johnson was smoking a pipe. He explained that he was unable to smoke cigarettes since the damage to his jaw meant he couldn't keep a cigarette between his lips, however, he could comfortably hold a pipe up to his mouth.

As the battle raged, Allan moved around among the flaming wreckage of the battalion's ammunition trucks and carriers. The wireless trucks were abandoned in the streets as movement became suicidal. Communication between HQ and the companies became impossible, as the runners were fired at whenever they tried to move in the open. No longer was the battalion making a co-ordinated defence of Hazebrouck, instead there were simply 'penny packets' of infantry desperately attempting to hold off the enemy for as long as possible. The survivors of D Company watched as German troops advanced towards the convent, yet they could offer no assistance. All the exits to the house they were defending were covered by enemy machine-guns, all they could do was watch the fate of their beleaguered comrades.

Eventually, the battle closed in on the defenders of battalion HQ. No longer did Allan need to go outside to find wounded to bring to the convent's cellars, he could simply fetch them from the upper floors. At one point he found himself manning a Bren gun, convincing himself it was correct for a medic to bear arms in defence of the wounded. By dusk, stragglers from throughout the battalion had made their way back to battalion HQ for the final assault. Every available man was ready to fight and all the cooks and drivers were upstairs manning rifles and machine-guns. As the enemy assault continued, fire took hold of the upper floors of the convent and the defenders were forced to move down to continue the battles from the lower floors.

By dusk news had reached Hazebrouck that elements of the BEF were being withdrawn to Dunkirk but it meant little to those within battalion HQ. Escape was impossible. All they could do was to sit tight inside their flaming position and pray for a miracle. Watching from D Company's position, it became clear the defence of Hazebrouck was doomed: 'The forward movement of the enemy could be observed by light signals which they fired as they advanced along each street, and I soon realised they were closing in on BN HQ from three sides.'[6] Still the men within the convent continued to defy the enemy, firing their weapons and slowing the advance. Their defiance cost them dear: 'Apparently by some pre-arranged signal four or five enemy bombers came over town and ruthlessly bombed the area.'[7]

Those watching soon realized the bombers were devastatingly accurate. An officer watching the scenes later wrote: 'I then witnessed the most despondent scene of all my life . . . not 50 yards away was our battalion HQ which was simply being blown to pieces. Planes came down so low they couldn't fail to miss it . . . at that moment the entire place was dead, there wasn't a soul to be seen anywhere. I felt an utter wreck after seeing this.'[8] With the terrible work complete, the planes flew off, leaving the Wehrmacht to complete the destruction of the convent. Six tanks closed in, firing into the already burning building. Suddenly there was a terrific roar as the entire building collapsed. Still the tanks advanced, firing into the rubble as if to advertise their devotion to the cause of destruction. Then slowly a section of infantry appeared from the shadows, their every movement silhouetted against the flames of the burning town. No longer did they need to take cover. There was no one left inside to offer resistance. The defence of Hazebrouck was over. One last obstacle on the road to Dunkirk had fallen.

Yet, the battle was not over for some within the convent. Despite the pounding of the HQ, Les Allan had kept working. Bloody bodies had filled the cellars, dust had been shaken from the ceiling, coating the wounded men in a film of dirt, but his work went on:

The artillery had got the range. For the last hour we were down in the cellar for our own safety. We were keeping our heads down hoping to avoid the shelling. The convent was in flames, so the blokes upstairs were fighting in the gardens. They fought to the very last – at least to the end of their ammunition. It was a last ditch stand, the Germans invited them to surrender but they refused. We couldn't give the wounded much treatment. We just had first aid bandages. All we could do was to stem the bleeding. We just helped those we could treat. But they were good – they were resigned to their position. We told them we'd get them out as soon as possible. I think the fact we didn't desert them helped to ease their minds. None of us would have deserted them anyway – even if we wanted to there was nowhere to go.

Trying to ignore the roar of the bombers and the crackle of the flames, he made one final effort to help the wounded. As he tried to leave the cellar his world, quite literally, collapsed around him. For a brief moment the hideous roar heard across the town terrified Allan – and then it was over. Silence engulfed his world.

By 9.30 p.m. the whole town had fallen silent. Hazebrouck, along with its defenders, was a dead town. As the remnants of the battalion scattered northwards towards Dunkirk they had no idea of the fate of those left behind in the ruins of the convent. Just twelve officers and 200 men of the Buckinghamshire Battalion reached England. The commander of D Company took almost a week to reach the coast. Some of the stragglers who made their way northwards were captured before they could get away. A party led by Lieutenant Powell from D Company reached Dunkirk one day after the last boats had departed. The group led by CSM Baldrick reached the Dunkirk perimeter but were taken prisoner.

How long Les Allan lay in the ruins, he would never know. Eventually he came to, as two German medics grabbed his inert body and dragged him upstairs into the street. Nursing a head wound, he sat in the street wondering what had happened. All he knew was that somehow he had survived. As the ceiling had collapsed he had just been leaving the cellar. The arched stone entranceway had taken the brunt of the collapse and remained standing – with him beneath it.

As he slowly regained consciousness there were none of his comrades to be seen. It seemed no one else had been pulled from the rubble that had buried the wounded men he had been caring for earlier. Nor were there any of his fellow bearers, or any of the infantrymen to be seen. He was alone. Dumped onto a lorry, he was driven to a French field hospital. As he struggled to make sense of what had happened, he realized someone had bandaged his head – when or who, he couldn't remember. At the field hospital an English-speaking German officer took away the haversack, arm-band and papers that identified him as a medic. As soon as it became clear Allan was walking wounded he was separated from the French prisoners. Still alone, he was placed onto a truck and driven to a reception area for British prisoners. In the weeks, months, then years, that followed he never met another survivor of the defence of Hazebrouck, a battle that the German Army described as having been carried out 'in a manner truly worthy of the highest tradition of the British Army'.[9]

However, if some Germans rushed to praise the efforts of the British Army, there were plenty who did not hold the defeated men in such high esteem. Some believed their own propaganda that they were superior to all others. In their minds the prisoners were worthless specimens who deserved nothing more than to be beaten and humiliated. Initially, many prisoners found it was common for the German front-line infantrymen to treat the defeated British with respect, as Peter Wagstaff discovered:

There is no doubt there is a vast difference between the treatment by the fighting soldier at the front and the adminis-trative bastard at the back. I remember I found myself at a German gunnery colonel's HQ. He looked at me and stood to attention and then gave me a bottle of beer. I also remember

sitting on the pavement of a railway station, as we waited to be
put into cattle trucks. A whole lot of German troops passed us,
they were young lads – I don't suppose they were more than 18
or 20. And somebody lobbed a cigarette into my lap. He did it
quite secretly.

Similarly, Eric Reeves discovered the fighting men who took
him into captivity treated him fairly. Some men from his regiment
were even offered lifts by German motorcyclists who dropped
them off at the enclosures for prisoners, rather than leaving them to
walk. Indeed, Eric Reeves was initially shocked at being so well
cared for by his sworn enemy. He soon discovered not all Germans
were so concerned about prisoners: 'The next day the B-Echelon
troops turned up. They kicked us all the way up the road.'

For some, such mistreatment became a regular feature of the
round up. At Hesdin five British officers were singled out and
forced to stand in the gutter. Three were wounded and one was
suffering from a fever. The French and Belgian medics who passed
through the streets were refused permission to help the wounded
officers, instead the German soldiers stood and jeered. After four
hours of humiliation, two of the officers were finally taken away by
ambulance. An hour later the remaining officers were eventually
allowed to rest.

Elsewhere five British officers and forty other ranks were forced
to spend a night in a cowshed that was deep in liquid manure. The
policy of deliberate humiliation, particularly of British officers, was
widespread. Soldiers found themselves laughed at by their captors,
many of whom seemed so much taller, physically fitter and better
equipped than the exhausted POWs. Senior officers found themselves forced to stand to attention when speaking to junior German
officers. Captain G.S. Lowden, captured at Rouen in June, was told
by his captors that all officers would have their rank badges
removed and then be sent to salt mines. Once the British had
been defeated, his captors informed him, the prisoners would be
held as slave labourers for thirty years. The threats were com-

pounded by the promise that if any officer attempted to escape, five other officers would be shot as a reprisal. Such claims hit the already battered morale of the prisoners, although the next threat was even more worrying for Captain Lowden: 'our women folk at home would be equally treated and those found to be of suitably Nordic stock would be reserved for breeding purposes . . . my own wife, being partly of Scandinavian stock, was practically certain to be amongst the favoured ones!'[10]

If it was not enough for the defeated British to see the modern tanks, guns, half-track carriers and automatic weapons of the enemy, they also had to endure Germans armed with cameras. Like tourists taking holiday snaps, their captors seemed obsessed with taking photographs of the battleground and the men who had lost the battle. One group of prisoners found camera-wielding Germans lining up to photograph their bare backsides as they used the open latrines. It was just the beginning of the degradation they would suffer in the months and years that followed.

To some of the survivors such behaviour seemed little more than gesturing compared to what they had already witnessed. After all, what were kicks, punches or humiliation compared to the fury of mass murders? In May 1940 there were two incidents that have, in the post-war years, come to sum up the brutality shown by the SS towards defeated British soldiers. The massacres at Le Paradis on the 27th, and at Wormhoudt the following day cost the lives of scores of soldiers who had given their all in battle and then surrendered.

When the survivors of the 2nd Battalion Royal Norfolk Regiment, surrendered they were filled with the same sense of trepidation shared by all prisoners. They were marched away, their helmets and equipment taken from them, then sent to a nearby farm, Le Paradis. Their treatment at the hands of the 1st Battalion, 2nd Infantry Regiment, of the SS Totenkopf Division was rough, but initially no rougher than that experienced by many prisoners. Wounded men were kicked to their feet, others were hit with rifle-butts and threatened with bayonets. But it was what followed that was so different to the majority of POW experiences. Around

ninety of the Norfolks were marched to a brick farm building with
a pit running along the outside. When they saw the two machine-
guns pointing towards them it was clear they were to be executed.
There was nowhere to run or hide as the machine-guns poured fire
at the helpless men. Eventually the bullets stopped and the
survivors could hear bayonets being clipped to rifles. The survivors
then heard the ringing of pistol shots and the sound of bayonets
being thrust into screaming men. Others had their skulls smashed in
with rifle-butts, a sight that appalled some of the Germans who
discovered the massacre site. Some of the badly wounded men
pleaded to be finished off, desperate to be released from their
agony. Slowly the cries of the wounded and the noise of gunfire
died down as the SS finished their deadly labours. When the attack
was finally over just two men were alive. Privates Bert Pooley and
Bill O'Callaghan had somehow survived, despite both being shot
and having been checked over by the SS men. When night fell the
two men were finally able to escape the scene.

In the aftermath of the defence of Wormhoudt a group of
survivors from the 2nd Battalion Royal Warwickshire Regiment
were herded towards a barn. Those unable to walk were simply
shot where they lay. In common with so many of the defeated
troops, the fifty or more who were hustled inside the barn were
exhausted and apprehensive. All knew the terrible reputation of
their SS captors. At the entrance to the barn stood a German soldier
who spoke with an American accent. The actions of this man,
taking out a hand grenade and preparing it to be thrown, convinced the prisoners of their intentions. Believing they were to be
executed, Captain Lyn-Allen asked for permission for the men to
have a last cigarette. The request was granted, then the Germans
began firing machine-pistols and throwing grenades into the barn.
Two of the grenades had little effect on the assembled men since
Sergeant Moore and CSM Jennings threw themselves onto the
grenades, absorbing the blast but sacrificing their lives.

The SS then called for the survivors to leave the barn in groups
of five. As they left they walked six or seven paces, then were shot

in the back by the Germans. Realizing their fate, the following groups refused to move, causing the Germans to continue throwing grenades into the barn. When they believed their work was done the Germans departed. Yet they had not been thorough enough. Some of the men had survived despite their injuries. Some had feigned death, others had suffered sufficient injury to lose consciousness and appear dead. One, Private Albert Evans, had escaped from the barn when the Germans threw the first grenades. Along with Captain Lyn-Allen, Evans – his arm shattered by the first grenade – made for the safety of a copse, where they sheltered in a pond. Soon a German appeared and fired at the two men. The captain received a fatal wound and slumped into the water. Two bullets then struck Evans in the neck and he too collapsed into the dirty pond. Believing his quarry dead, the German departed. Some minutes later, Evans regained consciousness. Amazed he had survived, he crawled away, being hit again by a stray bullet fired during the execution of others at the barn.

Albert Evans was incredibly fortunate, he was found by a German ambulance unit who treated his wounds and saved his life. Others who survived included one from the groups taken outside, he had been hit then feigned death. Some of the survivors within the barn were eventually saved by a German anti-aircraft unit who turned up and treated their wounds. Another man was actually blown from the barn by a grenade and shot in the face, but he too somehow escaped death.

The first reports of the Wormhoudt massacre reached London via letters from an officer who met survivors of the incident whilst in hospital in Ghent. At first Lieutenant Kenneth Keens did not believe the man's story, the shocked survivor of the massacre being unable to remember any of the names of his comrades. However, as the days passed, three survivors, Edward Daly, Albert Evans and Private Johnson recounted the same version of events.

Although the incidents at Wormhoudt and Le Paradis became widely publicized in the post-war years, they were not isolated incidents. There were plenty of other murders and acts of violence towards prisoners right across France and Belgium. When Lieutenant Keens reported the Wormhoudt massacre he also pointed out stories he had heard of similar incidents on a smaller scale. One wounded officer from the Worcestershire Regiment told Keens he had watched as his men were lined up against a wall and executed by SS troops. He was then also shot but somehow survived. French sources later also revealed that twenty-one Scottish soldiers had been discovered in a mass grave. Each corpse displayed neck wounds suggesting they had not fallen in battle but been executed by their captors.

Some of the many murders and massacres were later reported to London by prisoners via the Red Cross, others remained only in the memories of the men who had been fortunate to survive. Fred Gilbert, serving in the 8th Battalion of the Warwickshire Regiment – whose 2nd Battalion became victims of the Wormhoudt massacre – watched as his captain, whose last minutes of battle had been spent trying to clear his jammed revolver, attempted to surrender: 'He'd got his hands up and the German officer just shot him. His hand was up and the bullet went straight through the palm and blew his hand off. It was bewildering, I didn't know what was going to happen next.'

The officer was fortunate, the German officer then waved his pistol and signalled to him to walk away to join the other prisoners. Others were not so lucky. In the aftermath of the defeat of the 4th Battalion of the Royal West Kent Regiment in the Forêt de Nieppe, a number of soldiers were murdered by their captors. Corporal Bertie Bell, a reservist who had spent five years in India during the 1930s, Corporal Theroux and Privates Shilling, Mills, Daniels, Carter and Lancaster, were rounded up by soldiers from the SS Totenkopf Division after they were found sleeping in a farmhouse. Paraded from the farm in single file, the men were taken into the forest. Uncertain what might happen next, Bertie Bell kept a careful eye on their captors, who all seemed to have their rifles at the ready. Suddenly one of the SS men jumped up and hit Daniels and Shilling with the butt of his rifle then spat at them. Bell tried to intervene, hitting out at the German, but the intervention of a German officer prevented any further action. At that moment Bell heard the officer bark out an order. Though unable to understand the words, he was certain of their meaning and threw himself to the ground as shots rang out around him: 'I lay perfectly still and held my breath. A few seconds later there were three revolver shots. I then heard the Germans walk away. Remaining in my position for some five minutes more, I got up and looked at my comrades.' What he saw shocked him: 'I saw that one revolver shot had hit Private Shilling and blown half his head off. The other two shots appeared to have been aimed at Private Daniels who was shot in both eyes.'[11]

For the whole of the day he remained hidden in the forest, only returning to look for the bodies the next day. He discovered all evidence of the execution had been removed. For five more days he hid in the forest, attempting to find food and water. Eventually he was hidden by French farmers and joined up with two other survivors of the battle. Six months later Corporal Bell and Second-Lieutenant Parkinson of the Royal Sussex Regiment reached Marseilles and were interned by the Vichy authorities. They escaped and reached Gibraltar in April 1941.

Another who survived the vicious attentions of victorious Nazis was Private John Cain of the 2nd Battalion, the Manchester Regiment. He was part of a Vickers heavy machine-gun crew fighting in the rearguard. At 5 a.m. on 26 May their position was overrun by advancing tanks and infantry. Cain and his fellow machine-gunners Johnson, Phillips and Hodgkins, along with the platoon runner Private Maish, soon found themselves prisoners. Although wounded in the left shoulder, Cain helped Johnson, who had been wounded in the foot, to the supposed safety of a house, whilst Privates Maish and Hodgkins carried Phillips, who had been wounded in the hip and groin. Confronted by Unteroffizier Karl Mohr, Cain refused to reveal his regiment, defying the German by revealing just his name, rank and number. Ominously Mohr told him: 'We have means in the German army.'[12] When Private Johnson heard the German's words he turned towards him, only to be shot in the stomach by Mohr, who fired his rifle from the hip.

The unwounded Hodgkins jumped at Mohr in a futile attempt to stop his murderous intentions but was cut down by a burst of fire from another German armed with a machine-pistol. His right breast was shot away and he had a bullet hole in the centre of his forehead. Accepting his fate, Cain looked towards one of the Germans and then flinched as he heard the bang of the rifle. The bullet tore into his cheek, throwing him unconscious to the floor. When he regained consciousness he was surrounded by the corpses of his friends and was being assisted by a German medic who revealed to Cain the identity of the man who had murdered his friends and then left him for dead. Unteroffizier Mohr was captured by the Americans at Landau in the last weeks of the war. Efforts were then made to bring him to the UK to face trial for the murder of Privates Johnson and Maish.

Although the shooting of prisoners was witnessed across the battlefields of France that summer, few incidents were as bloody as the reported killings of British soldiers at Colpaert Farm. The incident was reported by Madame Ghoris, a refugee from Lille. She watched as a unit led by an officer known to her as Oberleutnant von Pingsaft, found four British soldiers hiding in a barn:

One of them was wounded and had to walk with two sticks. The Germans forced him, as well as the three others, to raise their hands and made them march, hitting them with batons. The Germans, in order that we should not witness this, made us enter the houses. A few moments later three Germans came to the house and asked for water to wash their hands and forearms which were covered in blood. The Germans said they had just cut the heads off the four British soldiers.

Denise Besegher was also present when the Germans entered the kitchen, noting how one was carrying a bayonet in his bloodstained hands: 'He asked for soap, water and a towel to dry himself, and said that the four "Tommies" had had their necks cut, making a gesture with his hand, just as if he had himself done it.'

The horrors did not end there. A local miller, forty-one-year-old Achille Boudry, was forced to bury the corpses of British soldiers who had fallen in the battle around the farm. As he worked he noticed that one of the men was still alive. He reported this to the German supervising the burial. Instead of rescuing the wounded soldier the German simply told Boudry to collect the man's wristwatch and to continue with the burial.

Whatever treatment they faced, most of the prisoners shared similar experiences. First there were the searches carried out by their captors. Some prisoners frantically scraped hollows in the earth to bury grenades or bullets they had in their pouches and pockets, fearful of the reaction of their guards if they were discovered. Guards walked among the prisoners, knocking off their helmets. One soldier recalled a guard knocking his helmet to the ground, then kicking it. The guard looked down at the dented helmet and declared: 'That's how good your English steel is.' During the searches many prisoners were forced to discard all of their equipment. Small packs, ammunition pouches, belts, great-coats, gas masks and groundsheets littered the areas in which the prisoners gathered. Many lost their waterbottles and mess tins, meaning they would have nothing in which to collect food and water in the days ahead. So too they lost their army sewing kits – housewives, as they were known – that would be desperately needed in the months that followed.

There was little they could do to prevent the losses. It was a brave man who dared complain to his captors. Most among them were too exhausted, or simply too relieved to have survived, to worry about what they were losing. For most, it was not the concern over equipment that was lost. Instead, all that mattered were their personal possessions. What they did not want to lose were their wallets, watches, rings, letters from home and, above all, the treasured photographs of their loved ones. For those able to save their personal possessions, these would bring immense comfort in the long years ahead. Despite his guards searching for anything that could be a potential weapon, Bill Holmes was able to save a small pair of scissors. These he kept for five years, using them to cut the hair of his fellow prisoners.

For a few, the losses during these initial searches had an effect upon their destiny. Under the Geneva Convention no medical personnel could be treated as prisoners. They were officially 'protected personnel', whose duties should only be the treatment of the sick and wounded. Indeed, many medics fully expected to be sent home to the UK after all the wounded had been cared for. For Les Allan there was no hope of such treatment. As the German officer explained to him that he was a prisoner, he tore away the armband and haversack marked with a Red Cross. Likewise, he took away Allan's army paybook, which identified him as a stretcher-bearer and 'protected person'. It was an action that would condemn him to years of working in farms and factories, rather than using his skills to care for the sick.

Whilst thousands of newly captured men huddled in barns or sprawled out exhausted on the bare earth of fields – comforted only by the relief they had survived both the battle and the round up by their captors – other prisoners were already facing up to the reality of existence as a prisoner of the victorious Nazi armies. Even before the battle for France was over some unfortunate POWs found themselves forced to start work for their captors. Although such behaviour was expressly forbidden by the Geneva Convention, groups of freshly captured men were sometimes made to assist the Germans with their continuing efforts to defeat the Allies. On 26 May, one group of Royal Army Service Corps soldiers were forced at gunpoint to operate a ferry across a canal that was standing in the way of the advancing Germans. They were made to haul rubber dinghies back and forth by way of a rope, allowing enemy troops to cross the canal and continue their pursuit of the retreating British forces. Appalled by the notion of aiding the enemy, some men attempted to resist. All they received for their efforts were bayonet wounds to their legs.

At the end of their labours, the soldiers were finally searched by their captors. When the turn came for Lance-Corporal Stanley

Green to be searched he reached out to try to prevent the guard from taking away his family photographs: 'Thereupon another soldier who was carrying a German hand grenade – of the type carried at the end of a short stick, popularly known as a "potato masher" – struck me across the face with the grenade. I was knocked out and when I came to some time later I found I was bleeding freely from the nose and mouth, that my underlip had been cut right through and that two teeth had been knocked out.'[13] Dragging himself to his feet and checking his pockets, he soon realized the teeth were not all he had lost. Also gone were a pound note, a gold ring, a silver cigarette case and the gold watch he had just received from his parents for his twenty-first birthday.

Following the search, Green and his fellow prisoners were made to carry German corpses to a graveyard, while other German soldiers laughed and jeered at them, with scant respect for their own dead. Then, at pistol point, the prisoners were forced to dig graves and bury the German dead.

Whether they found themselves working for the enemy, nursing their own wounds, blessing their fortune to have survived or cursing their fate at being left behind in France, around 40,000 soldiers of the BEF found themselves in captivity by the time the last boats had sailed from Dunkirk for home. In fields, farms and village squares, as the prisoners were assembled ready to begin the long journey into captivity, few really knew what lay ahead. Would they be treated fairly or be tormented as slave labourers? For Bill Holmes, who had 'missed the boat' at Dunkirk, the answer would soon become apparent: 'And then we got five years of hell.'

CHAPTER THREE

The Fight Goes On

'Where's the officer?' . . . 'Dead.' . . . 'Where's the sergeant?' . . .
'Killed.' 'Where's the corporal? . . . 'Killed.' . . . 'Who's in charge?'
They pointed to Lance-Corporal Rose, who was in command of the
whole platoon.

David Mowatt, Seaforth Highlanders

Along with the last boats, all hope of rescue had slipped away for
those men who remained around Dunkirk. Though the heroic
men of the rearguard, left behind in France, had marched wearily
into captivity, the battle was not yet over. Despite the post-war
presentation of the events that summer, the British role in the battle
of France did not end as the last of the little ships sailed for home or
when the rearguard ran out of ammunition and raised their arms in
surrender. Instead, right across northern France remained a multi-
tude of BEF units who had yet to play an active part in the
campaign. Many were reserve formations, rear echelon units –
supply units, engineers, pioneers, transport companies – but they
were all still soldiers, and all still needed to get to safety. If Britain
was to survive the fall of France it was clear they would need every
available man to defend against the Nazi menace.

However, they were not all the so-called 'useless mouths' of the
rear echelon, non-fighting units. As the evacuation ended from the

beaches of Dunkirk, there remained an entire front-line division whose role in the campaign was not yet complete. To the south, still fighting alongside the French, were the officers and men of the 51st Highland Division. During April the division, under their commander Major-General Victor Fortune, who had served with the Black Watch during the Great War and with the Seaforth Highlanders during the inter-war years, had moved into the Maginot Line, near Metz, and come under French command. It was a move designed to strengthen Allied solidarity, but one that would cost the Highlanders dear.

The 51st Division began the war as home to some of the finest regiments in the British Army, among them the Black Watch, the Gordon Highlanders, the Argyll and Sutherland Highlanders and the Seaforth Highlanders. Even their divisonal artillery included the proud 1st Royal Horse Artillery, who had sacrificed their beloved horses just a couple of years earlier. By war's end the division had served in France, in the victory at El Alamein, invaded Sicily and Italy, fought in Normandy and been among the first troops to cross the Rhine. However, in 1940, all that was a long way in the future and the division had plenty of fighting to do before it could win those battle honours.

Like every regiment in the British Army, the Highland regiments were fiercely proud of their heritage, but they also had a distinct identity that made them stand out amidst their peers. Each regiment retained its own tartan, either worn on kilts or trews, and displayed distinctive headgear. There were tam-o'-shanters with their distinctive red hackles, Atholl bonnets and glengarries which made them stand out from the khaki-clad crowds. Such was the glamour of the Highlanders that at the outbreak of war large numbers of Englishmen – particularly Londoners – volunteered for Scottish regiments. By 1945 some Scots regiments, their numbers depleted by years of hard fighting, contained less than 50 per cent Scotsmen.

The traditions of the Highland regiments had survived for many years, proudly protected by a succession of commanding officers.

Even with war looming they still paraded in their kilts. It was a prestigious world that officers did not intend to sacrifice just because there was a war on, and the traditions applied just as firmly to the waves of conscripts, Territorials and 'foreign' volunteers. One Territorial serving in a Highland regiment recalled standing to attention at parade whilst his officer used a cane to lift their kilts to check the men were not wearing underwear. Since the unit were in makeshift accommodation at the time they did not muster on a parade ground, but instead lined up along the seafront at Carnoustie. Each parade was accompanied by the cheering of the girls from the local jam factory who came to watch the display, lying in the sand to get a good view up their kilts.

Yet the Highlanders were a hardy breed. It would take more than exposing their manhood to deter them. They were known as tough fighters, solid in defence and enthusiastic – some would say bloodthirsty – in attack. By tradition they came from lonely crofts, highland farms and windswept coastal communities. More recently they had come from the great cities of Glasgow and Edinburgh.

None was more typical of the Highland soldier than nineteen-year-old David Mowatt. Born in 1920, he had enjoyed a hard rural upbringing in one the remotest parts of the United Kingdom. The farms and villages of the Black Isle, to the north of Inverness, were as far away from the bright lights of the big cities as it was possible to get. War had opened the eyes of men like Mowatt to a world far removed from the empty Highlands of their youth:

> I was brought up the hard way. It was a rough life – no bicycles – I ran everywhere. Cross fields, over fences – I was a real country bumpkin. We lived on a big farm – my father was a foreman-horseman – there was a brook near the farm. I lived off the land. In the summertime at 4 o'clock in the morning I'd be away catching trout by hand. At 5 pm I'd come back and I'd share my catch with the other houses on the farm. Then my mother would dip the trout in rough oatmeal and fry them. It was as sweet as honey.

When the tide of the Cromarty Firth was out, Mowatt would wade through the waters, feeling for the fish underfoot and catching them. His biggest haul in one day was eighty-two.

A born countryman, he could catch eels by snaring them on the riverbank. In the summer he snared rabbits in the field. In the winter he would trap them by searching where they had burrowed beneath piles of horse dung and diving in to grab them: 'I'd come home from school with my school clothes covered in dung. My mum gave me a terrible telling off – but she always cooked the rabbit.' It was an idyllic life, but one that could not last forever. At the age of fourteen Mowatt left school and began life as a labourer on a local farm. Life continued to be hard, working all hours with just Saturday nights free to enjoy dance night in Cromarty. Cycling the five miles to town, on the bicycle he could now afford with wages coming in, Mowatt met with his mates to drink two pints of beer before the dance. The two-pint limit was imposed since they could afford no more. It was one of these evening trips that would seal their destiny:

I was 17 by then. All ten of us were in the pub and who should walk in but the recruiting sergeant. They were encouraging boys to join the TA. The man behind the bar said to him 'By God, cast your net now and you'll get the lot of them!' We all signed on, took the 'King's Shilling' and spent it on two extra pints each! We thought we'd join the TA and get a holiday – there were no holidays on farms in those days, it was seven days a week all year round.

They were right, they did get a holiday in the form of a week-long camp outside Dundee, but being a Territorial didn't change their lives. It simply meant they were even busier than before, spending even more evenings cycling through the empty lanes to Cromarty to attend evening drill sessions. It would be another year before war would finally tear Mowatt away from the Highlands. The news of war came at a fitting moment for a born countryman:

I was in the field cutting the harvest. We'd just given up the horses and it was the first – and last – harvest I had a tractor to use. I had cut two fields and I was half way through the last field. All of a sudden I could see the old farmer walking towards me. I thought, what's happened? I switched off and he said 'Pack up. Go home. Get into your uniform and report to the nearest drill hall.' I said 'Why?' He said 'You've been mobilised.'

Dressing in his uniform, with its smart Seaforth kilt, he cycled to town to meet his fellow Territorials. Within hours they were on a boat heading for the regimental headquarters. Like so many of his fellow soldiers, it was the last he would see of his Highland home for five long years.

Initially the division was stationed in northern France before later being transferred to the Maginot Line as part of plan to foster co-operation between the British and their French allies. Prior to the move south the Highlanders enjoyed the experience of being away from home. One recalled spending evenings in Lille during the phoney war:

Me and my mate Paddy used to go to the brothels. One night we were in a nice bar, Paddy fancied this African girl. So he went upstairs with her. I waited for ever such a long time for him. I thought he must be having a good time – it'll cost him a fortune! There were a couple of French officers in there and one of our sergeants chatting at the bar. Then all of a sudden this African tart came down, gabbling away in French. I asked her 'where's my mate?' With that she whacks me across the face! I thought 'what have I done?' So I pushed her over. Of course these French officers get up. They had no chance. They came at me. I picked up a chair and hit one of them, then I put a nice boot in on the other one – just where it hurts the most! He went down. I turned to go. Then this other French squaddie came up to me. He was in dead trouble. Bang! I head-butted him. He went down – straight out. So I ran. I found Paddy. He said he hadn't been enjoying it so he tried to take his money back – she'd tried to take his cap, so he'd escaped out of the window. Another night we went out to a bar. Again he went upstairs with this girl. When he came down he looked strange. He'd only knocked off this bloody great French clock and hidden it under his battle-dress! As we go out of the door this bloody thing starts chiming! So the girl behind the bar realised what's happening – she sent this French sergeant after him. That did no good – Paddy just bashed his head against the door. Goodnight! Down he goes. So we run down the road with this clock. The funny thing is, we'd had a few too many beers and on the way back he dropped it and smashed it.

The high life enjoyed by some of the soldiers didn't last forever. Once the Highlanders were transferred to the Maginot Line, they received an introduction to the real war – one that was far removed from that enjoyed by most of their comrades during this period. Once in position, the Highlanders soon discovered that the so-called 'phoney war' was in fact very real. The notion that the BEF was idle from September 1939 until 10 May 1940 was a fallacy. There was plenty of activity for the infantrymen stationed in the *ligne de contact* seven miles in front of the Maginot Line. There were trenches, command posts and listening posts to be dug. There were telephone lines to be laid. There were positions to be camouflaged. And above all else there were enemy soldiers a few hundred yards away.

The Highlanders were kept busy as they awaited the inevitable enemy assault. They occupied forward posts, from where they could observe activity. There was the vital role of gathering intelligence to build up a picture of the strength of the enemy facing them. Most importantly, the intelligence officers attempted to establish whether the Germans were building up their forces ready to attack. The troops listened for the sounds of vehicles and tried to work out where they were going. They also watched all enemy movements – counting the Germans as they moved in and out of houses and calling down artillery fire against any groups of enemy officers they spotted. They listened to the sounds of picks and shovels as labourers built defensive positions. From their own cold, damp positions they watched for which buildings showed signs of occupation – smoking chimneys were a tell-tale sign – laboriously counted and timed the sentries on duty in the enemy lines and counted the flares that hovered in the night sky. More ominously, they listened intently for the peal of church bells sometimes used to mask the deadly crack of sniper rifles. There was also the threat of enemy aircraft. On 21 April, C Company of the 7th Argylls reported five enemy aircraft brought down by infantry fire.

To fulfil the vital the task of gathering intelligence, the forward platoons of the 51st had to carry out intensive patrols along the front. David Mowatt, with the 4th Battalion Seaforth Highlanders, remembered their role:

We were in the Maginot Line to gain experience. We were going out on patrols – it wasn't all fighting. It was skirmishes and recce patrols. The boys didn't like that because they weren't allowed to fire. They were just looking at the enemy. They'd have rather been firing. They wanted to be able to defend themselves. We were keen, we were trained for it. We knew we would go into action at some point and we were ready. Of course, we didn't have a clue really.

Each night patrols sneaked out into no man's land looking for signs of whether the Germans were occupying their own forward positions. They searched for enemy telephone lines, then cut them to hinder communications. They looked for signs of new barbed wire being laid and searched the ground for any footprints that indicated enemy activity. At other times they went on hunts through woods and orchards, trying to locate the snipers that plagued them. Even when these patrols met no resistance they still faced danger since the enemy regularly shelled woodland in which they believed the British troops to be active.

The nightly patrols, and the serious reason behind them, was remembered by one soldier. Like so many youngsters, Jim Reed had joined the army to escape the boredom of his job in a Sheffield foundry. When he first visited the army recruiting office he had been immediately sent out again by the sergeant, who told him that at seventeen he was too young to volunteer. However, he did offer one piece of good advice, telling Reed: 'Go out and come back in and say you are 18!' By spring 1940 Reed found himself in an outpost in front of the Maginot Line, serving with the Seaforth Highlanders:

We got broke in gently. A section of us were in a dugout. At night one man would get blacked up and go on patrol. We'd look for Germans and they'd look for us – but I never found any. There was just a bit of shelling – it was noisy. At mealtimes one of you would have to go down with a canister to collect the food. It was a dicey, you had to be careful, because there was a German out there. Sometimes he managed to get the odd one. Once one chap has been shot you realise it's not a game anymore. It makes you a bit careful.

The Highlanders soon got an opportunity to take part in more aggressive patrolling when they sneaked forward to snatch prisoners, to attack enemy positions or to harass the enemy patrols that also used the cover of darkness to gather intelligence. In early May 1940, Second-Lieutenant Orr-Ewing, of the Black Watch recorded the activities of his fighting patrol:

About 40 yards away from me I saw 3 men running from the woods towards the stream, I opened fire with my Beretta and 2 men dropped. Immediately, heavy firing from at least four tommy guns opened up on my flank. My patrol and I all dropped flat and continued to fire and throw grenades. About 8 to 10 men then left the wood and opened fire. More men from the wood also fired on us. One man advanced towards us but was severely hit in the stomach. At least two more were hit by grenades as we heard them screaming. The enemy threw stick grenades, one landing near my bearer and me, cutting us both and temporarily blinding me with blood owing to a cut above my eye. Owing to the fact that our ammunition was running low and their superior numbers, we withdrew about 60 yards under covering fire . . .[1]

Despite the dangers of such actions, some of the patrolling troops were able to make light of their activities. One officer, calling himself 'Bashful', wrote a colourful account of a patrol. The action began as he opened fire upon an enemy patrol: 'The enemy were very rude and fired back with automatic weapons and also had the bad manners to throw a stick grenade . . . This annoyed "Bashful" no end so he played the game and pumped plenty of lead out of his weapon. The enemy retired discomforted and, "Bashful" hoped, wounded; two grenades were bunged at them as they hastily hastened back from whence they came.'[2]

As these encounters showed, it was not just the British who made nightly excursions into no man's land. Forward positions of the Lothian and Borders Horse reported hearing German patrols in the woods communicating by using owl and frog noises. Sometimes it was the German patrols whose aggression was fully displayed. In the final days of April the forward platoons of the 1st Black Watch in Hartbusch Wood came under attack by enemy patrols. The attack came in just after midnight, signalled by the stark white light of a magnesium flare fired from the woods. One platoon was able to keep the enemy at bay using grenades and well-aimed bursts of Bren gun fire that scattered the advancing Germans. The other platoon found repulsing the assault was less simple. Under a hail of mortar bombs and machine-gun fire that seemed to be coming from posts that had been unoccupied a few days earlier, the enemy attacked from both flanks and then from the rear. In the light of the flare an estimated 100 Germans charged their position, throwing grenades and firing machine-pistols. Bizarrely, it seemed none of the Germans were wearing helmets and seemed to be wearing overalls. Then an attack came from the flanks, the Germans using a ride through the woods that had concealed their advance.

The Highlanders' Bren gunners opened up a steady beat of fire, keeping the enemy at bay. Some brave men ran from cover to collect grenades and boxes of ammunition to keep the guns firing. In desperation the platoon commander fired a flare to signal SOS. It took twenty minutes for their signal to be answered. Despite the delays, caused by the difficulty of raising the carrier platoon from their beds, the arrival of the carriers saved the day. They moved forward, pouring rapid fire into the German patrols, scattering them and sending them back towards the German frontier. Two nights later another attack was made against the Black Watch's forward posts and three men were wounded when a grenade was thrown into the platoon HQ.

These activities were just a prelude for what was to come in May. The aggressive patrolling and night-time attacks on isolated outposts – followed by increased artillery activity around 9 May – masked the fact that the main assault was due to the north, through Belgium. At 7.45 a.m. on 10 May, Major-General Fortune passed the news to his front-line battalions that the enemy had launched an assault into Luxembourg, Belgium and the Netherlands. The news was passed on with the instruction that the troops were to move into battle positions – or as their French leaders put it, they were to be *mis-en-garde*. As the positions in front of the Maginot Line became a hive of activity, with all spare vehicles withdrawn a safe distance, ammunition rushed to the forward platoons and nervous men quietly accepting they would soon be thrown into battle, some responded with the characteristic phlegm of the officer class of the period. In the positions of the Royal Scots Fusiliers, the battle diarist noted the news of the German invasion with the simple words 'The balloon is up.'[3] Elsewhere, as he recorded the momentous news in the battalion war diary, an officer of the 1st Black Watch added the words 'Leave cancelled yet again.' There was an unconscious irony and sense of sad prophecy in his choice of comments. The location of the German assault, bypassing the positions of the 51st Division, meant they would see little action in front of the Maginot Line. Yet it would be years before most of them would get another chance to see their homes.

Despite light-hearted comments noted by the diarists, the division's situation was less than certain. As soon as the news came of the German assault, the commander of the 6th Battalion Royal Scots Fusiliers, Lt.-Colonel The Lord Rowallan, contacted Major-General Fortune to plead that his unit not be used in any forthcoming operations. He was blunt in his assessment of the situation. Quite simply his battalion was underequipped, undertrained and unready to face the enemy. They were not the only ones. As the men of the Royal Northumberland Fusiliers prepared their Vickers heavy machine-guns for the forthcoming battle, they could not fail to notice the words stamped into the sides of some of the weapons – '*For Drill Purposes Only.*' As one of the gunners, Jim Charters, a former miner and pre-war Territorial, remembered: 'We weren't prepared for war. It was a hopeless position, we were short of every damn thing. We took those "drill only" guns to France. It wasn't a good start.' He was right, it was an inauspicious start to what was to be a fraught month of fighting.

Although the main battles were taking place to the north of them, it didn't take long for the men of the division to begin to react to the changing situation. Drivers stopped using convoy discipline and instead sped along roads, failed to keep gaps between vehicles and rushed through villages in clouds of dust. Officers noticed their men had hair that needed cutting. In the days following the German assault Major-General Fortune complained about his men taking off their jackets and discarding their headgear. As he pointed out to all ranks in the division: 'The pride of a well disciplined unit is for all ranks to act in times of emergency exactly as they do in times of peace.'[4]

Yet it was not the changing attitudes towards discipline that really counted. What mattered was the attitude to war and the creeping violence that entered their world. Enemy patrols, though few in number, now used aggressive tactics – firing and moving to appear more numerous – to draw fire. By constantly infiltrating between the forward positions they were able to disturb the British troops all night long, increasing the frustration for the men whose days and nights were spent in dirty, damp and dangerous holes, far beyond the safety of the Maginot Line.

For the men of the 51st Division these early encounters were their first real taste of war, and many of them were relieved that it was a gradual introduction. Dick Taylor, a Territorial from Berwick-on-Tweed, approached war in a sanguine manner:

> When war came I was just anxious to get to France, I didn't have any real thoughts about what was going to happen. It was youthful enthusiasm. When we were mobilised I didn't have time to think, it was a change from working behind a shop counter! In France we were gradually introduced to war. I was in a trench – there were 4 or 5 of us – we could see the Germans in the distance. A few shells came across but it was nothing to worry about, in fact it was just a bit of a laugh. I was not nervous, I just accepted it.

His comrade Jim Charters also remembered his first experience of coming under fire: 'It was a shock the first time we got mortared. But what can you do? You just got down as far as possible in your hole. The survival instinct just takes over.'

On the day following the German assault into the Low Countries the 1st Black Watch came under heavy artillery fire and encountered an enemy patrol during the night, as they attempted to sneak through the lines. The men in the forward posts waited until the enemy were moving between their positions then opened fire, hitting the leading Germans, who were walking openly, obviously not expecting to meet any resistance. The patrol scattered and ran off under the cover of smoke: 'Two men were obviously hit and lying exposed in the open . . . they were considered dead but three bursts were fired at them with obvious effect but producing no movement. One man who had taken refuge in what appeared to be a shell-hole, attempted to crawl out, was obviously hit by a rifle bullet and fell backwards.'[5]

The division's gunners were soon embroiled in battle as well. The two forward troops of the 17th Field Regiment Royal Artillery fired 1,289 rounds of high explosive in the course of a single day. Previously, the regiment had laid claim to being the first British gunners to fire shells into German territory when they had gone into action on 6 May. Yet this activity came at a price and they lost one man killed, three wounded and one man with shell shock as a result of bombing and enemy counter battery fire. Peter Royle, a lieutenant serving with the regiment, recalled the incident: 'I well remember seeing my first dead man as one of E troops' trucks came back through our positions with a dead gunner on board. He was covered by an army blanket but his boots stuck out and the sight of these haunted me for days.'[6]

During this period the light tanks of the Lothian and Borders Yeomanry also had their first taste of action. At 6.30 p.m. on 11 May they took part in a reconnaissance patrol through woodland in front of the division's positions. They were soon spotted by the enemy. As one tank commander later recorded, they advanced along a road before veering off cross-country:

This meant crashing through some barbed wire. We skirted round the left hand corner of the wood about thirty yards out, and 80 yards between tanks. There was a considerable amount of shelling and gun fire . . . Made a quick inspection of the tank. I found that the camouflage net had been set alight by the exhaust and was burning . . . Shells were bursting very close and my spotlight was blown off. At this point my tank got bogged and I found the crew of number 3 tank hanging on to the outside. Whilst getting into position the number 2 tank got bogged, endeavouring to tow us out.

Still under fire, the crew worked quickly to put wood under tracks to grip in the mud, but just minutes later they got bogged down again. Realizing the dangers of remaining in the open, they left the tanks, first removing the firing mechanism from the guns. The next day they returned to fetch the tank, only to discover the towrope was caught in its tracks. As they attempted to free the tangled ropes they were again shelled by the enemy. This time it was with deadly results, leaving one man dead and one wounded. Efforts were also made to locate the other tank that had been lost the previous day: 'No 2 tank was found in the morning to be well out in No Man's Land. It was visited. Both tracks were off, one could not be found. The tank had been hit by a shell, the turret was twisted, and no doors could be opened.'[7]

Casualties continued to mount in the days that followed. Lieutenant Peter Royle later wrote of his memories of enemy artillery fire: 'This was the first time I had experienced shell fire at fairly close range and I soon began to know by the whining each shell made as it came towards me exactly where it would land – in front or behind. On this, my first night under fire, my fear was tinged with a certain amount of excitement because it was something new. The more I was shelled during the war the more frightening it became and the less exciting.'[8] The long-term effects of this eventually led Peter Royle to experience battle-fatigue during the campaign at Monte Cassino in Italy in 1944. He was evacuated back to the UK and spent the rest of the war in an artillery training regiment.

The division took ninety casualties in three days, with doctors performing fifty operations. On 13 May the Seaforths lost one man killed and two wounded when a fighting patrol ran into a German patrol. The same day the Black Watch suffered the deaths of three men with a further six wounded. As the Germans continued with their 'aggressive patrolling' the men of the 4th Black Watch reported enemy troops using flamethrowers in attacks on forward positions. David Mowatt recalled how the deaths of comrades initially had a major effect on the newly blooded infantrymen: 'My friend Murdo MacRae was the first to be killed in the battalion. We were mates, we'd been called up together and used to share our cigarettes. We were in the line and the Sergeant Major sent me on a stupid errand. I went to the Sergeant at Company HQ and said "You wanted to see me." He told me he hadn't called for me. While I was gone they were burying my mate.' It was a sensitivity that was soon washed away in the tide of violence that followed.

The tanks of the Lothian and Borders Yeomanry were also soon back in battle as they were sent forward to support the troops in the forward posts. Once more, they came within range of determined enemy gunners:

> No1 tank came into the view of the enemy and we were fired at by an anti tank gun, one shot hitting the track and wounding Cpl Akers, the gunner, in the leg. We tried to turn right and get under cover, but probably the track came off and the turret was out of control. Cpl Akers made a gallant effort to turn the turret so that I could get the gun into action, but at that moment we were hit by HE coming through the turret, killing Cpl Akers instantaneously and jamming the guns.[9]

Then the number two tank was hit, killing the commander and disabling the guns. The remaining crewmen got out and valiantly engaged an enemy patrol with their revolvers before wandering in the Grossenwald Forest and both getting wounded by shrapnel, until they were finally located by stretcher-bearers.

Although the men in the forward positions did not know it, the war was not going well for the British and French. Though they were standing firm against probing enemy attacks and aggressive patrols, it was a far cry from the vicious blitzkrieg inflicted elsewhere. With the entire front in danger of collapsing, Highland Division were told they were to pull out from their positions in the *ligne de contact* and join the French reserve – ready to be sent wherever they would be needed to stem the Nazi advance.

On 15 May the withdrawal commenced, although it would be some days before all the British units were fully disengaged. As the 7th Argyll and Sutherland Highlanders pulled back towards the *ligne de recueil* they found the enemy in hot pursuit. Two men were killed and six wounded as the final platoons pulled back. It was not until the 23rd that the French 33rd Infantry arrived to take over positions from 2nd Seaforths.

At first the division withdrew to positions just in front of the Maginot Line and then moved back safely to the rear. As the division pulled back, many among the troops were astonished by what they witnessed. France was under attack but behind the front life seemed to continue as normal. John Christie, a twenty-year-old artillery signaller, who a year before had been a bus driver in Aberdeen, found his regiment passing through a town whose population was making the most of the warm, early summer weather: 'People were gathered at what was obviously a type of Lido, bathing and basking in the warm sunshine of the afternoon. I remember thinking at the time, how can they be so calm and relaxed as if the war was a thousand miles away instead of just up the road.'[10]

The calm was deceptive. Christie and his colleagues were heading into the unknown – retreating towards an unknown destination, oblivious to the chaos and confusion that was engulfing the rest of the British Army. Stranger still, considering the desperate situation being experienced by the BEF in Flanders, on 24 May the 51st Division became part of the French reserve. The sanctuary of these rear positions did not last long. The war caught up with the men of the Middlesex Regiment – a machine-gun battalion attached to the division – on a break during the withdrawal, as machine-gunner Jim Pearce remembered:

We didn't stop long anywhere. We were pulling back all the time, we'd had no contact with the Germans yet. I was wondering what was going to happen, but we just accepted it. Then the Germans dive-bombed us one time. I was having a

shower. I ran downstairs, got dressed and got my rifle. I ran out
and people were firing rifles at them – I don't know why, it
never did any good, we never got any of them. They bombed all
around us. It was the first time we'd been under fire. It made me
think the war was catching up with us.

It was soon clear to all that the German advance was too fast and
the situation too fluid for units to remain out of action for long.
They were needed at the front and orders soon came for the
division to relocate, joining the French 2nd Army in northern
France. The move was confusing for the troops – they had been
informed they were heading towards the front but everywhere
they went there seemed to be French troops heading in the
opposite direction. Yet, day by day the Highlanders continued
to move, passing through Gisors and Sézanne, crossing the River
Bresle, until on 1 June they reached the line of the River Somme
near Abbeville. It was just miles from where men like Eric Reeves
and Ken Willats had 'gone into the bag' almost two weeks earlier.

With the rest of the British Army reeling back towards Dunkirk
and the French seemingly on the verge of collapse, it was little
wonder the Highlanders found their movements misted by chaos
and confusion. The officers of the 6th Battalion Royal Scots
Fusiliers searched desperately for information about the division
so they could link up with them. Adrift in a fog of conflicting
orders and instructions, their commanding officer later described
how he felt the 51st Division had neglected them: 'They do not
seem the least bit interested in us or our affairs.'[11] When they finally
reached Neufchâtel he again looked back and contemplated the
extraordinary situation they were in: 'Still no word from 51 Div,
nor is it possible to get in touch with them . . . So ends the most
extraordinary move. 400 miles across France without one intelli-
gible order from anyone. Whole division practically lost during this
time.'[12]

This sense of confusion was shared throughout the division. It
was normal for the other ranks to be ignorant of the situation but

their officers expected to be kept abreast of their orders. The
Lothian and Borders Yeomanry travelled in three separate groups as
they moved north ready to join the French. The party taking their
tanks by rail were told they were being moved to an unknown
destination, but should be prepared to be attacked by both air and
ground forces during the journey. On the 25th the advance party
arrived at Vitry. Here they discovered they were less than welcome. It had been badly damaged by enemy bombers and the
officer in charge of the town was found to be inefficient and
excitable, seemingly desperate to force the troops away as quickly as
possible. Moving swiftly on to Gisors, they soon discovered the
road party was lost and the rail party was fifteen hours late.

Finally arriving at St Léger, the exhausted men bedded down for
the night in an empty house. They were soon rudely awakened. In
the middle of the night Major-General Fortune arrived, also
looking for a bed. He was heard opening doors, then moving
on once he realized all the rooms were occupied. Heading to the
top floor, he was heard to say: 'Come on David, we'll get fixed up
in here anyway.' Instead, upon reaching the top floor he discovered
two officers in the only bed and another one sprawled across the
landing. The next morning the general told the astonished officers:
'As a matter of interest this is Divisional HQ.'[13] The officers were in
for a further surprise when they asked an intelligence officer on the
HQ staff if he knew where the rest of their unit were. He was
unable to answer, but Major-General Fortune later kindly informed the advance party they were in completely the wrong
location.

Such gentlemanly encounters masked the reality of the desperate
situation faced by the 51st Division. They were attached to a
foreign army, were part of a collapsing coalition and were growing
increasingly isolated by the withdrawal of the rest of the BEF from
Dunkirk. But such details meant little to the men in the front lines.
All knew they were members of regiments with proud traditions –
ones that were shared by their divisional commander. It seemed
clear they would soon be making a stand.

Arriving near the line of the River Somme, the division began to ready itself for the inevitable action. Initially the Argyll and Sutherland Highlanders advanced in the wake of French troops attempting to retake Abbeville, taking over positions previously occupied by a French cavalry unit. Once in position, they were shelled by the enemy. This was not a barrage intended to harm them but something more ominous. They were registration shells, aimed at ensuring the enemy had their range ready for when they would bombard the positions in advance of their inevitable assault. It was a taste of what was to come. The message was reinforced when two men in civilian clothes entered their lines. They were anti-aircraft gunners who had become separated from their unit, dressed in civilian clothes, then swam the Somme in an attempt to rejoin their unit. They reported to the Argylls that significant enemy forces were concentrating on the opposite bank of the river.

Outside Abbeville, a platoon of Seaforth Highlanders took up position in a graveyard. They had a wonderful view across the gently rolling country – for two or three miles they had a clear view of anyone who approached towards the British line. It was from this location that Jim Reed spotted the enemy advancing in their direction. At first they were nothing but dots on the horizon. Soon it was clear that men and vehicles were coming towards them. The tense infantrymen kept low in their slit trenches, not wanting to reveal their position, not wanting to fire until their bullets would have maximum effect. It was simply a matter of holding fire until the enemy were caught in a trap – except that one soldier had other ideas:

> This reservist couldn't wait. They were still a couple of hundred yards away. He stood up and started firing. He was pleased with himself. I said 'You'll bring some shit down on us now.' He said 'No, they won't have seen that.' But a couple of minutes later they got our range with mortars and they were dropping all around us. Fortunately we got a recall. But he never learned his lesson, he got killed two or three days later doing the same thing.

If he'd kept still – keep quiet till you can kill them without them seeing you – he'd have been ok. It was foolish, that's how most of them got killed. Some learn, others don't. Luckily I was learning by then.

The story was the same across the divisional area. It was clear the vast enemy forces ranged against them would soon close in for the kill. One artillery unit reported the chilling sight of enemy bombers passing just fifty feet (fifteen metres) above their heads. Others reported bombers and fighters circling their positions as if just waiting for the order to attack. Furthermore, every battalion commander in the division found his men stretched out over a front that seemed far too large to defend. The tanks of A Troop of the Lothian and Borders Yeomanry were assigned a 2,000-yard front, with just sixty-five men and three carriers. To bolster their defences they positioned an abandoned French tank in the line, hoping its puny 2-pound gun might help to ward off any enemy advance.

On 30 May a reconnaissance patrol of the Lothian and Borders Yeomanry set out to recce the area between the towns of Eu and St-Valery-sur-Somme. They were informed the enemy had a bridgehead over the Somme but were given no further information as to how far their advance units had penetrated. It was an eerie experience for the crews as they drove across a landscape where signs of war were predominantly the graveyards and memorials to the victims of the Great War. Even when they found bridges prepared for demolition there were no Allied troops anywhere to be seen. But they did locate telephone wires that had seemingly been cut by enemy troops. Furthermore they met civilians who informed them the Germans were so confident of victory they had borrowed bathing suits and gone swimming in the sea. Chillingly, the civilians also reported approximately 1,000 German soldiers in St-Valery-sur-Somme. The only signs of Allied activity were a few French marines, armed with nothing heavier than rifles, who were occupying a lighthouse, whilst at Le Tréport they discovered a handful of British troops hanging around in the town square. Their only contribution had been to open all the swing bridges to hold up the German advance.

Here it was intended they would make a stand and attempt to counterattack the enemy forces to their north. On 4 June, as the final survivors of the Dunkirk perimeter were being rounded up, the men of 152 and 153 Brigades went on the offensive. With the support of French tanks, they advanced upon the enemy bridge-head over the River Somme. Like so many attacks launched in the weeks before, it was a failure, despite the furious efforts of the artillery to support them with the gunners of the 17th Field Regiment firing nearly 650 rounds in just three hours. Nearly 600 fighting men were lost from 152 Brigade, with the 4th Seaforths and 4th Cameron Highlanders taking the bulk of the casualties, as the French tanks were picked off one by one by determined German anti-tank gunners.

It was the first serious action the Seaforths had seen. For Jim Reed the story of the battle had begun the previous evening when his sergeant had informed them they would be going into action the next morning. They would be advancing with fixed bayonets – a sure sign they could expect close contact with the enemy:

We had tea in the early morning, were given picks and shovels and then we advanced. We reached the edge of this wood quite easily. Then the trouble started. We'd thrown away the shovels – we couldn't carry these big things and carry a rifle with fixed bayonet. We came under a bit of fire then we got half way through the wood and it started to get a bit heavy. We could hear tanks battling away at the other side of the wood. Then we got some really heavy stuff coming down on us, but having thrown our picks and shovels away we had to try to dig in using our bayonets. The shelling lasted for about two hours. We lost about half a dozen men killed from our platoon and quite a few were wounded. That's a lot for one platoon. I remember at the end I went looking for my mates because we'd all scattered. I

found one of my friends who'd had his throat torn out. But you
soon forget it because after that we got in quite a few skirmishes.

The attack was the first time the Highlanders were thrown into a
major action. It was a day that had a profound effect on each man,
as David Mowatt remembered:

I shot a couple of Jerries. I was going along the riverbank and
there was a platoon of them on the other side – so I had a couple
of bangs at them. Then they scarpered – but I'm bloody sure I hit
them because I was 'dead-eye dick'. I thought 'I've got to get
you first mate!' We were taught 'shoot first, ask questions later'.
You were a soldier and your rifle was your best friend – that man
over the other side isn't! But that was the only time I fired my
rifle. As the company runner I had other work to do. At another
point I saved my mate's life – Eckie MacPherson. I'd just come
back from an errand and I bumped into him in an orchard. I
heard a shell coming over – I shouted 'Down Eckie!' I threw
myself down. The shell landed and blew Eckie high up into the
air. God knows how high he went. He landed – bang – exactly
where he'd been standing. He was out cold – I got underneath
him and lifted him. I carried him down to the aid post. I said to
the orderly 'Careful with him, he'll fall to pieces.' I couldn't look
at him. I told the medic what had happened and he said 'By God!
He's lucky to be alive.' Every year until he died Eckie'd be at the
regimental reunion with a glass of whisky waiting for me and say
'Here's to the man who saved my life.'

The following day the Germans made a determined effort to
push the Highlanders back from the Somme. The 7th Battalion
Argyll and Sutherland Highlanders were particularly hard hit at
Franleu. It was later described as the 'blackest day in the history of
the regiment.'[14] The Germans launched their attack in the early
hours of the morning. When the news reached battalion HQ they
at first believed it to be patrol activity, but the men who were sent

to investigate found large numbers of enemy troops surrounding the village. Communication for the Argylls became difficult as the enemy cut telephone wires around the village.

It soon became clear the entire position was under threat and the Bren gun carriers were positioned around the HQ as a final line of defence. With enemy snipers infiltrating into the village, anti-sniper patrols were sent out. The situation deteriorated as the artillery HQ in the village of Ochancourt was captured, leaving the Argylls without effective support.

In the confusion the reserve company was sent forward but didn't know the way and were soon lost. When one officer got out of his truck to check a signpost he was shot in the back by a sniper and severely wounded. With its last hope lost on the way to the village, the battalion HQ came under fire from heavy mortars. Some relief was felt when the heavy machine-guns of the Royal Northumberland Fusiliers were heard engaging the enemy. The respite was short lived and at 4.15 a.m. they saw the green white-green white flare that signalled someone's position was surrounded. From the C Company positions the troops could see around 1,000 enemy forming up on three sides of them. Elsewhere D Company were attacked first by enemy cavalry, then by light tanks backed up by cavalry and motorcyclists. The company's Bren gunners did sterling work, ensuring that short, accurate bursts were enough to prevent the enemy from crossing open areas, but it was not enough to turn the tide of battle. From the observation post in a church tower enemy mortars were spotted being brought up on horse-drawn wagons, accompanied by more troops arriving by truck. The newly arrived mortars took a serious toll, concentrating their fire on the battalion HQ and on the hedgerows concealing the Bren gun positions. Their deadly fire soon destroyed the wireless truck and one of the ammunition lorries. As the high explosive rained down, the wounded were sent into the HQ cellar. Here they received little assistance since there was no one to treat them, the medical staff having earlier been evacuated as the result of a confused signal. The bearers attempted to stem the bleeding and

make them comfortable, helped by the valiant padre, Captain
MacInnes. When enemy snipers were picking off men collecting
water, he had insisted on being the only one allowed outside. As
the day progressed, the men in forward positions were issued with
chocolate and water as their only sustenance.

At 2 p.m., with the sounds of the neighbouring battalions under
heavy attack, the Argylls could see a large formation of troops
massing nearby. At first it was hoped the 1,200 soldiers were the
expected relief from the Black Watch. They soon discovered these
were enemy forces preparing for a final assault upon the village. For
the rest of the afternoon A Company and the HQ were able to
continue to defend their position in Franleu. Enemy advances on
the village were repulsed thanks to a section of Royal Northumberland Fusiliers machine-gunners and the sterling work of a
single mortar crew.

Relief was attempted by French tanks and a detachment of Black
Watch but these were unable to advance due to enemy resistance.
At 5 p.m., with all hope of relief extinguished, a mortar bomb
struck the last remaining ammo truck, blowing up and flattening
the area around the HQ. Major Younger, who had organized the
defence, was hit in the head and eye. Captain Robertson was hit in
the leg, and forced to bandage his own legs. Lieutenant Mackay,
who had organized the observation post and arranged the feeding
of the men, was peppered with shrapnel. RSM Lockie, who had
led the earlier anti-sniper patrols, was also hit and CSM Dyer was
severely wounded in the arms and legs.

With their situation desperate, the Argylls were ordered to
withdraw to the village of Bouvaincourt. The difficulty was that
the forward companies were unable to disengage and retreat –
indeed they could not even be contacted. The surrounded B
Company were unable to withdraw and nothing more was heard
from them

At 6 p.m. Colonel Buchanan, realizing the situation was hopeless, gave permission for any men who wished to attempt to break
out. Two carriers were able to get away, as did some trucks

crammed with men, many of whom were wounded. Some platoons never received the message since they were cut off in the village. All of C Company, whose position faced the main thrust of the assault, were posted as missing. Only the colonel and the padre were left unwounded. Having spent all day offering comfort to the wounded, MacInnes refused to leave them to their fate. At the end of the day he remained inside, along with thirty wounded, the colonel, the French liaison officer and other officers. Mortar bombs continued to land around the HQ and soon all the trucks around it were ablaze.

In the days that followed it became clear the battalion had been mauled beyond belief. Only D Company, minus the platoon that had earlier fired the surrounded signal, and some from the battalion HQ had been able to extract themselves and withdraw. By the end of that one day's fighting the battalion had lost twenty-three officers and 500 other ranks killed, wounded or missing.

That same day the Lothian and Borders Yeomanry also found themselves under attack. At first it was just patrols who advanced on their positions. Their initial approach took them towards the abandoned French tank. Realizing the British troops were waiting, the first German soldier raised his hands in surrender – until one of his comrades shot him for being cowardly. The second German soldier was then shot by waiting men and the patrol scattered. With the Germans safely behind a ridge, the French gun was used to fire over the ridge where they believed the enemy to be. So far so good – or so it seemed. A patrol was sent to make contact with the forward posts, but it never returned.

With the enemy far from beaten, heavy artillery fire struck their positions, as one of the officers later recorded: 'After each burst I heard groans. Finally it stopped. At least three men had been killed and about 15 wounded. Two carriers were loaded and sent off . . . whilst the last carrier was being loaded and the wounded attended to, the Germans appeared at very close range running and firing tommy guns . . . somehow all the wounded and all the guns were got away, there were nine on the last carrier.'[15] The intense fire took its toll on both the physical and mental resources of the regiment. Cohesive activity and coherent thought were impossible as the troops struggled to stay alive. In the haste to withdraw, some men, positioned in relative safety within a house, did not hear the order to retreat and were left behind. By the time the mistake had been noticed it was too late to go back and the men were abandoned to their fate.

Soon enemy dive-bombers joined in the fray, their bombs screaming down onto the tanks and crews assembled in the village of Ballilleul: 'Result – little left.'[16] One of the regiment's squadrons lost forty men out of a total of just sixty-five. As one officer of the regiment later noted: 'All ranks discovered the use of a hole in the ground, the deeper and narrower the better.'[17]

Despite the losses suffered by the division that day, the Highlander's ordeal was far from over; 4 June may have seen the end of the Dunkirk evacuation but in Normandy the Highlanders were only at the beginning of their ordeal. Whether infantrymen, tank crews, pioneers, drivers or gunners – officers, NCOs or riflemen – every man of the division was in the firing line. The gunners of the 17th Field Regiment had initially been firing at targets over 8,000 yards away. The range had fallen to 6,000 yards, then fallen again to find themselves firing at targets to their left and right. Eventually the targets they were given were to their rear. At Escarbotin one battery of the regiment found themselves virtually surrounded and firing incessantly at a rapid rate. Unable to fight on, they took the firing mechanism from the guns and withdrew on the gun tractors. Elsewhere C Troop were sent with rifles and Bren guns to help protect A Troop, who were firing at the enemy at point-blank range. Despite the help, they were soon surrounded and captured. Another battery reported coming under mortar fire at a range of 1,000 yards whilst enemy machine-gunners fired at them from the rear. With further resistance pointless, one battery gave a surprisingly cheery final message over the wireless: 'Cheerio, coming to join you.'[18]

As the gunners pulled back they came under attack from the air. Peter Royle later wrote of the experience: 'I lay on my back in the

open field and watched the JU87s screaming down vertically
before loosing off their bombs and zooming away. I watched
the bombs leave each plane – sometimes two, sometimes four, at a
time – and they always seemed to be aimed at me personally. Of
course they never were, and I always breathed a sigh of relief when
they went on and hit somebody else.'[19]

With units throughout the division coming under increased
pressure, it was little wonder that some found themselves split off
from the main force – isolated and seemingly abandoned in the
chaos. Two companies of the 8th Battalion Argyll and Sutherland
Highlanders found themselves holding a lighthouse and school
buildings at Ault, near St-Valery-sur-Somme. They were soon
engaged by German tanks which were able to remain under cover
whilst still being able to bombard their positions. Initially it seemed
the assault was 'frightening but not dangerous',[20] but as the fire
increased it soon became clear their position was untenable. Quick-
firing cannon peppered the school and lighthouse, causing casualties from shell splinters and causing French sailors within to
surrender en masse. Despite this surrender, the enemy did not
press home the attack, one officer considering this to be because it
was merely 'an exhibition of frightfulness to give us a sleepless night
and a foretaste for the next day'.[21]

Fortunately for the Highlanders, they did not await the final
assault. Instead they withdrew overnight towards Le Tréport in
hope of rejoining the division. The orders for the night march were
that if attacked they should fight to the last round, then try to
escape. Any wounded, if they were unable to be moved, were to be
left behind. Luckily they met no enemy resistance during the night
and the next day they laid up in open countryside. With little
shelter, they were forced to lie in the oppressive sunshine, unable to
move for fear of revealing their positions.

At nightfall they headed west, coming under fire from German
sentries who soon scattered into the night when the Highlanders
returned their fire. Alerted to their presence, the Germans sent
spotter planes firing parachute flares across the countryside to

illuminate the area. Avoiding the light of the flares, the two companies were able to continue their journey and eventually reached positions held by the Black Watch.

With any hope of driving the enemy back over the Somme at Abbeville extinguished, the division withdrew to attempt to hold the River Bresle. The Highlanders were reinforced by A Brigade, consisting of the 4th Border Regiment, 5th Battalion Sherwood Foresters and the 4th Buffs, who had been sent north from Rouen to help hold the line, along with 900 reinforcements for the infantry battalions. But they continued to come under intense pressure. Again David Mowatt found himself in the thick of the action:

It was bloody terrible, it was difficult for me as the company runner. I had to be in contact with the three platoons – we'd be pulling back and reforming and my first job to find where they were. The River Bresle was my worst time, but I'd got to get to the platoons. My old platoon, No 16, were holding the bridge. Word came through that Jerry were on the other bank of the river and the artillery were going to shell them. So our company had to pull back behind the railway embankment for safety. I had to go to tell them to pull back.

He reached the bridge and gave the message to the defenders, then was forced to dash to reach another platoon in an exposed position:

I went out but I was under heavy machine gun fire – there were bloody bullets everywhere. I got behind the iron wheels of an old railway engine. Bullets were coming at me and pinging off the wheels, landing just in front of me. So I crept out. I did the old trick of putting my tin hat out on the end of my rifle. Nothing came – they were still firing at the other end of the train. I was safe! So I got up and ran across this level ground. Suddenly I saw this ditch and dived into it. It was full of old engine oil from the trains! But I was safe. So I crawled down and reached the next platoon. I gave the message to the officer but he warned me it would be difficult to reach the next platoon since they were covered by machine guns – but I had no choice.

Continuing to crawl along the oil-filled ditch, Mowatt eventually reached the next platoon, where he asked for the officer. The reply shocked him: 'He's dead.'

What came next was even less comforting: 'I asked "Where's the Sergeant?" They said "Killed." So I said where's the corporal and again they said "Killed." So I said "Who's in charge?" They pointed to Lance-Corporal Rose, who was in command of a whole platoon. I told him they'd got to get back over the embankment. So we all crawled back so the machine guns couldn't see us.' Reaching the embankment, the lance-corporal – uncertain of his new-found role as a platoon commander – asked Mowatt what he thought they should do: 'I told him no one had spotted us so far, cause we were in the long grass. I said we should get all the boys over together, if we went in ones and twos we'd be spotted. So we rushed over the top and all of us reached safety.'

If David Mowatt thought he had indulged in enough heroics for one day, he was wrong. With the tide of battle turning against the 51st, every man was required to go beyond the call of duty. Arriving back at the company HQ, he was informed he would have to return to the bridge to collect the Bren guns left behind during the withdrawal. The company commander sent him and a mate, Jock Swanson, to join an officer in a carrier. They were to rush to the bridge and return with the guns to complete the mission:

It was a straight road, down an incline, to the bridge. We went about twenty yards and the carrier stopped. I could see paint chipping off from the inside of the carrier – it was armour-piercing bullets coming through. The driver was killed, so was the officer and the Sergeant, Kenny Ross, was screaming his head off. He couldn't get out, his legs had been shot to pieces. I said to Jock 'Try to get the Sergeant out, I'll nip down and get the guns. So I ducked down over the bank, fetched the Bren guns and ran back to the carrier. When I returned Jock was still struggling to pull Kenny Ross clear. But between us we managed to pull him out. Jock carried him on his shoulders and I carried the guns, and we managed to get back to the company HQ.

With the tide of battle turning against the Highlanders there was no choice but to retreat. Or as Jim Pearce, a loader on a Vickers machine-gun put it, in the words of a song popular at the time, it soon became a case of 'Run rabbit run'. During the phoney war, when they had sung that song the troops had envisaged Hitler and his forces running away. Now they realized that was not going to happen. As Pearce soon discovered, the only running the Germans were doing was directly towards their positions: 'I was feeding the gun – we kept firing but they kept coming in waves – they didn't seem to give in. I felt horrible – think about it, we were killing all these people – but they wouldn't stop coming. We were just firing and firing. Oh dear. But you do it automatically. Looking back, it doesn't seem possible but you've been trained to do it. Your nerves take over. You have to defend yourself – you want to save yourself.'

It was clear if the Highlanders continued to take casualties at such a high rate they would soon be but a shadow of a division. By 7 June the 7th Battalion of the Argyll and Sutherland Highlanders reported their depleted force consisted of just five officers and 130 other ranks. Only the remains of D Company and the men from the rear echelon were still fighting. With their situation reported, they lost two more men killed and 11 wounded before the day was over.

Through the valiant sacrifice of the Highlanders, the division held the line of the River Bresle until 8 June. Then, with the news that enemy formations had broken through in the south, cutting them off from their supply base at Rouen, it became clear their position was no longer tenable. The following morning, the arrival of Royal Navy representatives to discuss the evacuation of the division from Le Havre, marked the end of the uncertainty. It was now no longer a matter of how long could they keep fighting, rather how soon could they make their escape.

As the division fell back from the Somme valley, the Highlanders conducted a fighting retreat. Their world was absorbed by the battles they fought. There was no time for thoughts about the rest of the BEF. To them, Dunkirk was just the name of a Channel port – just another French town – the growing legend of the evacuation was unknown and meaningless. Unlike their comrades who had sailed home, they were not yet safe. Their war continued to take a heavy toll. Hour by hour, day by day, the division established new positions, engaged the enemy and then withdrew, always uncertain where they might be heading.

For the soldiers it was a harrowing time. Lack of food, lack of sleep, sheer physical and mental exhaustion, meant few could ever build up a clear picture of all they experienced in those final days of battle. Even if they could summon up the strength to keep marching – walking mile after mile in a virtual daze – all realized they could not continue to fight unless assistance was forthcoming. One battalion reported the daily ration was just two sugar lumps and two tablespoons of mixed carrot and potatoes per man – hardly enough to keep them awake, let alone keep them fighting. Food and cigarettes would have cheered them but without replenishing their ammunition supplies the battle would be a foregone conclusion. So it was with despair that officers of the battalion admitted they had been unable to find the trainload of ammunition that had been destined to supply the Highlanders for their retreat to the coast.

As they marched, fully exposed, along the straight roads – with nowhere to shelter but beneath the flanking poplar trees – the Highlanders faced the same hazards their comrades to the north had faced during their retreat to Dunkirk. 'We got quite a few German planes coming over,' recalled Seaforth Highlander Jim Reed, 'and they dive bombed us. I began to take things seriously when one or two of the lads got killed. Someone would tell you "So and so got shot this morning." So you'd think, I've got to be a bit careful here.'

Like their comrades who had fought in Flanders, the High-landers were affected by these aerial attacks. As Jim Charters, a machine-gunner in the Royal Northumberland Fusiliers recalled: 'Seeing refugees being machine-gunned and bombed was the worst moment of my whole war. The Germans did it to impede our retreat. It was a shock to see it, but after the first few days we got used to seeing people getting hurt. Mortars and Stukas were the things we feared the most. The bombs had their sirens on and howled when they were coming down at us. But during the retreat I think we were in a stupor most of the time.'

For many it was the terrible sense of helplessness that had the greatest impact upon them. Seaforth Highlander Jim Reed also watched as dive-bombers destroyed columns of refugees, machine-gunning the women and children as they scattered to reach safety. When the attacks were over there were civilians – old men, women and children – all crying for help. There were upturned prams scattered amidst the corpses and wounded people pleading for assistance from the British soldiers. But there was nothing they could do, there were no medical supplies to be given away and no time could be lost on the retreat. Jim Reed's words expressed the sense of regret felt by the troops as they left the civilians to fend for themselves: 'They were helpless. You want to help them but there's nothing you can do. It was the saddest day of my war.'

As most soon realized, there was little point concerning them-selves with the casualties they saw, there were more pressing issues for them as they retreated. Dick Taylor, whose first experiences of enemy fire had been treated lightly, noticed a change in attitudes as the retreat progressed: 'It wasn't serious until the retreat started. We were being harassed, we were chased all the way. It was all pretty quick – we were taking up positions trying to help anybody who was in trouble. But I wasn't particularly nervous, it was just one of those things you accepted. It was just when shells dropped close by you'd get quite a fright.'

For the exhausted but undeterred men of the 51st Division, any light-hearted moment, however brief, was something to be savoured. As the Seaforth Highlanders fell back towards the coast David Mowatt did his utmost to provide some relief for his comrades:

There were times when I could see the humorous side of what was happening. I was getting up to all sorts of tricks. I would go into a house and pinch a bottle of rum. I'd always get something for the lads. They'd be waiting for me – 'What you got us this time?' – I'd get loaves of bread, I'd search wagons that had been blown up. I'd find tins of bully beef and fill my jacket up. But by this time we were on our bloody knees. Marching – pulling back – holding the line. One night I went to this big house, went up to the attic and found three brand new bikes. I thought 'I'll take those back to the company.' Let the boys cycle rather than march. I showed them to the company commander and he said 'Mowatt, do as you bloody like!' So by the time we got back to St Valery every man in the company had a bike.

As Mowatt and his mates cycled towards the coast all they could think of was reaching safety. It may not have been perceived as in the finest traditions of such proud regiments to be withdrawing from the battlefield but it was the only way of surviving. To fight on was tantamount to suicide. Escape was their only option. Yet even the hope of escape was diminishing by the second. They did not know it, but Major-General Fortune had already made a fateful decision. When he had been told to withdraw to Le Havre he made the conscious decision to do so side by side with his French allies. He was part of a French Corps and believed that if they could fight and die together they could withdraw together. As a result, with the French relying on horses in place of mechanized transport, it would take longer to reach their destination. With their trucks, carriers and artillery tractors, the Highlanders could have made a lightning retreat to the port; however, this was not a time to be sacrificing their French comrades. It was a noble gesture that would cost the Highlanders dear in the days that followed.

CHAPTER FOUR

The Death of a Division
The 51st Highland Division at St Valery

Our officer, Captain Wright said 'Barber, you were a signaller. See if you can get a frequency on that set.' I still remember it. 'This is the BBC' – you know, the old toffee nosed way of talking – 'The BEF have been successfully evacuated from Dunkirk.' I thought what a load of bollocks.

Gordon Barber, Royal Horse Artillery,
51st Highland Division

And so the 51st Highland Division fell back towards Le Havre, expecting an evacuation. Some had been told what had happened at Dunkirk. Others were unaware of the scale of the defeat inflicted upon the Allies but, as most would later realize, ignorance was bliss. Had they known the punishment inflicted on their comrades in the north, they might have felt even less certain about their own ability to resist the surging enemy advance.

By the time of the retreat, the so-called Highland Division was far from the homogeneous organization that name suggested. The infantry battalions in the division may all have been from the Highlands, but many of its other units reflected the diversity of the modern army. The Sherwood Foresters, the East Kents and others had joined the division during the retreat.

Other incomers included the 101st Light Anti-Aircraft Regiment, who were attached to the Highlanders near Abbeville. They joined other non-Scottish formations like the pioneers of the Norfolk Regiment, the machine-gunners of the Middlesex Regiment and the 1st Royal Horse Artillery, whose prestigious gunners had been among the first units to arrive in France back in September 1939.

Within these regiments were a wide selection of men whose role alongside the Highlanders would be largely forgotten – first when the defeat of the 51st Division was widely ignored to concentrate on the 'victory' at Dunkirk, then secondly when those highlighting the sacrifice of the 51st focused upon the events of June 1940 as a tragedy for Scotland. Whilst the greatest burden of the slaughter was borne by the Scottish infantry, thousands of those who fought in the retreat to St Valery owed no allegiance to the Highlands. Indeed many were from backgrounds as far removed as imaginable to the wild northern lands from where men like David Mowatt had come.

As the 1st Armoured Division moved into position at Abbeville they were accompanied by the 44th Battery of the 101st Light Anti-Aircraft Regiment, formerly the Finsbury Rifles, a Territorial unit from the heart of London. With them was an ambitious young bombardier who had already been 'at war' for eighteen months. Fred Coster had joined the Territorial Army in early 1938, a patriotic reaction to the German annexation of Austria. In October that year, in the midst of the Munich crisis, he was called from his bed in Stepney, East London and told his unit had been mobilized. For nearly a year they found themselves, armed just with First World War Lewis guns, defending the skies above Kent. They were still there on the morning of 3 September 1939 when the very first air raid sirens sounded – marking the start of the Second World War.

Fred Coster was a typical Cockney – he was from a poor but respectable family and had an indefatigable spirit that saw him through the hard years of the 1930s and into the harsh realities of wartime life. His naturally cheery confidence – or cheek as some might have called it – was amply demonstrated whilst working as a junior lift operator in a City of London office. Hearing there was a job on offer in a firm of stockbrokers, he walked out of the lift, still clad in his work uniform, and presented himself in the office asking for a job: 'I think the manager gave it to me because of my cheek. So I became a stockbroker's clerk.' However, by June 1940 the streets of London were behind him, as he prepared himself for his first battle outside Abbeville.

Not far away was another young gunner, also preparing for his first battle. Like Fred Coster, Gordon 'Nobby' Barber was from a poor London background, having been brought up in two rooms in Anerley with his parents and five siblings. Fired from his job as a laundry delivery boy, he could not accept the enforced poverty of his parents' existence, so made a difficult but rational decision when his father questioned his plans for the future:

He asked me 'When are you going to get a job?' I didn't know. I was eighteen, I was fed up being an errand boy, I was getting older and I hadn't got the brains to get a better job. I said I wanted to see the world. He told me to buck me ideas up. He started to give me a lot of mouth and I was getting fed up with it. I said 'It's no good you talking – you've never had a job. You've been unemployed for a bloody hundred years!' He lost his temper with me and said 'Do you a bit of good to get in the bloody army! That'll make a man of you.' That was when it clicked.

With the idea planted in his head, Barber went to visit a friend on leave from the army. The man warned him that the training was hard at first but once that was over there were great opportunities to travel: 'I thought "Oh, sod it. I'll join the army." So I went up to Woolwich to join the artillery. They signed me in and I went home, told Mum and she burst into tears. It was the 3rd of January 1938. It was a month before my 19th birthday.'

Just as so many other young men would discover in the years that followed, Barber found life in the army was far removed from the glamour of recruitment posters:

> It was bloody hard in the army. It was a rough life. 'Cause we were Horse Artillery we had to march holding a whip. We were supposed to keep it straight but mine never was. There were three of us, all the same – right idiots. That was the type went in the army in them days. I wasn't the best at pickin' things up. I was worried about my passing-out parade. I thought I might get chucked out. How they punished you was by getting all of the squad to do everything again, so me and my two mates weren't popular. But the other blokes taught us how to do it. We had to practise in the barrack room – all the time. You'd be going to the loo and someone would shout 'Take that bloody whip with you and when you're having a piss make sure you're holding it straight!' I took a couple of good hidings from that lot – and I gave a few out an' all. It was rough in those barracks!

Despite the initial difficulties, Barber began to settle into life in the army. He prided himself on his appearance and made sure his kit was laid out perfectly for inspections. The new recruits learned to polish their boots till they gleamed. Their brass buttons and buckles shone like gold and the creases of their trousers were razor-sharp. It didn't matter that he had to spend hour upon hour scrubbing and polishing. It seemed he was coming up in the world and the hardships of home life were far behind him. There was a shower block for the recruits – no more filling up a tin bath in front of the fire. Plus he had three sets of clothing, one on, one in the wash and one pressed and ready in his kitbag: 'And it was all my own, nothing second hand and no sending your only suit to the pawnshop.'

Unlike the volunteers and Territorials, many of the regular soldiers were far less enthused by the thought of war. During the 1930s patriotism had played less of a role than poverty in deciding who joined the army. Men like Barber had joined to get off the dole queue, to feed their families and, most importantly, to restore their personal pride. Army life may have been hard but it certainly offered them a future. However, with the army retreating through France, that future seemed less than certain.

One thing was certain. Death was not choosy and war soon stripped away the old divisions between Territorials, regulars, conscripts and reservists. Whereas, just months before, many regulars had laughed at the TA's 'weekend warriors', and TA men had scoffed at the poorly educated and cynical old regulars, now they were all in it together. What mattered was not where a man had come from but what he could offer. The parade-ground creases of the regulars or the inept drilling of the newly conscripted militiamen meant little to men fighting for their lives.

Fred Coster's first time under fire showed him how survival was a lottery. He had just arrived at his gun position when Stuka dive-bombers appeared above and released their deadly cargo: 'We were firing like mad at them. But we couldn't keep up with the Stukas. We could see our shells bursting around them but we just couldn't hit them. We tried to follow them down. It was absolutely frustrating, we'd trained hard then found we hadn't got a weapon that could engage their planes.'

Unable to drive away the enemy dive-bombers, Coster and his fellow gunners soon realized their position was hopeless:

This one plane came down at us and we had to take cover. I ran and dived onto the ground. One poor chap took cover in the worst possible place – beneath the gun. A Stuka came down and machine-gunned his legs off. Then a bomb took his arm off. This poor chap was mangled, we rushed him to the aid post but he died on the way. He was a very religious fellow and he was the first one to die. I don't know if you can read anything into it! To see his death was a big shock. That's when I realised it was a damn serious business.

These were experiences shared throughout the division. Gordon Barber and the gunners of the Royal Horse Artillery were also getting used to the reality of war. The phoney war may have been an enjoyable period for Barber but the first weeks in action soon removed any remaining glamour. The very first time the regiment deployed their guns one man was killed when a gun rolled back over him. Part of the problem was the guns were too heavy for their mountings since they were 25-pounder guns mounted on the carriages for obsolete 18-pounders. In their first action one of the guns exploded. It was not what Barber had joined the army for: 'I didn't go out there for a war – I went into the army for a good time. I thought it had been a good time, we'd been there eight months without firing a shot!' It was clear the good times were too good to last. Barber spent his first night of battle in an orchard near Abbeville, sheltering from incoming shells:

I thought we wouldn't need a deep trench, the trees will protect us. I spent all night listening to shit falling all around us. Trees and branches were coming down everywhere. I nearly dug meself down into the ground. This bloke Roberts was praying – 'I want to go home!' – he'd lost it. He was beneath me crying about getting home to see his wife and all that bollocks. I thought 'What's going to happen here?' In the morning there were shell splinters everywhere.

The following day was no better:

We went into action. We were sending it up pretty heavy. I'd been on the gun for so long – I was firing it – that when I came off I was deafened. I was sent down to fetch some ammunition. As we walked down I heard a crash – right in front of our gun. One of our blokes Coppin, who used to be a groom when the regiment still had horses, shouted out 'I've been hit!' We rushed to him, picked him up to take him to the medics. I picked him up by the shoulders and my mate got his legs. As we lifted him I noticed one of his arms was just hanging off. I can still remember all the blood running down over my uniform and all the tendons hanging out from his arm. Do you know what he said to me? 'When they take me arm off, tell them to keep my ring and give it to me.' I thought 'Oh my God!' Then he said 'Have you got a fag Nobby?' So I shoved one in his gob. There was nothing left of his arm, it was just hanging on by a bit of flesh. As they took him away I told the medics about his ring and said 'I'll see you later.' But I never saw him again, I found out later he'd died – a bit of shrapnel had hit him in the side.

As the division retreated from the Somme, the enemy never seemed far behind. Gunners recalled stopping, dismounting, getting the guns into action, then hitching up again almost as soon as a few rounds had been fired. In the haze of exhaustion, they did their best to keep firing – hoping the guns would hold off the enemy just long enough for everybody to reach safety. The frenetic nature of the retreat was soon revealed to Fred Coster when one of the gunners in his regiment engaged the enemy with his Bofors gun whilst it was still being towed. This was not something they had been taught on the training grounds of England – it was just pure reflex action by men who were desperate to escape.

Despite the situation, the troops had all begun to learn, battle itself was not the worst thing they experienced. Once battle started they had something to do – riflemen had to keep firing, machine-gunners concentrated on firing, loading and rapidly changing barrels, gunners kept raining down high-explosive on the enemy, even the officers were so engrossed in giving orders there was little chance their minds could dwell on what fate had in store for them.

It was only before battle that their thoughts wandered, filling their minds with the horrors of what might happen. This tension was unavoidable, gripping at their souls. During the retreat, Fred Coster spotted one group of soldiers he would never forget:

I went into 'No Man's Land' on a motorbike. I had to get one of our guns back – it had been left behind. So I went to look for it. As I was going through the line I saw a group of Northumberland Fusiliers. They were digging in and just standing in the trenches with rifles. I said 'You know what you're up against, don't you?' They nodded – tanks would soon be advancing in their direction. As I went back past these poor guys in the trench, I said 'Good Luck!' But I knew they wouldn't have any luck. They didn't survive.

The sacrifice of the Fusiliers, who awaited the inevitable assault without weapons that could harm the advancing tanks, reflected so much of the quiet heroism demonstrated that summer. What thoughts must have gone through their minds as they awaited the attack? All hopes for the future were submerged beneath the knowledge of what awaited them. And yet, like so many of their comrades had done during the retreat to Dunkirk, they stood firm, ready to do their duty. The sense of hopelessness was not lost on Fred Coster as he rode onwards, towards the hoped for sanctuary and salvation supposedly awaiting in St Valery.

Whilst the division's infantrymen and gunners continued in their desperate attempts to hold back the enemy – each playing out their own personal dramas – elsewhere important decisions were being made. These were decisions that would seal the fate of so many under Major-General Fortune's command. Realizing they needed to fall back to Le Havre ready for evacuation, Fortune made an important decision. Unless their route to the port could be secured there would be no chance of evacuation. If the Germans arrived at Le Havre first all hope of escape would be lost and if the division had to fight all the way to the town he knew they would be decimated. On 9 June, with the nearby city of Rouen captured by the enemy, General Fortune despatched a collection of units to secure the line of retreat to Le Havre. This force was based around the fresh A Brigade that had been attached to his command just days before. Ark Force, as it was to be known, would hold the line between Fécamp and Bolbec, receiving its name by virtue of having first been formed in the town of Arques le Bataille. It was an appropriate choice of name – just like Noah's Ark, this was to rescue them from the flood of enemy forces rushing towards the Channel, and ensure they could all sail to safety. Consisting of the 4th Black Watch, 7th and 8th Argylls, 4th Buffs, 4th Border Regiment, 7th Sherwood Foresters and 6th Royal Scots Fusiliers, the unit established its headquarters in Le Havre's Rue Félix Faure, under the command of Brigadier Stanley Clarke DSO.

Despite the rapid organization and deployment of Ark Force – travelling overnight to avoid the unwanted attentions of the Luftwaffe – they were doomed to failure. Through no fault of their own, there was no available unit capable of holding off the enemy and holding open the escape route. For on 10 June, as Major-General Fortune made the decision to withdraw to Le Havre ready for evacuation, they received the worst possible news. Sweeping northwards from Rouen, the enemy had reached the Channel coast at Fécamp, cutting off the beleaguered Highlanders from their only possible place of evacuation. Within sight of the German Panzers which had reached the clifftops, were British ships embarking troops. With the divisional artillery in support, the tanks engaged the ships at Fécamp, hitting a destroyer and ensuring the harbour could be used for no further evacuations. From these clifftops the Germans could also look northwards across the Channel towards their next target – England. All they had to do was finish off the armies left behind in France and their victory would be sealed.

It was clear there was no way the already weakened Highlanders, short of ammunition, food and men, could break through the line of Panzers that stood between them and escape. Fortune had already warned the War Office that he had just two days' worth of rations left and requested that, since they could not come to the navy at Le Havre, the navy should come to them when they managed to reach the coast. With little choice in the course of action, the decision was taken to save all who could be saved and, rather than sacrifice the men in a pointless attempt to drive back the enemy, Ark Force were ordered to pull back into Le Havre to await evacuation. Whilst some of those deployed to form Ark Force were little more than battalions formed from scratch, others performed their duty to the highest degree. One company of the Border Regiment, along with a company of Sherwood Foresters, failed to receive orders for withdrawal. Instead they fought on, defending positions at crossings on the River Bresle, denying their use to the enemy. They held on until 13 June when they were finally beaten by the Germans' employment of heavy mortars.

Attached to Ark Force were the remnants of the 7th Argyll and Sutherland Highlanders, who had suffered so much in the previous days. By now they were reduced to little more than a skeleton formation – not really a battalion, rather a few survivors of the front-line companies attached to the untried troops of the B Echelon. Bombed by Stukas on the night of the retreat, the shrieking bombs had a great effect on the nerves of the men, especially since so many of the troops had not previously been bombed. It was clear to all that they could do little to hold off the enemy. To all intents and purposes, Major-General Fortune and his Highlanders were alone.

Cut off from the base at Rouen, blocked from reaching Le Havre and with their backs to the Channel, there was nowhere for the division to go, apart from the fishing port of St-Valery-en-Caux. It was no more than a small harbour, unable to offer moorings to the larger ships that had made the Dunkirk evacuation so successful. Nestling in the shade of wooded hillsides that led down from the cliffs around, the quaysides were lined with houses and cafes. And so, late on 10 June, Fortune ordered his division to withdraw into St Valery to await evacuation. The move was to be made carrying only essential equipment. In order to make space for as many men as possible, all non-essential kit was jettisoned. Greatcoats, large packs and blankets were left behind and even the division's artillery was rationed to just 100 rounds per gun.

Despite these efforts, which ensured lorries of the divisional RASC could carry the necessary fighting men, the move did not go entirely smoothly. In the dark many units found themselves on routes that had not been allotted to them, choking the roads. The situation was also complicated by the arrival of French transport, much of which was horse-drawn, which strayed onto roads and slowed down the withdrawal.

Arriving in the port on the morning of the 11th, Fortune ordered the infantry battalions to form a box perimeter around the town. His battalion commanders were informed they would hold the line during the day and then be withdrawn to the port under cover of darkness. The 4th Seaforths, 5th Gordons and 1st Black Watch held the perimeter from the nearby seaside village of Veules-les-Roses to Fontaine-le-Dun. To the west, the line was held by the 1st Gordons, 4th Gordons and 2nd Seaforths. With everybody convinced, wishing, or simply praying, that the Royal Navy would soon be coming to rescue them, the troops began to follow the orders to destroy their vehicles. As at Dunkirk, the town became surrounded with the wrecks of cars and trucks as drivers drained radiators and oil tanks, smashed open batteries and slashed tyres. Following the orders of Major-General Fortune, only the Bren carriers were to be retained for the final rearguard.

However, the Highlanders were not the only ones who had reached the area. That morning General Rommel and his tanks also arrived to the west of St Valery, seizing the high ground that commanded a view of the area. They did not waste the advantage they had gained. As the divisional HQ arrived at 11 a.m., the Germans opened up with a ferocious artillery barrage and aerial bombing that served to underline the desperate situation the Highlanders were in. Fred Coster and his column of anti-aircraft guns arrived just in time to witness the bombardment: 'When we got to town there were loads of lorries there, there were no tanks and we didn't see any heavy guns – just our ack-ack guns. There were British and French infantry everywhere. The gun tractor pulled up and another army wagon pulled up behind us. He couldn't have seen our gun barrel, it went straight through his windscreen and smashed his face in – he was screaming in pain.'

The driver's screams were in direct contrast to the peaceful scenes in the town ahead. It was a location so far untouched by war, but this situation did not last long:

> St Valery was an ordinary seaside town, with rows of lovely, colourful, painted houses in the distance. It was undisturbed. Then the Germans saturated it. We were in an open square. We could do nothing except take shelter. As they were bombing these lovely coloured houses were being lifted up complete then collapsing to the ground in ruins. Then they started machine-gunning us. There was a bit of a lull. I looked up and saw this old Frenchman. It looked like he was out for his morning constitutional walk – he couldn't care less! Then they started bombing again and I kept my head down until it was all over. When I looked again the town was an absolute wreck. All within minutes.

As the divisional headquarters moved into the town they found the town hall in flames and the post office, originally chosen for division HQ, was also untenable. The bombing was the cue for the Germans to close in on the town from the dominating western heights. Despite the odds being stacked heavily against the surrounded Highlanders, they were in no mood to capitulate, as Fred Coster remembered:

> I was watching from behind as my mate, who was number 2 on a gun, prepared for action. Just as they got the gun ready three tanks came into view. These were damn great tanks, like nothing we had seen before – not like our army's little ones. They engaged the first tank – shot at it, killing the crew and putting it out of action. Then the second tank slewed round, so they fired at it and put that one out of action. The third tank turned round and drove off. All the time the tanks had been machine gunning our guns, their bullets were splattering off the front of the gun. My mate was thrown

back from the gun onto the ground. Several of us ran forward to man the gun, but he got up, jumped back on the gun and started firing again. He was covered in blood and shouting 'You bastards!' at them. I think a bloke like that deserves a medal – but of course he didn't get one.

Although those tanks had withdrawn, the Germans were not disheartened and soon advanced again, this time with infantry. Again Coster and his comrades were ready: 'We were really in amongst it. The Germans started to arrive in lorries. They began to fan out in the field. We used the gun to destroy them. We fired at them – we could see arms and legs flying everywhere. They retreated. That's how we were holding the town.' He later tried to explain his emotions at being embroiled in such intense action. His explanation showed why men like his friend could continue to fight against the odds: 'The only thing that goes through your head is "I've got to get that man!" You've got to fight. This is it – you have no time for anything else – no time to be nervous. You've got to survive!'

In the close-quarter fighting around the town there were terrible scenes. In the St Sylvain and Le Tot positions, infantrymen fought from house to house to prevent infiltration by the enemy. Some groups, including the 'Kensingtons' and the Northumberland Fusiliers even managed to drive the enemy back to the woods outside the town. The fighting became intense, taking its toll on both attackers and defenders. Positions came under fire from tanks, mortars and artillery as the Germans chose to probe their defences rather than risk all-out attacks. One soldier later wrote of watching a Bren gunner emptying an entire magazine into an unsuspecting German. As the man lay dead upon the ground a British officer approached and fired into the back of the man's head – just to make sure. These were vivid images for men who had already seen plenty of fighting in the previous weeks. In another incident, a British soldier was hit by machine-gun fire that stitched up his spine, causing his body to arc upwards and then collapse in an obscene heap. Every man fighting witnessed such scenes of death and destruction. Everyone experienced the terror, horror and exhaustion so typical of the modern battlefield.

The story was the same all around the town. With the entire perimeter under threat there was no time to worry about troops and weapons being deployed in their correct roles. Anyone who could hold a rifle held one – whether cooks, gunners, mechanics or drivers. There was no way the proud Highland regiments, with their long, prestigious histories, would surrender without a fight.

In the course of 11 June, around 1,000 prisoners were taken by the advancing Germans, but still they had not broken the defenders' spirits. As long as they had arms, ammunition and hope, they would continue to defend the town. From their positions above St Valery the Germans watched as the British constructed barricades in the harbour and moved up guns ready to defend the area. It was clear Fortune and his men would not accept the offered terms of surrender made by Rommel on the evening of the 11th. Instead General Fortune focused his efforts on ensuring the navy came to their rescue that evening. As he told the War Office, the shortages of food, petrol and above all ammunition meant that the night of the 11th would mark the final chance to get them home.

That evening, the Germans assaulted the town with an unprecedented fury, their artillery raining down shells upon the harbour, in the hope of demoralizing the defenders and hampering any attempted evacuation. Over 2,500 shells struck the town and were followed by further tank attacks aimed at penetrating the defences. Under these sustained attacks there was little chance of the division holding out much longer. With ammunition running low, numbers of dead rising ever higher and little hope for the wounded if they did not get rapid treatment, it was clear the end was approaching.

With swathes of the town in flames or in ruins, the division began to withdraw to await evacuation. As the infantry held their front-line positions, the division's support troops moved towards the beaches and harbour in hope of finding ships waiting for them. Though few of the troops realized it, the Royal Navy made genuine efforts to ensure they were rescued. Many of them would not discover the truth until many years later and, instead, they believed they had been abandoned to their fate. Fred Coster only discovered the navy had tried to rescue the division more than sixty years later, when he read an obituary of one of the ship's captains. Prior to that he never believed the navy had attempted a rescue.

For the tank crews of the Lothian and Borders Horse the withdrawal into St Valery was a fraught affair. German artillery spotter planes were seen above the village of Cailleville, resulting in violent shelling that caused several casualties. At midnight the regiment mustered in the village, destroyed all vehicles, then were marched to St Valery to await embarkation planned for 4 a.m. From two miles out they could see St Valery where two pillars of red smoke were spiralling into the night. As they tried to find a route to the harbour they found themselves getting lost in the twisting lanes of burning buildings. Columns became separated, with groups coming face-to-face with each other after going the wrong way up alleys. But like so many disillusioned men that night, they soon realized there were no ships waiting. Illuminated by the glow of blazing buildings, under star shell bombardment from enemy artillery on the cliffs above and standing in an area that kept being swept by machine-gun fire, the troops were in a hopelessly exposed position.

When it was time for the 101st Anti-Aircraft Regiment to head to the harbour for evacuation, Fred Coster was told to pass the news to the various batteries: 'I saw this motorcycle sitting there and thought that would make it quicker. I started it up and the officer jumped on the back. As we went down the road he was shouting out to the gunners telling them where to muster. It was night time by then and the place was in flames.' The flames may have illuminated the roads but they also helped to silhouette Coster, making him an obvious target: 'As we passed a blazing van I heard a shot whizz past in front of me. I realised they were shooting at me. I revved up and sped away and as I did a shot went past behind us. The officer said "Take it easy!" I didn't answer him but I thought "We're going to get our heads shot off here!"'

Having received the message, the men began to muster on the beach to await evacuation. It was not to be. Milling around at the water's edge, Coster and his mates looked out across the misty waters, eagerly anticipating the appearance of ships out of the gloom. But nothing came. Out in the Channel 207 ships of all sizes were waiting for the order to sail to St Valery. Most had spent the day in the waters near the coast but had been driven further out into the Channel by German gunfire. By the night of the 11th they were still waiting to rescue the Highlanders but there was little they could do when fog closed in around the approaches to the port. With just sixteen of the 207 vessels equipped with wireless, they were forced to rely on communicating by signal lamps, and with limited visibility there was quite simply no way of communicating between the craft and organizing the evacuation. Around 3 a.m. General Fortune ordered that the men should leave the harbour area and head back to their positions above the town. Disappointed, the gunners of Fred Coster's regiment made their way back inland where they were to return to their guns and take up new positions to defend the town.

With ammunition running low, the situation began to get increasingly desperate. Major-General Fortune wanted the infantry to attack at dawn, to push the enemy back far enough so that the harbour area could be held for one more day to allow for another attempted evacuation. Yet there was precious little they could do. As Major-General Fortune was requesting the navy to use their guns to suppress the enemy, many of the division's gunners were destroying their weapons so they couldn't fall into enemy hands. As Gordon Barber made his way into St Valery from his gun positions he couldn't help but be astounded by the wreckage that seemed to surround him, either dumped in roadside ditches or smouldering on the verges:

It was the biggest cock up I've seen in my life. Blokes were getting killed everywhere. They wanted volunteers to go into town to find small arms, so we went. The idea was, we were going to fight our way to the beaches. The outskirts of the town were a mess. We found these four French officers in their car, like they were asleep. But they were stone dead! They had all their medals on. All I remember was going into a broken shop and finding this big box of stockings. I thought 'When I get home with these I'll be rich!' Then I found a bag full of fruitcake and tins of Ovaltine. So I kept them as well.

There was little chance of the division making good its escape. The town, with parts of it flattened and in flames, seemed deserted. There were no boats in the harbour and few civilians in the streets. Instead there was just the detritus of war – corpses, wrecked vehicles, scattered boxes of food and ammunition and, above all else, the lost and bewildered soldiers of all nations. Middlesex Regiment machine-gunner Jim Pearce was surprised to find himself approaching the front lines only to see Frenchmen going the opposite direction loaded down with tins of British rations. The situation was not helped by the knowledge that their own stores of food and cigarettes were being blown up to prevent their capture by the enemy. Given the circumstances, no one could blame the Frenchmen for taking the food. Such was the chaos that food had to be found wherever it was available. There was no time for scruples. Gordon Barber returned to his gun position, still clutching the stockings, fruitcake and Ovaltine he had 'acquired' in the town.

Upon arrival, Barber handed over the weapons he had found, just one box of hand grenades. His officer, Captain Wright, then asked him to try to pick up any information from the wireless set, and that was when Barber, working his way through the dials, heard the self-congratulatory BBC announcement of the successful evacuation of Dunkirk.

It was clear to both Barber and Captain Wright that their war was coming to an end. A gun battery without shells, small arms or ammunition could not fight on. Not only that but the single box of grenades Barber had found were useless. As an infantry sergeant told him: 'It would have been a good idea to bring the detonators.' Barber's admitted ignorance was a reflection of how poorly prepared the army was: 'That was another balls up! I wasn't to know. I'd never used a bleedin' hand grenade in my life.'

In the circumstances there was but one choice, as the captain soon explained: 'I can't give you any more information. We are now going to be taken prisoner of war. You can do as you like.' This was all the information he needed. It was 'every man for himself'. Not wanting to be taken prisoner, Barber and his mate Paddy mounted a motorcycle: 'It was all "pie in the sky". We hadn't got a clue where we were or where the Germans were or where we were going to go. It was all a big mess. We were all young kids – 18 or 19. We didn't know what we were doing.' Despite their ignorance, they made the conscious decision to escape and roared off into the unknown.

The situation was the same all around the town. Eventually the gunners of the 101st Anti-Aircraft Regiment also realized their guns could defend St Valery no longer. Their orders were to keep firing until they had just two shells remaining. These two were then fired together, the detonation of the second shell destroying the gun. Unfortunately, one of the sergeants forgot to use an extended lanyard and managed to destroy the gun and seriously injure himself. With the Bofors guns out of action, the gunners were ordered to take their rifles and rejoin the battle as infantrymen: 'We were ordered to take up positions behind a low wall,' recalled Fred Coster. 'We were facing a wood waiting for the Germans to come through it. Some of the boys had even fixed bayonets. Suddenly a man beside me slumped down – he'd been shot. The fire was coming from a ruined building behind us. It was a Fifth Columnist – he shot another one. Then my mate Harry Champion turned and fired. Out of the window slumped a man dressed in a French uniform. Harry said "You won't shoot any more you bastard!"'

On the morning of the 12th, there were few among the

Highlanders who believed the fight could go on much longer. Dick Taylor had manned many defensive positions in the last few days but by that morning it was clear the fight was over. The previous day they had come under attack by enemy tanks and attempted to resist the attack with machine-gun fire. It was hopeless – one moment they heard the order 'Open fire' then the next order they heard was 'Every man for himself!' With no hope of escape, Taylor and his mates made their way to the high ground above the town but soon came under fire. Taking shelter behind a monument, they stayed low and hoped no one could see them. When one French soldier raised himself above the ground he was immediately shot in the chest. After nightfall, they returned to the town in the hope that the Royal Navy might be able to get boats into the harbour under the cover of darkness. Wounded men were laid out on stretchers awaiting evacuation, but there were no ships. That night Taylor slept in a local cinema before rising in the morning and making his way back up to the high ground and rejoining a detachment from his own regiment. There he and his comrades simply spent the last few hours waiting for the enemy to arrive to take them prisoner. His comrade Jim Charters recalled that, on the morning of the surrender, he soon realized any further resistance was futile since he had just half a belt of ammunition left for his 'drill purposes only' Vickers machine-gun.

The situation was much the same for the men Major-General Fortune had chosen to to reclaim the ground around the town. Orders were given that the 23rd Field Regiment Royal Artillery should provide supporting fire. However, it was soon discovered many of the gunners had already stripped the breach blocks from the guns to prevent them falling into enemy hands. Despite the difficulties, some of the remaining gunners set to work to restore the guns to working order. Deprived of artillery cover, the infantry continued with the planned attack. As they advanced they found surrendering French troops crossing their path, preventing them from engaging the enemy. Under cover of the chaotic conditions, enemy tanks and infantry were soon able to outflank the

Highlanders, surrounding the advancing infantry and forcing their surrender.

As dawn broke that next morning, the Germans watched as some troops attempted to continue the evacuation from the steep cliffs to the west of St Valery. Many became committed to one last desperate effort to reach safety. Surrounded by an ever-encroaching enemy they clung to the hope of rescue by Royal Navy vessels in the Channel. In desperation, some of the forlorn soldiers fell to their deaths whilst attempting to descend the cliff faces. Both British and French soldiers began to crowd around on the clifftops, anxious to reach the beach below to board a boat back to England. In their haste to escape the enemy some tried to descend the cliffs on ropes that were too short for the job. They were left dangling in the air, lacking the strength to climb back up and unable to lower themselves any further. There they hung until their strength had gone, they lost their grip, and crashed onto the rocks below.

Not all of the men fell to their deaths accidentally. In some locations, as the troops attempted to lower themselves to safety, German soldiers arrived on the clifftops. Although the men descending the cliffs were in a hopeless situation, some of the Germans showed them no mercy. David Mowatt remembered: 'They had tied their rifle slings together to make ropes and the Jerries came along and were cutting them. These were ordinary soldiers! SS, you could imagine doing that, but not ordinary soldiers. It was murderous.'

Seeing the dilemma, others raided the lorries that had brought them to the clifftops for anything that could help them descend to the beach below. One group, waiting at a fissure in the rocks, took the ropes that held the canvas covers on their trucks and joined them together. Eventually the rope was long enough to lower men the whole distance, this was then secured at the clifftop. Private Watt, serving with the Royal Engineers, remembered the scenes: 'The method used was to pass a loop over a man's head, he then walked backwards down a very steep incline and lowered himself over the edge, the men at the top lowering him hand over hand.'[1]

The journey down the rock face was a perilous one for the already exhausted soldiers. The rocks were muddy, making it easy for them to lose their footing. Private Watt soon discovered how difficult the descent would be: 'Eventually my turn came to go down . . . I was fully dressed, overcoat, full equipment – less my pack – my clothes being sodden with rain, my rifle slung. I had grave doubts about the strength of the rope as I must have weighed a considerable amount, but there was no time to hesitate.' Slinging the rope over his shoulder, he walked back and gave the signal for the others to begin lowering: 'I risked one look then closed my eyes quickly. It was a very unnerving descent as I kept twisting one way, stop, then twirl the other way.'[2]

The survivors who gathered on the beaches prayed for salvation but none came. Around them they could see the bodies of those who had fallen to their deaths from ropes that had not been long enough for them to reach safety. With nowhere to take cover, they faced assault by German dive-bombers and came under increasingly heavy fire from snipers who had taken up positions further along the clifftops. As time passed, machine-gunners joined in, raining fire down onto those who dared expose themselves on parts of the beach. Finding themselves trapped by the advancing enemy, one group even took shelter in a cave, intending to fight it out from behind a barricade of rocks. When the Germans eventually reached the cave the men within realized their situation was hopeless. A few hand grenades thrown into the cave would cause chaos. They made the only sensible decision and surrendered.

Despite the dangers, other waiting troops began to wade out to sea, attempting to get onto the rowing boots that were ferrying men out to a destroyer waiting offshore. This ship was their only hope of escape. It was also firing its heavy guns towards German batteries on the cliffs and drawing some fire away from the desperate soldiers. Yet it was not enough. With shells continuing to land among the men on the beach, Private Watt and his mates decided to join the swimmers attempting to reach a French trawler waiting offshore. Discarding their equipment and rifles, stripping off all their uniform except their trousers, Watt and his mates swam out towards the boat.

Despite the strong currents they reached the trawler and climbed up a rope ladder onto the decks. In an attempt to stop the boat being swamped by desperate soldiers, sailors on board the trawler cut the rope ladder, sending men tumbling down onto the swimmers below. What happened next revealed that those on board were no safer than those struggling through the surf:

> A shell landed right amidships, apparently in the engine room. There was a terrible noise of escaping steam. Two quick firing guns on deck were still firing madly away . . . We could feel the shock as several shells hit the ship, mostly about the water line . . . Then they opened up with anti-tank guns . . . holes started to appear in the sides above our heads. Men all around were hit, very few escaping injury. Some were killed at once and many dying after only a few minutes.[3]

The men on board faced a terrible dilemma. Surely if they remained on board they would be killed. Yet looking into the water around them, they could see swimming men being hit by rifle fire from the cliffs. With the boat ablaze and slowly sinking the survivors began to help the wounded men onto the decks. All they could do was to pray that salvation might come, but neither Allied nor German vessels appeared to save them. Some men even tried to build a raft to help ferry the wounded ashore, but it sank as soon as it was launched.

Realizing the wounded would not survive in the water if the boat went down, the troops raised a Red Cross flag to signal to the enemy that the men on board would resist no longer. Eventually, a German officer appeared on the beach and called out to the survivors. All the able-bodied men were to swim ashore and leave the wounded on board. If they did not comply immediately they would be fired upon. Their situation was hopeless. There was nothing they could do but to swim into captivity.

As the bedraggled men dragged themselves from the water, a German officer stood on the beach offering them a swig from a bottle of spirits. One of those who pulled himself up from the water was Frank Norman, of the Royal Corps of Signallers, was only seventeen years old. He had volunteered in June 1939 at just sixteen, falsifying his age to show he was eighteen. Like the rest of his comrades, he was to endure five long hard years of captivity – in Frank Norman's case working in the mines of Silesia.

As the walking wounded were taken away from the beach for treatment, the other survivors were given blankets and overcoats and put into a straw-filled bivouac for the night. Exhausted, they slept through an artillery barrage that landed around them. Such was the extremes of hunger experienced by these men, they were forced to scavenge for grain amidst the straw of their bedding.

As this drama was being played out another ship was also sacrificed in the desperate efforts to rescue the division. The Dutch motor barge *Hebe II* was sunk off the French coast with eighty soldiers on board. There were no records of any surviors.

Not all those on the beaches were quite so unfortunate. Others were able to reach boats, such as the three officers and seventeen other ranks of the Lothian and Borders Horse who escaped by boat from the port of Veules. Similarly, thirty-one pioneers from the 7th Norfolks were picked up by HMS *Harvester*. When he rescued them from the beaches the commander of the ship told the lucky men it was no longer safe to attempt to reach the harbour of St Valery.

The events of the morning of 12 June remain confused. Some reports quote the French capitulation as forcing General Fortune to surrender. But when one flag of surrender was seen fluttering from a steeple close to the divisional HQ, Fortune insisted it be torn down and the perpetrator arrested. When the French officer responsible was found he explained that he was simply following his own general's orders. Other sources quote incidents of French white flags being torn down by enraged British officers, then British officers crying when Fortune ordered them all to lay down their arms. Some British troops even recalled the vision of a British fighter flying above their positions displaying a white flag. What was clear was that the French had informed Fortune of their intention to surrender. It left the Scotsman in a hopeless situation. Without the French fighting side by side with his men there was no hope of holding out for another day. It was a stark choice – surrender or die.

Despite Major-General Fortune's defiance and hope to keep fighting long enough to effect an escape, the situation was wretched. His infantry had not been able to push back the enemy from above the town and with the clifftops occupied by the enemy any evacuation would most likely result in a slaughter, costing the lives of both his men and the sailors he had hoped might come to rescue them. At 11 a.m. Fortune received news from England that the previous night's evacuation had been called off due to fog. Yet by that time the news was irrelevant. Half an hour earlier Major-General Fortune had already notified the War Office of his intention to surrender.

Most of the divison went quietly into captivity, knowing further resistance was futile. One group of soldiers, exhausted after a day of close-quarter fighting, bedded down in a field, sleeping through the night without sentries to watch over them. They awoke to discover they were surrounded by German tank crews who quickly spotted them and took them prisoner. Elsewhere others continued to fight. Each man became embroiled in his own personal war. The notion of escape filled the minds of many, whilst others hardly seemed concerned about the slim chance of slipping across the Channel. For some the desperate battles around St Valery were simply them following orders – they knew it was the duty of each man to fight on for the honour of his regiment and his country. For others it a sign of personal defiance, a way of showing the enemy they were not beaten. For many more it was just a desperate fight for survival. Whatever happened, few seriously contemplated the possibility of being taken prisoner.

When the moment of surrender came, a deathly quiet fell over the troops. The gunners of the 23rd Field Regiment were still working to ready their guns for the attack on the Germans' clifftop positions when they heard the news. Rather than load and fire their guns, they were told to line up in a field ready for the surrender. Within a minute of receiving the order the gunners noticed a German tank entering the field. One man then shot himself, preferring to take his own life rather than be taken prisoner.

As the Germans began to round up the survivors of the 51st Division, most of the prisoners began to follow the shouted orders of their captors without daring to question them. Northumberland Fusilier Dick Taylor recalled that the process of surrendering was like anything else in the army: 'You do as you are told – you don't think about it. I threw the bolt away and destroyed my rifle. Elsewhere they were already dumping trucks into the sea so I realised everything was in chaos and our position was hopeless.' Each man was submerged beneath waves of his own emotions. Bewildered by the speed of the collapse, Jim Pearce marched into a barbed wire enclosure still carrying his rifle over his shoulder. The German guard knocked it from his shoulder, without Pearce even breaking his step.

Such was the depth of feeling that some soldiers felt a rage they could not express, barely able to suppress their anger that the division had been defeated. A few openly wept at the disgrace of defeat, whilst others were disgusted to see the behaviour of some among their comrades. John Christie found himself looking on in awe at behaviour he felt out of place in a modern war. He watched as officers changed into their dress uniforms ready for the surrender. It seemed ridiculous, within a formation that had not eaten a hot meal for a week, to be so concerned about appearances: 'It could have been done in order to put on a "good show" for the Germans . . . I don't go much on "good shows", anyway I had more important things on my mind like how I was going to get out of this mess.'[4]

Others felt numb with disgust, fear, hunger, exhaustion or the simple relief they had survived. For days they had fought for the right to escape from France. Each step back towards the coast had been a step towards salvation but it seemed they had been betrayed. The whirl of emotions experienced as the enemy approached to take them prisoner was shared by every able-bodied man in the division, leaving most barely able to express what that moment had meant to them. Fred Coster attempted to explain his feelings: 'We were ready to fight but then the French surrendered and that was it – we gave up. There was no option. We would all have been massacred if we had fought on. We were numb – we were tired. We were wondering what was going to happen. What went through my mind was perhaps they would murder us. They lined my unit up in the field with a machine gun facing us. We were just standing there.' The gunner that approached Coster expressed the thoughts silently shared by each of them: 'There was one little fellow, he came running up and said "Bombardier, they're not going to shoot us are they?" I said "Of course not. They wouldn't dare to!" He was happy and went off laughing. But I started to feel a bit timid. I thought they might shoot us, but I couldn't tell him.'

Cut off from the rest of the division, with no way of communicating with General Fortune or the other senior commanders within St Valery, the 2nd Seaforth Highlanders at the St Sylvain position continued to fight their own battles. On the 11 June it had been estimated the remnants of the battalion were facing around 100 enemy Panzers. It was an ominous situation for the exhausted and lightly armed infantrymen. Despite their desperate situation they continued to fight hard.

Realizing that the Seaforths would not surrender without a hard fight, the German commanders decided on an unorthodox tactic to convince them to lay down their arms. Central to the German plan was Colour Sergeant Edwin Fields, known as 'Gracie' to his fellow Seaforths. After more than a month in the front lines, Gracie was exhausted and had finally been captured, along with a wounded sergeant and a young private. As a senior sergeant, he was selected for an unpleasant task. A machine-pistol-wielding German NCO appeared and forced him onto the front of a tank. With the German behind him, and a gun pointed at his back, the sergeant was driven towards the Seaforths' positions. Some reports have the tank advancing under the protection of a white flag. Other reports suggest no white flag was shown. In any event, as they reached a crossroads close to the forward positions, the tank was hit by a burst of gunfire. Still, the worried sergeant had no choice but to remain on his perch – if he stayed his own men might shoot him, but if he ran the Germans would certainly shoot him.

Recognizing who it was seated on the front of the tank, the Seaforths held their fire, watching as their Gracie was driven ever closer. Eventually he was released and the tank withdrew towards the enemy lines. Reporting to the battalion HQ, the message he carried was simple. The Seaforths were in a hopeless situation. The rest of the division had surrendered and they were surrounded. If they did not stop resisting they would be bombed into oblivion.

But surrender was not an option for the proud Seaforths. Sergeant Fields refused to return with the message to the Germans. Instead he chose to remain with his regiment as the decision was taken to split up and attempt to reach safety. During the attempted escape, Colour Sergeant Fields managed to reach the coast but was taken prisoner. Whilst in captivity he was able to report the incident to General Fortune.

One of those men who watched the arrival of 'Gracie' Fields was Jim Reed, the under-age soldier from Sheffield who had volunteered to fight as a Seaforth Highlander:

It was a real shock to see 'Gracie' strapped on that tank. Then a sergeant came round and told us the division had surrendered, but that the Seaforths weren't going to surrender. It was our last battle. We were in close quarters fighting, holding the upper floor of a farm, overlooking a sunken road. A German half-track came along and stopped opposite us. I had one magazine – half-full – for the Bren gun. My mate said he'd take out the Machine gunner and I'd get the driver. I could see him clearly – he was just 10 ft away. We fired down onto them. As soon as I hit the driver the half-track ran down and crashed into some woods. We didn't waste any more ammo on them – anyway I only had a couple of rounds left. We could hear them calling to us to come and take them prisoner. We didn't bother. That was just hours before we were taken prisoner.

Eventually it became clear such resistance could continue no longer. Jim Reed had used some of his final magazine on the crew of the half-track and realized there was little else he could do:

We had no choice. What settled it was the wounded. They were in a barn and that got bombed. We said we would hang on until 6pm to see what happened. It was not worth carrying on. There was nothing for the 2 inch mortars, we had no ammunition. We could do nothing and we needed to save the wounded. We had to surrender but we had no idea what was going to happen. We realised how exhausted we were. We'd had no food that day and hadn't slept for two or three days. But when we finally surrendered it was the worst moment of my life.

The 4th Seaforths found themselves in no less desperate a situation. In the trenches of his company HQ, David Mowatt's company commander made the decision to go to the beach to check out the rescue situation for one last time. Mowatt and another man accompanied the major. Making their way down the rough path they discovered there was no possibility of escape and, returning to their positions, it was obvious to all that they had no choice but to surrender or be wiped out. When the moment came it was strangely numbing for the last of the defenders: 'We just waited for them to walk in. Rommel came up – he was on one of the first tanks to come through – he spoke to us. He said "I hope you will be treated fairly and that you will not be too long as a

prisoner of war." He was right there at the front with his troops –
he probably knew we'd had it! He knew he was safe.'

Despite the German general's words of sympathy, as the remnants of the St Sylvain defenders were rounded up there was little
mercy shown to those who had fought so long and hard. Some paid
a harsh price for their defiance. One group, including two officers
and five other ranks, were forced to sit on the bonnet of a car,
despite there being room inside, as they were driven for twelve
miles (twenty kilometres). It seemed they were being deliberately
paraded as trophies of war. The senior officer in the group, Major
James Murray Grant, the grandfather of the actor Hugh Grant,
noticed the pistol pointed at him throughout the journey, reminding him of the treatment of 'Gracie' Fields, whose ordeal he had
witnessed. With the surrender of St Valery a strange calm settled
over the town. Jim Charters and his comrades abandoned their
hopeless positions, destroying their guns as they left, then assembled
in the town square. They arrived just in time to watch as General
Rommel came into town on the leading German tank.

In scattered groups, sharing their last cigarettes, the exhausted
soldiers simply hung around the harbour awaiting orders. For most
it would take days for the reality of what had happened to sink in.
Instead, with numbed emotions, they watched as the German
troops took control of the town they had hoped would be their
escape route. Frustrated British officers watched as German soldiers
strolled along the quayside and their commander Major-General
Fortune was photographed beside the battle's victor, the soon to be
legendary General Erwin Rommel.

So the entire 51st Highland Division went 'into the bag'.
Leaving his Vickers machine-gun behind him, Jim Pearce joined
the lines of prisoners: 'There were dead soldiers all around us. Some
were people you didn't know but some were my friends. It was
hard to see your mates were dead, but you had to just accept it. You
can do that when you are young. Luckily my brother had survived,
so I had someone to support me.' Thousands of men like Pearce
and his brother were herded into barbed wire enclosures hastily

erected by the Germans to house the incoming prisoners. Some
arrived in the pouring rain. Already exhausted by the week of
fighting and dejected by defeat, their pitiful situation was heightened by the weather, especially when their captors insisted on the
prisoners handing over the gas capes and groundsheets that were
helping to keep them dry.

As they passed through the wire they were searched for any
remaining sharp implements, like knives and scissors. Some men
lost cigarette lighters and matches. Vast piles of abandoned equipment were piled up as the dejected and defeated men faced their
first day in captivity. A wave of helplessness and hopelessness swept
over the Jocks as they slumped down onto the grass and contemplated what lay ahead of them. As the prisoners assembled some
were in tears, others were praying, most were too tired to show
emotion. John Christie later described the consensus of opinion:
'The general feeling was that we had been "sold down the river"
and "left holding the baby". Don't forget that for a week we had
been listening to the details of the evacuation at Dunkerque and
being told of how all the stops had been pulled out to make it
succeed.'[5] In the eyes of all those who went 'into the bag' that day,
Christie was right. The 51st Highland Division had fought on,
against hopeless odds, to ensure the survival of others. As a result
the survivors of an entire infantry division marched off to face
almost five years in captivity.

CHAPTER FIVE

The Wounded

In battle you will live dangerously and you will feel the stark grip of fear; you will be unarmed amid violent, indiscriminate lethality; to you the hurt and the frightened will turn for easement and comfort; through your devoted service the profession of medicine will gain added dignity.

From a speech given to medical students about to join the Royal Army Medical Corps during Second World War

As the remnants of the BEF marched into captivity there were many others in no fit state to embark on a long journey by foot. The vicious battles that raged across France and Belgium resulted in vast numbers of wounded soldiers who were left behind in hospitals, aid posts and casualty clearing stations. Some were so badly wounded they were hardly aware they were now prisoners – many were unconcerned about the fate of the BEF, focusing instead on their own physical situation. Unable to leave their hospital beds, they had no time to trouble themselves with the outcome of the war. Others had wounds which had been sufficient to result in their exit from the battlefield. Yet these same men were now considered fit enough to join the exodus towards the Reich.

There was a third group also left behind to the mercies of the enemy. In the aid posts and hospitals were a group of soldiers for whom the defeat of the BEF did not mean the end of their duties.

The surgeons, doctors, medics, orderlies, stretcher-bearers and ambulance drivers were still focusing on the survival of the wounded who had been sacrificed in the retreat. Wounded men – regardless of their nationality – should be treated with respect. Medical treatment should be given wherever and whenever possible. The Red Cross was a symbol that stood out above all others. Regardless of their rank – whether senior surgeons or lowly stretcher-bearers – medical staff provided a standard of care to the utmost of their abilities long after the majority of the BEF had escaped across the Channel. From men like Les Allan, transferred away from his company to become a bearer simply because his commanding officer knew he had first aid training from his time with the St John Ambulance, to Captain MacInnes, the padre with the Argyll and Sutherland Highlanders, who remained behind with the wounded since all the medical staff had already been withdrawn, the wounded would have much reason to be grateful in the years ahead.

The medic's status as 'protected personnel' was enshrined in Article 9 of the Geneva Convention: 'If they fall into the hands of the enemy they shall not be treated as prisoners of war . . . They shall be sent back to the belligerent to which they belong as soon as a route shall be open . . . They shall carry out their duties under the direction of the enemy; they shall preferably be engaged in the care of the wounded and sick of the belligerent to which they belong.'[1]

Although large sections of the Royal Army Medical Corps – RAMC – were members of the Territorial Army they considered their organization to be highly professional. The RAMC was one part of the army that had undergone many changes during the inter-war years. The changing weapons of war – in particular the use of shells that exploded with a greater force than those twenty years before – called for a new system of care.

Wounded men would be immediately removed from the front lines by stretcher-bearers whose task was to deposit them at the regimental aid post. There they would receive first aid. From there they would be collected by RAMC stretcher-bearers, transferred to

ambulances and taken to an advanced dressing station. At the ADS
the wounded would be given any immediately required treatment,
then classified into three categories. The first group were men
suffering from shock, who were taken to a field dressing station to
be given blood transfusions and other treatments for their condition. The second group, those requiring immediate attention, were
sent to an advanced surgical centre where they could be given
emergency operations. The third group, those fit to travel, were
sent to a casualty clearing station. These were equipped to give all
manner of treatments, including x-rays. Following treatment, all of
the wounded were transferred to a forward general hospital from
which the lightly wounded could receive treatment prior to being
returned to their units and the more serious cases could be
transferred to a base hospital.

Graham King, a pre-war Territorial, serving with the 13th
Casualty Clearing Station, had a good understanding of the
modern treatment methods and how the RAMC had changed
during the inter-war years: 'Medics always seemed to be despised.
They got the idea we were sitting on our arses way back from the
front just waiting for the casualties to come in. That might have
been right in the 14-18 war, but with what had happened in the
Spanish Civil War they found the quicker you treated patients for
secondary shock they had a far better the chances of survival. So we
were placed up near the front, treating casualties as they occurred.'

Every man captured by the Germans in May and June 1940
experienced the same emotions: shock, bewilderment, fear and, in
a great many cases, loneliness. These were combined with thirst,
hunger, sleep deprivation and an all-engulfing sense of mental and
physical exhaustion that numbed the prisoners. Such was the
hunger experienced by one wounded man that he ate a hunk
of bread – green with mould – he had pulled from the mud of a
farmyard. If the physical and mental impact caused emotional
turmoil for the fit prisoners, the shock was far worse for the
wounded men. Not only did they have to cope with the impact
of captivity but they had to do it whilst enduring physical pain and

often the knowledge they might either succumb to their wounds or never fully recover.

The scenes witnessed by many wounded as they made their way slowly to get treatment left an indelible impression. Fred Gilbert, shot three times prior to surrendering, had to march past the twisted corpses of the rest of his section as he made his way to an aid post. Another soldier recalled being transported by his captors on the front of a tank and seeing the charred corpses of his fellow soldiers in the doorways of burning barns. The horror of such scenes, combined with the pain of their wounds and the fears of what might happen to them, created a general sense of hopeless isolation for the wounded men.

The experience of being wounded and captured was recorded by Geoff Griffin, a twenty-two-year-old, serving in the Royal Army Service Corps, who was sent to defend a canal to the east of the Dunkirk perimeter. Whilst exposing himself in order to fire at the enemy he noticed another German swing a machine-pistol towards him: 'I felt as if someone had knocked me down with a tank and I fell backwards into the trench, with blood streaming from four bullet holes in my left shoulder. Yes, the German had missed my head, so I lived for that moment in time. Strangely, I felt no pain.'[2] In an effort to help stem the flow of blood from Griffin's wounds, his mate tore away his tunic and applied field dressings to his shoulder. When his mate attempted to leave the trench to get assistance he was immediately cut down by a burst of machine-gun fire.

Griffin later wrote of the hours that followed: 'Somehow I survived the night, drifting in and out of my delirium, praying and imagining myself back home with my parents . . . Darkness faded into light and I awoke to complete silence except for birds singing . . . this is it, I thought, this is death and hopefully it's heaven.' The very silence confounded him and he looked around, to discover he was still alive, left all alone in the aftermath of a vicious battle. One thought filled his mind: 'Had the war ended?'[3]

Unsteady from the loss of blood, he rose to his feet, putting on his helmet and picking up his rifle. He soon dropped the rifle, realizing his wounds rendered him incapable of firing it. Standing on the edge of the trench, he surveyed the scenes: 'Bodies of my friends littered the garden and there were many lifeless forms on the canal bank further away.' He came across the surreal sight of two men beside a Bren gun, one as if ready to fire it, the other kneeling ready to reload the gun. He tapped one on the shoulder only to see the man topple over. Both the men had been killed by blast. Eventually, searching for food, he found a house full of dead and wounded, most of whom had crawled in to seek shelter from the battle they had been no longer able to contribute to. There Griffin awaited the inevitable arrival of the Germans.

Wounded in similar circumstances, Fred Gilbert didn't have to wait for the Germans in order receive treatment. Instead, at gunpoint, he was waved away into a village where an aid post had already been established. There he was joined by a handful of other survivors of his unit. Arriving in the village, they were struck by the irony of what happened next. British artillery – the supporting fire they had asked for to help drive back the enemy from their positions – finally landed around them. But it was too late, the battle was over:

> We were driven to the village school where they had set up an aid post. There were two British medical officers. They were patching blokes up and cutting arms and legs off – just throwing them into a bucket. This horrid place was packed and they were using a trestle table to operate on. I had my arm, side and ear bandaged up, I was covered in blood – I was a mess. There were plenty of lads in a bad state – worse than me. The doctors said to me 'You're alright, you're only wounded!' I was glad to get out of there it was more like a slaughterhouse than a surgery.

Blessing his good fortune, Gilbert moved into one of the school rooms and was mobile enough to go outside to escape the tragic scenes within. What he saw only helped to increase his despair:

The thing that made me feel sick was when I went outside. The whole French army seemed to be marching past. They were prisoners. This endless column – four abreast – seemed to be going past from dawn to dusk, there were thousands of them. They were carrying food, all with their full kit. They were all clean and tidy. I thought to myself 'God, I've been fighting to save you bloody lot!' Then I looked at our boys with their torn, blood stained battledress, unshaven and hungry, no equipment, nothing, all of them wounded, some of them incomplete. They had given their all to try and save France. It made me so sad and, in a way, bitter.

Doing his best to forget what he had seen, Fred Gilbert attempted to offer whatever assistance he could to the more badly wounded men: 'The floor was absolutely full of bodies – blokes with arms and legs missing. I had marked my space – I could stretch out, I was lucky. There was a bloke lying next to me who had lost his arm and his other hand was damaged. He couldn't get up. He wanted to go to the loo, so I had to help him. I only had one arm. I had to pick him up enough to get him into a position to do it.' Yet if these scenes of suffering were enough to tax the more resilient of men, it was about to get worse: 'There was just a narrow pathway through the middle of us. They came and put a wounded bloke in the way, he was laid right up against me. I said "You can't put him there – what if we want to get up?" The bloke said "Don't worry, he won't be there long. I think he might be dead now." He didn't last the night. It wasn't very pleasant sleeping next to a corpse – having to climb over him to get to the loo.'

Despite these conditions, Fred Gilbert was fortunate to receive such swift treatment. Any delays risked the increased possibility of infection. For those with abdominal wounds, the reality was that they faced death if their wounds were not treated within six hours. Prompt treatment was also vital for those wounded who came in contact with the soil because of the increased chance of gas gangrene.

The stretcher-bearers were the vital link to rapid treatment, and of all the medical staff were the men in the greatest danger. They were the ones, like Les Allan at Hazebrock, who crawled out into the open to pull the wounded men to safety. They were the men who braved incoming fire to save the lives of soldiers who were no longer able to save themselves. Theirs was an intense world, one in which they had to face everything the enemy threw at them without having the means to protect themselves. As the BEF fell back on Dunkirk, these front-line medics were among the hardest pressed of all the troops. They had to face the harsh reality of saving men to whom they could sometimes offer little more than the most basic first aid. It was combined with the realization that when the wounded could not be moved someone would have to stay behind to assist them. At the Mont des Cats this had cost the medics dear. As the troops retreated from the hill they had to watch the enemy blasting the monastery and the aid posts within.

As possibly the only survivor of this final bombing of the convent cellars at Hazebrouck, Les Allan – despite his wounds – soon found himself joining the march into Germany. He was not alone. As the Germans began to round up prisoners across France and Belgium there were plenty of instances of wounded men being refused transport on the journey into captivity. Outside Arras a group of walking wounded were sent on a twelve-mile (twenty-kilometre) march, without food, that lasted twenty-four hours. In one group of marchers was a sergeant with a shattered arm and a private with a wounded foot. Their officers found a German officer who spoke English and requested that food should be given to the men and transport provided for the wounded. As soon as they had completed their request the German turned and walked away without reply.

Another group of walking wounded found themselves abandoned in the middle of a French village. For three days they waited for the Germans to come to offer them medical treatment. When treatment finally came they were roughly treated by the German doctor, who pulled off their bandages causing them to cry out in pain.

One of the wounded men who was forced to join the march into Germany reported that such were his injuries that he could hardly walk and had to hobble along supported by his mates. As he was so slow he was beaten across the back by the guards who marched with the column. He was later given transport into Germany but arrived at his final destination to be left outside in the rain, despite his wounds, sleeping on the bare earth.

These were not isolated incidents. When Captain Derick Lorraine was wounded in the leg he was moved by ambulance towards Cassel. However, the ambulance was captured by the enemy and the driver was taken away as a prisoner – itself a clear breach of the rules concerning medical staff. With the driver gone, the four wounded men inside were left without treatment for two days. When the Germans eventually returned to the ambulance Captain Lorraine was not offered immediate assistance, instead he was taken away to help force the surrender of a British unit holding out nearby. Lorraine insisted he was too badly wounded to walk but the Germans refused to accept his excuses, waving a revolver at him to demonstrate the consequence of his refusal.

Realizing any resistance was futile, the captain – covered by the rifles of the German soldiers – made his way to the position, a large concrete blockhouse that was holding back the enemy advance. He shouted to the men inside not to reply to him, hoping they would continue to defy the enemy and not see his actions as treacherous. Using Lorraine as cover, the Germans then approached the blockhouse and poured petrol into the rubble, igniting it with hand grenades. Despite the efforts of the Germans, and the blackmail enforced on Captain Lorraine, the platoon within the blockhouse continued to resist. They eventually surrendered after four days of hard fighting. For three of those days they had no food and for the last thirty hours of the siege the building was on fire.

The unfortunate captain was not alone in being denied treatment. All across Belgium and France those patients within aid posts, casualty clearing stations and hospitals were given a cursory inspection by their captors to see whether they were really in need of further treatment. Anyone whose wounds were not considered deserving of further care was told what they should do – in no uncertain terms. Cyril Holness, a company runner, was wounded during the retreat through Belgium. His introduction to battle was violent and bloody:

> I was crawling along a trench and I can remember my officer jumping on top of me when we were bombed. All the young soldiers outside the trench were killed by blast. It was terrible to see. Two of my colleagues were shot down beside me. I was wounded in the neck by shrapnel, it wasn't too bad but I thought it was my ticket home. We were in makeshift beds in the aid post. My pal Jimmy Bryant was next to me, he'd been badly wounded – he'd got a fractured leg and everything. I was waiting for the ambulance to come back for me. I thought our pals would be coming to take us home. But it never came. Next thing I knew there was a German with a great big revolver shoved up my nose. I thought I was dead, that they would bump us off. My mate looked up and asked him for a fag. The German went beserk. I said 'You'll get us shot, Jimmy!' The German looked at my neck said 'Nix' – nothing – and ripped the dressing off. That was the end of my treatment.

With aid posts being overrun, the men within them and the field ambulances which transported the sick were increasingly in danger. With the Wehrmacht driving through the Allied positions there was no longer a definite front line behind which the medical staff could feel protected. As a result the staff of the field ambulances faced some of the greatest dangers on the battlefield. In the flat lands of Belgium and northern France this left them hopelessly exposed as they rushed their patients from aid posts to field dressing stations. As one observer noted, the ambulance crews found it difficult to maintain the balance between keeping out of the range of the enemy's field guns and keeping in range of the casualties. Furthermore, like so much of the BEF, the RAMC had gone to war with ambulances that were often unfit for their purpose. Many were mechanically unreliable and unable to cope with the weight of travelling fully loaded. Some of the RAMC stretcher-bearers were forced to march towards the front line since their vehicles could not carry them. It was a less than auspicious start to a violently dangerous campaign. A further problem was that some ambulances had nowhere to store a bedpan during their journey. Nor were there sufficient bedpans to allow one per ambulance.

There were other problems for the staff of the ambulances. Such were the realities of war the Red Cross symbol was not respected by everyone on the battlefield. Some soldiers even reported seeing German doctors armed as if ready for battle. John Forbes Christie later wrote of seeing German ambulances being used to ferry fully armed troops into battle prior to the defeat of the Highlanders at St Valery: 'From the British point of view the idea of pushing forward armed infantry in ambulances with Red Cross markings would be "just not on", even though winning the battle depended on it. In the language of the day such a move would have been classed as "just not cricket". War never was and never will be cricket.'[4]

If ambulances could be used as weapons of war they could also become targets. Wounded men from the Warwickshire Regiment were killed when the ambulance they were travelling in came under attack. There was no mercy shown to the stretcher cases. The ambulance doors were slammed shut by the Germans, trapping them inside. The ambulance was then set on fire, killing all of those within.

The experience of being targeted whilst within an ambulance marked the turning point in one young medic's war. Norman 'Ginger' Barnett was a Territorial soldier serving with 133 Field Ambulance, attached to 133 Brigade of the 44th Division. Barnett had never planned to become a medic, quite simply circumstances had thrown him into the job. He had only joined the TA because a friend had suggested it would be a good idea. Their main concern was that if conscription was introduced they might be sent to work in a coal mine. Anxious to avoid this fate, Ginger and his mate had tried to join the Royal Artillery, only to find the local TA unit was full up. Then they visited their local barracks and offered their services to the Queen's Regiment. Again they were told there were no vacancies. Eventually they were told to volunteer for the RAMC, whose local unit was based in a wooden hut in a Croydon back streeet. Their fate was sealed.

Just a year later Ginger Barnett found himself in Flanders where he and his fellow ambulance men were soon introduced to modern warfare:

> The first casualties I ever helped pick up were in an air raid on Béthune. We were just shipping men to aid posts and taking civilians to hospital. We were 'blooded' there. There were some horrific wounds coming through. I can remember the first one we picked up. It was a civilian woman. The whole of the muscle on her leg had been torn away. You could virtually see the bone. But after that you quickly got used to it. Later on we were seeing bullet and shrapnel wounds. You just put M&B693 powder on it, slapped a field dressing on and got them back as fast as possible. Some of them took it well, but some didn't – crying that they were going to die.

With the 44th Division falling back, Barnett and his comrades continued their bloody tasks, until they were in the shadow of the Mont des Cats. Here, like so many from that division, Barnett and his comrades faced their final action. By that time the Mont des Cats was in enemy hands, giving them a perfect vantage point from which to observe the surrounding area. Barnett was travelling in a loaded ambulance when it reached a crossroads. Instructions were swiftly given for them to take one particular road to avoid the enemy: 'Sod's Law – we went the wrong bloody way!' From nowhere small arms fire began hitting them as they came under fire from SS troops:

> In the end we were surrounded. We had stopped and bullets were coming through the canvas sides of the ambulance. I said to

the sergeant 'C'mon lets get out of here!' But he told me to wait for orders. I thought 'You're joking!' He told me to pile all the blankets up the side of the lorry. But it didn't stop the bullets – they were firing tracers through the side of the ambulance. They set fire to the ambulances. So we slit the sides of the ambulances and dived out into a ditch. It was every man for himself, you just got out and ran after the bloke in front of you, hoping to get to some sort of shelter.

As the ambulance crew dived for cover there was nothing they could do to help those wounded trapped within the burning vehicles: 'That was the first time I'd ever smelt burning flesh. It was bloomin' horrible.'

Crawling to safety, the shocked medics reached the cover of a farm where they awaited their fate: 'The first German I saw had a tommy gun, he had bandoliers of ammo round himself and a steel helmet. Was I frightened? Christ, was I? Oh yeah, I was scared bloody stiff. I was "tom titting" myself! I really thought it was going to be the end of me. My mate said to me "Well Ginger, I think this is going to be our lot." Christ, I was frightened.'

With war raging across the front, British medical staff found themselves swamped by the casualties who had safely escaped from the front lines. At one hospital 1,200 patients were received in a single day. The surgeons worked in four teams, each undertaking eight-hour shifts. Even when off duty the surgeons had little time to relax, since they still had to eat and were supposed to scrub up for an entire ten minutes prior to operations, plus they found themselves continually interrupted in their endeavours as they scuttled for shelter during seemingly endless bombing raids. When one hospital was finally ordered to evacuate, the senior surgeon was found to be finishing off an operation whilst wearing an unsterilized tin helmet.

One of those who became well acquainted with the realities of surgery under battlefield conditions was Ernie Grainger. A pre-war insurance surveyor in the City of London, Grainger had joined the

Territorial Army in 1938, a period when junior staff in the City were encouraged to serve their country: 'It wasn't compulsory, but God help you if you didn't.' Having originally dreamed of being a doctor, joining the RAMC (CCS) was a simple choice – life with 10th Casualty Clearing Station was the closest he would ever get to realizing his ambition. Thus he had trained as an operating room assistant (ORA), a position in civvy street that would be held by a theatre sister. Their role was to assist the surgeons, mopping up blood as the surgeon worked, holding clamps in place and generally fulfilling whatever tasks the surgeon found for them.

The clearing station was established in the Belgian town of Krombeke, just miles from Dunkirk, when it began to receive casualties. For the next few weeks Grainger and his eighty or so comrades worked incessantly to save the lives of the wounded of every nationality on the battlefield:

> We were well trained – we were like para-medics. In the BEF medics were pretty thin on the ground, so you had to take over and do lots of work you didn't expect. We were permitted to do a lot more than civilians could do during surgery, like stitching up wounds. We were also allowed to administer morphia without a doctor's permission. Sometimes the surgeons were so busy that they did the essential part then left us to clear up – they didn't have time. They were doing amputations, then they'd take out some shrapnel and leave it to us to stitch it up. We weren't concerned with the cosmetic aspects of surgery, we were just keeping them alive. It was crude – but it was effective. We were so busy, but of course on top of all the wounded we'd still be getting people with appendicitis! While we were doing all this, clerks were labelling the wounded to keep a record of them.

There were men shipped straight from the front lines by the field ambulances, whose staff had done little more than staunch the blood flow with bandages and hastily applied tourniquets:

We were in a few old houses, we had a few tents and a marquee as an operating room. That was all. During the retreat we were treating men from the units who were retreating and the men who were fighting in the rearguard. The Germans had the 88mm gun. It was a vicious weapon. When the boys got hit with that they really got cut to pieces. So all of a sudden you'd get fifty or sixty casualties in an hour coming in. It wasn't a surprise to see a man with his leg amputated or with a load of shrapnel in his stomach. We just expected it. We thought we'd be frightened of blood, but for some reason we weren't.

Alongside the British wounded, 10th CCS also accepted large numbers of French and Belgian wounded. Although they might have expected a language barrier, there were no problems – most of the wounded were too badly hurt to be able to worry about what was happening. All that mattered was that they were being treated and might therefore survive: 'If they were in pain, we gave them a shot of morphine or some chloroform, knocked them out and got on with the job.'

Despite the urgency of their surgical work, all the staff at the clearing stations had another vital task to fulfil – to prevent the spread of infection in wounds. Though they could not always work in aseptic conditions – after all, who could keep the interior of a marquee full of men direct from the battlefield spotlessly clean? – but they could make sure infections were spotted and dealt with as early as possible. There was no shortage of such infections arriving with men who had been wounded in the fields of Flanders: 'The biggest problem was gas gangrene. It's caused by soil infected with animal waste getting into wounds. It was terrible. There was nothing you could do about it – they were immediately an amputation case. It didn't take long to set in. You could smell it a mile away. Once you've smelt gas gangrene you can never forget it. The smell stays with you.'

Grainger and his fellow medical staff worked around the clock, cutting men open, extracting shrapnel, cleaning wounds, removing amputated limbs, stitching wounds – hardly able to care about anything that was taking place outside the green marquee that had become their home. Sometimes with three or four surgeons working at once, they were doing operation after operation, just stopping for a brief rest after every few patients, then returning to continue their bloody tasks. Grainger and his fellow ORAs, doing work reserved for surgeons in more peaceful days, were forced to learn the job quickly.

Hour after hour, day after day, the teams worked to save the lives of their patients so that they could be swiftly ferried back to the general hospitals established in the rear areas:

Eventually we found ourselves in the front line. We were absolutely knackered. We were with the Norfolk Regiment and they really hammered the Germans. So much, that when they captured the Norfolks the Germans shot a lot of them. It was pretty vicious, it wasn't a gentleman's war by any stretch of the imagination. But we were so busy we never knew what was happening outside our tent. We never knew anything about being defeated. It came as a big shock. We didn't even know they were near us. We were at work in the operating theatre and all of a sudden a German medical officer came in, said 'For you the war is over' and then watched us working.

Though shocked by the arrival of the German doctor – who arrived with a stunningly modern mobile operating theatre that was towing a trailer used for x-rays – the staff of 10th CCS could not stop to worry about their fate. Instead they carried on working, treating whatever wounded arrived, and working side by side with the German medical staff. As Grainger recalled: 'We carried on for five days, working side by side – it was just medicine. Yes, we knew they were Germans and we weren't very happy about being prisoners, but the German doctors were very efficient. We stayed there until they decided the war had passed by and then we were treated as prisoners.'

Despite the efficiency and speed with which Grainger and his fellow medical staff had worked, the carefully planned system of swiftly passing wounded men down a chain of aid posts and hospitals to ensure their rapid and effective treatment could not function perfectly. With the BEF and its allies retreating at speed, the medical staff were met with all manner of difficulties. Quite simply, at no time was the BEF holding static positions long enough to put the system into complete use. Some medical units found they had hardly reached the front line before they were forced to pack up and move backwards. To avoid this problem many of the hospitals were positioned further away from the front lines than had been intended. At the forward dressing stations the question was how long should they keep working before closing down and joining the retreat? If they waited too long they faced treating all the wounded but being captured. If they withdrew too soon they would condemn some among the wounded to death, but would also ensure they were available to function at the next battle. It was a difficult choice for any commander to make.

Such was the chaos of the retreat towards Dunkirk that one column of ambulances, caught in a traffic jam, were told they would have to carry all their patients over a bridge in order that it could be destroyed to prevent the enemy's advance. After the bearers had toiled through the night to get the wounded men safely over the river – resulting in the patients spending a night in the open – the news was given that the bridge was not to be blown. Similarly, Ginger Barnett's unit had wasted hours trying to find a river crossing since so many bridges had been blown. As he later recalled: 'It wasn't organised chaos – it was just chaos.'

One of the units caught up in the chaos was the 13th Casualty Clearing Station, as Graham King recalled:

Our unit was unfortunate really. We were supposed to be moving up to the front. We were cut off by the sweeping movement of Rommel's division. We had about 100 miles to move but we had no transport. We couldn't move any of our equipment. We'd sent the more mobile stuff ahead. They were going to prepare the ground. We were supposed to bring the heavy stuff up afterwards, once they'd prepared the ground. But we were having to march up. On the way we met some French medics who were retreating. They told us the Germans were ahead. But our colonel said 'My orders are to go St Pol so we will make our way on.'

Despite the colonel's understandable desire to reach his destination, the odds were stacked against the 13th CCS. Splitting into three separate groups, each group tried to find a way through the Germans to reach the rest of the unit: 'That's when it all came unstuck. We'd been wandering around in the wilds trying to make our way through. We had very little food – just our iron rations. Loads of the blokes had eaten them before we even started, so they had nothing. The rest of us had to share our food with them. So that cut down how long we could survive. We were absolutely starving and getting weaker with it.' On 23 May, now desperately hungry, King and his comrades decided to barter for food in a French village: 'We got eggs and bread and milk. Whilst we were sat at the roadside eating and drinking a German patrol came up. We wondered if someone had gone and told the Germans. We weren't a fighting unit so we couldn't fight. They just rounded us up. I later discovered the ones who had gone ahead with the light section actually got away from Dunkirk. But when they got back the 13th CCS wasn't reformed. I suppose they thought it was unlucky.'

King and his fellow medics were refused permission to remain in France to fulfil the role they had trained for, and since they had no medical equipment, the Germans made no effort to treat them as protected personnel: 'We were just treated as ordinary POWs. You couldn't do anything about it, especially when there's a man pointing a gun at you. When you're captured no one says to you "Well done, old boy. Sorry you've found yourself in such a mess. Would you like to sit down and have a cup of tea." War's not that simple.'

King and his comrades began the long march into Germany:

After much to-ing and fro-ing, we were herded into columns and were marched off . . . This was a calamity as we had been given no food and were forced to find sustenance from the fields we passed, if there was anything left. From the back of the column one could see a brown mass moving along to a distant green field. As the head reached there, it hesitated and then spread out over the green until it covered the field. This seething mass then began to retreat, leaving a field of dark earth as all the crops had been harvested. For those who were at the rear there was little chance of getting any kind of adequate foodstuff and they became weaker . . . One evening I bartered with two French Moroccan soldiers for a cigarette tin of stewed stinging nettles. We settled on two cigarettes and an English shilling. Very tasty were the nettles. Eventually, our captors got things organised and began to give us barley soup, which looked like bleached porridge and army bread covered in green mould – but eaten with relish.

If getting used to the realities of captivity was tough for those captured on the battlefield, it was perhaps worse for those who had had no opportunity to create their own destiny. Those who were patients by the time they were captured were already helpless and could think of nothing but survival – any notion of evading the enemy was but a distant dream. However, among the patients there was one group with a particular sense of bewilderment. These were the men who had reached the supposed sanctuary of Dunkirk only to be taken prisoner in the hospitals that lined the evacuation beaches. For them it was a case of 'so near, yet so far'. At the beginning of the evacuation the wounded had been given priority, being carried onto ships by stretcher-bearers. Later, even when evacuation became more difficult, both walking wounded and stretcher cases had been helped out onto the waiting ships. However, as the situation worsened, it became more difficult to get the wounded on board the boats. Quite simply, many were too sick to be moved.

Others who found themselves left behind in Dunkirk hospitals were men who had safely reached the beaches only to be wounded while they awaited evacuation. Among them was Leslie Shorrock, who was wounded in the back when German artillery shells landed amidst the sand dunes. His battledress tunic running with blood, Shorrock was helped by two soldiers who dressed his wounds, then two French sailors – wearing berets and striped jumpers – helped him to the nearby French sanatorium that was being used as a hospital. As he arrived at the red brick building he noticed there were fully armed British soldiers in trenches around the building, as if expecting an imminent assault.

What he found, he later described as 'hell upon earth'.[5] Inside, the entire floor was covered with the wounded, groaning in pain. To Shorrock the sound of their pain mingled in with the hellish cacophony of war – German planes screaming down from the skies, naval guns firing, shells and bombs exploding. Elderly nuns comforted the injured, doing what little they could to ensure the dying men were as comfortable as possible. As one worked she had tears streaming down her face. Elsewhere a priest in full robes administered the last rites to soldiers as they lay dying on stretchers.

Having fallen asleep, Shorrock awoke to find himself being lifted onto the operating table of a makeshift theatre. Around him were French surgeons whose aprons were covered with blood. Shorrock was fortunate the doctors still had gas available to put him to sleep for the duration of the operation. When he came round he was confronted with the sight of a corporal he had met the previous day. Then the man had taken pity on him and they had shared a precious cup of tea. Now he was on a stretcher minus one arm.

The wards were thick with the terrible stench of unwashed bodies, dried blood, open wounds and urine from men unable to reach the toilets. Although many among them were too badly wounded to care about their situation, others remained wholly aware that they were all but helpless. Out on the sand dunes they had been able to run and take cover from bombs and shells, but within the hospital they could do nothing to escape from the deadly rain of high explosive that poured down upon Dunkirk. Leslie Shorrock realized their helplessness when two shells hit the neighbouring ward: 'It was horrible, the glass in our ward shattered and the resultant pandemonium from the helpless wounded was unbearable. There was smoke, debris and screams coming from the ward that was hit.'[6] As they lay there, the corporal beside Shorrock grabbed his hand and said, 'This is it,' then he hid his head under the pillow and said goodbye. When the doctors and nurses entered from the wrecked ward the horrified looks on their faces reflected the carnage they had witnessed.

Two days after the bombing, Shorrock noticed that everything had fallen silent: 'I looked out of the window onto the small pathway between the wards and saw, with very mixed feelings, a middle aged German soldier slowly riding along on a bicycle. I knew what that meant . . . We knew that it was over, that we were now prisoners of war.'[7] Shorrock was about to discover the reality of the Germans' attitude towards wounded prisoners. Their captors entered the ward and observed the amputees and men too sick to be moved. Reaching the less badly wounded Shorrock, the German looked at him and shouted, 'Raus!' – telling him it was time to get up and leave the hospital. But first he had to find some clothes to replace the hospital gown he was wearing. The only clothes available were French, consisting of boots, a pair of short trousers, striped socks, a striped seaman's jersey and a tasselled cap. In this ludicrous apparel he began the journey into captivity.

The most fortunate of the wounded prisoners were those who were already patients in, or taken to, established British military hospitals. In these they were treated by doctors who could speak their language and, more importantly, were prepared to listen to them and treat their wounds without exception. They also had their own ambulances, beds, orderlies and vital supplies of medicines. If they were to receive first-class treatment anywhere it would be in their own hospitals.

In all these hospitals decisions had already been made to evacuate some of the medical staff whilst leaving others behind to look after those patients who could not be moved. In some cases there were simply not enough vehicles left to transport both patients and staff. The the decision over which staff should stay and which should go was made in different ways. Sometimes volunteers were called for, alternatively the men drew straws or flipped coins. Often all married men were exempt from remaining behind.

At 17th General Hospital in Camiers, where the British medics treated both military and civilian casualties, six officers and thirty other ranks were detailed to remain behind. Territorial Army medic Bill Simpson was one of those who volunteered to stay with the prisoners. One of his comrades, who had been detailed for evacuation, was left behind because he was so busy he missed the transport. When it came time for Simpson and one of his friends to make the choice over who should be left behind, the decision was surprisingly easy: 'We just shrugged our shoulders and came to the conclusion that he would go and I would stay. It was one of those cases of heads you win, tails I lose.'[8] Simpson and the remaining medics worked to remove the bodies of the dead from the hospital where they had been mixed up among the living. Their corpses were then buried in slit trenches in the gardens. As the medics moved among the dead they found few were properly laid out, instead they were simply lying rigid in the positions they had died in. Such was the foul aroma given off by the abandoned corpses that the wounded complained the drains must be blocked. Later the stench of gangrene grew so strong that Simpson remembered crossing the ward to avoid the smell.

The wounded men added their own smells to those of the corpses. Compound fractures were treated with plaster of Paris casts, which soon drew suppurating flesh into the plaster, giving it a 'high' smell compared to that of over-ripe Camembert cheese. Yet it was a small price to pay for the chance to recover from wounds. Bill Simpson later wrote of this awful period:

> While all this was going on the surgeons were operating trying to deal with the more urgent cases first. The sum total of suffering in that main ward was simply unbelievable to someone like myself who was seeing it for the first time. I recall a badly wounded elderly woman, close to death, with a large notice pinned to her bed clothes, 'Useless to operate.' A patient drew my attention to the man in the next bed to him who seemed to be in some sort of trouble. Just as I got to him, he coughed up something from the back of his throat and died. And so it went on.[9]

In another tragic incident a distraught Belgian woman came into the hospital asking to see her dead child. The medics could not convince her not to go in to view the corpse. Once she had seen the child she was surprisingly able to compose herself and calm down. By night the medics listened to the voice of a sick Frenchman calling out 'Vive la France.' In response a British voice piped up, 'Can't someone kill that old bastard?'

As the battle grew closer to the hospital so the tragic scenes continued. Some of the hospital's own ambulances reappeared after coming under fire, bringing back the wounded they had earlier tried to remove. For Simpson it was a defining moment: 'I always regard that day as the longest and certainly the worst I ever had to endure in the whole war . . . There was an overwhelming feeling of desolation . . . the BEF did not stand a chance against the German war machine . . . I realise that 22nd May 1940 was the day I really grew up.'[10] When the final moment came it was something of an anticlimax for the staff of the hospital. The first Germans who arrived told the staff they were surprised the hospital had not already been taken over. As a result they simply checked to make sure the German patients were receiving suitable care and then moved on, leaving just a guard at the door.

With the Germans in control of the hospital, the first job for Bill Simpson was to make a list of all the patients. In the days that followed the situation began to change. Wounded prisoners started to arrive from across the region, including Leslie Shorrock, who arrived just in time to experience the declining rations that resulted from the Germans taking away the hospital's entire food stores, leaving them with nothing but stale bread.

The shortages of food may have been a problem for the wounded men and the hospital staff but it was nothing compared to the shortages of medical supplies. At one hospital there was no access to x-rays for an entire month. Elsewhere prisoners were treated in a hospital which was without any anaesthetic. Instead, in a throwback to the early days of the nineteenth century, the patients were made to drink cognac to dull their senses prior to operations. Even before the shortages the use of anaesthetics had been restricted to giving injections rather than the preferred use of gas. The dangers of an explosive, inflammable gas bottle in use so close to the battlefields could not be contemplated. This did not make the work of the anaesthetist any easier. If patients received too much they risked stopping breathing, with the tongue falling back to choke them. Too little anaesthetic and the patients, though unconscious, would not relax their muscles fully, making the surgeons' work increasingly tricky.

Furthermore, both doctors and nursing staff were forced to begin to use medicines with which they were less than familiar. Scrounging from the Germans, or using what could be found from the French or Belgians, they sometimes found themselves embarking on uncertain treatments. Every army seemed to have its own way of treating wounds and, as a result, its own medicines for the purpose. At one hospital, staff found them-selves administering a purple antiseptic liquid to open wounds, similar to the Lysol they normally used, but they could not be certain. Elsewhere doctors used Rubiazal, a French version of the more familiar Prontosil, to prevent infection in wounds. One patient died because the doctors' lack of knowledge about the drug resulted in them over-administering. They were also forced to improvise. Another treatment for open wounds was acriflavine tablets dissolved in water.

One commodity that needed to be kept in constant supply was the blood needed for transfusions. The BEF had refrigerated stocks of whole blood and stocks of dried, powdered plasma. It had been believed the whole blood could only be stored for fourteen days until further research showed its life span was four weeks. As the shortages began to bite, some doctors continued to use stored blood that had been extracted up to seven weeks earlier. With these precious stocks dwindling, desperate measures were used, including the direct transfusion of blood from healthy men to patients. With no stocks of blood or plasma available, it was the only solution for the hard-pressed doctors. Using a Joubelert machine, the donors whose blood group matched those of the needy patient were joined to the recipient. The constant need for blood took its toll on the donors, in particular those whose blood type made them universal donors. It was not just the blood loss that affected the donors – in one hospital they were also given a bottle of champagne each as a reward for their efforts.

Conditions within the hospitals led to tragic scenes in which wounded men drew their last breath in an unfamiliar, and sometimes hostile, environment. The plight of the dying, and the need to offer them some dignity in their final moments, made a lasting impression on all of those who witnessed the scenes. Sent to hospital for treatment to a wounded hand, Second-Lieutenant Peter Wagstaff later wrote of entering a ward to find a dying British soldier: 'The poor devil was unconscious and there was nothing I could do. I felt so utterly inadequate, so useless, but that I had to stay with him until the last. And when he had gone I remember trying to give him that semblance of repose by closing his eyelids; his left eye closed without any trouble but the right eye, in spite of all my gentle attempts, kept springing open. I could not even give him that simple service.'[11]

As the 51st Highland Division withdrew to St-Valery-en-Caux, their casualties mounted. Two entire field ambulances teams were at work within the perimeter; 152 Field Ambulance had its dressing station within the town and 153 Field Ambulance collected wounded men in the nearby village of Blosseville. A local French doctor, Dr Aureille, treated some of them within his own home because of the lack of hospital beds. Hoping to find a place of safety for his wounded, one of the British doctors, Major E. Walker, made a reconnaissance of St Valery. To his dismay there was nowhere he could safely transfer them to – too much of the town was burning or unsafe. Unfortunately for Major Walker the wounded were already in ambulances, sitting out in the open, totally exposed to enemy fire. There was nowhere for them to go, they could neither move forward nor go back. Hopelessly exposed, they soon came under mortar fire that hit one ambulance, killing the men in back. Even as the bearers tried to remove the wounded from the ambulances, the Germans continued to fire on them.

There were simply not enough established hospitals to take all the patients. As a result, the wounded were treated in whatever buildings were deemed suitable. Conditions were such in one hospital that the wounded men who were able to walk were forced to use an open latrine above which they had to perch whilst holding onto a rope suspended from the ceiling. At Le Touquet the wounded were housed in the local casino, with operations taking place in what had been a rich man's playground. Within the casino's plush rooms the figures of French nuns who were treating the wounded seemed strangely out of place. They were joined in Le Touquet by captured British medics, among them Ernie Grainger and his comrades from 10th CCS who had been marched from Belgium: 'We were on the wards with German medical staff. The patients were a mixture of French, German and British. There were lots of French colonial troops. The Germans didn't treat the French Africans very well at all – they were just left to die. I don't know why. They were segregated, we weren't allowed to go near them to give any treatment. I guess their attitude was "What the hell are you doing here fighting us?" But the Germans were still treating us well.'

The role of the religious orders cannot be overstressed during this period. All across the region Catholic nuns provided medical services for the wounded soldiers, often in their own establishments that had been taken over for the military. One detachment of the RAMC reported how the Germans transferred them to a French Catholic college where all the wounded were given beds with mattresses and neither medical staff nor patients were interfered with by their captors. Others in hospital noted how gas gangrene patients were rapidly separated, so that the stench of their wounds did not affect the rest of the patients.

Geoff Griffin, wounded as he fought to hold back the Germans from the Dunkirk perimeter, was one of those whose hospital treatment was as good as could be expected in the circumstances. He was initially taken to a convent in Bruges, where he heard French-speaking doctors discussing the possibility of amputating his arm. He argued against it, insisting they attempt to save his arm in order that he might one day be able to return to his pre-war job as a coach-builder. They informed him that the shoulder joint was shattered, the muscles severed and there was just skin holding his arm in place. But as a result of his pleadings, they agreed to attempt to save it.

From the convent he was sent to a military hospital staffed by British medical personnel. On the staff were British nurses who were married to Belgians. Griffin noted their names – Mrs Somerlink, Jenny Williams, Helene Boudens, Madame Lams – so that some day someone might be able to repay their kindness. Although the German guards prevented the nurses bringing food to the soldiers, they did not interfere with medical care, meaning the men were able to begin the long, slow process of recovery.

The misery and physical incapacity of the prisoners was reflected by the measures Griffin was forced to go to in order to help his fellow patients. With food in short supply, one of the guards allowed him to scrape the insides of the soup pot, although it was not easy since he was: 'encased in plaster from neck to waist, with my left arm at an angle of 90 degrees, it was no easy task climbing into boilers to extract perhaps a tiny bowl of soup to share amongst 20 starving men.'[12]

Although large numbers of the German medical staff showed the utmost respect to the wounded men left behind in the aftermath of the defeat of the BEF, others held them in contempt and deliberately mistreated them. In July 1940 the first reports of the poor treatment given to some of the British wounded began to reach London via the Red Cross in Switzerland. The Swiss stressed that the reports came from more than one source and that the British were being badly treated and often given no care at all by their captors. Even those friendly civilians who attempted to give water to the wounded prisoners were forced away. A Madame Odier of the Red Cross reported that the condition of wounded British soldiers in French hospitals was 'deplorable, because of lack of food'.[13] The following month reports from the still neutral Americans also reached London. When a representative of the American embassy in Brussels had attempted to visit the wounded receiving treatment in Belgium the Germans refused permission for the visit. Using information gleaned from local sources, the embassy staff were able to report: 'Owing to lack of food, the condition of British wounded prisoners in northern France were deplorable.'[14]

At the hospital in Boulogne rations were no more than a daily issue of soup and biscuits. Furthermore, two-thirds of the British medical supplies were confiscated by the Germans, as was the hospital's entire stock of cigarettes. At Malines Captain Ironside – the son of General Ironside, the Chief of the Imperial General Staff – died as a result of his mistreatment. Despite his cries for help, the assistance that could have saved him was not forthcoming. Instead the other wounded men in the hospital had to listen to his cries whilst being forbidden to help him.

Between June and October 1940 around 1,000 wounded Britons were treated at the College of St Augustin at Enghien in Belgium, where Allied doctors used whatever French and Belgian medical supplies were available. There were too few beds so some patients had to sleep on stretchers, and they were constantly hungry. However, that was not the worst of the problems for patients and staff.

Dr Peters, the German administrator, quite wisely left the treatment of the wounded to the Allied doctors and medics. However, by leaving one particular German in charge at the college, Dr Peters ensured that the treatment given was not as good as it could have been. Feldwebel Walter Scharping was a middle-aged man from Stettin on the Baltic whose behaviour made life a misery for some of the patients. He stopped some of the wounded from receiving any treatment at all, leaving them in a fly-infested room. The list of his offences did not stop at refusing treatment. He was even seen to punch one patient, and the wife of the local mayor, who was attempting to make arrangements for the Red Cross to assist the wounded, reported: 'I myself saw him kick one of the prisoners with his feet in the belly and drag him into a cellar . . . On another occasion I saw Scharping beating the interpreter . . . Scharping hit the prisoner with a book on the head.'[15] When one prisoner escaped from the hospital and was later returned, Scharping also beat that man, leaving him with severe bruising. The German told civilians he wished he had a machine-gun to make his prisoners march faster. At another hospital this behaviour was matched by a German guard who fired a machine-gun at any prisoner who dared to approach the hospital windows.

In one particularly vicious display, Scharping was seen to beat up a patient and then force French prisoners to join in and complete the beating. Such was his control of the hospital, the Frenchmen were unable to refuse his orders. The German's attitude towards the patients was also shown when the local population attempted to bring in food for the wounded prisoners to supplement their meagre rations. As a result he simply stopped giving the men their rations. Such was the vindictive nature of Scharping that he left bread to rot rather than issue it to his hungry patients.

However, one thing that was clear was that he did not discriminate – he treated British, French and Belgian prisoners with the same severity. Others made deliberate efforts to discriminate in their treatment, seeming to attempt to cause resentment and factional disquiet among even the sick and wounded. In one case two wounded Britons were forced to clear out latrines by hand, whilst French prisoners looked on. If it was disgraceful that the Germans discriminated between wounded soldiers on the grounds of their nationality, it was even worse when French medical staff behaved in the same way towards their allies. One man reported how he and his fellow wounded had their wounds dressed by a French medic. He attempted to get all the British men discharged from hospital whilst offering impeccable care to his fellow Frenchmen.

One of those who suffered discrimination was Ernest Lister, a member of a supply company of the 51st Division. He was wounded whilst driving an officer from his company. Lister was unconscious for three days and then awoke in a hospital at Bruyères, near Épinal. He discovered he had been wounded in both the leg and head and that whilst unconscious he had undergone trepanation. He was then transferred to St Dié. When he arrived at the hospital it was discovered that he was British. Lister later reported the treatment he received from the German officer who received incoming patients: 'His attitude seemed sympathetic. At that time I was wearing the jacket of an old French uniform. The officer asked my nationality in French which I understood sufficiently. When I replied that I was English he threw the charts and photographs away and went on to the next case.'[16]

Whilst in the hospital Lister received a daily ration of a bowl of barley but since he was too weak to eat he had to be spoon-fed by a fellow patient. With no treatment forthcoming from the Germans,

Lister also had to rely on the French prisoners to change the bandages covering his wounds. United Nations reports into war crimes described his treatment as 'remarkable for callousness and discrimination against him'.[17] This discrimination was noted by Leslie Shorrock who at first found himself in a hospital full of French patients. Here he received coffee for breakfast, then mashed potatoes, meat, sausage, carrots, bread and wine during the course of the day. Only after being transferred to the British hospital at Camiers did he notice the paucity of rations.

A report into the behaviour of the Germans at the British military hospital in Boulogne emphasized the 'systematic discrimination against and inhumane treatment of British prisoners of war . . . It cannot be too strongly insisted that the actions of the Germans at the time reflected complete disregard of obligation towards prisoners of war for which, it is submitted, they should be made accountable.'[18]

As the days and weeks passed, military hospitals across France and Belgium began to disgorge the wounded men the Germans considered fit to be transferred to Germany. Though still wrapped in bandages, weak from hunger, and often clad in little more than the ragged remnants of their uniforms, large numbers were forced out onto the roads to begin the march east. One officer captured at Calais spent three months in hospital at Le Touquet prior to being forced to march to Germany. Upon reaching Wesel, he and his fellow marchers were put on a barge that was then pulled down the Rhine by a pleasure steamer.

Not all were allowed so long in hospital to recover. Many of the less seriously wounded men had received little more than cursory treatment before beginning the march. Many of the wounded joined up with the columns of healthy men being led away from the battlefield. Despite his wounded back, Leslie Shorrock spent just ten days in hospital before being sent on the march, joining up with the columns of men captured at St Valery and eventually travelling into Germany by barge. At the end of each day's marching he had to get someone to dress his wounds. Eventually he found a kindly German guard who allowed him to travel the final miles of the journey in a lorry.

As the months passed, reports reached Britain, via the neutral countries, of British servicemen in hospitals throughout France. There was a group of sixty Glasgow Highlanders in a hospital at Laval, whilst at Rennes there were thirty-six wounded men who had lost their uniforms and equipment as a result of the bombing of the town. At Tournai 157 wounded Britons were found in a former Belgian army barracks, whilst a further 420 were found to be receiving treatment in Lille. The reports also began to record the eventual movement of the wounded soldiers. In November 1940 nearly 1,000 were moved from Belgium to Thuringia and Hessen in Germany, leaving just thirty-two men in Belgium who were still to sick to be moved.

Such moves often also took the British medical staff away from the most needy of wounded prisoners. The medics knew they were needed by the men being moved to POW camps but they also knew the sick men being left behind were in desperate need of care. At Camiers, Bill Simpson had to say goodbye to a middle-aged sergeant who had been under his treatment. The man's face was an awful colour, a sure sign that he would not live much longer. As Simpson went to leave the man pleaded with him: 'Don't leave us to die, sergeant. Please stay.'[19] But Simpson – like so many of his fellow medics – had no choice but to leave.

With so many patients departing, life began to change for those doctors who were left behind. By December 1940 doctors in the Rouen area had the passes which had given them freedom to leave the hospital confiscated by their guards. It seemed they were no longer being treated as protected personnel, more as prisoners. Protected personnel status entitled them to repatriation under the Geneva Convention when their duties were over, so it was essential their identification papers were in order.

When Ox and Bucks stretcher-bearer Les Allan had been pulled from the ruins of Hazebrouck his armband and medic's haversack had been taken away, removing any way he had of proving he was a protected person rather than a fighting man. It was to cost him dear. Unable to prove himself a member of the medical staff, he was condemned to five years in the farms and factories of the Reich, working like a slave for the Nazi regime.

Whilst those serving with the Royal Army Medical Corps – RAMC – were able to prove their status, many others were not so fortunate. Most stretcher-bearers and infantry medical personnel had nothing to show their duties, their paybooks simply indicating their belonging to infantry battalions. Many ambulance drivers could only prove membership of the Royal Army Service Corps and were unable to show evidence they had spent weeks ferrying the bloody wrecks of wounded men between the front line, aid posts and hospitals. To avoid any confusion some hospitals made efforts to identify the men. At the 17th General Hospital in Camiers a stamp was made and put into each man's paybook identifying him as 'protected personnel'. At the same hospital efforts were also made to create new paybooks for some of the wounded. The new books gave them a revised religious identity, no longer showing them to be Jewish and thus preventing the possibility of discrimination by their captors.

The haphazard nature of the reports reaching the UK regarding those men in hospital placed a great strain upon the families of the wounded. Although the Red Cross did their best to record the names of all the men entering Germany's system of POW camps, passing the names on to the British authorities, finding out details of the sick was not so simple. With the men spread across France and Belgium, many had not been officially recorded as prisoners. The family of one man received their first indication of his fate when they received a photograph of him via Spain. It was a relief to see he was alive, but a shock to discover his leg had been amputated. In September 1940 Geoff Griffin's family received notification that he was 'missing, presumed killed'. The army were even preparing to pay out a pension to his family until a letter came via a Red Cross nurse. Relieved by the news, his father ran all the way to the home of Griffin's fiancée to show her the letter. Eventually, the War

Office accepted that he was still alive, cancelled the pension and restarted his pay.

With the war in France finished, and the majority of wounded prisoners transferred to Germany, the protected personnel had done their duty and now looked forward to going home, ready to continue their healing work. They would soon have a rude awakening. There would be many long years of work ahead of them before they would be heading home.

CHAPTER SIX

The First Men Home

Now, without fully comprehending why, we were on our way back to Blighty.

Joe Sweeney, waiting to board a ship at St Nazaire[1]

The good, the bad and the indifferent.

British infantryman describing the stragglers heading west across France[2]

As the last valiant defenders of St Valery were rounded up and marched off into captivity, scattered groups – some in pairs, some alone, some in organized groups – continued to make good their escape from France. Just as the story of the BEF had not come to a close as the last of the small ships set sail from the beaches of Dunkirk, neither had the story reached its climax with the defeat of the Highlanders at St-Valery-en-Caux. In the two weeks following 'the miracle of Dunkirk' and a week following the surrender at St Valery, the evacuation of the BEF continued, with over 160,000 Allied soldiers – including British, French, Belgians, Poles, Czechs and Canadians – escaping via the ports of Le Havre, Cherbourg, La Pallice, Brest and St Nazaire. Some were even ferried along the Loire from Nantes to reach open seas. The confusion of the continued retreat across France, the mayhem of the conflicting political and military orders passing between England and France, the chaotic scenes at the evacuation ports, the carnage experienced as German bombers pounded the final boats bound for the UK – all combined to create a series of ignominious events that were initially covered up, then eventually ignored, since they failed to fit into the glorious story of the Dunkirk evacuation.

The BEF had two main bases, the northern one at Rennes and the southern one at St Nazaire and Nantes. St Nazaire was the main storage area for ammunition and frozen meat, whilst the base at Nantes was the centre for motor transport and drivers. In addition there was the medical base at Dieppe. From these base camps and hundreds of smaller centres, thousands of soldiers were rapidly heading away from the battlefields, either in hope of evacuation back to England or simply in the hope that someone, somewhere, might give them orders. Everywhere the front lines were fluid, with one French commander later admitting that every report seemed to be out of date by the time it could be acted upon. It was little wonder that, on the same day that General Fortune reluctantly surrendered his division at St Valery, the French commander General Weygand told his government they should begin negotiations for an armistice. For the soldiers of the BEF, such political machinations were far from their minds. Instead they were occupied with nothing more than personal survival.

For those men of the BEF left behind in France, just as for those who had escaped via Dunkirk, survival meant one thing – evacuation. The first of the next wave of evacuations was already underway as the Highlanders were being sacrificed in and around St Valery. As the final pockets of resistance were being mopped up by Rommel's forces, one small group of survivors made their way along the coast to the nearby village of Veules-les-Roses, where they could see a ship offshore. Not knowing if the village was held by enemy, they made their journey by night. When they arrived at Veules they found five groynes – three for the French and two for the British – from which the evacuation was continuing. From there they were able to embark.

Like a mini-Dunkirk, small boats from the larger boat offshore ferried men to safety. As they waited they were bombed by the Luftwaffe and shelled from the direction of St Valery. A few French soldiers comforted themselves by firing rifles at the enemy aircraft. There was little hope of doing any damage but it made them feel safer to know that at least someone was fighting back. When the evacuation was completed, and the small British group had returned to their regiment, they were counted. A total of three officers and seventeen other ranks were all that remained of the entire regiment. The rest had either perished in the battles around Abbeville and St Valery or were already making their way into captivity. In total, more than 2,000 British and 1,000 French soldiers made their escape from Veules-les-Roses.

As some men attempted to escape across the Channel, others tried to escape southwards through France. Most were soon captured but others were successful, reaching the south coast after weeks or months of travelling. Taking to heart his officer's order of 'every man for himself', Gordon Barber and his mate Paddy headed off on their motorcycle.

> We'd gone about twenty miles and I told Paddy I was thirsty. So we stopped in the next farm. As we pulled up he said 'Jesus Nobby – it's full of Germans!' These bastards were all 6ft 4 tall – stormtroopers, covered in guns, with grenades stuffed down their boots! They had bloody great motorbikes with machine-guns mounted on them. Paddy said 'Let's get out of here, quick!' As we turned around I said to him 'Stay where you are!' They had guns pointed at us and I was going to get shot in the back at any moment. I said 'Let's give up.' These Germans said 'For you the war is ended' and they meant it.

Whilst Barber and his mate began the march into captivity, others faired better. When the Germans had struck at Abbeville, cutting off men like Eric Reeves and Ken Willats, the rest of the

2/5th Queen's Regiment had escaped across the River Somme. Those who could swim stripped off and swam across, pulling their rifles behind them. The non-swimmers were forced to make the crossing as best they could, using an improvised guide rope made from rifle slings – many perished during the crossing. Eventually the survivors reached Cherbourg and returned to England on the SS *Vienna* on 7 June.

The rail network was soon crowded with slow moving trains, filled to capacity with soldiers, that snaked their way across northern France. So busy were the railway lines, that most trains moved at little more than walking pace. Soldiers who wanted to urinate were able to jump down, relieve themselves, then run alongside to rejoin their mates.

The problem for the trains was the inevitable attention of the Luftwaffe who roamed, often unchallenged, through the skies above France. Every so often, the men within the trains would hear the roar of engines and the rattle of machine-gun fire as those men stationed on the train roofs to provide anti-aircraft fire opened up. Each time the fighters swooped down, the soldiers would jump from the trains and scatter across the fields in search of cover. The biggest targets for the roaming fighters and bombers were the railway yards where trains carrying both men and supplies inevitably halted. Gunners seldom had time to get their weapons into position to offer covering fire, leaving the trains open to attack, and the soldiers running for cover.

Inevitably, such attacks led to men getting separated from their mates and losing their units. Some would not find them again until they returned home. Men recalled being given orders to do no more than head for Channel ports or to head west until they met someone else who could give them instructions as to where their unit would be reforming. One man recalled being told to drive by the position of the sun and that if he reached a river crossing that was blown he should simply abandon his truck and swim the river. The same man later found himself directed into Dieppe, riding into the port on the running board of a civilian car. Instead of finding an active military garrison, with a fully functioning port, he discovered a dead town.

Included among the units retreating across France were some that had only recently arrived there. The 2nd Royal Tank Regiment had only sailed to France on 23 May – days after men like Eric Reeves and Ken Willats had already been captured. By the time they arrived in Cherbourg it already seemed to many that the battle for France was lost. Boulogne and Calais were under siege, the army was reeling back towards Dunkirk and the alliance with France was faltering. Yet for Fred Goddard, his crewmates 'Dusty' Millar and Bill Meadows, and their commander Lieutenant York – or 'Yorkie' as they called him – there was no indication of the chaotic situation they were heading into.

Goddard was a regular soldier, who had been born and raised in Haywards Heath. His home life had been miserable, with his family seemingly unconcerned for his welfare. Although his father no longer beat him regularly, by the time Goddard left school he continued to interfere with his life by preventing him getting the apprenticeship he wanted and instead sending him to work in a shop. In late 1938 he had been forced to sell his beloved motorcycle to pay for the dental work that had seen seventeen of his teeth extracted. Then, to make matters worse, he was told to attend his old school to be issued with a gas mask. Goddard's memories of his schooldays had been less than positive and it was to be a pivotal moment for the twenty-one-year-old: 'I got up there and looked at the gate. I thought "I'm not going in there" and I just decided to walk on down to the recruiting office. It was a Saturday morning – and I never went home again. I enlisted in the Royal Tank Regiment.'

The decision to elect for service in the tanks was a simple one. He was told his lack of education would keep him out of the RAF but that he would have plenty of opportunity for technical training in tanks. Furthermore, the recruiting sergeant – whom Goddard knew from the local pub – thought that at just five feet four inches tall he was the ideal size to fit inside a tank. In many ways he was representative of so many of the army's recruits during peacetime.

He just wanted to get away from home and make something of himself. For the first time Fred Goddard felt his life was beginning to settle down. Discipline was strict but it was preferable to the life he had left: 'The training was hard going, you had to parade at 5 a.m. for breakfast. You had to wash and shave. I joined in November and you had to break the ice on the water tubs.' It toughened him up but quickly he got to like it, even the discipline, although he wasn't the 'King and Country' type: 'It wasn't patriotism that drove me into the army. It was my home life that made me join. It was somewhere to go to get away from home.'

By May 1940 Goddard felt he was ready for war. The regiment was well trained and had expected to go to France months earlier. Although they had missed the start of the battle they were determined to play their part in whatever came. For Fred Goddard it would not be his first time fighting Fascism – back in the mid-1930s he had taken part in street fights to prevent Oswald Moseley and his Blackshirts from holding rallies in Haywards Heath. Then he and his mates had been successful, forcing Moseley to drive away as local gangs attacked his car. This time the enemy was somewhat more formidable and, as the 2nd Royal Tank Regiment (RTR) approached the front lines, Goddard could only hope for such a success.

The tanks moved north towards the front, first by train and latterly by road. On 25 May they got their first glimpse of the destructive power of modern warfare, passing through the already bombed town of Neufchâtel. As they detrained they were relieved to see the operation was being covered by RAF fighters, circling in the skies above them. Later the same day orders had come for them to move north towards the River Bresle to support the French 5th Army. In an ominous warning of what was to come, they moved forward with severe thunderstorms breaking above them, soaking the roads and rendering their wireless sets virtually useless. Two days later the regiment saw its first action, losing nine men and five tanks, with a further four tanks lost to mechanical failure.

With the Germans still pressing, Fred Goddard and his fellow 'tankies' soon found themselves falling back from the front. On 2

June they were moved by rail to Louviers, then put into harbour
under the cover of woods near Rouen. Having witnessed German
air raids on Rouen, the 2nd RTR were given the order to move,
advancing to Beauvais before falling back again in face of the
advancing Germans. On 8 June Lieutenant York's tank, with Fred
Goddard driving, was accompanied by one other tank and a scout
car to guard a bridge over the Seine at Gaillon. The next day they
rejoined the battalion, having knocked out four enemy tanks, two
mortar teams and an artillery battery. It had been a heroic stand but
there was no point in remaining to hold the position – both the
tanks had used up all their ammunition.

The Germans were pressing hard, and the regiment was forced to
retreat in hope of escaping. Fred Goddard recalled the scenes as they
withdrew: 'Nobody knew what was happening. We didn't know
where we were going, but we got held up by the French cavalry,
they were retreating. And they were shooting their horses. We were
held up,we couldn't get through. We were given a bearing by our
commanding officer and we just went off on our own.' Their tank –
call sign 'Bolton' – became separated from the rest of the regiment
and Yorkie decided they should pull over into the cover of a
wooded area. The crew were absolutely exhausted and he knew
they needed to get some rest and have something to eat. Each man
would do a one-hour shift of guard duty, manning the radio to
listen for any further orders. Goddard took the second shift, sitting
on top of the turret listening to the chattering of other tank
commanders over the wireless. They knew that the others were
not far away, since they remained in contact by radio: 'The louder
they were, the closer they were.' However, in the darkness there
was no way of finding their comrades, even if they could hear them
engaging the enemy about a mile away. It was whilst listening that
he heard the news of the death of one of his closest friends – as he
talked to the man's tank commander. As Goddard sat there he could
hear the enemy guns getting closer and closer.

With one of his colleagues taking over the wireless, Goddard
was able to rest. It was not long before he was awoken and told to

climb silently into the tank: 'By this time the Germans had come into the wood. I was lying in this ditch – it was raining hard, soaking me – and I could hear the Germans talking. One of the crew woke me up and I could hear them. It was pitch dark, you could just hear their voices, you couldn't see them – and they couldn't see us.'

Safely inside the tank, Lieutenant York gave him the order to contact the commander and inform him of their position. The reply that came through was a shock to the waiting crew: 'They told us to destroy the tank and make our way to the coast on foot.' It was the first indication of the dire situation they had found themselves in. With orders that they should escape any way possible, the four men packed their personal belongings. The job of blowing up the tank was left to Lieutenant York: 'The cruiser tanks had been designed so you could flood them with petrol. We had 200 gallons in the back, so Bill opened the taps and filled it with petrol. Then Yorkie fired a flare down into the tank. That set it on fire. All hell was let loose – the ammo started blowing up. But we were on our way out of the woods. We were actually passing Germans but it was pouring with rain and it was so dark they didn't know who we were. So we walked from there, all the way to the coast.'★

Le Havre, the evacuation point of choice after Dunkirk, was chaotic and fraught with danger. Arriving at the port on 11 June, the drivers of the 7th Argyll and Sutherland Highlanders rammed their trucks into each other to disable them. They were given specific orders that the trucks should not be destroyed by fire so as not to alert the enemy. Frustrated by the seemingly pointless destruction of so many serviceable vehicles, some officers drove

---

★ In his published memoirs Fred Goddard stated that he was evacuated from Brest, from where the organized elements of his regiment were indeed rescued. However, the author believes Goddard was actually evacuated from St Nazaire since his account includes vivid recollections of German aerial activity and the bombing of ships in the harbour. Records show that no Allied ships were lost to bombing at Brest.

trucks westwards in the mistaken belief that they might be able to save the vehicles by embarking them elsewhere.

On 12 June the orders came for those waiting at Le Havre to be evacuated. Orders were clear, the troops were to keep good order – there was to be no talking and no smoking. With the seemingly incongruous codename of 'Whoopee', the evacuation commenced. At the Quai d'Escalles the 4th Black Watch boarded SS *Amsterdam*, whilst at 2 a.m. the 7th Argyll and Sutherland Highlanders were loaded onto SS *Viking* and SS *Tynewald*. As the Black Watch waited at the quayside, they watched RAF Hurricane fighters engage a group of Heinkel bombers. To their relief the fighters shot down three of the menacing bombers. By the morning of the 13th more than 2,000 soldiers had been transported to England. At the same time over 41,000 tons of stores had been transported out of the town by rail, destined for St Nazaire.

Although the relieved remnants of the 51st Highland Division's Ark Force boarded ships at Le Havre, they were not sent directly home. To their dismay, a decision had been taken that a new BEF was to be formed further west. As a result, 8,000 soldiers were shipped to Cherbourg. With France still fighting, the British government had reached the conclusion that the BEF should be reconstituted at Cherbourg and continue the fight alongside their French allies. To form the core of this new force the 52nd Lowland Division and the 1st Canadian Division were hastily shipped to Cherbourg. A commander for the reformed BEF was appointed, Sir Alan Brooke, who had shown himself to be a capable corps commander during the retreat to Dunkirk and was one of the rising stars of the British Army. Arriving at Cherbourg on the evening of the 12th, Brooke soon found himself having to come to terms with the reality of his position. Though he was not convinced of the wisdom of the reformation of the BEF and of further French plans, the hope was for the British to stall the Nazi advance and retain a foothold in France. Initially expecting to concentrate his forces around Cherbourg, Brooke soon discovered the French planned to form a redoubt in Brittany, using the Atlantic ports to re-supply the

force. In their minds this would ensure the Allies retained a
foothold in continental Europe.

Though shortlived, the plan to fight on interrupted the passage
of the units from Ark Force. Arriving in Cherbourg on the 13th,
they were sent to the town of Tourlaville where they were
expecting to go back into action. Changing circumstances would,
however, see them returning to Cherbourg the following day. One
retreating soldier recalled seeing Canadian gunners advancing
rapidly into France, as if eager to reach the front line. They shouted
at the retreating troops, asking why they were heading in the
wrong direction. Later the same day he saw the same Canadians
heading back to Cherbourg, travelling even faster than before.

On Saturday 15 June the British took a decision that would
shape Anglo-French relations in the years ahead. Brooke received
the order that he and his reformed BEF were no longer under
French command. Thus the planned 'Breton Redoubt' was abandoned even before it had begun, being revealed to be nothing
more than a fantasy conceived by commanders who were no
longer in effective control of their armies. Instead of concentrating
in Brittany, the remaining British forces were to continue to fight
alongside any French units in their area but their main task was to
ensure the escape of as many British troops as possible. It was an
order the allowed those troops remaining in France to breathe a
collective sigh of relief. It was clear to so many of those in charge on
the ground that there was little hope of fighting on. Even before
the final evacuation order had been issued, Brooke was convinced
any further resistance would be futile. French generals had informed him that organized resistance by French forces had already
come to an end. It was clear the available forces were insufficient to
resist the Germans any longer.

It was an emotion shared by many others. Whilst in Cherbourg,
Lt.-Colonel The Lord Rowallan, commanding officer of the 6th
Royal Scots Fusiliers, heard of the capitulation of the 51st Highland
Division. He wrote that it was an 'inevitable end to attempts for six
weeks to hold corps front with a depleted division'. He went on to

criticize the failure of organization during the retreat across France: 'Morale of most men in Brigade almost non-existent. Many first class men sacrificed to indecisive orders or none at all. Staff work throughout incredibly bad.'[3] As Brooke knew, if the British attempted any further resistance, the remaining units would share the same awful fate as the Highlanders.

This final evacuation of troops from France was given the codename 'Operation Aerial'. The Royal Navy, under Admiral James, the Commander in Chief Portsmouth, were given command of an operation that saw the British merchant fleet, escaping French naval craft and all manner of commandeered boats, converging on the west coast of France hoping to bring off as many men as possible. Unable to supply sufficient protection craft, James was unable to organize a system of convoys, instead he sent whatever was available – troopships, storeships, coasters and Dutch barges – to rescue whoever they could.

For those units concentrated around Cherbourg, escape was relatively simple. In just two days, a total of over 30,000 troops were evacuated from the port, with the final ships leaving as the Germans entered the outskirts of the town. For those elsewhere it was a task that would involve much exhaustion and heartbreak. As the German Army rolled across France, Allied soldiers found themselves desperately travelling from port to port in search of escape. Some units started off attempting to reach Le Havre, only find it already occupied, then headed for Cherbourg only to discover that too had fallen. One group from a petrol company in the 44th Division, who had been on the beaches at Dunkirk before, realizing they were unlikely to get away, moved south. Somehow they slipped through the thinly held German lines and were eventually evacuated via St Nazaire. For many such small groups, it became a desperate game of cat and mouse as they tried to keep one step ahead of the enemy.

Despite the lucky escape of Ark Force from Cherbourg, not all among its ranks were evacuated from the northern ports. At midnight on 11 June, the 17th Field Regiment, Royal Artillery, whose gunners had fought so hard, and suffered so much, alongside the Highlanders during the battles between the Rivers Somme and Bresle, were ordered to move south-west towards Nantes. The order was a great relief, just twelve hours earlier they had been ordered to fight to the last man and the last round. But with the fate of the Highlanders sealed it seemed pointless to sacrifice anyone else. Travelling via Caen and Avranches, the remnants of the regiment arrived in Nantes four days later. On the 15th they were told that since France had capitulated they had '48 hrs to clear out!'[4] In fact, there would be two more days before the French requested an armistice, but to the men on the ground the message was clear – the front had crumbled and escape remained the only viable option. Receiving such blunt orders, there was nothing they could do but head, along with thousands of others, towards St Nazaire.

Many soldiers found their flight hampered by the lost and leaderless, some of whom – both British and French – seemed to have given up all hope of escape. Some towns seemed to be crowded with drunken gangs, all fully armed and many ill-disposed towards any displays of authority. One soldier recalled being sent into a town to work as a security guard at a gentlemen's club. The owners were prepared to pay armed British soldiers to prevent intrusions by unwanted elements. The manager had come to the arrangement with a sergeant at the local British base, who provided guards in exchange for payment. The same soldier later found himself asked to escort a bus driven by a nun, carrying girls from a Catholic boarding school from Rouen to Argentan.

Even those men who did their best to remain disciplined were caught up in the chaos. Most found that whatever money they had been carrying soon ran out. Those who were unwilling to steal food discovered that, in order to eat, they could offer their services to cafe-owners and do the washing up in return for a meal.

Food became the question on every man's lips when he reached a base or checkpoint. When one man asked a sergeant where he could get food he was told to hold out his cap as a corporal dished out raisins by hand from a sack. Most resorted to the time-honoured military tradition of foraging. Effectively, that meant scrounging from civilians, searching abandoned farms, picking fruit from orchards and vegetables from fields or stealing. Some attempted to shoot rabbits, only to discover the impact of a .303 bullet left little worth cooking. One group used their lorry as a battering ram to smash down the wall of a French Army store, only to discover their loot consisted of box after box of tinned baked beans.

Fred Goddard had originally been told to head for Cherbourg and he and his crewmates had set out across Normandy on foot to reach the port. Relieved to be moving westwards, they also knew the German guns were getting closer:

> We never went as the crow flies – sometimes we had to double-back on ourselves 'cause the Germans had got in front of us. We just walked. One night we went into a farmhouse, but the French were very wary of us because lots of Germans had been infiltrated into France dressed as squaddies. But this one family took us in, they were really good to us – we'd only asked for water for a wash and a drink – but they gave us a meal. I think that was the start of the French resistance. The next day they took us down to the Seine in a van and set us on our way.

Although the four men walked for what seemed like days on end, they did get another opportunity for mechanized transport. Finding an abandoned French tank that appeared to still be in working order, they commandeered it and made their way in the direction of Le Havre. They were soon stopped by a French officer who, though perplexed to see the Englishmen driving a French tank, explained that they had no chance of reaching Le Havre. Instead, he told them, they should join with him in fighting a rearguard action on the banks of the Seine. They prepared positions beside a demolished bridge, joining with a mixed bag of British and French stragglers. Goddard's crew checked their guns and waited:

> The Germans came in from the east with lorries and infantry. They got to the river and we were firing at the lorries. I was

surprised at how much firing there was from our side and quite a lot of damage was inflicted on them. They must have been prepared for a rearguard and for the bridge to be blown. They brought up several tanks to return fire. The next thing they were launching pontoon boats filled with infantry. Most of the rear-guard were now retreating on foot. Yorkee gave the order to Bill to turn around and get moving. We headed away west. It would take the Germans some time to build a temporary bridge and to get their tanks across. That French officer had done a good job.[5]

It was not unusual for troops of all nationalities to get mixed up during the retreat. Despite the efforts of most men to remain in groups of fellow countrymen, inevitably the marching columns became mixed. Some men recalled being in groups that seemed to be filled with all nationalities. Despite their governments having surrendered, soldiers from the armies of Belgium and the Nether-lands joined the British and French as they retreated. Rather than accept captivity they had elected to seek sanctuary in England, in the hope of rejoining their army if it reformed. Also on the roads were soldiers from Czechoslovakia and Poland, men who had escaped from their homelands when the Nazis had occupied them. They had been formed into units by the French and, like the Belgians and Dutch, were looking for another base from which to continue the struggle for freedom. Soldiers whose earlier experi-ence of war had been in the company of their fellow nationals were shocked to see so many different uniforms and hear so many languages as they headed west.

Making good their escape, Fred Goddard's tank soon ran out of petrol and they were once more forced out onto the roads on foot. The alternative was to give up and go into captivity, a fate none of them relished:

We had no idea what was happening from day-to-day. What was going through my head? I don't know. It's surprising, I never thought about being killed. We kept off the main roads because of the refugees – and other soldiers of all nationalities were on the roads – but they were being machine-gunned by Stukas. So we walked through woods and over fields. We kept ourselves to ourselves, just the four of us, we'd decided to do that at the beginning. We washed and shaved in streams, fortunately it was June so the weather was warm. I was exhausted. But we kept our spirits up because the crew remained together. We were used to each other. But we got so tired – I was sleepwalking half the time! I was lucky, I had a couple of pairs of socks. Each day I'd wash one pair out in a stream, then hang them round my neck as we were walking, so as they'd dry. Changing me socks as often as I could really helped me. Also, we were still wearing our tank overalls, rather than battledress – it wasn't very comfortable. Luckily we still had our greatcoats and wrapped ourselves up in them to sleep at night. We thought we'd get away at Cherbourg, back where we'd first landed in France, but the Germans got there before us.

The discovery that the Germans had advanced to Cherbourg came as a shock to them. At first they spotted a military policeman directing traffic on a road heading in the direction of the town. Lieutenant York observed the policeman through his binoculars and casually informed his crew that they were right, he was an MP, the only problem was that he was a German. There was nothing for it, they turned around and resigned themselves once more to finding an alternative port. Fortunately they discovered they were not the only troops heading away from Cherbourg: 'That was the only time we got a lift, we were picked up by an army lorry. This bloke had been landed at Cherbourg but he'd only just got out before the Germans arrived.' Gladly accepting a lift, Goddard and his mates climbed onboard and were finally able to get some rest.

As the remnants of the BEF – some in fully functional units, others in ragged bands of stragglers, many more hitching lifts in any vehicle heading west – converged on France's western ports, the final evacuations got underway. There was a sense of dreadful urgency in the need to escape. One anti-aircraft battery arrived at Brest pulling two guns behind a Ford tractor they had comman- deered from a French farm. On 17 June the inevitable happened and the French capitulated, with Marshal Pétain broadcasting an appeal for the French to lay down their arms whilst an armistice was negotiated with the victorious Germans. This was the culmination of the process of collapse that had been unfolding before the British politicians and generals. Britain's abandonment of the planned Breton Redoubt and the removal of the BEF from French command were the result of the unshakable belief that France would capitulate. For all the later French complaints about betrayal, the British action had saved 160,000 men from captivity or death.

Despite the end of official Allied unity and the appeal for the French to surrender, many among the French forces continued to work alongside the British to complete the evacuation. At Brest the French attempted to form two defensive lines, the first in an arc 100 miles (thirty kilometres) from the port, the second forty miles (twelve kilometres) away. The British reached the port in large numbers and were soon evacuated, with most having safely departed by 17 June. As in the other evacuations, vast amounts of material had to be abandoned in order to make space on board ships to carry the men. One artillery officer, sent ahead by his commanding officer to find out about arrangements for evacuation, was told they should destroy all their weapons and then proceed into the port by lorry. They were forced to destroy the six 3.7-inch heavy anti-aircraft guns and four Bofors guns that they had lovingly towed all the way from the Pas de Calais. The officer who gave the order was blunt, there was no time to be sentimental, if they did not destroy the guns and arrive in the port ready to embark by nine that evening, they would most likely end up as prisoners of war. When the artillery officer protested that they had not pulled the guns 400 miles only to blow them up, he was given written orders.

By the morning of the 18th over 28,000 British and Allied troops had disembarked in English ports. The operation was carried out despite the attentions of the Luftwaffe, who endeavoured to mine the waters around Brest. Hard-working French minesweepers kept the channels open, allowing the final ships – including those carrying the French gold reserves – to escape. With the evacuation complete, Royal Navy shore parties began the destruction of essential port facilities and the deliberate firing of the remaining stocks of petrol, causing a spiralling plume of thick black to obscure the skies above the departing ships. The Germans entered the town on the evening of 19 June.

The situation at Brest was repeated at other ports in western France; 21,474 soldiers were rescued from St Malo, another 2,000 escaped from La Pallice and around 19,000 were picked up at smaller ports. However, the busiest evacuation port was St Nazaire from whose quaysides over 57,000 soldiers were evacuated. It was also the scene of greatest disaster of the entire evacuation from France.

From the 16th onwards the port of St Nazaire became crammed with soldiers and civilians all hoping for a passage out of a country that was obviously on the brink of defeat. Even before the troops entered the town they were struck by the chaos. As the 17th Field Regiment Royal Artillery reached the outskirts of the town on 17 June they were given orders for the destruction of their vehicles. The vehicles were soon rendered unserviceable. However, they were told the guns should be retained and manhandled to the docks for embarkation. When they arrived at the quayside they were informed the guns could not be loaded and they too should be destroyed. Unable to wreck the guns effectively, the gunners left them on the quayside with just their dial sights removed.

Such were the scenes when the exhausted Fred Goddard and his mates arrived at the port. Outside the town they found field after field of British vehicles, all abandoned by the escaping troops. The confusion over what the Royal Navy could transport back to England prevented large numbers of vehicles and vast stocks of essential war materials from being rescued. Instead hundreds of brand new vehicles and guns, and millions of rounds of desperately needed ammunition, were abandoned in France. After his return, one soldier wrote home: 'don't say anything about it . . . the papers don't say anything about the cars and tanks which were left in France, it must have cost millions. But as I say, keep it dark, or I will get shot, and that's not very pleasant is it?'[6]

As Fred Goddard passed the field of vehicles he watched some men break away from the column and defy orders to take motorcycles, deciding it would be more comfortable to ride into town rather than walk. Elsewhere soldiers fired rounds from anti-tank guns directly into the cylinder blocks of vehicles as a spectacular way of disabling them. Fred Goddard was by now content to walk the final few miles:

> There were brand new lorries and staff cars – but all we cared about was that along as we got away we'd live to fight another day. That's what actually happened! We lost Yorkee about five miles outside the port. We were sitting on this bank beside the road – I was changing my socks again – and some other officers were there. They said we were going to form up in threes and march into town. Of course that was only any good until the Stukas started up! So Yorkee was at the front of the column with the other officers. Then we lost Dusty as well. They were asking for volunteers to blow up and wreck all these vehicles outside the town. But they only wanted reservists, not regular soldiers. They wanted all the properly trained blokes to get home. It was a relief for me – I said to Dusty 'It's a relief to get away from you.' But then he actually got home before me and Bill did! But it was a tremendous sense of relief – thinking we might actually get away.

On the first day of the evacuation over 12,000 troops were evacuated and during the night vast amounts of stores were removed from the port, with the RAF patrolling the skies above. Yet in the days that followed the situation in St Nazaire became increasingly fraught, first as the French surrender was announced and then as visits by the Luftwaffe became increasingly frequent. As queues of anxious soldiers snaked their way along the quaysides – looking desperately out to sea for the small boats ferrying men out to the larger ships offshore – they were besieged by civilians hoping to secure a place for themselves on whatever vessel might be leaving.

Though this evacuation saved large numbers from death or captivity, there were other activities that were less heroic and were subsequently swept under the carpet, for they hardly showed the British Army in a positive light. One of those who later recorded his disgust at the behaviour of some of the soldiers was Sergeant S.D. Coates, an instructor from the army's Small Arms School. It was not until more than sixty years had passed that he wrote of his experiences, believing it was a shameful episode of which he was not very proud and one which he believed should not be given much publicity.

Having left Chanzy barracks near Le Mans, Coates eventually reached the holiday resort of Pornichet, outside St Nazaire. There, attempts were made to organize the assembled stragglers into ad hoc battalions, with Coates put in charge of a platoon. On 15 June they were told to leave the camp as it was being evacuated. Coates soon became disillusioned with the behaviour of the British troops following the announcement of their impending departure: 'large numbers rampaged through the camp, looting the NAAFI stores and anything else to hand and respirators were being discarded from their haversacks to make room for looted cigarettes, beer etc. it was a scene I had not imagined possible. I was appalled and disgusted.'[7]

At another depot near St Nazaire the soldiers discovered a train carrying cases of spirits, including army issue rum. Soon gangs of drunken men were seen running riot through the camp. It seemed their frustration with the defeat, retreat and chaos of the BEF was firing their fury. Angered by the failure to provide transport home, the mood of the drunks – mostly still fully armed – seemed set to get violent. It was only the quick thinking of one soldier that prevented a complete breakdown of discipline. Seeing an officer failing to control the crowds, he suggested they should set fire to the straw that had been used to pack the spirits in the wagons. The resulting fire spread quickly, consuming the first wagon then spreading to its neighbours. It had the desired effect of driving the drunks away from the spirits but had one unexpected result. The fire caught a wagon being used to transport ammunition, that soon began exploding, sending bullets whizzing across the railway yards, driving back the crowds.

The following day they marched to St Nazaire, the warm weather soon resulting in the column leaving greatcoats, blankets, equipment, helmets an even rifles in their wake. French civilians scavenged at the roadsides, picking up whatever the troops abandoned. A few, Coates included, marched in full kit. Exhausted, he kept marching, preferring the exertion of carrying the kit rather than the shame of abandoning it.

At St Nazaire the weather was glorious, with civilians strolling around watching as the troops queued to be ferried out by destroyers to the waiting passenger ships, the *Georgic* and HMT *Lancastria*. Despite how close salvation seemed to be, Coates continued to be shocked by the behaviour of the soldiers. As the air was rent by the noise of explosions, he watched the queuing troops flee in panic, knocking aside civilians as they ran for safety. Waiting for transit out to the *Georgic*, Coates watched as one woman was pushed aside and her child's pram was sent crashing to the ground. He also saw British soldiers cowering on the malodorous floor of a urinal: 'I think then I was almost ashamed of the uniform I wore.'[8]

From 5 a.m. on Monday the 17th, British troops began to load into the *Lancastria*. Among them was Charles Raybould, a corporal in the 2nd Sherwood Foresters. The Foresters had fought a desperate fifty-mile rearguard action, in which soldiers had abandoned their cumbersome belongings, such as greatcoats and blankets, leaving behind anything that weighed them down and delayed their flight. All they cared about was clinging on desperately to their weapons and ammunition, knowing they might be called to fight at any time. As they retreated it seemed that discipline had begun to disappear, with soldiers calling their NCOs by their Christian names and vice versa. One corporal was spotted irreverently saluting a pig as it trotted past the marching men. Men were answering back to the NCOs and, it seemed to Raybould, had started to display a civilian outlook as they realized they were getting closer to home.

As they lined up along the quays, Raybould was struck by the feeling that it would soon be a case of 'every man for himself'. With discipline at best strained, and with soldiers from all manner of units – in particular, the Pioneer Corps, Royal Army Ordnance Corps and Royal Engineers – packing the port, it seemed that chaos was waiting to sweep the area. When one corporal tried to get Bren gunners to set up their guns in anticipation of an attack from the air, the men ignored his orders and openly threatened to dump him into the harbour. Despite such open insolence, every time enemy aircraft appeared above the town all manner of weapons opened up at them. Ack-ack guns fired rapid bursts into the skies, with the explosions of their shells accompanied by the steady thudding of Bren guns and the rattle of rifle fire. Exhausted infantrymen frantically filled magazines with their remaining rounds, passing them to the hard-pressed Bren gunners.

The scenes were watched by Fred Goddard:

It was like a miniature Dunkirk – all hell was let loose. The Stukas had got it to themselves – there were no English planes anywhere. We made for this ship but the Stukas were dive-bombing and they got it just before we got to it. A Stuka dived down. I thought he was going to crash onto the ship but he pulled up and dropped his bombs. One of those I saw go straight down the funnel. There was a terrible explosion. I'd never seen anything like it – the ship went straight down so quick. But as we came back from where the ship sunk we spotted a 'coaler'. The skipper had a loud hailer and he said he was coming in but he wasn't going to tie up. But if anyone wanted to they could jump onboard as he went past! So Bill and me jumped – it was quite a long way down. There were about forty men on the deck of this boat. The captain couldn't take any more. Some men that jumped from the harbour missed the deck. One or two we managed to pull onboard, but the rest just sank straight down. The skipper told us 'I can't take any more men. Don't pull anybody else out.' These days people forget anything else had happened after Dunkirk.'

Goddard was one of the lucky ones; he had made it safely to the port and found a boat that had avoided the attentions of the Luftwaffe. Others were not so fortunate. At St Nazaire the hopeful troops soon became embroiled in one the greatest maritime disasters of the entire war. Despite the bombing, the queues at St Nazaire gradually moved forward, the men making their way slowly towards the boats waiting to ferry them to safety. Joe Sweeney was one of the servicemen who, along with 200 other men, arrived at the HMT *Lancastria* by tug. Upon boarding he was pleasantly surprised by the orderly nature of the arrangements that had been made for the soldiers. He gave his name, rank and number to a waiting seaman and in return received a card allocating him to sleeping quarters and telling him when to go for meals. In total, the sailors handed out almost 6,000 of these cards. The *Lancastria* had once been a liner with the prestigious Cunard company. As a result, the comfort offered in the saloons and restaurants was in stark contrast to the conditions the troops had experienced in the weeks retreating across France. The luckier ones found themselves in the First Class dining rooms, at tables laid with crisp white linen and gleaming glasses and water jugs, as they sat down to a meal of sausages, mashed potatoes and coffee. Yet it was little more than an illusion of civilization and they were soon reminded of the reality of their situation.

In the mid-afternoon the *Lancastria* was subjected to a vicious aerial assault. German planes machine-gunned the decks, sending troops running for cover whilst bombers aimed their deadly cargo

A pre-war soldier of the Territorial Army displaying his kit
at Wannock camp, Sussex, during summer 1939.
This illustrates the differences between the German and
British armies in the 1930s – this soldier's uniform and
equipment are First World War issue.

The retreat through Belgium and France – British troops passing the burning wreckage of an allied
aircraft. Such scenes became depressingly familiar throughout May and early June 1940.

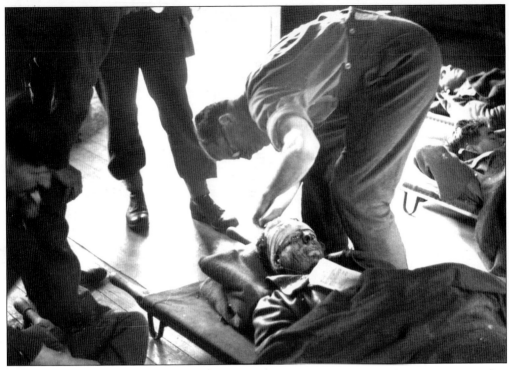

A British medical officer attending a wounded soldier at St Maxent, May 1940. In many cases, the wounded who were too sick to be moved were left behind to be treated by the Germans.

Vast amounts of equipment had to be left behind in France, with soldiers forced to destroy anything of use to the enemy. This soldier is seen breaking open petrol cans with a pickaxe prior to withdrawing.

Soldiers of the 51st Highland Division defending the line of the River Bresle, 7 June 1940. One man is using a Boyes anti-tank rifle, a design that was already obsolete and of little use against anything except the most lightly-armoured vehicles.

Burning houses on the waterfront at St-Valery-en-Caux. With the town under heavy fire from the enemy, there was little hope of evacuating the Highlanders from the harbour.

British and French prisoners of war being marched from the cliff tops to the west of St-Valery-en-Caux. Most were initially treated well by their captors – something that soon changed.

A mixed group of British and French prisoners of war are marched into captivity by the victorious Germans. The photograph is from the private collection of Field Marshal Erwin Rommel, who may have taken this picture himself.

A column of British POWs photographed near Calais in June 1940, their faces displaying the misery and uncertainty of life as a prisoner of war. Nearly 40,000 British soldiers experienced these long marches into Germany following the defeat of the British Expeditionary Force.

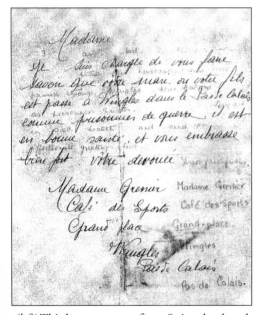

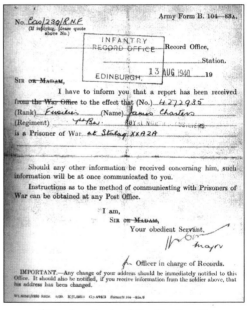

(left) This letter was sent from Switzerland to the parents of Northumberland Fusilier Jim Charters, who was captured at St-Valery-en-Caux. It was written by a Madame Grenier who had been passed a scrap of paper by Charters as he marched through her home town in the Pas-de-Calais. By the time the letter reached his home, Charters' parents had been told that he had died in battle. (right) The official confirmation letter, telling the Charters family that their son Jim was alive and a prisoner of war. By the time they got this letter they had already received Madame Grenier's letter.

N° 215   Série X   Empreintes digitales
(À défaut de photographie)

PRÉFECTURE DU PAS-DE-CALAIS

Signature du titulaire

Seuron Jean

CARTE D'IDENTITÉ

Nom : *Seuron*
Prénoms : *Jean*

Né le *9 mai 1921*
à *Pernes en Artois*
Département du
Pas de Calais
Domicile : *à St Pol.*

A *St Pol*, le *8 Décembre 1939*

Par délégation du Préfet,
Le (1) *Maire*

SIGNALEMENT

Taille : *1 m 70*   Nez : *moyen*
Cheveux : *Chatains*   Forme générale du visage
Moustache :   *ovale*
Yeux : *bleus*   Teint : *coloré*
Signes particuliers : *Néant*

(1) Maire ou Commissaire de police.

The forged identification card acquired by John Christie following his escape from a column of POWs after his capture at St-Valery-en-Caux. He used the document to reach Marseilles, where he was interned.

Eighteen British evaders are picked up off the coast of North Africa by the British destroyer, HMS *Kelvin*. Among them is John Christie (see page 249), who had escaped from a POW column in northern France then made his way south into unoccupied France. Disguised in the uniform of a French Foreign Legionnaire, he had made his way to North Africa before travelling to Casablanca and boarding a ship destined for Portugal.

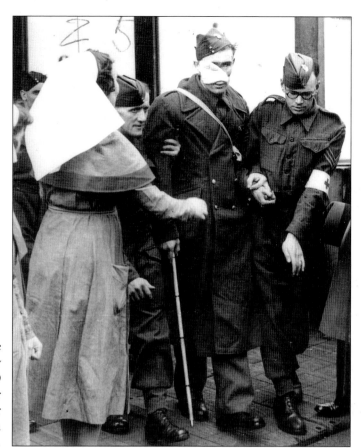

After many false starts, the repatriation of men seriously wounded during the 1940 campaign finally got under way. This blind soldier arrived home via Sweden in October 1943.

Eric Reeves (front row, far left) at Stalag 21D, 1941. Typical of the period, the soldiers are wearing a mixture of uniforms from various European countries.

British POWs, most of whom had been left behind in France in 1940, photographed following their liberation by American troops near Gotha in May 1945. After almost five years in captivity they were finally about to make the journey home that had been denied to them at the time of the Dunkirk evacuation.

on the easy target of the large liner. Some of the soldiers were ordered onto the decks, armed with their rifles, to fire on the attacking planes. Their brave efforts were wasted as the bombers soon gained the upper hand.

RAF Sergeant Wally Hewitt had just made his way onto the decks when the planes began to target the *Lancastria*. He took cover as a bomber appeared above them:

> The gunners on board turned their fire on it. While they were firing another bomber dived down from the rear. There was a rush of men for cover. I was knocked onto my knees in the doorway I was near. I did not see the plane but knew it had dived low as the bomb's whistle lasted only about three seconds. It was followed by a terrific crash and then a series of roars from down below. A sheet of flame seemed to strike me in the face. I was lifted up then crashed down again. I was stunned for a minute. I then forced my way clear of a number of bodies that were on me.[9]

Having bandaged his wounded brow and aided a soldier with a broken shoulder – whom he lowered into the sea – Hewitt found a lifebelt and swam off from the already submerged deck.

Also on board the *Lancastria* was Charles Raybould, whose own luck had sufficed during the Luftwaffe's attacks on the port. He and his mates were given tickets allocating them space in a saloon at the front of the ship. The relief they felt as they settled down in expectation of returning home did not last long. Raybould was standing in a queue to get a drink of lemonade when a bomb struck: 'A lightning infra-red blast skittled us like ninepins. I felt as if a very large blow lamp had been held at my head. Half-conscious I forced my trembling legs over inert bodies, groaing bodies . . . my tortured lungs were shrivelling fast in the oxygenless air . . .'[10]

The searing blast left Raybould in no doubt that the situation was desperate and he immediately began to look for a way out:

'men were babbling snatches of prayer like frightened children in the dark. Dying voices called the names of their loved ones. Men became animals, fighting and snarling towards the small aperture of light which would feed and cool their dying but burning lungs . . . Screams came up from a large crater which could be seen in the light.'[11]

Those on the decks were stunned by the bombs. One dazed soldier recalled how he could feel debris crashing down onto his steel helmet. As the noise subsided he raised his head but could see little but a red hot glow that pierced through the clouds of smoke and dust. Within seconds he moved backwards, away from the heat, and noticed crowds of soldiers jumping overboard. The soldier, though badly burned, realized there was no time to waste and joined the jumping men.

At the stern the situation was very different from these chaotic scenes at the epicentre of the blast. As the bomb struck, Joe Sweeney didn't even realize what had happened. To him it seemed like another close shave. Then suddenly the ship lurched to port. This was an obvious signal that something was wrong and he decided to leave the saloon where he had previously bedded down. The corridors were packed with soldiers, all attempting to reach the decks with rifles still slung over their shoulders and packs firmly on their backs. As the crowds attempted to find their way through the narrow corridors, the lights went out and the air was filled with the shouts of frightened men. Again the ship lurched, this time to starboard. Water began to flow into the corridors, sending the men charging towards the port escape routes. Swee- ney, spotting an opening in the crowds, dashed up the starboard stairs but was soon followed by others who had also sensed an opportunity to escape.

Charles Raybould was lucky, there was no hesitation from the men at the front of the boat who had so narrowly escaped the bomb's ferocious blast. Nor was there any delay as they made their way to the decks. Realizing the ship was doomed, soldiers began stripping off their uniforms and diving overboard. Elsewhere he noticed a young padre descending into the depths of the ship, telling those who tried to stop him that he had to do God's work. Men watched in disbelief, realizing it was suicide to go down into the chaos below. Whilst the padre was gripped by faith, others abandoned all hope. Knowing the ship was sinking, one non-swimmer shot himself rather than facing a slow death by drowning.

Raybould joined the crowds who had decided to risk the waters in hope of swimming away before the *Lancastria* slipped beneath the waves. Diving overboard, he hit the water and screamed in pain. The bomb blast had torn his hair from his scalp, blistering the skin. Now the salt water seared his wounds, leaving him in agony. Accompanied by a sailor, he swam for safety, urged on by his companion telling him they needed to get as far from the ship as possible or else they would be dragged down as the ship went under. Reaching a safe distance, he watched as crowds of soldiers continued to leave the stricken ship. As he bobbed in the waves, he could see small figures still clinging to the immense steel sides of the ship. Other survivors watched in admiration as a Bren gunner continued firing at the attacking aircraft in the final moments before the *Lancastria* disappeared below the surface.

One of those who found himself clinging on to the *Lancastria* was Joe Sweeney. Along with hundreds of others, Sweeney had reached the relative safety of the deck. No longer trapped below decks, Sweeney faced another terrifying dilemma – he did not know how to swim. Initially he was not unduly concerned, believing that the ship's demise would be a lengthy process. However, it was sinking rapidly by the prow, with the stern beginning to rise from the water. He had to act quickly or be trapped as the rising stern made jumping increasingly dangerous. Around him he noticed men throwing anything that could float into the water, in hope that there would be something to hold onto once they had dived overboard.

Looking down into the water, Sweeney could see hundreds of heads bobbing up and down, some being struck by the chairs and tables being hurled through the air, ostensibly to save them. Men were seen sinking under the surface, never to appear again. It seemed that the chaos of the situation had engulfed Sweeney. The air was filled by the hissing of steam escaping through pipes, the banging of the anti-aircraft guns and the screams of the soldiers. For Sweeney this was a pivotal moment in his war:

> There are times in one's life, when stock must be taken; when one weighs up what has been accomplished; when one dreams of future achievements. One searches for the meaning of life. For me, this was one of those moments. I pondered; I wondered. I wondered why innocent women, children and old folk had to endure the privations and sufferings of total war . . . My whole life seemed to scuttle by in a flash. I asked myself whether this was my last day on earth. Alas! I arrived at no solutions at all.[12]

All he knew was he needed to get into the water to escape the sinking liner. Watching as men jumped, some sinking into the depths and others bobbing back to the surface, he realized he was not alone. Others were hesitating, each man wrapped up in his own personal whirl of emotions. Around him some men began singing – mainly popular military songs – that were soon taken up by the mass of soldiers still on board the stricken ship. It was now or never. Sweeney removed his jacket and boots, hiding his jacket in the desperate hope that the boat might not sink and that he might be able to retrieve it later. Than came the moment of truth.

Unable to wait any longer, he ran towards the rails and jumped, hoping to get as far away as possible from the ship's side. His efforts were wasted and instead he slid down the steel sheets of the ship's side plating towards the water. As he slid he could feel the rough, rusty metal scratching at his naked back. He came to a halt on the casing of the propeller shaft, where he soon realized he was not alone. Around him were a number of soldiers – some fully clothed, arguing that their uniforms would keep them warm in the water, others naked, fearing that the heavy serge uniforms would drag them under. Still some forty feet above the waves, the men solved their dilemma in the soldier's favourite way – they lit cigarettes. The group sat there smoking and contemplating their dilemma until the ship suddenly lurched. Abandoning their cigarettes, the men began throwing themselves into the water. Sweeney, forgetting his modesty, tore off his trousers and jumped: 'When I hit the water, I seemed to go down and down for an eternity . . . I extended my arms upwards. I held my breath till the lungs seemed near to bursting. And I finally, when I popped out of the water, I seemed to keep on rising. Then I plopped. I jerked my arms like paddles. I tried floating on my back . . . a voice close by screeched in terror, "I can't swim!" "Neither can I!' I screamed back in equal terror.'[13]

One man tried to hold onto him, pulling him under. All he could do was to fight the man off, battling with him until the petrified soldier slid beneath the water. It was a frantic time, survival was all that mattered. This was the perfect time to learn to swim and Sweeney kicked and swung his arms, desperate to reach a plank to which four men were already clinging.

Watching these scenes was Charles Raybould. He saw the final men leaping to safety just moments before the *Lancastria* sank beneath the waters. Beneath him he could feel the ominous dragging current of the water pulling him towards the sinking ship, threatening to drag him under with it. As they watched their comrades dragged beneath the waters, Raybould and the survivors around him, wept openly, realizing just how close they had been to sharing their fate.

Kicking away from the wreck, Joe Sweeney reached the dubious safety of the floating plank, which was his only hope of salvation. One man was already lying across it, making it harder for the others to hold on. For a full seven hours he refused to move. Another soldier was holding on with one arm, his free arm supporting a third man who was in obvious pain. The fourth soldier remained until he spotted a destroyer and, telling the others he was a strong swimmer, he struck off towards it. The naked men were all covered in oil from the now sunken ship. Around them were live men without lifejackets who were desperately trying to stay afloat. Elsewhere were dead men wearing lifejackets, whose lifeless corpses bobbed along on the waves. Later it was discovered that many of these had jumped from the decks wearing their lifejackets and broken their necks upon hitting the water.

Charles Raybould watched as a fellow survivor began swimming for the shore, then, realizing his strength had deserted him, the man waved goodbye and dived beneath the waves, never to be seen again. With an officer by his side, Raybould managed to get hold of a floating board, only to lose sight of the officer after a German fighter strafed the waters around them. Despite the thousands of men in the sea, most of the survivors were struck by how few men seemed to be around them. In reality there were lifeboats, rafts, rescue boats and other ships in the waters – some of which were prevented from assisting the survivors since they were too busy attempting to fight off enemy aircraft. Yet the men in the water seemed hardly aware of their presence.

Alone in the water, Charles Raybould's thoughts turned to his comrades who had been lost in the sinking. There was the mate he had seen jump from the decks in full marching order, surely knowing that, encumbered by so much kit, he would sink straight beneath the waves. In his loneliness he began to think of giving up, accepting his fate, and drifting off into a damning sleep. He was saved by a voice coming across the water as a soldier swam to his side to join him holding onto the life-saving plank of wood. Another man tried to join them, before he too disappeared beneath the waves.

Eventually salvation came. At first Raybould and his comrade watched as a ship approached, only to see it blown up by bombs from the German aircraft. Eventually, just as it seemed they would never be saved, another ship approached: 'Soon a grey sleek destroyer came into view . . . HMS *Havelock*; bold and British mistress of the waves; Rule Britannia. An insignia of safety and protection.'[14]

Charles Raybould was safe. However, there were plenty more

for whom rescue seemed almost unthinkable. Still hanging onto his own plank, Joe Sweeney saw the plight of the man who was supporting the injured soldier. The strain was obviously weakening him and so Sweeney offered to help. For the next few hours they took turns to keep him afloat. As night approached they realized the chances of surviving through the hours of darkness were small. With the light fading and the waves beginning to rise, it was clear that rescue – if it were to came at all – must come soon: 'In the creeping darkness, we could only see one tiny boat. By then we had given up all hope of being spotted. It took time before we realised that this insignificant craft was getting nearer and nearer. Salvation seemed to be coming closer.'[15] Soon the boat came alongside them and ropes were lowered to pull the injured man onboard. Using his last ounce of strength, Sweeney eventually slithered over the side onto the lifeboat.

For several hours the crew of what was one of only two of the *Lancastria*'s own lifeboats to escape from the stricken ship, had searched the waters for survivors. Time after time they had filled up, taken the survivors to a larger craft, then rowed off to look for more of the desperate men as they swam or trod water. Yet, by the time they rescued Sweeney, their energy had sapped away. No longer able to row, and with the pitiful naked survivors unable to offer any assistance, the boat was left to ride the waves in the hope that they might soon meet another craft. They were lucky, eventually they were picked up by a French fishing boat and taken back to St Nazaire. The four soldiers who walked ashore were just a handful of the 2,000 survivors – out of around 6,000 who had been ready to set sail earlier that day. It was a sobering end to a day that had seen the French government request an armistice.

The situation in St Nazaire was now even more confusing. With the loss of the *Lancastria* many of the remaining troops were convinced the end was near and that no more ships would be coming for them. Some accepted the inevitable and settled down to drink themselves into oblivion and wait until they were taken prisoner. Others decided to leave the port in the hope of finding a boat elsewhere. Some even acquired transport, took to the roads and began the journey towards neutral Spain.

One group who left St Nazaire reached a nearby harbour, whose name none was later able to remember. The situation was far removed from that they had left behind them. There were no German planes in the skies above them, there were smartly dressed British officers organizing the loading of troops into an old steamer. There were even military policemen checking the identification of every man boarding the ship. There were also refugees attempting to secure a passage, including a group of Jewish families. A British officer stood firm, refusing to allow anyone except Britons or Allied military personnel onto the boat. One of the Jewish families made an offer to the British officers. They were willing to pay a soldier £1,000 to marry their daughter and take her to safety. They even had a rabbi on hand to carry out the ceremony. A British officer soon put a stop to the plan. He explained that no British soldier could legally marry without their CO's permission.

Back in St Nazaire, men continued to find a passage home. Still naked, and unconcerned about his nudity, shipwreck survivor Joe Sweeney headed towards a bar. What he saw before him seemed to characterize the chaos of the BEF's final days in France: 'I felt I had entered the anteroom to Hades. The bar and eating areas were chock-a-block with troops. Most were standing, packs still on backs, rifles still slung. Some sang; some shouted; some screeched; some swore. Of course, all were drinking. They were drowning their sorrows . . . All were well aware that the morrow would settle their fates, up to heaven, down to hell, home to Britain or to 'lagers' in Deutschland.'[16]

In the back room of the bar he met the owner, who gave him some cigarettes and a half-bottle of brandy, then sent him on his way. He met a teenage girl who kindly went to fetch clothes for him, handing him a flannel shirt and a pair of riding breeches that belonged to her brother. In this curious apparel, that he had to tear open to get to fit him, he was directed towards the harbour by an officer of the Royal Navy, who advised him there might still be a chance of getting home. Eventually he was able to board a collier, and the next day he arrived safely in Plymouth. As he finally left the boat, he was struck by the contrast between his own ridiculous outfit and the splendour of the band of the Royal Marines who were playing at the quayside. He also realized that the assembled crowds were laughing and clapping at his comical appearance. Sweeney was not alone in reaching England in a pitiful state – nearly all of the survivors of the *Lancastria*'s sinking disembarked barefoot.

Outside Falmouth, the boat Fred Goddard was sailing on ran aground, having to be pulled off to refloat and reach the harbour. Goddard and the rest of the soldiers on board weren't worried, all they were cared about was that they were home. The journey had been scary, sitting on the deck: 'So it was a relief to see the coastline of Britain – but it wasn't a relief a few days later when I was back in camp and saw the physical instructor. He started getting us back into shape! You can imagine what shape we were in after that march. It took a month to get us fit again. Then they sent us straight out to Egypt!'

Sergeant Coates, the small arms instructor who had been so appalled by the behaviour of the British soldiers around St Nazaire, recalled arriving at Liverpool and watching a perfectly turned-out section of Guards arrive at the quayside to take some of the British soldiers into detention. The reaction from the troops was immediate. From the deck of the *Georgic*, which had been at St Nazaire at the same time as the ill-fated *Lancastria*, they began pelting the Guardsmen with whatever came to hand – bottles, tins and all types of rubbish. Under the hail of missiles the Guards were forced to retreat. Such encounters with officialdom were not unusual, some soldiers even reported not being allowed to disembark until Customs and Excise officers had checked them. Fred Goddard remembered hearing soldiers shouting and swearing at the customs man who seemed embarrassed once he discovered where the troops had come from.

Despite the dreadful scenes in St Nazaire when the *Lancastria* went down, her fate had not marked the end of the story. Evacuations from the port continued throughout the next day with 23,000 soldiers sailing for Plymouth on the morning of the 18th. News of more troops converging on the port meant further boats had to be rushed there to take away anyone left, with 2,000 Polish soldiers leaving later on the 18th. That day also saw the departure of some 10,000 soldiers from the nearby French naval base of La Pallice. The next day a further 4,000 Polish troops were also rescued from the base. Despite the French surrender the Royal Navy continued to send craft in search of stragglers, finding more Czechs and Poles in the days that followed. The final troopship sailed on 25 June – twenty-one days after the Dunkirk evacuation had drawn to a close. Operation Aerial had seen a total of 144,171 British and nearly 50,000 Allied soldiers evacuated from France.

As the soldiers arrived back home, there was little time to celebrate their return, instead they were hastily packed off to camps across the country to rejoin their units. For some it was a strange time, arriving back at empty barracks that had once housed comrades who had been killed, wounded or were simply, like so many thousands, missing. One battalion that had formed part of Beauforce recorded just one officer and twenty-six other ranks returning after the campaign. In the days that followed the arrival home there was a terrible realization among some of the returning units that many of their comrades had been lost when the *Lancastria* had sunk. The gunners of the 17th Field Regiment realized that the first groups to depart from Nantes must have been on board the stricken liner when she went under.

Others returned with a feeling of frustration. Unlike the Dunkirk arrivals, who had come home to a wave of public adulation, the later evacuees found themselves unacknowledged. Some reported being treated with disdain, despite the fact that their fight had continued for weeks after the Dunkirk men had arrived home. Arriving at depots they were annoyed to find quartermasters demanding they hand over their divisional insignia, as if erasing the history of who they were and where they had been.

That was not all that was erased during the final days of June 1940. The terrible loss of life when the *Lancastria* went down was not revealed to the British public for many years. The news of what had really happened in the BEF's final hectic days was considered too depressing for public consumption. Somehow, it seemed to sour the sense of joy that had accompanied the escape from Dunkirk. Having grabbed victory from the jaws of defeat, it was too soon to allow another defeat to darken the horizon. Instead the official news was that the later evacuations had been a great success, allowing thousands more men to return home to continue the war.

Yet there were some for whom there was no joy in the return of the army from France. Evacuated soldiers later reported seeing women waiting at ports to see whether their own husbands, sons and boyfriends were among those returning. Clutching photographs of their men, they waited patiently for the ships, then scoured the crowds of soldiers as they disembarked, always hoping their loved ones would be there. In between handing out food to the returning men, they pressed forward with their photographs, eagerly asking the soldiers if they knew their man – just desperate that someone could give them some news. For some it would be many months before the news they had been waiting for finally came. For others, the return of the ships marked the last hope they ever had of their men returning.

CHAPTER SEVEN

The Long Way Home

At this camp we were made to work, carrying stones etc, and those who fell behind were lashed with thorns and sticks.

Testimony of a British officer interned in
the concentration camp at Miranda, Spain[1]

As the 40,000 POWs settled down to contemplate life in captivity, there was another group of survivors of the BEF who had escaped neither via Dunkirk nor the western French ports. Scattered across France were small groups of soldiers who had somehow missed the boats home yet had also managed to avoid capture. Throughout 1940, these 'evaders' faced up to the realities of their situation as they attempted to either settle into life in France or to make their way home. As the British embassy in Spain later reported, these evaders had refused to accept captivity in German hands and had gone through incredible hardships, with a singular purpose: 'to get home to England, not to see their families, but to begin to fight again against the Germans'.[2]

Some of those at large in France and Belgium were men who had been wounded and left behind as their units retreated. By-passed by the enemy, they treated their wounds as best they could and attempted to find shelter, many being taken into local homes and hidden by civilians. Others were men who had escaped from the columns of prisoners by jumping into ditches and hiding. John Forbes Christie, the bus conductor from Aberdeen, later wrote of his escape: 'We chose a spot on a slight rise on a right hand bend in the road. Telling our fellow POWs around us that we were going, they closed in on the corn, which was growing right down to the edge of the roadway . . . There were whispered "Good Lucks" from the lads as we crouched low and entered the chest high corn.'[3] Accompanied by his mate Arthur, Christie darted into the field and began an adventure that would eventually take him to North Africa.

Some were simply men who were lost and alone, having somehow been missed by the advancing enemy and never having received orders to retreat. Discovering they could not reach Dunkirk without breaking through the enemy lines, they made their way cross-country and survived by pinching and plundering from the homes, shops and fields of France. They tried milking cows or dug up vegetables to cook on the stoves of abandoned homes. They picked spring greens and ate them raw, which had the effect of increasing their thirst.

Few of the evaders could have reached safety had it not been for the courage of the French civilians who fed them, housed them, gave them clothing, false papers and transported them from safe-house to safe-house. Many of the French people had good reason to help the stranded British soldiers, after all many French sons were also away from home. Parents could but wish that someone, somewhere would offer similar kindness to their sons. These eager French civilians formed the basis of the eventual escape routes that developed in the following years, spiriting numerous Allied airmen away to safety. The routes through France took in a bewildering range of buildings. Some evaders found sanctuary in churches and convents, whilst others preferred the anonymity provided by brothels whose madams had a long-established tradition of asking no questions of their guests. A few found shelter with noble families who were able to house the evaders in palatial splendour, whilst the majority were more accustomed to the barns and cowsheds of poor French farmers.

However, not all encounters with civilians were encouraging. One group of evaders encountered the mayor of a French town who insisted they should hand over their weapons before continuing on their way. Despite stealing civilian clothes to disguise themselves, they were soon captured.

Another group who were captured by an enemy tank crew were simply told to follow the tank. At the first opportunity they darted off into cover, returning to the Allied lines a few days later. Two tank officers rejoined the Allied lines after disguising themselves as Belgian refugees. At one point they were captured by Germans, who failed to search them properly for weapons. The two officers waited for an opportunity then shot the Germans and escaped again. One group took a lift in a civilian car, replacing their military headgear with civilian caps in case they encountered any Germans. One officer who listened to the accounts of such evaders described the antics of the men who sneaked cross-country to rejoin the BEF as 'boy scouting'.

Most of these evaders were alone or in twos and threes. Only a few remained as cohesive units. One such unit was a group of eight Seaforth Highlanders who had managed to slip through the enemy lines at St Valery. With an officer in command of seven men from his platoon, they soon became known to their French hosts as 'Snow White and the Seven Dwarfs'. The problem for larger groups was keeping together when sneaking through the countryside. One group contained a soldier whose hearing had been damaged in the battle at St Valery. As a result he kept going missing since he could hardly hear instructions.

There were many hurdles for these evaders, not least of which were the rivers that lay between them and their planned journeys to safety. Since the Germans guarded all bridges that had not been destroyed during the Allied retreat, there was no way for the evaders to cross without getting their feet wet. Some were lucky to secure rowing boats, but often the men chose to avoid boats since that meant entering villages where they could not be certain of avoiding the enemy. Where possible, men built rafts from barn doors or improvised ropes from webbing straps to help the non-swimmer. Soldiers needed to get their clothes to the opposite bank but it was dangerous to swim fully dressed in heavy wool. So they swam rivers pushing their boots and uniforms ahead of them, bundled up on makeshift floats. Unfortunate men who lost their uniforms during these river crossings were forced to raid civilian homes to find replacements.

Among the most optimistic of these evaders were the men who decided that the simplest way to reach safety would be to make their way to the coast, steal a boat and head north across the Channel to home. One British officer reached the coast opposite Jersey, only to hear the frustrating news that it had been occupied just three days before. For John Christie and his mate Arthur the first few days of their journey were spent in a state of confusion. Wearing overalls they had found during the march, they travelled by night, attempting to use the stars to guide them. In the darkness they almost stumbled into an enemy flak battery, but were fortunate to spot it as it opened fire on a British plane. Each day, they called at houses to find food, sizing up the occupants and only telling them their true identity if they appeared trustworthy. They soon realized they would need plenty of luck if they were ever to reach safety. Reaching the coast near Hardelot they, like so many others, discovered there was little chance of finding a boat and decided to head inland to find an alternative route home. The decision was taken to head to St Pol, where Christie had made friends earlier in the year when his unit was based in the area. There they waited until it appeared safe to move on.

Another officer with the same idea at least got near a boat. Captain Guy Lowden was a veteran of the Great War who, prior to the collapse of the BEF, had been based at the vast British depot in Rouen. Whilst at Rouen he had witnessed many lost and lonely soldiers arriving at his base, all hoping to rejoin their units. Captain Lowden was captured on 8 June, only to escape from one of the marching columns five days later. He had then attempted to find a boat to cross the Channel and fallen in with a group of British soldiers who promised Lowden they knew where to find boats and had an escape plan. What followed was farcical:

> The boat house, lavishly described by the troops as full of the most magnificent craft and stocked with every conceivable marine requirement, proved to be rather a tumbledown affair, well above high tide, and containing only some flashy racing cockleshells, all badly holed. Of a number of boats drawn well above high water and all too heavy for us to shift, the motor craft had no motors, the sailing craft no sails, and in short the grand stories of these ridiculous chaps were so much baloney! . . . Served us right for taking the troops' word for everything – bless their stupid hearts.[4]

Now he was among the lost and lonely, hiding in the woods with a fellow British officer. Whilst in hiding he wrote a succession of letters to his wife that he hid in the hope that they might one day reach her. In his second letter the captain wrote of his experiences in his early days as an evader:

> I think we've done all the traditional things – hidden in barns (all escapers do this, right through history); lain and trembled while the enemy rummaged about the sheds where we lay, miraculously missing the one place where we were; stumbled suddenly on enemy sentries in villages or air fields on the downs, and beaten a panic stricken retreat. At one place there was even a pretty girl who brought us food – rich and delicious food, in plenty, with great hunks of fresh white bread in a basket. Yes, I think all conventions have been honoured.[5]

Still hoping to find a way back to England, Lowden and his comrade travelled by night, keeping to the woods to avoid the farms whose dogs were prone to howling when disturbed. By day they hid in barns, sometimes with the acquiescence of the owners, or simply concealed themselves anywhere they could stay warm and dry. One day saw them hidden in a vegetable pile whilst farm labourers worked around them. Lowden and his fellow escapee soon recognized they were not the only soldiers in hiding in the Pas de Calais. As he noted, every wandering labourer clad in blue overalls seemed to recoil when addressed in French, thus revealing himself as a British evader. The soldiers spent their spare time either sleeping, scavenging for food, or searching for fellow Britons who had resided in the area since the Great War. Some were even hidden by British men who had deserted during the Great War and had been living under an assumed identity ever since.

For the men in hiding, certain factors played havoc with their morale. All picked up bits of news about the course of the war but seldom was this anything more than rumour. With no access to regular information channels they had no way of verifying what they heard. When news was seemingly good they felt a brief lifting of spirits only to be depressed once the news proved to be untrue. Derrick Peterson, in hiding with a group of over twenty fellow soldiers, recorded the news he received on 30 May: 'The simply terrific news that Italy, Turkey and America were in the war against Germany!' The following day he wrote: 'Further news was that Dunkirk had been completely destroyed and Calais taken – that London had been completely evacuated and that the Germans were within five kilometres of Paris.' The bad news kept coming and on 9 June he recorded the rumour that King George had been taken prisoner and Chamberlain was dead. More rumours fed their see-sawing spirits: 'News of Russia having attacked Germany and taken over all of Poland! Turkey smashing up Italy! British apparently retook Calais, Dunkirk and Boulogne!'[6] A week later Peterson even heard that the Americans had supposedly landed at Brest with two motorized divisions.

Those who received their news direct from civilians with access to radio sets soon realized that Britain was in a perilous situation. Should they risk everything to attempt to reach home, or simply sit out the war in hiding? For some the question of trying to find a route home was irrelevant – what difference did it make where they were, if the Germans would soon be occupying Britain anyway?

Others remained certain that it was their duty – or indeed their destiny – to report home to rejoin the war as soon as possible. One of those who never gave up hope of returning home was Captain Guy Lowden. After spending the early summer of 1940 sneaking around northern France attempting to steal a boat, Lowden was captured by the Gestapo in August whilst hiding in the northern city of Lille. At first they threatened to execute him as a spy since he was wearing civilian clothing. Instead of carrying out their threats, the Gestapo threw him into a cell where he was detained in solitary confinement until February 1941.

In the darkness, Lowden could hear the cries of a madman in the adjoining cell. He could hear the sounds of other men receiving beatings from their captors. It was an ominous sign. Was his neighbour a lunatic or a sane man driven mad by captivity and torture? Day upon day, Lowden faced interrogation from the Gestapo, always careful not to reveal the names of the kindly French people who had given him shelter. His cell was five paces long and four paces wide. It had one small window and no artificial light. He had a single blanket and a straw palliasse to sleep on. Through the dark, damp days of winter the captain survived on a diet of soup, coffee and bread.

After six months of enduring the misery of solitary confinement, Lowden was fortunate to be transferred to Oflag 9. Maybe it was his advanced age that prevented the Gestapo from inflicting more severe punishment on him, since others were not so fortunate. At the prison in Loos a number of British escapers and evaders were held in detention. Among them was Corporal Norman Hogan, a reservist who had been called up in September 1939. He had been wounded during the last week of May 1940 and sent to hospital in Boulogne, then to a convalescence depot in the seaside resort of Paris-Plage. After escaping from the hospital he went on the run until he was captured by the Gestapo and imprisoned at the civilian prison in Loos. For five months Hogan was held in solitary confinement. In all that time he was never given an opportunity to exercise. Instead, like Captain Lowden, he spent his hours awaiting the next interrogation.

The methods employed by the Gestapo were less than subtle. They tried planting documents on Hogan, hoping he would feel pressured to reveal the names of those who had assisted him. When he refused to talk he was kicked and beaten by military guards. When he tried to complain about their behaviour he was beaten again, losing a tooth in the process. After five months of mistreatment, Hogan was released and sent to a POW camp. In 1943 Hogan was repatriated to the UK as a result of his wounds and the mistreatment inflicted on him by the Gestapo. Another of the evaders held at Loos prison, Private Hoyle, faired better. He was also severely beaten by the Gestapo, but when he was transferred to a POW camp he was able to escape and reached home via Gibraltar.

Between September 1940 and March 1941 thirty-five evaders were captured in northern France and held in the prison at Loos. One of the thirty-five was Lance-Corporal Robert Dunbar of the London Scottish. He had been captured at St Valery but had escaped on the ninth day of the march into captivity. After being at large for three months, posing as a Belgian refugee and working in a French cafe, he was eventually captured. Initially held at Loos, he was then transferred to Lille where he was interrogated by the Gestapo who knocked one of his teeth out with a pistol-butt. At his trial his French helpers were sentenced to a year's imprisonment and he received five months in solitary confinement. The sentence was carried out at Frontstalag 190 near Stuttgart. He survived on black bread, one cup of coffee and one bowl of soup a day, which left him so weak he could hardly move around his cell.

Despite this treatment Corporal Dunbar was not disheartened. Two days after his release from solitary confinement he escaped from the stalag and made his way to the south of France. From there he crossed into Spain where he was interned before being released upon the intervention of the British military attaché in Madrid.

In February 1941 a report reached London suggesting that as many as 1,000 British soldiers remained in hiding in villages around Brussels, with one valiant Belgian industrialist collecting money to ensure the men could be fed. In April that year thirteen Belgians were tried for harbouring British troops. One man and one woman were sentenced to death whilst others received sentences of up to eight years' imprisonment. In September 1941 another report arrived from Spain giving the figure of 5,000 men believed to be in hiding or working on farms under assumed identities in the towns and villages of the Pas de Calais.

Derrick Peterson, who remained in hiding throughout the summer, continued to record the rumours that wove their way around the men's emotions. Through June and July he had heard stories of a German invasion force of 60,000 men heading for Britain that was foiled by a secret British 'death ray'. On 1 August he heard that the Germans had used poison gas over British cities. Fortunately the stories were nothing more than that.

The question of what course of action the evaders should take continued to vex every man among them. Those who had settled comfortably into life on French farms knew that, if they were caught, their hosts faced savage reprisals. That summer, signs were posted across France threatening execution for anyone caught harbouring Allied soldiers. A few men chose to put their travel plans on hold in order to assist their hosts with gathering the harvest. They felt it was all they could do to help repay them for their kindness.

Once such considerations had passed, there was the question of what the best route home would be. It seemed ridiculous to some to even consider walking south – to Spain or Switzerland – when home was little more than twenty miles away across the Channel. Surely, they reasoned, a boat would have to become available one day. Other groups discussed whether the safety of neutral Switzerland would be worth having to spend the rest of the war in internment. Some argued that would mean swapping the freedom of occupied France for the captivity of a neutral country. For many southern France – the unoccupied zone of Vichy – was their best bet. At least there they would be able to attempt escape to North Africa or Spain and Gibraltar.

As the year progressed the soldiers also realized they would not be able to spend the entire winter hiding in woods and barns. They would need permanent shelter to survive the cold. One evader estimated there were at least a dozen men hiding within a mile of his location. Each man needed to be fed and each mouth was a drain on their hosts. So, with such thoughts in mind, most of the evaders gave up on the notion of sailing home and prepared themselves for the long trek south. Derrick Peterson, who had faithfully recorded all the rumours about the course of the war, was one of the men who joined the march south. With just two companions, out of an original group of twenty-three evaders from his regiment, he took a haversack of food and began the long trek to the south of France. He and his comrades travelled by day, always attempting to look like farm workers, an image that was helped by carrying farm implements.

How to look like French civilians rather than British soldiers was something that perplexed many of the evaders. In the early days following the German victory some continue to brazenly wear their uniforms and walk around French villages as they had done back in the days of the phoney war. If they hoped to remain free they had to change these habits – if not for their own sakes, then for the sake of their French hosts. Even in civilian clothing they had to make sure they did not march like soldiers and had to remember that French farm labourers would never be seen with highly polished boots. Similarly they had to forget the daily shaving habits of the British Army and develop facial hair. More importantly, the evaders had to learn to walk, sit and gesticulate like Frenchmen. However, above all else, the soldiers needed to at least learn to grasp the basics of the French language. The most successful evaders tended to be those who could read road signs and railway timetables, who could order food and drinks in cafes and ask for assistance from French civilians. Some chose to adopt the identity of foreign labourers as cover for their poor command of French, claiming to be Flemish-speaking Belgians in search of employment. Some of the most proficient French-speaking evaders even dared to engage German soldiers in conversation. One evader started a conversation with a German only to discover the German spoke no French. The British soldier asked if the man spoke English, which he admitted he did. The two men then conversed in English until the British soldier departed, leaving the German blissfully unaware he had just been speaking to an English evader.

Fortunate to escape the attentions of the Germans, John Christie and his mate Arthur spent the entire summer of 1940 in hiding in the northern French town of St Pol, where they soon became aware of large numbers of troops amassing ready for the intended invasion of southern England. Despite these ominous troop build-ups, the local people disregarded their own safety to take the two Britons into their homes. Christie later wrote of this spirit of co-operation which seemed so far from the bickering between the politicians of the two Allied nations that had marred the military campaign: 'One thing my travels taught me at this period of my life was that there is a tremendous amount of goodness going around. It's only when you are really down that you get a chance to find out.'[7]

As the summer months passed, they began to make preparations for the journey south. Like all evaders, their intention was to reach Vichy France in the south. But first they would need passes and identity cards to allow them to travel. Their friends stole passes from the Germans to make counterfeits, concentrating on finding a copy of the necessary pass to leave the so-called Forbidden Zone around the French coast. The stamps for their passes were made by cutting up the rubber heel of a shoe with a razor blade. The ink was obtained by extracting blue dye from a sheet of carbon paper.

By August 1940 they were finally ready to begin their journey: 'We set out that first day with high-hopes and it was goodbye to cross country travel, because armed with our false papers we decided that we could travel on the open roads once more.'[8] The irony of their first few days travelling was that some locals were reluctant to help them since they had accepted the truce, and were not enamoured with British soldiers attempting to continue the war, whilst they were able to hitch lifts in German convoys who allowed the two make-believe Frenchmen to travel in the backs of their trucks.

Although months had passed since the two men had been at the heart of the defeated army, it was not long before they were once again reminded of the scale of the defeat. Passing through Amiens they witnessed a compound filled with the detritus of war: 'It was a huge concentration of artillery of all shapes and sizes, mainly British. Some of the guns had been "spiked", that is done by exploding a shell inside the barrel to burst the metal. The majority of them appeared to be undamaged . . . It brought home the measure of the massive amount of equipment that the British Army had lost to the Germans.'[9]

Many of the evaders preferred to avoid the big cities, but Christie decided Paris was the perfect place from which to head south. Quite simply, a city was easy to hide in – people were too concerned with their own problems to worry about two itinerant labourers who claimed to be heading south to find work in the grain harvest. Their main problem was how to avoid the crowds of German soldiers out on the streets. But they soon noticed the Germans were too busy visiting tourist sites and taking photographs to worry about them. One French-speaking evader later wrote of how he deliberately misdirected Germans who asked him for street directions.

Paris was also a city ravaged by war. The Germans may not have needed to fight their way into it but they had still made a vast impact. The requisitioning of French industrial goods caused ripples throughout France. Vast numbers of locomotives and railway wagons had been commandeered, leaving transport in short supply. Even French horses had been pressed into service for the enemy. Bread rations had fallen, shops were bereft of consumer goods and the sale of alcohol was restricted. There was also a curfew in force, limiting the movement of any would-be evaders during the hours of darkness. Such were the deprivations caused by the defeat and division of France that the death rate in Paris rose by 24 per cent.

These conditions encouraged the growth of a hostile population, some of whom welcomed the British evaders and were eager to offer assistance. There were also Irish citizens with links to the UK, Americans and Polish émigrés who were more than willing to do anything to assist the army of a country still fighting the enemy. William Broad, a British officer in hiding in Paris whilst looking for a way to get his party of soldiers away from France, was one such man taken into the care of French civilians. He began to circulate openly in their company, dining in some of the best restaurants in Paris. One night in Maxim's he found himself enjoying his evening meal when Reichsmarschall Hermann Goering entered the room and sat down to dine.

Christie and Arthur were given food and shelter in Paris by a disabled French Great War veteran, who provided them with the ever-popular British dish of egg and chips. Welcome as it was, food and shelter was not all they needed. If they were to reach the south of France in safety they would need enough money to feed themselves and pay for train tickets. It was decided that the best source of funds would be the American embassy, which was still operating in the city. Using their forged French identity papers, the two soldiers gained entry to the embassy, where they met a Mrs

Deacon. She listened to their story and proved willing to assist. Handing them 600 francs each, she advised them to leave the city as soon as possible. They took her advice and that night they boarded a train at the Gare de Austerlitz heading for the town of Angoulême.

On leaving Angoulême, the biggest problem was how to cross the demarcation line into the unoccupied zone without being apprehended. Forged identification papers were not enough, a special pass was needed to make the crossing legally. As a result most evaders attempted to cross in secret. It was not an easy process, nor was it helped by the fact there were no detailed maps available that showed the precise location of the border. After an attempted night crossing, during which they got lost, John Christie and his mate decided it would be safer to cross in daylight, when there was less chance of accidentally bumping into a patrol. Daylight, meant they could see the border and, keeping a German camp within their view, at a safe distance, the two men passed safely into Vichy France. They were not yet home, they were not yet free, but at least they were safe, for the time being, from the Germans.

Not all the evaders were able to make a safe crossing. After weeks of walking, Derrick Peterson and his comrades passed safely into the unoccupied zone of France. It seemed they were free, but five miles into Vichy they were picked up by French police, marched back to the demarcation line and handed over to a German patrol. After thirty-two days in a POW camp Peterson made good his escape in the company of a French artilleryman. From October 1940 until March 1941 he managed to evade detention within France. After arriving in the unoccupied zone for the second time, his French companion was forced to rejoin his unit and sent to North Africa, whilst Peterson teamed up with a fellow Briton who had escaped from a POW camp via the sewers. During this period he was assisted by the Americans. A letter from the American consul in Lyon detailing his escape from the stalag had actually reached the Peterson home before his parents had received official notification that he was a prisoner. In October they wrote to the

Home Office, asking if it would be possible to forward money to their son. They received the reply that the Americans were funding him to the tune of £10 per month. Peterson's relieved parents immediately offered to repay all the American money. In April 1941 the two men crossed the Pyrenees into Spain and walked to Gibraltar. That month another two soldiers reached Gibraltar. It was Seconnd-Lieutenant Parkinson of the Sussex Regiment, accompanied by Private Bertie Bell, the only survivor of the massacre of British prisoners in the Forêt de Nieppe.

The Americans were not the only nationality able to help the evaders from the BEF. As a neutral state, the Irish retained diplomatic facilities within France. This opened up an obvious course of action for some evaders. Those with Irish heritage were able to request Irish passports. By claiming to be civilians trapped in the south of France they were able to acquire the necessary documentation to make the journey out of France, through Spain and into Gibraltar.

Arriving in Marseilles, the evaders had a number of options. Some men went straight to the Red Cross for assistance, visiting their canteen to get a hot meal. After days and weeks of walking, a hot meal was the one thing they needed more than anything else. Once that was finished they gravitated to the American Seaman's Mission at 35, Rue de Forbin, where they were able to collect money from the amiable Church of Scotland minister who ran the institution. Reverend Donald Caskie had been the minister at a church in Gretna, Scotland, prior to moving to France in the late 1930s. Following the fall of France he had moved south to Marseilles to assist the stranded British merchant seamen, airmen and soldiers who had congregated at the Seaman's Mission in hope of shelter before finding a way home. Though a sign outside the mission read 'Civilians and Seamen Only' it had become a beacon for soldiers arriving in Marseilles. Indeed, 100,000 French francs had been made available to Donald Caskie by the British government for the relief of the British soldiers. Once settled at the mission, the evaders gravitated towards the port to seek a way out of France by boat. But although the quaysides were full of ships, each one was guarded by French police and troops. There seemed to be little chance of either stowing away or finding a berth on a ship.

From the mission the kindly minister used his own money to forward mail to the UK via American diplomatic channels. It was a vital channel to ensure that the families of the evaders received the welcome news that their husbands and sons were alive and safe. The wife of Lance-Corporal Fred Verity, of the East Lancashire Regiment, received a telegram sent from Marseilles on 10 August 1940. It informed her: 'Fred safe in Marseilles'[10] and had been sent by someone named Osborn. The message amazed Mrs Verity since she had already been officially informed of her husband's death. One officer used the minister's mail service to request the Foreign Office repay £17 he had borrowed from the American consulate to aid his journey to Marseilles. He need not have worried since they had already requested financial assistance from the Americans. In addition, the Foreign Office asked the American embassy in France to hand over $100,000 to the representative of the Quakers in Marseilles in order that he too could assist the evaders.

In the early days following the defeat of the BEF, some evaders who reached Marseilles made contact with Polish soldiers in the city. In August 1940 the Polish legation reported that there existed a group of fifty destitute British soldiers in the city who were entirely reliant upon the generosity of their Polish allies. The Polish camp, in the Queen Victoria Memorial Hospital, became a haven for men who intended to escape since the Poles had no intention of handing anyone over to the French authorities and – unlike the French – had little interest in whether their behaviour upset the Germans. They even attempted to establish an escape network involving sending Britons to Spain on passports provided by the Polish consul.

Also assisting evaders to leave Marseilles was Captain Charles Murchie of the Royal Army Service Corps. He ran a team of twenty-five guides who operated from the area around Lille. Their task was to send evaders on to a 'reception centre' in Paris. From there, the men made their way into the unoccupied zone. Initially, Murchie sent men from Marseilles to North Africa by boat, until London requested he begin to send them via Spain. By early 1941, the system he had established operated smoothly. Captain Murchie's northern guides brought men across the Vichy border and submitted to him expenses claims for costs incurred during the journey. He also gave the guides money for their fares home. So successful was the system that Murchie was forced to give up his endeavours. He had simply become too well known to be able to continue to operate. He found men arriving from as far away as Brussels and asking for him openly by name. When French attention became too great, Captain Murchie was himself forced to flee to Spain, taking with him a British sergeant who had been his assistant and André Minne, a Lille cafe-owner who had made five journeys to Marseilles as a guide to evaders.

When John Christie arrived in the unoccupied zone he took a train to Marseilles and then telephoned the American consulate. By February 1941 the US consul had provided assistance to 400 British soldiers who had escaped from the occupied zone. However, not all the men seeking assistance received the advice they desired. When John Christie and his companion finally reached the port, the consul advised they hand themselves over to the French authorities at the local barracks of the French Foreign Legion.

The barracks to which they were sent became a vital waypoint in the evaders' journeys to freedom. Located in the old port, the Fort St Jean was famed as the Foreign Legion headquarters and its main recruiting base. Entered via an iron bridge across the harbour waters, the seventeenth-century fort was on a rocky island, totally surrounded by water. By January 1941 Fort St Jean was home to eleven British officers, forty-nine NCOs and 175 other ranks.

Some evaders initially found themselves interned in the Ste Marthe barracks, a detention barracks for the Foreign Legion. Conditions within the camp were appalling and there were no toilet facilities. Instead they had to use the prison yard that was swilled down each morning. Other evaders were interned in the Fort de la Revère in Nice where the senior British officer, Captain Whitney, reported to the Foreign Office on the 'absolutely unbearable'[11] conditions, the cases of tuberculosis and the suspicion of German infiltration. A similar situation was found in the internment camp at St Hippolyte du Fort, near Perpignan, where a soldier turned up calling himself MacBrendan. Back in the UK checks were made on his identity. No records could be found of his birth, or his claimed service in the British Army during the Great War, or of his having been served military intelligence with the BEF.

Once inside Fort St Jean, John Christie found himself directed to the room that was to be his home as an internee. He would be sharing it with about twenty other ranks, including a fifty-five-year-old veteran of the Great War, whilst three officers were housed in a separate room. Others within the fort slept in cells, to which the doors were fortunately left open all day. Each morning the men rose at 7 a.m., ate breakfast at 8 a.m., then paraded at 9 a.m. For the rest of the day there was little for them to do. The internees were allowed to give their parole and go into town, with officers allowed out at any time and other ranks allowed out between 6 a.m. and 9 p.m. Once in the town, they were free to visit the Seaman's Mission and were able to collect the money that was available via the Reverend Donald Caskie.

Although it was a vast improvement on sleeping in woods and barns, life in the fort was far from comfortable. The internees reported they were in desperate need of extra blankets and winter clothing. The treatment experienced by some of the sick internees was also not up to accepted standards. One soldier, a Private Street, was interned in the hospital at St Hippolyte du Fort. He had lost an arm during the battles in northern France and had also suffered serious chest wounds. Fellow internees noted his health was failing fast since French doctors were unwilling to operate on him.

In general, however, conditions of internment, whilst not comfortable, were at least not onerous. As the French described it, this was a case of *liberté surveilée*. In the words of escaping Britons, it was 'rough and ready'.[12] After weeks or months of scrounging food they could at least expect French military rations that included a litre of red wine per man per day. At St Hippolyte, two British soldiers even requested permission to marry local women they had befriended whilst on visits to the town. In particular, the other ranks were pleased that the officers made little effort to enforce order upon them. Instead of taking control, they appeared to live their own lives until the time came for them to disappear and head towards freedom. It was just as well, as John Christie noted: 'We remained very much a collection of individuals. We had reached Marseilles very much under our own steam, either singly or in pairs and none of us was very inclined to give up any part of control over our own destiny.'[13]

The independent nature of the men who had made their way safely through occupied France to the unoccupied zone meant that few among them were prepared to sit out the war in the stupefying boredom of an internment camp – especially when the camp was filled with lice and some French guards were stealing their food parcels. When they went into the town many faced a hostile reception from locals, especially French sailors who were angered by the British sinking of French ships at Oran. One or two, in particular the sick and wounded who had been promised repatriation, made no attempt to escape the fort. However, for the majority leaving France remained their aim. Using the same independent means that had brought them south, the internees gradually slipped away to make their way home. One officer approached the commandant at Fort St Jean and informed him he wished to withdraw his parole. The commandant understood exactly what he meant and replied: 'So you're off again – good luck.'[14] On another occasion, when the commandant met up with a British medical officer who had been returned to the fort following an unsuccessful attempt to stowaway on a ship, he told him: 'Better luck next time!'[15]

The nearest British territory was Gibraltar. From there, escapees knew they would be able to report to the authorities and eventually rejoin their units. The preferred route of escape from France to Gibraltar was via Spain, paying up to 1,000 French francs per man to be smuggled over the Pyrenees to Barcelona. Some evaders even found themselves accompanied by French guides who did not ask for money, instead they requested the soldier assist them to reach England in order that they might join the Free French forces of General de Gaulle.

The aim of the evaders was to be able to reach a British consulate or the embassy in Madrid before they were detected and interned by the Spanish authorities, but they were to discover that it was not simple either to cross the border or to remain anonymous once within Spain. First they had to reach the border in safety. It was not just a case of joining a train in Marseilles and alighting once it had crossed the Spanish frontier. During the summer of 1940 the American authorities had been able to assist by passing word to an American representative in Port Bou, just over the frontier in Spain, giving the likely time of arrival for escaping British soldiers. However, the French authorities soon became aware of the numbers of men attempting to escape into Spain and made sure that thorough checks were made on train passengers. As a result it became necessary for men to leave trains a few stops before the border and continue the journey on foot. One group even took a train to Perpignan, then hired a taxi to take them to the Spanish border.

Although routes could be found that avoided French police patrols, the problem was that the border ran along the Pyrenees, forcing men thousands of feet up into the mountains to avoid checkpoints at road crossings. Following cart tracks and rough mountain paths, they trudged for days to cross the mountains. Even in the summer the temperatures dropped as they climbed up the rocky mountainsides. From the dizzy heights of the mountains they could look down to the blue of the Mediterranean – to a world of fishing boats and seaside cottages – and wonder how it could be so cold where they were. When the skies were clear, the piercing sun seared their skin, leaving it dry and burnt. Then when the clouds closed in on them they were chilled to the bone in their inadequate clothing. In the upper reaches of the mountain range they could at least find plenty of water – as long as they first broke the ice on the rocky pools. Those who engaged the services of local shepherds were guaranteed a journey that took in familiar paths and winter shelters. For the men who travelled alone it was simply a case of going up one side of the mountains and hoping they could find a safe path to descend into Spain.

Yet there were greater dangers than getting lost amidst the peaks. Spain was under the government of General Franco, whose victory in the Spanish Civil War had been facilitated with the assistance of the Nazis, who had used Spain as a testing ground for the same military tactics that had brought Poland and France to their knees. Though neutral, Spain was not guaranteed to give a safe passage to soldiers attempting to reach Gibraltar.

Some evaders headed directly to the nearest big city, Barcelona, where they hoped to retain their anonymity in the cosmopolitan crowds of the port. Like Marseilles, Barcelona was another port city famed for having a vast underworld in which fugitives could take refuge. As a city in a neutral country, Barcelona offered another incentive. Upon reaching the British consul, the escaping soldiers were able to acquire civilian documentation and continue towards Gibraltar. By December 1941 the consul in Barcelona had assisted forty-six soldiers from the BEF who had reached his office without being apprehended. Initially these evaders were sent to Madrid by train; however, this practice was stopped after the Spanish authorities began searching trains between the towns. As a result the consul thought it simpler to deliver the men using his own car, which had diplomatic immunity.

Many of those who escaped over the mountains soon encountered patrols of the Civil Guard. Showing a distinct lack of understanding of the situation in Spain, when apprehended, some of the soldiers even asked Spanish policemen to direct them to the

nearest British consulate. It did not take long for them to realize
such assistance would not be forthcoming. Taken into custody, the
soldiers soon found themselves crammed into the filthy cells of
local police stations. Under Spanish law they should have been
arrested and committed to court under a warrant of arrest for
'crossing the frontier clandestinely'.[16] Those carrying foreign currency could also be charged under regulations prohibiting the
importation of currency to Spain. In reality, few were ever actually
charged. Between August and November 1940, the British consulate in Barcelona recorded that a total of seventy-three British
soldiers had been detained upon entry to Spain. It was reported that
a large proportion of them were men who had slipped through the
enemy lines at St Valery.

Some arrived in prison to find fellow Britons they knew from
Marseilles who had been captured earlier. The threadbare clothing,
matted hair and filthy skin of these men soon warned them there
was little hope of a swift return home. The cells were seldom big
enough to accommodate the ragged gangs of soldiers. The diet was
inadequate. One cabbage provided soup for fifty. The cells were
unlit and the latrine buckets overflowed. Some were housed in
prisons that were already crowded with political prisoners from the
Spanish Civil War. One such prison had been constructed to house
two hundred men but actually held over a thousand. At the Prison
Habilitada Palacio Misiones in Barcelona British prisoners shared
the facilities with thousands of Spanish citizens who were oppo-
nents of Franco. Whilst held there the British soldiers heard the
executions of Spanish prisoners who seemed to have been picked
out at random. In another prison it was noted that some Republican prisoners were men who had been wounded during the Civil
War, including amputees whose wounds had not yet fully healed.

One good point about Spain was that, despite Franco's victory in
the Civil War, the nation's political loyalties were still divided and
the country was gripped by an economic malaise that had caused
widespread poverty. Thus not only were escaping British soldiers
able to count on a measure of assistance from sympathetic civilians

but they could also bribe their way out of trouble. One officer, who found himself and his men held in a gaol where the guards even allowed a whore to ply her trade among the prisoners, was able to bribe a guard to make contact with the British consul.

Eventually many of the interned soldiers were transferred to the concentration camps at Miranda del Ebro and Cervera. Covering eight acres and situated to the south of Bilbao, the camp at Miranda had become notorious following the defeat of the Republican forces in the Civil War. Often arriving with their hands chained together, the incoming prisoners had their heads shaved and were given filthy prison uniforms of rough cotton tunic and trousers. Within the concentration camp the British soldiers discovered men of all nationalities, some left over from the Civil War but most were soldiers of Europe's defeated nations who were planning to reach safety to continue their fight against the Germans. There were even a number of German deserters housed within the camp.

The regime was harsh, bordering on vicious. British officers complained of being lashed with thorns, whilst others recalled beatings with leather thongs and sticks. Inmates were flogged for minor offences and one favoured punishment was to force offenders to march around the camp carrying a stone-filled sack. The British embassy reported that many inmates, who did not appear to be slacking in their work, required treatment for weals after being attacked by whip-wielding guards. Some inmates were also employed to break stones used for road building, although the British were usually put to work peeling the endless piles of potatoes that were served to them at mealtimes.

At night the men slept in two layers, the first in two lines on the floor and the second on a wooden shelf running along the walls. Blankets were shared one between two and the many of the men slept naked to avoid the lice that inhabited their prison uniforms. If a man wished to use the latrines at night he had to remove any clothes and wrap a blanket around himself when he left the hut. When one Scottish sergeant attempted to leave the hut without removing his trousers he was beaten with a rifle-butt and kicked repeatedly as he lay on the floor. Each morning the guards arrived with whips to raise the inmates from their beds, striking any man who did not move swiftly enough. Life within the camp soon took its toll on the mental and physical well being of the inmates. Their bodies became marked with open sores where they had scratched incessantly at insect bites. Some suffered nervous breakdowns, whilst dysentery and scabies became widespread.

Whilst conditions at Miranda were awful, at least the inmates were able to exercise in the open air. After incarceration in cramped, stuffy cells, simply to be out in the clear mountain air was thought glorious. They might have been surviving on pitifully meagre rations but just to be able to see the sky and taste the crisp air seemed a bonus. Meanwhile the British embassy was reporting back to London that the men at Miranda were living in conditions a great deal better than in the provincial prisons. They would have found little comfort in the ambassador's words: 'I have no reason to believe British prisoners have been treated any worse than Spaniards. The treatment of any prisoners in Spain is harsh; the Spaniard is naturally insensitive and cruel.'[17]

At the concentration camp in Cervera conditions were not so oppressive. The food was adequate and each man received a bottle of wine per day. Another bonus was that none of the British prisoners were required to work. The camp commandant stressed to the British consul that the soldiers were only delaying their eventual release by their constant escape attempts, tearing up bedding to make rope-ladders. This information was passed on to the senior British NCO and he gave his word no further escape attempts would be made.

On 12 September 1940 Lieutenant Hogg, Royal Engineers, sent a telegram from Spain to London: 'Stuck here with five others – Embassy very slow – can you help – Hotel Peninsula Gerona.'[18] Claims that embassy staff and consuls were slow to assist the men interned in Spain was refuted by the Foreign Office. Indeed, as it was pointed out, the British officers in the Hotel Peninsula were having all their bills paid directly by the consulate. The ambassador's official line was that there was little they could do to force the Spanish to release the men. Instead they preferred to press for ensuring all interned British soldiers were transferred to Miranda as soon as possible in order to be able to focus relief efforts. The diplomats were well aware of the pressure faced by the Spanish authorities to enter the war on the German side. They also understood that the Germans were putting pressure on Spain not to allow the release of the British internees. This made the situation tricky for the British ambassador

Rather than putting direct pressure on the Spanish, some thought it better to influence them indirectly. A letter from the vice-consul in Gerona requested that effort be made to publicize the sufferings of the prisoners in Spain. He requested that the embassy use British and American journalists based in Madrid to raise the subject. He wrote: 'If the public in England got wind of the manner in which British officers and men are being treated . . . there would be a fine shindy. Their only crime is that, after a 900 kilometre journey, facing every kind of hardship in an effort to get back and continue to fight for their country, they crossed into a neutral land without papers. There they find hardships equal to those of their long trek, without the stimulation of risk and danger.'[19]

Eventually, British inmates were released from the squalid hell of Miranda. The British military attaché in Madrid was able to visit the prisoners and negotiate their release in groups, according to how long they had been interned. However, some soldiers noted how the system for allowing the British to leave Miranda seemed to follow no discernible pattern. Some men left after just a few days whilst others remained in the concentration camp for weeks. In April 1941 the father of one man held at Miranda wrote to the Foreign Office asking for assistance. His son had arrived at the camp together with other soldiers with whom he had escaped from France. However, some of those men had already been released and had reached England. Another was in Gibraltar awaiting transport home. Despite their releases, the man's son was still languishing in the concentration camp.

Those fortunate enough to be released from Spanish camps were taken to Madrid and passed into the care of the British embassy. There they were bathed and fed with light meals, their weakened bodies being unable to cope with anything other than plain food. They were then given new clothes and most were housed in a hotel close by the embassy. In November 1941 the embassy reported they had twenty-two evaders actually living within the embassy. Such was the overcrowding within the building that plans were drawn up for the erection of an extension to be used to house soldiers passing through on their way to Gibraltar. From Madrid they were sent by lorry to Gibraltar, sometimes accompanied by other men who had manage to reach the embassy without being detected by the Spanish and therefore had to be hidden in the lorries for the journey. Once safely in Gibraltar, the soldiers were fully assessed by military doctors, allowing those in need of further treatment to enter hospital. All were given sulphur baths to kill lice and prevent the spread of scabies. Once fully recovered, the men were able to board ships and return to the UK to continue the war.

Whilst most of the internees preferred to attempt to reach Gibraltar via Spain, others attempted a more ambitious route, taking advantage of Marseilles' vigorous underworld networks. Through contact with a Hungarian civilian living in Marseilles, two British officers were able to purchase documents stating they were Romanians who had been serving as pioneers in the French Army and been demobilized. Using these papers, they were able to travel to North Africa. Upon reaching Casablanca the two men went to the American consulate and were issued with emergency British documentation. At the British Club in the city they made contact with civilians who were able to arrange visas for them to travel to Portugal, still using the Romanian ID papers. They later arrived safely in Portugal and were able to return home. One British soldier, Sergeant Wilson of the 13th CCS, had an even longer trip home. Having arrived in North Africa he travelled down the coast, finally arriving in Sierra Leone, where he reported to the first British base he could find.

John Christie also decided to make the trip across the Mediterranean. Having befriended a corporal in the French Foreign Legion, Christie decided he and Arthur would attach themselves to the Legion which was due to be transferred by ship to North Africa. Wearing borrowed uniforms, the two internees slipped out of the fort and boarded the ship waiting in the harbour. Following a three-day journey, the ship docked in Oran. Christie and his mate joined the legionnaires as they marched from the port, then left the column. Quickly changing into civilian clothes, they made their way to the Polish consul who helped them to take a train to Casablanca, where they sought the assistance of the Americans and received a temporary passport from the local consulate.

Having taken possession of their passports the two men arranged a passage on a ship heading to Portugal. Safely at sea, John Christie looked to the horizon and noticed something that soon took his attention: 'We spotted a wisp of smoke . . . Looking back, there wasn't a question in our minds about friend or foe . . . we knew that in this sector Britannia really did rule the waves! . . . The wisp of smoke soon materialised into the shape of a destroyer . . . as it moved round I could see the gun turrets rotate to "keep us in their sights". Next came the launch of their long-boat, crewed by four seamen with an officer in charge.'[20]

They were swiftly transferred to the destroyer, HMS *Kelvin*, which then steamed for Gibraltar. The crew of the *Kelvin* believed the Britons they had picked up were survivors from a merchant ship sunk by a U-boat and were astounded to discover they were actually the last remnants of the BEF. Once on board, Christie received the one thing he had craved for months: 'a cup of piping hot good old British tea!'[21]

These evaders were not the only soldiers left behind in 1940 who were able to complete the journey home before war's end. As the war progressed, increasing numbers of sick and wounded prisoners of war were finally repatriated to the UK. Under the Geneva Convention both the seriously wounded soldiers and the medical staff who cared for them should have been returned promptly. Article 68 of the convention stated: 'Belligerents shall be required to send back to their own country without regard to rank or numbers, after rendering them in a fit condition for transport, prisoners of war who are seriously ill or wounded.'

Unfortunately, the nature of modern warfare meant that there were lengthy delays and initially the British government found it was difficult enough to negotiate for repatriation with the French authorities, let alone the Germans. In March 1942 the French recorded turning back forty-three British internees due to be repatriated via the border with Spain as retaliation against the British for the bombing of French factories contributing to the German war effort. The War Office responded: 'it is intolerable that the Vichy government should give expression to their annoyance at what they well know to be a legitimate act of war on our part, by inflicting further suffering on those unfortunate men.'[22]

Later the French changed their reasons, stressing the refusal to repatriate the wounded Britons was related to the British government's failure to allow some French officers to return home. The Frenchmen, members of Air Mission B, were liaison officers based in London who had earlier been given access to military secrets and, as such, could not be safely returned to France.

Those men badly wounded during the battles in France were possibly the most piteous of all the prisoners of war. Among them were the men who had lost limbs or been blinded, or suffered debilitating stomach wounds. They did not face the prospect of recovering in the comfort of a hospital where they might be visited by their loved ones. Coming to terms with the knowledge that they would never fully recover was burden enough in any circumstances, but to face treatment by doctors who were pitifully short of supplies only served to deepen their discomfort, both physically and mentally.

The British medical staff desperately needed drugs and bandages, let alone false limbs and crutches. Furthermore, the conditions of imprisonment meant that wounds took longer than normal to heal. Due to the cold, damp, unsanitary conditions existing within many hospital facilities, wounds failed to close properly, continuing to weep or tearing open when they should have been fully closed. Infections were also difficult to prevent in hospitals where hygiene was almost impossible to maintain. If that was not enough, the medics also had to deal with diseases that swept through the masses of healthy prisoners who were living in filthy, cramped conditions.

Despite the stipulations of the Geneva Convention, it took three years for the first men to be repatriated. It had also been hoped that some of the more senior POWs would be allowed home. In 1941 a request was sent via the Americans that all prisoners who had also been captives during the Great War should be released. Another request was for the return of all prisoners over the age of forty-eight who had been captive for over eighteen months. Both requests were turned down. However, the subject was raised again in 1943 when Major-General Fortune asked that all 1914-18 POWs be allowed to go home. By this time those in government circles believed that no such move should be made until the seriously wounded had been allowed to come home.

Before any of the wounded soldiers could be repatriated they first had to be assessed by the Mixed Medical Commission, representatives of the protecting powers whose job it was to determine those men whose wounds were too severe to allow future military service. In some cases, such as blinded soldiers and amputees, it was clear who should go home. Many of these had already been assessed by the Germans as unfit for service, *Dienstunfahig* – DU – or as the patients referred to it 'definitely unfit'. In other cases, such as those with stomach wounds or serious diseases, the rules were less well defined. By December 1941 the Red Cross in Geneva had reported that of the 984 men they had examined 411 were suitable for repatriation.

Whilst waiting for assessment in the town of Treysa, one group of prisoners were appalled by the treatment given them by the Germans. They complained they were treated as prisoners rather than patients and described the care as 'disgracefully inadequate'.[23] Such was the paucity of rations that the British medical staff began to lose weight rapidly and they were forced to take regular rests whilst attempting to care for the prisoners. Among the sick men anaemia became a serious problem, but the only iron tablets available contained high levels of arsenic.

The first repatriation should have taken place in 1941. Negotiation commenced between Britain and Germany but they were soon deadlocked. The British requested that a Red Cross ship sail between Britain and either Lisbon or Marseilles. However, the Germans claimed that repatriation by sea was impossible since the waters around Britain were too dangerous for a ship to pass safely through. They insisted the ships should go to Canada, with any prisoners too sick to make the crossing instead being sent to Switzerland to be interned while they received further medical care. When these proposals were rejected by the British, the Germans asked whether it would be acceptable for the wounded of both sides to be transferred to neutral countries – British POWs heading to Spain and German POWs going to Eire. They would then be free to use Red Cross aircraft to transfer the wounded men to their home countries. This too proved to be unacceptable to the British.

With the negotiations deadlocked, a senior British Army doctor, Colonel W.A. Robertson – working at Reserve Lazaret Obermassfeld – requested that all soldiers cleared for repatriation be temporarily admitted to hospitals in Switzerland. Like so many who were aware of the plight of the wounded POWs, he was anxious they should be allowed to receive first-rate medical care in conditions that were not prejudicial to their health. He was not the only one pressing for action. Relatives of the men listed for repatriation were angered by the apparent procrastination by the authorities. As the Foreign Office admitted: 'Some of them even believe that the reason for the delay lies in the fact that the government does not take a sufficiently active interest in them.'[24]

In September 1941, in anticipation of repatriation, groups of badly wounded soldiers were transferred from their hospitals to camps in France. There was little doubt in the minds of many wounded that the journey home had become imperative. One wrote home from Stalag 9C: 'There are many wounded who need special treatment in England, and if they don't get home soo they may be ruined for life.'[25]

Rumours swept through the men as they realized they were being moved for a purpose. Back in London it seemed the scheme would go ahead and two hospital ships – the *Dinard* and the *St Julien*, were earmarked for the transport of the wounded men. It was proposed that the ships would sail between Newhaven and Fécamp, on the northern French coast. To prevent attack by air both the RAF and the Luftwaffe would be forbidden from coming any closer than ten miles from the two ports and a twenty-mile wide corridor was to be established across the English Channel. The proposed date for the operation was 4 October 1941.

The prospect of the journey home raised the spirits of the men. One recalled how the first move had been to a camp where he had the freedom to swim in a lake. It was a great relief to enter the cooling waters after the misery of a stalag hospital – even if he could only swim using one arm. Yet their hopes were dashed when news came through that repatriation negotiations had fallen through. On 26 September the Germans had suddenly introduced new conditions to the exchange. They would only exchange wounded British prisoners of war for the corresponding number of German prisoners. This was unworkable since there were over 1,000 British wounded soldiers or medical personnel in France awaiting evacuation. However, there were only 150 German soldiers in England who had been cleared for repatriation. To make up the numbers the Germans tried to insist that interned civilians should be returned to them. The British agreed that a limited number of civilians would be released, but they refused to agree to the

German demand of over 1,000. And so the negotiations foundered. The German wounded, who had already been embarked, were led back onto dry land and returned to POW camps.

In France, the news reached the British soldiers. Geoff Griffin, who had almost had his arm amputated following his capture in France, later wrote of his emotions upon hearing the news that he would not be going home: 'I suppose that most of us had experienced some disappointments in life, but at that moment there could not have been a more dejected lot of men than us. We slunk back to barracks and I know that I cried my eyes out, many of my comrades did the same.'[26]

Following this news, the prisoners were returned to Poland, where they were housed in a large warehouse that had been fitted with tall bunks. Orderlies had to organize the allocation of beds to make sure that the men who had to reach the upper bunks had enough limbs to climb up the ladders. Reaching the upper bunks was not the end of their problems, as Geoff Griffin discovered on the first night in the warehouse: 'We had just dropped off to sleep when there were terrible shrieks coming from the lower bunks, so those of us who could scrambled down to the ground to see what was wrong and found that the place was swarming with rats, and very large ones at that. They were biting the poor chaps in the lower bunks.'[27]

As Griffin helped to clear the rats from the room his wounds burst open again, resulting in his being transferred to hospital. When he arrived there, the hospital was so crowded he had to sleep in the corridor. For Griffin the long process of recovery continued, with doctors having to once again drain his wounds and remove more bone splinters. It was not until July 1942, more than two years after his arm was shattered by German bullets, that the wounds closed. They reopened the following year, necessitating one further operation.

The long process of awaiting repatriation left the wounded men plenty of time to consider their situation. Most realized they would never return to their pre-war jobs. Included among the wounded were a large number of men in their forties who had previously been manual labourers and who had been captured whilst serving in the Pioneer Corps. As a result the prisoners began to establish educational classes in order to increase their future employment opportunities with office skills such as book keeping and accountancy.

In the autumn of 1943 the first batch of disabled prisoners finally got the news they had long awaited – they were going home. After three years of wrangling the British and German governments had finally managed to come to an agreement. Following the Allied victories in North Africa, the number of POWs on each side had finally begun to even out. The agreed system was simple: the British transported wounded Germans across the North Sea, whilst the Germans took a corresponding number of British soldiers across the Baltic, with both countries exchanging the wounded in the port of Gothenburg under the supervision of the Swedish authorities.

One of the medics attending the sick men was Norman 'Ginger' Barnett, who had been captured in May 1940 after his ambulance was raked by German machine-gun fire. During his captivity he had built up a large collection of photographs taken at both Stalag 8B and at work camps. The problem would be how to get them home since he knew the Germans would not allow the photos to leave the country. Fortunately, he was a member of the camp band, playing the accordion at the regular concerts. He was able to insert the photographs inside his accordion, thus getting them through the searches prior to departure.

Like many others, Barnett had already been disappointed once, when the repatriation via France and Spain had been cancelled. As a result he didn't get his hopes up when the news came:

> We heard rumours about repatriation. At first I thought I wouldn't take any notice of it. Then the Feldwebel came to me and said 'I have news for you. You are going home.' I didn't believe him but he told me to get my gear together. The next morning they shipped me off to the Stalag. It was only when I

reached Lamsdorf that I knew it more than a rumour. Blokes were getting all their gear together. I was excited but was it going to come off? We'd been let down once.

After leaving Lamsdorf, Barnett was put onto a hospital train: 'There was me in this compartment with six berths. I had to look after these six men. The two men on the bottom bunks were strapped down. They were Polish. I was told to give them anything they wanted, so I gave them cigarettes. One of them started burning his forehead with the cigarette, he was mad. But also there were these smart Swedish nurses giving us white bread and milk!'

He had been right not to get his hopes up in advance of departure. As late as ten days before the exchange was due to take place, the Swedish authorities contacted the British with the information that they had intercepted German signals stressing that no decision had been taken by the Nazi leadership to actually allow the repatriation scheme to go ahead. In the final days before the operation commenced there were further practical issues to be covered, with the discovery that one of the German ships had too deep a draft to follow the proposed route and another ship, the *Stuttgart*, had been damaged in an American bombing raid on the port of Gydnia.

Despite these fears, a final date of 19 October was set. Arriving at the German port of Swinemunde, the prisoners and medical staff were loaded onto two ships – the *Meteor* and the *Ruegen*. Other groups, mostly mobile prisoners, travelled via Sassnitz and Trelleborg onboard ferries. Some of the repatriates enjoyed the luxury of being placed into cabins. It was a wonderful experience for the men to see stewards bustling around to assist them. It was a far cry from the days of living in rat-infested rooms. Among this first repatriation group was Geoff Griffin:

It is difficult to explain our feelings about what was happening but, having all had a luxuriating bath and a shave, we were ushered into a large cabin where a table was set with all sorts of cold meats, potatoes and salad, and we all immediately set to and tucked into the meal . . . we did not realise how small our stomachs had become so we could not do complete justice to the meal, although we were really hungry.[28]

At 10 p.m. on 16 October 1943 the ships sailed for Sweden, carrying 4,156 repatriates. The men onboard were swept by a wave of emotion as they realized that after more than three years of waiting they were finally free of the Germans and were actually going home. It was difficult for them to comprehend that they would soon be seeing their loved ones again. Arriving in Gothenburg three days later, the prisoners were amazed at the twinkling lights of the port after their world of blackout. Leaving the Swedish ship they were soon transferred to another vessel. On their way they exchanged friendly greetings with the similarly wounded Germans who were heading the opposite direction and for whom they had been exchanged. The British Legation in Stockholm reported back to London on the behaviour of the British soldiers:

The troops were unanimous in expressing their delight at the reception given to them by all the Swedes whom they saw or met. They were the object of enthusiastic demonstrations the whole way from Trelleborg to Gothenburg and the press was full of photographs and sympathetic anecdotes. To me the most poignant memory is of a Swedish band on the quayside playing 'Home Sweet Home' with hundreds of our soldiers hanging over the sides of the two big liners singing not boisterously but from the bottom of their hearts.[29]

Waiting in Gothenburg were two British ships. The hospital ship *Atlantis* was used for the most badly wounded of the soldiers, including the blind, stretcher cases and the mentally ill. The transport ship *Empress of Russia* was used for protected personnel. A third ship, the Swedish *Drottningholm* was also used for the repatriation of protected personnel. The British government had arranged a grant of £2,000 to be spent by the embassy in Stockholm to purchase comforts from the Swedish Red Cross. This money went on apples, razors, sweets, matches and illustrated newspapers for the returning men.

After the comfort of the liner, many of the soldiers were disappointed to see the troopship that the British had sent to collect them. Rather than beds they were supposed to sleep in hammocks – a difficult enough operation for a healthy man, let alone a man with one arm. Also, the steep ladders meant the men with legs missing found it almost impossible to reach the lower decks. Yet these were small concerns, all that really counted was that the ship was British and they were heading home.

Norman Barnett remembered the journey home: 'It was wonderful. But when we were off the coast of Norway the Captain came over the tannoy to say we had to get off the gun platform or else the Germans would open fire.' During the crossing each repatriate received a letter explaining what would happen following their arrival in the UK. The returning men were pleased to see they would be given twenty-eight days' leave as soon as possible after arrival. They were each to receive an advance of pay of £4. The soldiers were also issued telegrams and postcards which they were able to send free of charge to alert their families of their safe return to the UK.

On 25 October the ship finally docked at Leith in Scotland, where the disembarking soldiers were greeted by women who handed out tea and sandwiches – 'char & wads'. There were no family members waiting to greet them upon arrival. The army had deliberately kept families away until the men had been debriefed at a hotel at Turnberry. Geoff Griffin had just one thing to say about his treatment by the Germans: 'I only hope that the Germans involved were found and punished.'[30]

The process of bringing home wounded POWs and attempting to facilitate their recovery and rehabilitation was not an easy one. In two cases families who were overjoyed at the news their men were coming home had to receive the tragic news that they had died during the crossing of the North Sea.

There were also important concerns about how much the press could reveal. Special efforts were made to prevent publication of 'lurid horror stories'[31] about the treatment of prisoners that had been proposed by the *Daily Mail* and *Daily Express* newspapers.* The fear was that such exposés could jeopardize any future exchange of prisoners.

Others had more immediate concerns. The medical branch of the War Office found precious little material on the subject had been printed in the aftermath of the Great War. As a result they were unprepared for dealing with the mental state of the returning prisoners. Efforts were therefore made to gather the necessary information, with what was discovered during the repatriation schemes eventually being put to use when the mass of prisoners returned home. In 1943 Lord Phillimore, who had been a POW during the Great War, wrote to the War Office: 'Will you take it from me that their psychological state is rather a queer one? First they feel rather ashamed of themselves for having survived when their comrades were killed and for having played so small a part in the war.'[32]

What he claimed was soon discovered to be accurate. Even limbless veterans were found to exhibit psychiatric problems that outweighed their physical handicaps. Initial studies of repatriated men showed 'mild evidence of depression or neurotic difficulty' and that over 25 per cent of returning medical staff displayed 'incapacitating apathy and depression'.[33] Found beneath the mild symptoms were deeper issues that were discovered to have been masked by the euphoria of coming home. Quite simply, they hid their bitterness and hostility behind a superficial layer of protective cheerfulness. This was partly tied to their dreams of home and their expectations of what life might be. In their minds they had

---

* More than sixty years later both these newspapers did get such stories into print when they published features on the author's book *Hitler's British Slaves: Allied POWs in Germany, 1939–45.*

idealized 'civvy street' and the comforts of home. In reality, they returned to a country in the deep grip of rationing, one where they could find little escape from war's domination of their daily lives. One serving officer wrote to the War Office to express his concerns for the returning men. He spoke of their likely emotions: 'dis-illusionment on return home − the home of the man's fantasies maybe − is a most appalling factor and the problem affects all men who have been long away from home or very isolated.'[34] Around 20 per cent of all returning long term POWs were found to have difficulty adapting to life after their return from Germany, noting that the reality of day-to-day life did not match the romanticized version of home they had yearned for whilst in captivity.

One later wrote of walking down his street yet failing to respond to the greetings of his neighbours − quite simply he was over-whelmed by emotions and unable to react. Another admitted failing to attend a lunch arranged by his father in honour of his return. His reasoning was simple − he did not have to go, therefore he was not going to go. After three years of having his every movement dictated by outsiders he simply wanted to control his own destiny. It may have been difficult for outsiders to understand, but the men needed time to learn to live again. Norman Barnett recalled arriving home on three weeks' compassionate leave:

> I got home but mum was out. I stood at the front door and waited. Then I saw her walking down the road. She came running down. It was amazing. For Christ's sake, it was some-thing! That night I went out to see my uncle and aunt down the road. It was total blackout − but I could remember every single step down the road. It all came natural to me. But that night I couldn't sleep in the bed. I slept on the floor. For weeks I washed and shaved in cold water. I thought if I ever got caught again I'd have to learn it all over again. So I couldn't relax.

Of course, their mental state was not the only concern for the authorities. The returning men had very real physical needs to be cared for. There were false limbs to be fitted, others needed reconstructive surgery or had to learn how to cope with a life of freedom that was restricted by blindness. The repatriated men also had to be treated for their general physical condition after three years of captivity in appalling conditions. Studies revealed that around 11 per cent of the men had developed gastro-intestinal symptoms whilst in captivity, a result of their poor diets and living conditions. Recovery would not be a quick process for the men who had been wounded during the BEF's defeats of 1940, but at least they knew it was a process that would take place surrounded by their loved ones.

CHAPTER EIGHT

The Journey East

We were worn out. We weren't eating. We weren't drinking. We were just marching.

Bill Holmes, captured on the Dunkirk beaches

I saw a German officer shoot three wounded soldiers.

British soldier quoted in
United Nations War Crimes Reports[1]

The crushing defeat inflicted upon the British Army and its allies had shattered the myth of the quick war, 'over by Christmas', and the supposed invincibility of the British Army had been swept away by the tide of German military efficiency.

For all the desperate courage displayed by the army during the retreat, they had been pushed back, humiliated, then driven into the sea. Those left in France were exhausted beyond belief, racked by hunger, pitifully dishevelled, scared, bewildered and bitter. Moreover, they were about to face up to life as slaves to Hitler's dark dream of European domination.

Through May and June nearly 40,000 British soldiers joined the seemingly endless columns of marchers heading towards Germany. Alongside what appeared to be hundreds of thousands of French soldiers – including large and incongruous groups of colonial troops

– and groups of Belgians and Dutchmen, the battered remnants of the BEF marched into captivity.

There were numerous columns of men, taking hundreds of different routes. Yet whether they were in the single column, more than 8,000 strong, that left St Valery in the second week of June, or in the smaller, earlier groups captured in central Belgium, all shared the same numbing sense of despair and degradation.

There are few fully coherent accounts of what happened in those bitter days. Few troubled to keep record of their progress. Some made scribbled notes recording the names of the towns they passed through, a handful even recorded the distances they marched, courtesy of the road signs they saw as they trudged from town to town. Even those who had the energy to record such basic details had little inclination to record anything else. Most were too tired and hungry. All that mattered was whether there would be food at the end of the day.

The attitude of the victorious army as they marched their captives into Germany was summed up by what was overheard by Arthur Fleischmann, a Czech soldier captured whilst fighting in France. Listening to his guards, he heard one say: 'The English bear the blame for all evil and must be destroyed.'[2] It was a fitting start to what was to be a hellish period for the British captives.

However, for many the marches started as relatively easy. Large numbers reported that their original captors – the front-line infantrymen of the Wehrmacht spearhead – had treated them with sympathy. Tommy Arnott, captured at St Valery, was among a group who received unusual gifts from the enemy troops: 'On the first day after we were captured we walked a good distance. It rained all day and the Germans gave many of us umbrellas – not normally part of soldier's equipment even if it was wet.' Yet this generosity was short-lived. What soon followed was a bitter indication of what was to come: 'We had to run up hill shouting "Chamberlain!" in memory of our Prime Minister. A German wagon was filming this performance for propaganda as well as trying to humiliate us.' That night two men were shot attempting to escape.

In the initial confusion of defeat, it took time for the newly captive men to comprehend their situation. Many, though expecting to be executed in the immediate aftermath of battle, had been fairly well treated. There were some executions – some notorious like at Le Paradis or Wormhoudt, others less so, like the executions in the Forêt de Nieppe – but thousands of prisoners went safely into captivity. As many found, it was only after they came under the control of soldiers from the rear echelons that they really began to suffer. Having been captured by a perfectly polite, Oxford-educated SS officer, Eric Reeves noticed the changing nature of the guards: 'Along came the B-echelon troops. They were shoving us in the back and shouting "*Raus! Raus!*" – at that time we didn't know what it meant. We spent our first night in cattle pens. The next day we marched for six hours to a farm then for the rest of the time we always slept in open fields.'

One of the first observations made by Norman Barnett after he was sent back to the rear of the German lines was just how different everything seemed there. The German spearhead had been 'a crust' beneath which a very different world existed. Gone were the lines of modern trucks, the roaring columns of heavily armoured motorcycle combinations, the column after column of heavily armed and vicious-looking young soldiers. In their place came horse-drawn wagons, guards on bicycles and soldiers who seemed much older than those doing the fighting.

To many prisoners, it was the age of the guards that seemed to make the real difference in treatment they received. The younger soldiers, those on the battlefield, may have been more dedicated to their duty and convinced of their cause but they were enthusiastic in their pursuit of war. Once the battle was won they were, in the main, happy to move on to the next battlefield. The older men, many veterans of the Great War, seemed less than happy to have been recalled to the army. They felt they were too old to have been disturbed by this new conflict. They wanted to be at home with their families, not guarding the vast columns of prisoners who were heading to Germany. And it was the prisoners who paid the price for the obvious frustration of the guards.

As the marchers raised themselves from the fields and town squares in which they had been gathered following capture, all felt uncertain. Would they be put into trucks or be sent by rail? Would the defeat signal the end of the war or would they be held as captives for years? And, most importantly, when would they get food? In a field outside St Valery, David Mowatt soon received the answer to some of these questions: 'We were already on our knees, we were exhausted. We formed up and marched off. We couldn't believe it – there were thousands of us. There was a van with us, with a loudspeaker. As we passed through a village a voice came over the tannoy "You are not to accept any food or water from the locals." So we had nothing to eat or drink.'

Apart from food and drink, there was another important issue. Would they be able to maintain any form of military discipline now that they were prisoners? The issue of discipline was important. The role of their officers in enforcing order and controlling the men was vital. Yet, right from the beginning, the Germans took the definite step of ensuring officers and other ranks would be kept separate for as long as possible.

The prisoners leaving Calais were kept together at the start of the march, only being divided up once they reached the town of Marquise. Here the officers were taken away and then driven on to a barn. The next day saw them driven to the town of Desvres where they were put into a recreation ground surrounded by a high wall. The officers were put into a pavilion where they sheltered to await the arrival of the main body of marchers. Later that day the other ranks arrived and slumped down to relax, having marched through the night. Forbidden to use the tap, the thirsty soldiers had to wait for their officers to bring them water from the pavilion.

The next day both the officers and men were back out on the road. As they marched, they witnessed long columns of lorried infantry, all heading towards the front line. As they passed, the Germans jeered at the marching prisoners and took photographs to capture the misery of their defeat.

Having been soaked during a violent thunderstorm, the column eventually reached the hilltop town of Montreuil. Those still carrying their waterbottles rushed to fill them from the overflowing guttering of nearby houses. Again the officers were given preferential treatment, being sent to shelter in the appropriately named Café Anglais, whilst the other ranks were shepherded into a barbed wire enclosure in the town's market square. With the rain continuing through the night, some were able to take shelter in the local cinema whilst the rest were condemned to a night sleeping on the wet cobblestones. The following morning the officers were loaded into lorries, then driven to the town of Hesdin. As they waited for the marching column to catch up with them they were fed on bread and high horsemeat. Despite the smell of the meat the ravenous officers consumed it enthusiastically, knowing it might be days until the next meal arrived.

And so the officers' journey continued. Some days spent marching, on others they were carried in lorries. Some nights were passed herded into the shelter of factories or schools, others spent out in the open. One night was spent in a ditch – formerly used as a latrine – over which the officers built a shelter of sticks gathered from the surrounding countryside. Their misery continued as they approached the Belgian frontier. At Bapaume they were searched by screaming German officers who brandished pistols and took away their razors, pens, walking sticks, steel helmets and money. That night they were herded into a barn whilst the Belgian troops in the same column were left outside. The officers within had to barricade the doors to prevent a Belgian mob forcing their way inside.

There was an official reason for keeping the officers and their men separate – the Germans were obliged to do so under the Geneva Convention. However, there was another logic behind their actions. Although officers could help instil discipline into the massed ranks, they could also act as a focus for defiance. One of those officers who posed this risk was Captain Ernest Hart of the Royal Northumberland Fusiliers. Hart was the senior officer in a group of twenty-six men captured whilst holding a canal at St Omer. On the first day of their march a car drew up alongside the column, stopping beside a group of British prisoners. As the German officer left his car he launched a violent assault on the prisoners nearest him, kicking them as if to hurry them along the road. Seeing the assault, Captain Hart intervened, telling the officer he should treat the men as prisoners of war and show them respect. The German's response was immediate. He drew his pistol and fired three shots into the remonstrating captain. Hart fell dead on the roadside where his body was left as the column trudged on.

The daily marches varied in length. One man recorded how his group had marched from Boulogne to Hesdin, via Montreuil, a total of thirty-six miles (fifty-eight kilometres). They were given just one hour's break during the entire march. The Geneva Convention stated the maximum daily distance for any march should be twelve miles (twenty kilometres). As one soldier recalled, whenever he asked the guards how much further they had to go the answer was always the same – 'Three kilometres.' That became the terrible reality for the marchers – it always seemed that rest was somewhere in the distance, just over the next hill, in the next village, another mile, another hour, another day.

A group whose march began in Calais found themselves forced to march even further. They were on the road for an entire twenty-four-hour period, with breaks of just twenty minutes every three or four hours. At the end of their twenty-four-hour march they were given one hour's rest, then sent out onto the road for another twenty-four hours. During the entire period they were given no food. Those who fell out from the column were shot. This almost constant marching continued for six days. When the British government attempted to complain about the treatment given to the men in the columns they were brushed off by the Germans. Replying via Switzerland, the Germans stated they had 'no information regarding charges of bad transport conditions of British prisoners of war between places of capture and prison camps but will investigate further, if the British government can give information as to the date and place of alleged offences.'[3]

Some groups found themselves marching in circles. Suddenly, after miles of marching, they found themselves back in a village they had already passed through. It soon appeared this was a deliberate policy. They were being paraded through as many villages as possible to show off the fruits of the German triumph and reinforce the notion that the Allies had been hopelessly crushed. One of the circuits, taking in the towns of Douai, Cambrai, Valenciennes, Mons and Hal, lasted a total of fourteen days. A United Nations report later summarized the situation: 'It shows the state of the German mind in regard to this barbarous practice long since discarded by civilised nations.'[4]

Overnight stops were made in all manner of locations, a waterlogged field, a dung-covered farmyard, a dry weed-infested castle moat, or a sports stadium, depending on circumstances. In the main, the prisoners had to make do with sleeping outdoors, curled up on the bare earth, hoping and praying it wouldn't rain during the night. As one witness reported back to London: 'Men are kept in pens without any protection from the weather.'[5] It was not always the rain that proved a problem for the prisoners. At Jemelles 4,000–5,000 British and French prisoners were held in the open air. Under assault from the summer sun, they were forced to scrape holes into the hillside in order to escape its rays.

During the breaks in the march many prisoners began to regret the loss of their kit. Many had lost everything apart from the clothes they stood up in when they were captured. As Les Allan marched, mostly surrounded by Frenchmen, he could not help but notice some men far worse off than himself. He may have been wounded in the neck, and have lost all his kit, his papers and his battledress jacket but, compared some of the British gunners he saw on the march, he was well prepared. They had been manning their guns under the hot summer sun dressed in little more than boots, vests and shorts when they had been captured. A few were even topless. Yet they too, like everyone else, just had to keep marching, desperately hoping they might soon find some abandoned clothing to cover their exposed flesh.

The story was the same everywhere. Some had their steel helmets, but many did not. A lucky few had greatcoats that were a burden in daytime, but made for a comfortable blanket at night. Others blessed the groundsheets and gas capes they had saved to shelter them from the rain. But they were the minority. Those who had not lost their kit in battle had lost it when their captors had searched them.

As a result the soldiers picked up whatever they could find to make their lives more comfortable. For as long as they had the strength to carry kit, many broke into homes in the villages they passed through, taking whatever they needed. Some tied blankets and eiderdowns around their bodies with string, others slung pots and kettles over their shoulders so they might have something to cook food in – if they were lucky enough to find any. One officer, desperate for something to cover himself in the cold of night, found a discarded greatcoat. This was surely the answer to his prayers. Then he noticed it was heavily stained with the blood of its former owner. He preferred to remain cold rather than be wrapped in something a man had died in and soon abandoned the coat. Days later, the same officer watched as his comrades began to abandon their own coats as they became too tired to carry them any longer. One officer abandoned an almost new sheepskin-lined coat that had cost £10. However, despite the obvious value and use of such an item, no one had the strength to pick it up and carry it.

Weighed down by whatever little they were carrying, the troops craved nothing more than the short breaks and overnight stops that allowed them to rest their aching limbs – if only for a few minutes. Many soon realized there was a trick to ensuring they maximized the time spent resting. As Ken Willats remembered: 'The column was just one long trail of men shuffling into captivity. The trick was not to be at the back of the column. Because if you are at the back, when it gets to a rest stop you get there last. Consequently those at the back are only just arriving when the front of the column is told it's time to get moving again.'

The scenes of misery were spread across the region. One witness sent word via Switzerland of starving men clothed in rags held in cattle pens near Antwerp. His report also noted it was clear that the British soldiers were being discriminated against, and the French and Belgian troops were receiving favourable treatment. When the local Red Cross attempted to intervene they were told that if they wished to feed the British they would also have to feed the guards. Elsewhere there were reports of prisoners pushing wounded men in wheelbarrows.

Deliberate attempts to humiliate the British prisoners were also reported by the American nanval attaché who reported seeing British prisoners in the town of Cambrai. Many had had their boots taken away, others were dressed in a bizarre manner including: 'old bowlers crammed down, women's hats and articles taken from fancy shops in order to make them look ridiculous'.[6] It was little wonder the American embassy soon reported they were forbidden to visit the prisoners despite their position of being the protecting power.

Each night, as they fell to the bare earth to sleep for a few short hours, it seemed as if an awful burden had been lifted from their shoulders. Yet there was a down side to the experience. Though they craved nothing – except maybe food – more than sleep, they had to endure the terrible realization that the night would soon be over. Then they would rise once more and begin to march for another day. As the days passed this became something that weighed more and more heavily on them. The more exhausted they became, the longer it took to recover what little strength they retained, making it increasingly painful to rise from the cold earth and loosen their tight muscles each morning.

The nightly halts were seldom an opportunity for the prisoners to fully relax. Private Watt, marching from St Valery, later recorded: 'A lot of thieving took place in these camps. Coats were taken off sleeping figures, also boots. Haversacks were being stolen at every opportunity, just in case they happened to contain any food. We always had to have someone to look after our meagre belongings while the rest were on the eternal search for food.'[7]

There was something increasingly primeval about the behaviour of the prisoners as the marches progressed. In sandy soil, the prisoners were able to scratch small hollows to lower themselves into. When sleeping among trees they pulled small branches down to construct nests. In some places prisoners were forced into partially flooded fields. Here men fought each other for the right to rest at the top of the slope – the area that remained relatively dry. It was a bitter experience for those unable to fight their way to the top – but all now realized what counted from now on was the survival of the fittest.

The prison in the French town of Doullens was one location used for overnight stops. RAMC prisoner Norman Barnett had the misfortune of spending his twentieth birthday there. He arrived to find the prison had already been used by numerous men. As a result it was filthy and there was little food or water: 'It was a big compound. We were mixed up with these Senegalese troops. They must have been there some time 'cause they were well established, they'd even got food from somewhere. We only got water though. But they were dirty bastards – there was shit everywhere. And you were lucky to get somewhere to sit down. Luckily we were only there one night – I preferred sleeping out in the fields than staying there. I was glad to get away.'

As another column entered the prison, the new arrivals were greeted by the sight of German guards scattering biscuits to them from the back of a lorry. There were only enough for the early arrivals and those at the rear of the column went hungry. Arriving at the prison, some witnessed the Germans executing a sergeant who dared to remonstrate with guards for beating one of the men trailing at the end of the column.

Graham King, the medic who had been captured before he and his comrades had been able to establish their casualty clearing station, was among the men who spent a night in the dubious shelter of Doullens prison: 'By the time our group arrived the building was packed and we had to rest on the stony ground where we soon fell asleep. In the middle of the night a huge storm broke over us and in no time we were wet through. I thought of my mother and the way she would panic if any of us got wet. I was glad she wasn't able to see her youngest son completely drenched, no hot mustard bath, no dry clothing. He was on his own.'

Not every overnight stop was so fraught with danger. At Frévent marchers recalled arriving at a factory to be greeted by the sight of a perfectly attired sergeant-major of the Welsh Guards, complete with clean-shaven chin, who was holding a steaming cup of tea. It was a bizarre sight for men who had not had a hot meal or drink for over four days.

Of all the things experienced on the march into Germany, one thing made the greatest impression upon the prisoners. What mattered more than anything was the shortage of food. The marching may have blistered their feet and left their legs aching, but nothing was more important than the fact they often had almost nothing with which to sustain themselves. As a result, they relied on their meagre reserves of fat, something that was soon used up as they marched mile upon mile towards Germany.

The men captured at Calais were among the first to join the marching hordes. Their spirited defence of the port, against all odds, may have won time for the remainder of the BEF to escape. But all it had earned the defenders of Calais were bitter memories, exhaustion and hunger. Yet as they began to march there was little chance to satisfy their aching bellies. In such circumstances, even a single egg was manna from heaven. When Lt.-Colonel Ellison-MacArtney found one, he offered it to all his men in turn. Yet all refused, insisting their CO deserved that rare treat. On the sixth day of the march they each received a ration of thin barley soup with half an ounce of sausage. The next morning they received green and mildewed loaves that had to be shared one between ten. One soldier described his soup ration as 'nothing more than dirty water cooked in a pig-trough'.[8] The story was the same everywhere. It was the beginning of the process in which the hungry prisoners discovered that an empty belly was the one thing guaranteed to stop a soldier thinking of women. It was a bitter experience that would follow them for the next five years.

Those who eventually managed to pass reports of their ill-treatment back to the UK highlighted the poor food. For many, it was not just the question of rations being issued. As the almost inevitable soup was ladled out there were many who had nothing to collect it in. Having lost so much of their kit, they had no mess tins to hold out. Discarded rusting cans were pounced on at the roadside. Some improvised, holding out their steel helmets. One desperate man even took off his boot and held that out to receive his soup ration. When Fred Gilbert, already weakened by three bullet wounds and long days of marching, found himself in a food queue without a receptacle, he did the only thing possible, he stretched out his cupped hands and accepted a handful of soup. That was his entire ration for the day.

The men craved the taste of the nicotine that had always previously helped to suppress hunger, yet only the luckiest among them still had any tobacco. The pipe-smokers fared best. They crammed their pipes into the corner of their mouths and marched onwards, as Eric Reeves remembered: 'I didn't have any tobacco but I had my pipe. You can still suck on an empty pipe and get a lot of enjoyment, you get the taste and smell of nicotine.'

The last substantial group to join the eastward march were the men of the 51st Highland Division. Three weeks after the first prisoners had started marching, the Jocks rose from their barbed wire enclosure on the cliffs above St Valery. After a night in the open, one group of prisoners were fed raw salted herring and black bread. Such was the foul taste of the fish that most immediately threw it away. It would be the last time they would reject food, however sickening. The next morning the same men were given a cup of coffee and two British army hard tack biscuits. Another group watched as a German lorry drew up. Stopping beside the fence surrounding the prisoners, the Germans on board began to throw loaves of bread to the famished men. As the men fought over the loaves, scrabbling in the rain-soaked grass for a handful of crumbs, the purpose of their visit was revealed. As the Germans shouted, 'England *kaput!*' to their prisoners, the men looked up to see a film crew recording their desperate fights for the consumption of audiences eager to witness the German mastery over their British enemies.

The humiliation was just the start of their misery. In the course of their ten-day march, some remnants of the Highland Division did get the occasional food issue. During one stop a soup ration appeared but it was insufficient to feed everyone in the column. An officer made an announcement that the NCOs should divide the men into groups by their units and then draw lots for who would get the soup. The plan was that they would be ineligible for the next ration. Some men recorded receiving a pack of hard tack biscuits to share between three men each day and, as one man recalled, a cup of black liquid 'said to be coffee'.[9] Others, like Jim Pearce, received nothing more than a lump of bread, green with mould: 'So we lost weight rapidly.'

One group was offered rations by their guards on the proviso that they dug latrines for the column. Despite the lure of food they were simply too weak to break the shovels through the soil. Another were pleased to find they had stopped beside a duck pond. As many as possible pulled off their boots and wallowed in the murky waters, revelling in the relief it brought to their aching feet and filthy bodies

For those who retained some strength the nightly breaks meant an opportunity to beg, steal or scrounge whatever food was available. Dandelions, dock leaves, daisies and any other roadside weeds became a regular part of their diets. One man recalled boiling nettles in his tin helmet to make what passed for nettle soup. On another occasion the same man paid 50 francs to French colonial troops who had slaughtered a cow. His share of the kill was the unwashed tripe. Another soldier reported that his best night on the march was the one when he somehow managed to find a chicken. The chicken was soon killed, plucked and boiled in a discarded French helmet. Such fare was a luxury. One group of men marching from St Valery caught a dog and stewed it. However, the food carried by a group of French Moroccans was too extreme for even the most desperate British prisoners. The soldiers were aware that whatever the men were carrying was giving off a foul smell. When a German soldier made them open the sack, its contents were revealed. A rotten horse's head fell to the floor, alive with maggots.

The prisoners – dizzy from the effects of the encroaching starvation – consumed anything and everything that was vaguely edible. As they marched the they cut through the landscape like a cloud of khaki locusts. Fields and farms next to the roads they marched along became the scenes of vast foraging sweeps as the men desperately searched for anything edible. As Eric Reeves remembered: 'The only thing that saved me from starvation were the clamps of manglewurzels. You'd wait until the guards on their bikes were out of sight then you'd jump in and get as many as you can carry. Then you'd get back in the column and share them out with guys you'd never even seen before. So we ate them raw and unwashed.' For Fred Coster the experience was one that could never be forgotten: 'Eating these damn raw potatoes, most of the chaps got diarrhoea. They were dropping out of the column to go to the toilet all the time. It was very debilitating and disgusting. But that was how you had to live – or you'd go under.'

Gangs surged towards clamps of vegetables stored by the local farmers. Swedes, potatoes and sugar beet were pulled from clamps, the dirt brushed from them, then stuffed hungrily into the mouths of the marching men. It didn't matter that they needed to be cooked before consumption – few men had any way of cooking them, nor any matches to light a fire. Instead the foul-tasting raw vegetables were chewed and swallowed as enthusiastically as a gourmet meal.

As the columns passed through the countryside, whole piles of vegetables disappeared into the bellies of the marchers. Yet for many the appearance of the piles was as much a frustration as it was a relief, as Dick Taylor remembered: 'You'd see a clamp of vegetables in the distance, but by the time you got there it had all gone.' Even the condition of vegetables was of little interest, with some men recalling eating rotten onions taken from a roadside pile. Desperate for sustenance, David Mowatt joined the gangs that descended onto the vegetable piles: 'We reached this pile of turnips – all covered in soil – that heap had a life of its own, it just moved. It disappeared as we went past. We also got blighted potatoes. But they nearly killed us. I was very ill, we got diarrhoea.' As a trained chef, Ken Willats knew more about food than the majority of his comrades. Yet, just like the rest of them, there was nothing he could do but join the scavenging hordes: 'One time I picked up some crushed rhubarb from the road. I thought "I'll have that!" That was the length you were prepared to go to get something to eat. Rhubarb's not very nice uncooked, but when you are starving it's like nectar!' Whilst large numbers were hit by stomach upsets as a result of the poor food, there was another side effect suffered by those who had been forced to eat the most basic of roadside produce. As RAMC man Ernie Grainger remembered: 'Food! We ate grass. As a result, when you passed water it was green – because of the chlorophyll!'

Even the homes they marched past became fair game for the increasingly hungry soldiers. In one village Tommy Arnott and his mate ran to a house: 'There was an Alsatian chained to the wall so we went round the back and opened the door. The lady in the house had been baking bread – it was on a tray – big square loaves. She was going to put the dog on us but, by the time she got the dog, we ran off to the column clutching two loaves. Poor soul, we pinched her bread, but that's what starvation does to you.'

Driven to desperation by the lack of food, some men tried to get help. There were those who feigned sickness, hoping it might lead to better treatment. In one instance a soldier who found himself amid a large group of French prisoners discovered they had facilities for treating the sick. So he feigned a seizure, was carried to some farm buildings used as an aid post, then kept visiting the latrines to suggest he had dysentery. The ruse worked and he was able to get food from the French and a few days of desperately needed rest. After a few days rest he moved on, before trying the same ruse of a feigned seizure and finding himself put onto a truck carrying the sick.

One of those who wasn't feigning when he collapsed amidst the marching hordes was Eric Reeves. He was one of the men who was 'travelling light' – he had no greatcoat, no groundsheet, no mess tin and no waterbottle. All he had was an empty gas mask case and a small haversack. Everything else had been lost when he was captured. There was something else he was not carrying. Reeves was a small man, just over five foot tall with hardly any reserves of fat to sustain him as he marched day after day without food.

> After four or five days I was exhausted – I'd lost all my mates by this time – and we'd stopped for the night in a field. It was freezing that night and we were wet through. The next morning you could see steam coming off the blokes' uniforms as they eventually dried out. I'd had very little sleep and as I got up I just collapsed. I sank down to my knees. I heard a bloke say 'Quick grab him' and half a dozen of them picked me up. At this point there was an issue of soup going on to the Froggies. So they carried me shoulder high down the hill. The French and Germans were pushing us but the blokes said 'No he's sick – he's wounded' and they carried me right through the crowd. So we all got some soup.

It was a genuine relief for Reeves, who might otherwise had been left behind to face execution by the guards. Realizing there was at least some concern among both the French prisoners and the German cooks, Reeves and his new found mates decided it was worth repeating: 'We did it three times! One bloke would say "Hey, little-un, pass out, we're going to get something to eat." I never knew the blokes who were carrying me but they kept me alive. Helped me keep going for 21 days of marching.'

He was not alone in his increasing weakness. As the hunger and sickness began to bite, some men were forced to link arms to support each other as they marched. R.P. Evans, a private in the Gloucestershire Regiment, recalled offering assistance to one of the weaker men: 'A man walking just in front of me collapsed and a German officer was screaming at him and waving his pistol, so I put an arm around the man's waist and his arm over my shoulders and somehow coaxed him along for two or three miles, until a lorry came along picking up the stragglers. I often wondered what happened to that chap afterwards.'[10] He went on to describe the condition of his fellow marchers: 'The men's condition was indescribable, and with ten days growth of beard, and their faces caked with dust, seamed through with rivulets of sweat, they looked like beings from another world.'[11]

This result of using up their reserves of fat became a very noticeable side effect of the long days of arduous marching. In a letter that eventually reached the War Office, one prisoner summed up the misery of the period when he reported: 'You see we got nothing for the first 12 days, and had to do forced marching right through France and Belgium. I was taken prisoner after a great battle when we were surrounded for two days without water, and only gave up because of the cries of the wounded . . . the first time I had a chance to sit on a hard seat I found I had been living on my hips, then I noticed my breast had gone as flat as a pancake. I had used up all the fat I had . . . so I'm now just gristle and bone, but as hard as iron.'[12]

Whilst the physical effect of the incessant marching was shown on their bodies, the deprivations of the march also became evident in their clothing. Nights spent sleeping in the open soaked their dirt-encrusted woollen battledress with dew, covered them with mud and grass stains, and introduced the sort of creases that would have once brought any sergeant-major screaming down on them. Now no one cared what they looked like. Small rips and tears became gaping holes. Even their boots – that most had hardly ever expected to 'wear in' – began to wear out. David Mowatt, having been issued a brand-new pair of double-soled army boots just three weeks before he was captured, found the strain of the daily slog took its toll on the boots. By the time he reached Dortmund he had worn through the soles.

One of the few positive memories for the marchers was the attitude of the French, Belgian and Dutch women they encountered on their journey. Whilst a minority of civilians attempted to exploit the prisoners, selling food at ludicrously inflated prices to men who had not eaten for days, most were genuine in their efforts to help the marching men. Every man who made the fateful journey that summer can recall the courage of the women who lined up buckets of water for the prisoners to drink from. Even to hear a heavily accented voice call out 'Good luck!' was a tonic for the troops, helping to raise their spirits for a few brief minutes. One soldier described the effect of a welcoming Belgian crowd: 'overwhelming, and it gave us a boost and it encouraged us to straighten up and see it through.'[13]

Such was the clamour to come out onto the streets to see and assist the men that in the towns of Béthune and Lille the Germans used mounted military policemen to keep them away from the passing column. Elsewhere guards fired at the feet of civilians attempting to pass food to the starving men. In the pretty spa town of Forges-les-Eaux, the marchers were forced at bayonet point to run through the town at the double, preventing any contact with civilians. A man in the same column reported whips being used on soldiers who had dared to accept food from local children. It seemed there was no end to the vindictiveness of the guards. Passing through one town, Bill Holmes watched as nuns were beaten by German soldiers for daring to throw sticks of rhubarb to the passing soldiers. Elsewhere, British soldiers were lucky to escape with their lives when they attacked a guard who had assaulted a young girl who had passed food to them.

Despite these displays of viciousness from the guards, not all the

prisoners were convinced it was entirely their fault that the prisoners were starved during their journey. As Bob Davies explained of
his march from Calais to Germany: 'Initially we were well treated. I
think the Germans did not expect to have so many prisoners.
Therefore feeding arrangements were non-existent. So as we
staggered along the road we had to pick up swedes and potatoes.'
Blaming the collapse of the Allies and the enormous numbers of
prisoners for the food shortages was an understandable reaction,
one that may have been based in truth, but excuses were irrelevant
to the thousands who were starving. The Germans may not have
had enough food to provide them with a hot meal each day but it
was simply cruel to deprive a man the chance to accept alms from
the villagers who lined the French roads. Every prisoner on the
march witnessed women putting out water only to see a guard
cycle or walk past, stick out a boot and upend the pail. Eric Reeves
recalled the excuses the German guards later gave for their
behaviour: 'We'd been reduced to drinking water from ditches
because the Germans were kicking over the buckets. When I
complained the guard told me it was because German troops
weren't allowed to drink it unless they'd put purification tablets
in it. I thought, that's a likely tale! The way they kicked it over – it
was just spiteful.'

Wracked by thirst, the soldiers were desperate for a drink. Nobby
Barber watched in amazement as the men around him picked dead
pigeons out of a trough before dunking their heads in to drink from
the foul water. Fellow St Valery prisoner Jim Charters – his mind
numbed by exhaustion – recalled pushing lilies from the surface of a
pond in order to get a drink. Ken Willats explained how important
water became during the long marches along dusty roads: 'Survival
is a very emotive feeling. The progression of need in extreme
circumstances is water, food, cigarettes, ladies – in that order.
Without being offensive to the ladies, they come a lot further
down the list than water.' This desperate desire to find something to
drink even led some prisoners to confront the guards. Jim Pearce
looked on, astounded as one group of prisoners surged towards a

well to pull up a bucket of water. When a guard intervened the frustrated prisoners simply pushed him down the well.

Despite this desperate thirst, some prisoners tried to discourage their mates from drinking stagnant water. Fred Coster was one of them. He had been fortunate enough to begin the march still carrying his emergency ration, which was soon consumed – 'After all,' as he pointed out 'this was an emergency.' Despite his exhaustion, Coster still remembered some of his training: 'After 20 or 30kms we'd reach a village with a water butt. After that distance we were all terribly thirsty and the boys would rush to the water butts. I tried to stop them because of my medical training. I told them they'd all get dire diseases. They didn't listen. But of course they didn't suffer anything and I missed out because I didn't get a drink.'

For those who wouldn't drink stagnant water, the only relief came from the rain. It may have soaked their already weakened bodies, ran down and seeped into their boots, and softened the bare earth they would be sleeping on, but it brought relief to their throats. Marching men lifted their heads upwards, allowing the water to fill their mouths. They cupped their hand in front of their bodies and caught the falling rain, drinking it greedily from their filthy palms. Others dropped to the ground and lowered their faces into puddles, eager to drive away the dry taste of the dust that filled their mouths. Their throats relieved, the soldiers raised their soaking hands and rubbed their faces, washing away the grime acquired in days of marching. As the rain soaked their hair, they ran their fingers through it, rubbing the water into their sweat-stained scalps.

Among the marching men were some for whom food was more vital than water. Those nursing wounds needed to sustain themselves not just for marching but to ensure their wounds could recover. Without food, open wounds would take longer to heal. Cyril Holness, whose dressings – on wounds he thought would get him sent home – had been torn off by Germans who had appeared in the field dressing station, was one of those who had no choice but to find food wherever he could:

It was a tough old business, but you could still see the funny side sometimes. I was wearing a French jacket and trousers that I'd been given after leaving the aid post. As we went through Lille the women were raiding the pubs and cafes. We were calling out '*Du pain! Du pain!*' One woman came out with one of those long loaves, she undone my trousers and stuck the bread down my legs. They were telling us they'd rather we had it than the Germans get it. And there was a Scots bloke, he was as high as a kite – drunk on what they'd given him. Then these nuns – Sisters of Mercy – gave us socks and boots and cleaned our feet.

On the occasions that the local population were able to pass food to the prisoners their desperation was such that the prisoners often fought to guarantee a share for themselves. Bill Bampton, a soldier serving with the East Surrey Regiment, recorded how his mate received a package from a civilian: 'Suddenly he disappeared under the weight of other marchers all intent on having a part of the package. Charlie eventually reappeared, still clutching a handful of crumbs and a scrap of a paper bag.'[14]

For Jim Charters and his brother Jack, the assistance of one woman would bring far greater relief than they would realize for some time. Passing though one French village they handed over a hastily scribbled note to one of the women waiting by the roadside. On a page torn from a paybook, they had written their names and the address of their parents back in Ashington, County Durham. It was dangerous for the women to have any contact with the prisoners, indeed some men later recalled seeing civilians forced to join the marching columns for having dared to feed or talk to the prisoners. For Jim Charters, the bravery of such women helped revise his thoughts about their French hosts. As he watched them being pushed, kicked and hit with rifle-butts he could not but admire the fact that they still tried to assist the prisoners. As Norman Barnett remembered it: 'The Frenchwomen had guts – not like their menfolk!'

Of course, not all of the French civilians were charitable to the

British prisoners. Dick Taylor, marching away from St Valery, remembered: 'In some places French farmers stood there with shotguns to make sure their potato and turnip piles weren't pillaged.' The sight of farmers with shotguns was enough to deter even the most desperate of men. Yet in some cases opposition from the locals made little difference. Passing through a French village, Gordon Barber, who was no stranger to using his fists when necessary, found a butcher's shop: 'I had a few francs so I went in this little shop and saw this piece of meat hanging on a hook. I said "How much?" He said "No, no, no." So I slapped the coin on the counter, ripped the meat off the hook, right handed him – smacked him out of the way a bit sharpish – but he didn't go down. And I ran back into the crowd.'

The behaviour of the shotgun-wielding French farmers and defensive shopkeepers was a reflection of the relationship between many of the British prisoners and their French counterparts. There was certainly little love lost between the two factions. The efforts of the Germans to engender antagonism between the remnants of the defeated armies were helped by a mistrust that already existed among some of the troops. After a failed escape, Sergeant Stephen Houthakker was transported to Cambrai, where he was held amidst hordes of French colonial troops. When he later wrote of his experiences he did not bother to conceal his contempt: 'To my sorrow found myself thrown in with some of the most degraded and filthy men it has ever been my lot to meet. French Moroccans, Senegalese, Arabs, the scum of the world, members of the infamous Foreign Legion, tough men each and every one of them. Comforts of life and ordinary hygiene were as foreign to them as was fighting and honour.'[15] As a professional soldier schooled in the proudest traditions of the British Army, he could not reconcile military life with what he saw before him: 'In this hell I spent the two worst weeks of my existence. Lousy, hungry, depressed, but practising to the full the survival of the fittest theory.'[16]

Not all the British had such a low opinion of their allies. It was easy for both factions to blame each other – the British criticizing

French fighting abilities and the poor showing of the French High Command, the French cursing the British for heading back to the Channel coast and abandoning their allies to certain defeat. Yet some of the defeated armies were able to view the débâcle from a wider perspective. At St Valery John Christie joined a group of drunken Frenchmen. Christie was no more impressed with the Frenchmen than he was with the antics of some of the British, such as the officers who had changed into their best uniforms ready to surrender with honour. The Frenchmen offered him cognac, which he shared: 'I was duty bound to accept a swig to help maintain the very shaky entente cordiale. Don't get me wrong, I could see things from their side, it was one thing to fight and die for "*La Patrie*", quite another to die covering for us so that we could get off the hook.'[17]

Despite Christie's thoughtful assessment of the situation, there were very real reasons for the British prisoners to feel a genuine antipathy towards their allies. As the United Nations later reported: 'The fact that French prisoners of war, in much larger numbers, were comparatively well provided with food . . . tends to prove that the virtual starvation of British prisoners of war and the inadequate arrangements for their accommodation was deliberate.'[18]

It was an accurate assessment of the situation. Although there were genuine moments of kindness, such as when a German guard forced French soldiers to share their wine with British soldiers, most of the time the British faced appalling discrimination. Whilst the Germans kicked over buckets and beat back Frenchwomen attempting to feed the British, they allowed the French troops to accept gifts from the villagers. The story was replicated throughout the march. One group, who had begun their march in Calais, finished their first day's march in a stadium full of French and Belgian troops. They remained there for just one hour, then left again without being given any food. The following day, still unfed, they marched past their allies as they ate a meal of macaroni and army biscuits. It may have not been the most enticing of meals, but to the watching Britons it seemed like a feast – one to which they had not been invited. This became the pattern of treatment as experienced by the majority of marchers. The French received their rations first whilst the British were thrown the scraps.

The discrimination was noted by many among the columns. Eric Reeves was part of a group of around 5,000 British prisoners outnumbered three to one by French soldiers. Each night, as the column came to a halt, the Germans set up their horse-drawn field kitchen, allowing the famished marchers the comforting sight of its chimney smoking.

It was always soup, of a sort. Then they'd shout 'All of the English over here – Do not sit down. All of the French here. French first.' So the Froggies went off and filled their tins. Then the Germans would call us. The first blokes would get there and the lids would come down and the cooks would say 'All finished!' They did that every day. It was psychological warfare because eventually the boys started muscling in on the French and pinching their soup. So the Froggies hated us. The first bit of French I learned was '*Poussez pas*', Don't push – you'd hear them all shouting out when our blokes were going for their food.

Gordon Barber decided to take matters into his own hands: 'I saw the French getting issued dripping from these big vats. I had a French overcoat I'd pinched so I could go and get my share. As I came away with mine the French spotted my British jacket and I had to run for it. This Froggie went to grab it, he kicked my arm, so I nutted him hard. So I ran like bleedin' anything and got back to my mates.'

It was not only the humiliation of being fed from the French leftovers that made life increasingly unbearable for the British troops. Reginald Collins of the Gloucestershire Regiment re-corded the misery of being forced to march in a mixed column. The Frenchmen in the column were marched ahead of the British until a substantial gap had opened up. Then the Frenchmen were allowed to rest and the trailing British were made to run after them:

'To encourage us in this the German guards stood on both sides of the column swinging the butt ends of their rifles and sticks and clubs. This treatment lasted all day, the heat was intense and many prisoners fell at the side of the road from exhaustion. Those who fell were kicked until they regained their feet. For the whole of this day we had no water.'[19] This continued throughout the day with the British seldom allowed to rest, instead they were constantly marching or running.

In similar cases, British troops were made to run, then given a brief rest whilst marching French prisoners were allowed to catch up with them. Once the French had caught up, the British were forced to run again. One group recalled having to run to overtake French prisoners five times, all in the heat of the midday sun. Walter Kite, captured near Abbeville, later wrote of his experience of the march: 'On the march again at 0800 hours at the double. God what an experience – running uphill in the sweltering sun with the young German NCOs helping us along with their bayonets. A Tommy in front of me was bayoneted in the thigh and a Poilu killed just because he didn't hurry enough.'[20]

The antagonistic attitude of the guards heaped agony upon the misery of the marchers. As a government report later described it, the crimes inflicted upon British prisoners: 'seem to indicate systematic inhumanity directed against British prisoners of war'.[21] With no choice but to steal to stay alive, it was little wonder the prisoners came into conflict with their guards. Jim Reed, the Sheffield teenager who had been captured with the Seaforth Highlanders at St Valery, was prepared to take risks to ensure he was fed:

The Germans liked to show you who was the master. We had no food at all – we weren't given any food for about a week. So we scrounged food out of the shops. We just went in and grabbed stuff and ran out again. I saw one or two get shot. I got whipped by a German guard – he was riding by on a horse, keeping us in order. I had come out of a shop and he spotted me. He rode up and cracked me once or twice with his whip until I got into the crowd and got out of his way. But I kept hold of the food, I wasn't going to let go of that! It was us against them. I'd changed from a soldier into a thief.

Some paid a higher price than a whipping. On 16 June a private of the Cameron Highlanders was shot whilst attempting to reach a pile of sugar beet. Others in the same column watched as a soldier bent down to pull potatoes from the earth of a roadside field: 'Suddenly there was the sound of a shot and this man rolled over and did not move again.'[22]

In another incident a Scots soldier with wounded feet fell out of the column to rest, only to be shot and killed by a German NCO. One soldier captured at Calais recorded that he had witnessed the murder of six men who had fallen out of the column after collapsing. As one of those who had sufficient strength to keep a diary wrote of the march between Lille and the Belgian frontier: 'Treatment bad, stragglers being shot at.'[23] Another soldier later wrote of the German efforts to hurry the men at the back of his column: 'They consistently exhorted more speed and threatened us, finally shooting a few of the real stragglers. Thereafter, the speed of the column increased noticeably.'[24] Fred Coster remembered: 'Some would drop out and the Germans came along shouting "*Raus*". They told us the sick were being picked up by lorries. But we never saw any lorries. So we got the opinion they were being popped off.'

Having trudged wearily for mile upon mile, hardly able to distinguish one day from the next, David Mowatt had seen much in the week leading up to the capture of the 51st Division, but one act of savagery was to imprint itself in his memory:

We were going through this village and there was a Scots Guardsman in front of me. He was very tall, head and shoulders above me, still with his cap proudly on his head. He put his hand out to take some food from the villagers. Suddenly a guard struck out with his rifle butt and hit the man's hand. The Scots

Guardsman turned round and landed the finest right hook I've ever seen. It sent the guard flying, landing on the ground a couple of yards away. I said 'For God's sake get away! Take your hat off and change position! Get in another group.' He said 'No way' and carried on marching. About half an hour after the guard came up – he was right in front of me – he raised his rifle and shot the Scotsman through the chest. There was no hesitation. All because the man was too proud to take his hat off. It was terrible. You expect it of the SS, but this was just an ordinary Wehrmacht soldier. He just killed this man, it was a dreadful thing to do. The body was just left at the roadside . . . He was just left there and we all had to step over him. I don't know why he hadn't tried to hide. Maybe it showed his state of mind. Perhaps he'd reached the stage where he couldn't care less about living

Not all the marching men were witness to such acts of violence but all knew what was happening. Every day they would hear the gunfire as guards shot those attempting to escape. And every day men fell out from the columns never to be seen again. Eric Reeves recalled how the threat of violence was never far away:

I didn't see any executions, but I heard about it. We came to one place where the Germans shooed us all away. We heard that one of the guards had kicked a bucket of water over and a young Welsh Guardsman had given him a right-hander. So the guard shot him in the head. Another time, it was a beautiful day, and I was sitting on the side of a dry ditch. I was absolutely shattered. Then a guard came along. He shouted 'Get up!' and shouldered his rifle. Then a staff car drew up and this immaculate German officer got out and roared at him. The guard came to attention and then walked off. Then the officer threw three cigarettes at me and went off in his car.

Reeves was fortunate that the car had arrived just in time, allowing the officer to intervene and save him from one of the many acts of random violence that followed the marching columns.

The casual violence convinced most to keep their heads down and see the pointlessness of risking death for the sake a raw potato. One soldier recorded how the violence and deprivations had brought the British to a state of submission: 'A single shot fired over our heads brought instant attention from hundreds.'[25] It was an emotion reflected by Gordon Barber when he explained: 'You'd be surprised how resilient you are at that age. When you know that if you don't keep going you're going to die – they're going to fucking shoot you.'

In this situation it was little wonder few among the marching prisoners believed there was any point in attempting escape. In the early days of the march plenty had dived into the long grass at the roadside or dived into woodland. Most were soon recaptured and sent back to join the marchers. Others were shot and killed as they attempted to evade their guards. As the men grew weaker any thought of running away became unthinkable, it was strenuous enough to keep putting one foot in front of the other – hour upon hour – without contemplating the idea of dashing off to find cover. Growing increasingly weary, few were concerned about anything but their own survival. They also became increasingly cynical about the fate of those who took the chance, as Dick Taylor explained: 'I had no thoughts of escape, it was too dangerous. But if anybody else broke away you'd hear the shots. You'd just think to yourself "It isn't me." That was the attitude. One more dead man meant nothing, as long as it wasn't me. It was self-preservation – you're not bothered about anybody else. Heroes are dead people – it's better to live for your country than to die for it.'

There was a further concern. Most prisoners recognized how lucky they had been to survive the battle for France. They had seen their friends shot down or blown to pieces by high explosive. Why then take the risk of becoming another forgotten victim of war? Bill Bampton described the emotional pull against escaping: 'If it went wrong and we were killed, our parents would never know what had happened to us.'[26]

For so many of the marchers, it was a lonely existence. They were surrounded by thousands of men. All were sharing the same hideous experiences, all had known the horrors of battle and seen their friends slaughtered, yet they had no emotions to share. Instead each man became wrapped up in his own small world – a world that revolved around the desperate desire for food and rest.

Having witnessed the horror of a fellow prisoner being murdered just a couple of feet in front of him, and suffering the aching pains of hunger shared by every man on the march, David Mowatt began to feel the effects of all they were being forced to endure: 'I didn't have the strength to talk. We were all dragged right down. We were filthy – lousy. I can't describe the despair. It was terrible. The days just blurred into each other. We didn't know how far we were going to march – we were just going in circles.'

However, as he would soon discover, their ordeal was far from over.

CHAPTER NINE

The Journey Continues

Women came right up close to me and spat in my face.

Bill Holmes, captured on the Dunkirk
beaches, on his arrival in Germany

*I thought the war was over. We've had it. What's going to happen to
us?*

Jim Pearce, Middlesex Regiment,
captured at St Valery

As they approached the German border, the effects of the weeks of
marching took their toll on the physically and mentally exhausted
prisoners. They had been kicked, starved, beaten, humiliated and,
quite often, shot at by guards who seemed to have no regard for
their welfare. Quite simply, they had been treated worse than
animals – at least animals would have been allowed to graze each
evening. About to enter Germany, they would finally be engulfed
within a system that seemed hell bent upon their destruction.

The toil of the long marches – the aching muscles from days of
walking, the pain cause by sleeping on cold damp ground, the
empty bellies and shrinking waistlines, the blistered feet, the
calluses and carbuncles caused by equipment that rubbed – all
created a deep sense of despair for the prisoners. Unwashed, clad in

stinking, sweat-stained blouses that rubbed at their necks and heavy woollen trousers that scraped their crotches, leaving the skin red-raw, they marched onwards. Each step, that in their minds seemed to burst another blister and took their socks closer to disintegration, was an attack on their very humanity. When they found food they stuffed it into stubble-ringed mouths, through lips parched by thirst and burned by the sun. They looked at the hands that lifted the food to their mouths and could hardly recognize the filth-encrusted digits topped by nails deep in dirt. They cursed the sun that burned their skin, then in turn cursed the rain that soaked both them and the ground that was their bed. Each intake of breath brought the sickly sweet smell of the filth ingrained on their bodies. Then they endured the stench of what remained after they had been assaulted by the oppressive stomach cramps that signalled diarrhoea.

Less than two months before, Lord Gort, the commander of the BEF, had written: 'The morale of the troops is excellent and on that score I have no anxiety . . . the fears expressed in some quarters have proved groundless.'[1] Yet for the hordes of prisoners as they trudged towards Germany, such words were meaningless. The army may have retained its morale before war but, in the chaotic aftermath of defeat, the morale of those who had been sacrificed on the road to Dunkirk plummeted to a previously unknown level. It was no longer a case of whether Britain could survive, it was simply a case of whether they could survive as prisoners of the Germans.

The sense of defeat was compounded by the scenes they witnessed as they trudged towards Germany. Those with enough strength to moan cursed the army, the generals, the government – everyone – for their lack of preparedness. Others hardly dared think of what the defeat really meant. They feared for their wives – their lives – picturing them as the huddled corpses of refugees that had lined the roads of France during the retreat. They thought of the crying babies left orphan by bombing raids, of the bullet-riddled prams, then of their own families. They imagined stormtroopers kicking in their doors, sneering at their cowering parents, then laying down to rest in their beds. They pictured their streets in flames, their children as corpses – their world in ruins.

Yet if the hunger, thirst, exhaustion and violence were not enough to convince the prisoners of the German victory, there were other more subtle signals. One man, feigning sickness, found himself put onto a truck heading eastwards carrying a group of middle-aged German soldiers, all of whom displayed Great War medal ribbons on their tunics. As they headed home they were drinking looted French brandy whilst seated on rolls of stolen silks and soft furnishings. It was a sure sign of who were masters of the battlefield. Marchers were greeted by their guards informing them that England would be next and that, whilst they languished in captivity, their homes would soon be occupied by the victors of the battle for France. As if to add insult to injury, they also stressed that the German soldiers would soon be 'taking their girls out'.[2] As one group of marchers were told by a passing German officer: 'You go to Berlin – we go to London.'[3]

Each passing lorry seemed to contain at least one English-speaking humorist who wished to heap scorn upon the dejected British soldiers. Eric Reeves listened to their depressing comments: 'A cocky bloke would hang out and shout "Ja. You are going to 'Hang out your washing on the Siegfried Line' Yes, Tommy." So we hated that song! But it was depressing. There was silence on that march – you didn't think about anything.' The situation was even worse for the Londoners amongst them who had to endure boasts that the Luftwaffe was already flattening the English capital.

When reports reached London of the deliberate mistreatment, the British government soon recognized the criminality of what they had endured. The War Office was certain that charges would be bought against the German High Command for their deliberate discrimination against the British soldiers. How, they reasoned, could the Germans find food for the vast numbers of French prisoners yet fail to find anything for the relatively small numbers of British? It was not just the senior German officers whose behaviour

was condemned, those officers and men who had been in direct
charge of the columns were recognized as contributing to the
misery of the marching hordes. As one British report acknowl-
edged: 'The actions of officers and men in immediate charge of
prisoners of war was such that no pleas of superior orders, if
pleaded, could be admitted to relieve them of responsibility.'[4]
Effectively, the entire German military machine was responsible for
what had occurred: 'Blame must be apportioned between all ranks,
from the officer in supreme direction of arrangements regarding
prisoners of war downwards.' Furthermore: 'The mass ill-treatment
of prisoners of war would be seen to be a matter of policy or system
which would be laid down by the High Command.'[5]

 Yet, for the men about to enter Germany, as prisoners of a
regime that had already inflicted so much agony upon them,
thoughts of war crimes and any legal framework for punishing
their tormenters, were far from their minds. Instead, their thoughts
were full of more basic needs – food, water and rest. As RAMC
medic Graham King – who under the rules of war should have
been attending to the sick and wounded rather than trudging
country lanes – put it, they were 'hot, sweaty, exhausted, starving
men, struggling to stay alive and hold on to sanity if not hope.'

 As the march progressed, every single soldier grew increasingly
weak, both physically and mentally. The combined effect of their
defeat and the obvious disarray in the Allied armies was a potent
brew that delivered a blow to their morale. Though many among
the marching columns did their best to maintain morale the simple
truth was that most considered it to be the worst period of their
lives. Like many, Bill Homes, who had been so close to getting
away – beginning the march with the sand of Dunkirk still in his
boots – was struck by the enforced state of uncertainty: 'It took six
weeks for me to get to the POW camp. We were exhausted and
we never knew what was going to happen to us. I was full of
thoughts. I was wondering if I would ever get out of it. But the one
thing that helped was that I was still with some of my mates. So at
least we had a sense of togetherness. That made a lot of difference.'

The minds of others were engulfed in similar emotions. Bob Davies was among them:

> I don't really know what I was feeling. In the back of my mind was the thought that my mum and dad didn't know where I was. I was just one of thousands walking to Germany. I thought the war was lost. The Jerries made it clear to us that we were beaten – you didn't need to understand German to know what they were saying! What was to stop them getting over the channel? I was just thinking 'what's going to happen now?' But I don't think any of us realised we were going to be there for five years.

Back in January, when Ken Willats left home to report for training, he had hardly even imagined himself as a soldier, let alone dared to think he might end up as a prisoner. Yet as he marched, day after day after day, he realized he had to adapt to his new existence:

> It was survival of the fittest. The human body and the human being tend to adjust to the conditions that exist. Self-preservation was the predominant thought. One just thinks of oneself. Everything was new and unknown so we didn't really know if the war was over – or if it was just beginning. It was a strange time for us all. My feelings were dulled by the extreme physical conditions. To be honest with you, the morale was defeatist. There wasn't too much anger against the Germans – only when they kicked the buckets of water over. I think we all thought we'd been unlucky. Let's face it, we weren't trained soldiers, we were just there because we had to be. So we just thought it was hard luck.

Willats's memories of the final stages of the march reflected the feelings of so many. They had reached the end of their physical and mental tether, they were exhausted, filthy and starving. More importantly, they were facing something none had been prepared for:

It was the lowest point of the war. It was not so much physical as mental. It was my most desperate time. I didn't know what was in front of me. There was apprehension about what was going to happen to us. I can remember walking along in the pouring rain and a huge May Fly hit me right in the middle of the forehead. I didn't have the strength or the inclination even to raise my hand to wipe it off. I just trudged on with this bug on my face. So I must have been in a pretty low state. I didn't have much left. It was particularly bad for the regular soldiers. It hit them hard. I had the advantage of not being too patriotic. You hear stories about prisoners of war marching along in step – we didn't. We just meandered along feeling in the depths of despair. We didn't even talk to each other. We just struggled on. There was no enthusiastic – or patriotic – conversation with anybody.

Drained by almost three weeks of incessant marching, Eric Reeves began to reach a stage where it seemed he and his comrades were detached from the rest of the world:

We didn't know where we were going. It seemed it was all over. When you've blokes there who were captured at Calais and they said they'd been at the coast and not got away – we thought Britain had lost the war. We didn't know anything about Dunkirk, no one had heard of it. So we thought the war was finished. It was completely dispiriting. And the Germans loved to tell us we would never get home. They said we would have to stay in Germany and work for them forever.

As the marches progressed and more men began to join the columns, including those who knew about the Dunkirk evacuation, the situation began to seem even more desperate. Those men who had believed the initial defeats were merely a set-back were appalled to hear that the army had fled from France. For Les Allan, marching into Germany surrounded by starving men, all with 'the shits', their uniforms increasingly filthy, the realization of how serious the defeat had been was a blow. This was the lowest point, his morale was shattered, how could they ever recover?

Fred Coster shared these feelings. He was convinced the war was over and that Britain had been defeated. Yet, whilst he admitted it to himself, there was one group he wouldn't share his thoughts with: 'We didn't admit it to the Germans. If they approached us and said the war was over we laughed at them. But inside we thought Britain can't stand this. We were done for.'

Uncertain of what lay ahead, the vast marching columns began to converge on Germany. The routes they took were many and varied. The earliest prisoners, those captured before and during the Dunkirk evacuation, were directed to the Rhineland city of Trier from which they were entrained for stalags across the rapidly expanding Reich. Some marched all the way from northern France, passing through Belgium and Luxembourg, growing ever more exhausted with each footfall. Others were put on trains at Cambrai and Bastogne, completing their journey by rail. The men who went into captivity in the latter stages, including the 8,000 or so men of the 51st Highland Division took a more northerly route. Some were sent to the River Scheldt, from where they travelled by barge to Germany. Others travelled straight through Belgium to Maastricht in the Netherlands. There they too were put on barges to take a trip down the Rhine to Dortmund.

Those who entrained at Cambrai had to listen to the singing of German troops waiting for trains to the front. Laughing and jeering at the prisoners, they mockingly called out the words of 'Pack up your troubles in your old kit bag'. The irony was not lost on the prisoners, all of whom had troubles but most of whom had abandoned their kitbags in the fields and rubble of France. One group of officers, who had been separated from their men, were among those who joined the train at Cambrai. A group of sixty-five of them were crammed into a single cattle-wagon, the floor an inch deep in coal dust. When they complained about overcrowding, six of the men were allowed to leave. For the fifty-nine men remaining, the journey lasted for two days.

Other officers passed straight through Cambrai, staying overnight in a shed where the latrine seemed to have been used by all the thousands of prisoners passing through the town. The next day they were taken by truck to a barbed wire enclosure in a field beside a river. The dandelions that grew in the field made a welcome meal for the tired and hungry officers. It was not a restful night. All night they had to listen to the sound of their guards firing at the crowds of Senegalese troops sharing the field. The next day they found some relief, stopping for the night in the garden of an inn. Able to trade with Belgian civilians, they furnished themselves with soap, towels and toothbrushes as well as desperately needed food. It was not just the food that helped lift their morale. The Belgians helped raise their spirits by telling them that the British always lost the first battle but then won the one that really mattered – the last one. Then they laughed and said they would prefer that the British didn't always lose the first battle in Belgium.

This group of officers were lucky. Washed and fed, they were then transported by cattle-wagons to Trier, where they moved into a POW camp. They were made to travel with only forty-five men per wagon. It was far removed from the overcrowding most of the prisoners would experience when they left Trier.

The experiences of the prisoners in Trier differed from group to group. Some were marched directly through the city to the railway station, then sent on their way further into Germany. Arriving in Trier on 3 June, whilst the Dunkirk evacuation was still underway, the officers settled down to a dull routine of starvation rations in which weak vegetable soup was the most exciting food on offer. It would be another four days before the other ranks from their unit, who had not been travelling by truck and train, caught up with their officers and marched into the stalag. In that time they discovered the Germans were continuing to discriminate against the British, making them wait until last to be allocated bunks.

As the other ranks finally approached the stalag they passed vineyards whose workers paused to watch the dishevelled hordes using up the last of their energy to trudge uphill. Still their torment continued, as *hausfraus* leaned from windows to hurl abuse at the prisoners. One group were even serenaded into the camp by a German band that appeared to be playing for the pleasure of assembled German officers who were eager to enjoy the spectacle of the ragged rabble marching into captivity.

Within the stalag the prisoners were appalled by the conditions. The failing health of the marching men resulted in those with stomach upsets having used the grounds as a toilet, fouling the earth if they were too weak to reach the latrines. One of the men who was at first shocked as he entered the camp, soon found himself adding to the mess. It earned him a beating from a guard but, he reasoned, it was better to risk a beating than to foul his trousers. The paper used in the latrines seemed to be blowing all around the camp and the latrine walls were stained where those without paper had wiped themselves with their hands, then wiped their hands on the walls.

The issue of hygiene, though long forgotten during the march, once more became a concern. The filthy prisoners were desperate to wash themselves and welcomed the fact that showers were available to them. One soldier entering the shower block was amazed to see mirrors on the walls. It was a shock finally to catch a glimpse of an unrecognizable figure, with wild matted hair, a bearded chin and skinny body. That was not his only shock of the day. A fellow prisoner informed him he would need to keep watch on his uniform whilst he showered. He was astounded – surely no one would steal the wretched remnants of his uniform? He was wrong, it seemed the men within the camp would pinch every-thing and anything that was left unguarded.

And so began their introduction to life as prisoners of war. Just as on the march, food continued to be a problem for the prisoners. Arriving in Trier in the evening, with the rain pouring down, Ken Willats' column was marched to the stalag, where the word went round that food would be available: 'They said there would be soup for anyone who had a container. I still had my helmet so I joined this long, long queue. We stood there in the rain for hours. Eventually I reached the front where there was a hatch they were serving from. I put my helmet up to the hatch but he just said "Finished" and slammed the hatch shut. So I never did get any soup.'

Not all the groups of prisoners were given the opportunity to rest when they arrived at Trier. Instead of being marched into the stalag, they were sent straight through the city centre to the railway yards where they were soon loaded onto cattle-wagons to continue their journey. For many, passing through Trier was one of the lowest points of their entire experience as prisoners of war. For most this was their first time in a German city and their first opportunity to acquaint themselves with the people of a nation that would be their home for five years. It was an inauspicious start. This was one of Europe's great cities. It had some of the best Roman remains to be seen anywhere – an almost completely intact gladiatorial arena, a magnificent bath complex and the imposing Porta Negra. This enormous arch had once marked the very edge of Roman civilization. It was the gateway to the Roman Empire through which slaves had been transported westwards, destined for the slave markets of Rome. Now the journey had been reversed and a new horde of slaves made their way into the latest of Europe's empires.

Eric Reeves was among a group who reached Trier on 9 June – before the 51st Division had even surrendered. The journey from Abbeville had exhausted Reeves, bringing him to the point at which he cared little about what was going to happen to him:

We marched straight through the town. I can always remember going through the arch. It was a Sunday and all the women were in their best clothes – they had hats with flowers in them. We thought they were going to church. But as we marched through they were spitting and shouting things at us. It was degrading but you couldn't feel angry – you were like an outcast. We hadn't got a clue what they were shouting but the spitting was enough for us! It was a low point. But we'd reached the point where we didn't care — all we were interested in was food. You had to remember that at that stage nothing else mattered — no one ever talked about anything else. We'd forgotten about sex, all we concentrated on was food.

Too desperate to care about the hail of spittle and the venom directed at them by the Germans, Reeves and his fellow prisoners passed straight through the city:

> It was the end for us. We'd been through so much. But I'm sure the only thing that kept us going was that we weren't alone. There were about five thousand of us and we were all in the same boat. So you find the strength from somewhere to keep going. Also the biggest fear you have is of appearing afraid. You did everything you could to appear brave — you might have been dying inside but you never moaned or let them know. We kept silent. We were unwashed and unshaven — I hadn't got any shaving kit anyway. They marched us to a coal yard in a railway siding and that was where we lay for the night.

The celebrations indulged in by the local population as Reeves and his comrades entered the city were not an isolated incident. The prisoners' memories were centred around the physical and verbal torment they suffered. The final days of the march may all have blurred into one another but the experience of reaching Trier remained etched in their minds. The vast, swaying swastika banners, festooned above the baying crowds as they celebrated the subjugation of these remnants of the British and French Armies, all served to heighten their dejection.

It was as if everything had been designed to humiliate the prisoners. Old women spat at them, youths raised their arms in Nazi salutes and mocked the pitiful wrecks that shuffled through the city. Even the stark contrast between the Sunday best worn by the civilians and the filthy attire of the prisoners just served to deepen their misery. As Len Allan trudged through the streets on his way to the railway station, these scenes made a distinct impression upon him:

> The reception from the civilians was horrendous. The British never kick a man when he's down but they were the opposite. We were being humiliated. It was the period of the march that I shall never forgive them for. They were mostly women and children. You don't expect it from them. They were enjoying their victory. They were on Cloud Nine. But funnily enough, I never lost faith that we would win in the end. That was the one thing that kept us going. We said 'Keep smiling lads – one day we'll get our own back.' And it was worth it in the end.

Also arriving from Abbeville was Ken Willats, who was struck by the scenes: 'The reaction was awful. They were lining the pavements, spitting and swearing. We were presented as hostages of their success. It was a total picture of the Nazi regime. There were big flags hanging across the road. The civilians were at the very top of their enthusiasm – venting their hatred of us. They were jeering as if they had been whipped up. We were despairing.'

After just one night's rest, Graham King and his exhausted comrades were raised from their slumbers and marched downhill into the city of Trier. Once again they were given no food and sent on their way with empty bellies. The reception they received as they headed for the railway station was the same as that given to the others who had been greeted by earlier crowds: 'In spite of the early hour, the good German citizens of Trier were lining the streets to welcome us with stones, insults, manure, ordure, eggs (rotten) and anything else that could do us harm, the more serious the better.'

In the last days of June – almost a month after the completion of the Dunkirk evacuation and weeks after the first prisoners had passed through Trier – some of the 8,000 prisoners who had marched from St Valery arrived in the Belgian town of Lokeren. At Lokeren they were relieved to find themselves transported in small, open wagons on a narrow-gauge railway, packed thirty men per wagon. The train moved so slowly that civilians were able to approach and openly hand them food. Gordon Barber recalled being thrown a sweet cake that resembled cold Christmas pudding. In these wagons they crossed into the Netherlands.

When they arrived at their destination they were herded towards a coal barge. After an issue of bread, its surface dry and lined with mouldy cracks, they were crammed on board in conditions that would become familiar to so many of their comrades. Tommy Arnott watched as one group refused to enter the darkness of the hold: 'So the Germans turned their fire hoses on them. When the water and dust subsided they came out like the proverbial "niggers" – I shouldn't be using that word nowadays but it was ok then – and it fitted the description.'[6] Those remaining on deck blessed their good fortune. Those forced into the holds were trapped below in the darkness, since the ladders had been removed to prevent their escape.

Memories of these latter stages of the journey tend to be sketchy. Even those who had faithfully recorded the towns they passed through could do nothing once locked inside the holds of filthy coal barges. The journeys by narrow-gauge railway went from either Moerbeck or Lokeren, taking the prisoners to Terneuzen or Walsoorden, both on the River Scheldt. From there they travelled upriver, then through canals to reach the Rhine.

On the seventeenth day of their march, some of the men captured at St Valery eventually reached the Dutch town of Maastricht. Here they were allowed to receive food from the local branch of the Red Cross. What they received was like manna from heaven. Each man ate as much as he could, desperate to recover a little of the strength he had exhausted in the weeks before.

One of the groups greeted by the Dutch Red Cross reported that the half-inch thick slice of bread they received was all they had to sustain them on a five-day journey by barge. For the whole of the journey the prisoners, who were so tightly packed they were unable to sit down, were not given any water. Just as on the march, this group noted how the Germans had fed the French prisoners. This led to inevitable friction between the two factions since the British prisoners locked in the holds began to faint due to thirst and hunger.

At Walsoorden on the Scheldt, a group of 1,000 prisoners, including 300 British officers, were marched onto the Dutch paddle steamer SS *Konigin Emma* to complete their journey into Germany. Once they were all on board there was hardly any room to sit down. Both the holds and the unventilated decks were crammed with men. There was no food available for them except for an issue of mouldy bread. From the Scheldt they steamed through canals, then into the River Waal, through Nijmegen, then joined the Rhine before disembarking at Hemer forty hours later. The British officers were moved in groups of between twenty and forty men to a building where the rooms gave just enough space for each man to lie down on the straw-covered floor. For five days they shared the basic toilet facilities with a group of French colonial troops. After that ordeal was over they were sent, without rations, on a thirty-four-hour train journey to the stalag that would become their home.

Another group of 1,000 prisoners that travelled by river spent forty-eight hours in a coal barge travelling between Lokeren and Emmerich. Once again the British were sent in the company of French colonial troops. United Nations war crimes reports later stated that the racial mixing of the British troops with the French Africans was a deliberate attempt to humiliate them. Jim Pearce was one of the prisoners who travelled on a barge that had already been used for transporting men into Germany: 'It was shocking. The French Moroccans had been on it before us, they'd been to the toilet everywhere. It was filthy. It was awful. Then we got the fleas and lice.' Gordon Barber, his spirits lifted slightly by the help received from local civilians, found the next stage of the journey returned him once more to a state of extreme discomfort: 'They loaded us into the hold of this barge. That wasn't a pretty sight 'cause most of us got diarrhoea.'

Jim Charters recalled the toilet facilities being no more than a pole on the edge of the barge: 'By this time some of us were so weak that several of the men fell off the pole into the canal and had to be fished out.' As the boats sailed past watching civilians, they had to drop their trousers, hold on the edge of the boat and do their best to hang on as they emptied their bowels. Cyril Holness remembered his journey from the Netherlands on an old coal barge: 'This was when I started to feel really lousy. They degraded us. You just hung over the side of the barge, whilst people were walking past on the towpath. It was disgusting. We were all in a right state. That was my worst time.'

Fred Gilbert, still nursing the wounds that were wrapped in increasingly filthy bandages, remembered the cramped conditions:

They'd certainly forgotten how many people were supposed to go on a barge! There was room for everybody on the barge. A few people even found room to sit down – they were lucky. If you got space to lay down you were extremely lucky. I had my two feet of space and squatted there. You couldn't leave that space because someone would take it. Then you'd be stuck standing up. After a while I ambled about a bit and went down below decks. Two lads – silly things – got up from under a ladder. So I got their space and sat in that. They came back and saw me sitting there. They said a few things – I expect they wanted it back. But I wasn't moving. So I stayed and slept there.

Although the exhaustion of the march had been relieved by the chance to sit down and rest, the question of food was still foremost in the thoughts of the prisoners. Dick Taylor and his mate Stuart Brown realized it was vital to keep their strength up at all costs: 'We were down below. It was horrible – pretty rough. But you put up with it and make the best of things. We got an issue of raw potatoes and some of the lads started to peel theirs. I said to Stuart "Let's collect all the peelings" because I knew that later on we'd get nothing. So as they threw them away we got them and kept them.

It was astute because it meant we still had something to eat. It makes the difference between keeping on or going under.' Fortunate enough to be travelling on the upper decks, Fred Coster was able to make contact with the crew of his boat: 'We were lucky to be on a ferry. The captain was Dutch. I had an army watch with a luminous face. I heard he was flogging food so I went up to him and said "What will you give me for this watch?" He said one loaf of bread. I said "What about two?" He agreed so I said "What about three?" But he wouldn't budge. So I got these two loaves and took them downstairs and shared them with my two mates. That was our first food for ages.'

As the barges and ferries made their way through the waterways of Belgium and Germany, the prisoners celebrated these issues of food, however meagre. Dry bread was better than no bread – scraps were better than nothing – and just to be able to sit down as they ate, rather than devour raw root vegetables as they walked, was blissful. Fred Gilbert remembered the two 'meals' he enjoyed on the Rhine trip: 'We got bread with cheese and even butter. They were tiny pieces but because, we'd had nothing the day before, that was a jolly good meal! The second day we got the bread and butter, but no cheese. That was the daily ration. But it was food – hooray!'

As they travelled by boat many of the desperate prisoners began to notice some new companions had joined them. At first they scratched at their filthy bodies and thought it was just a reaction to being so pitifully filthy. Then they started to notice movement in each other's hair. They had lice. This was a new experience, some had known head lice as schoolchildren but it was nothing compared to the invasion of lice that arrived as prisoners of war. Leslie Shorrock, taken prisoner in a hospital beside the Dunkirk beaches, wrote of the lice: 'We were now in the grip of a savage tormenter, for we were all thoroughly lousy. Lice live and breed on the body, biting and drawing blood, invading every part especially those covered in hair. We constantly scratched and scratched, but these lice concealed themselves in seams of uniforms . . . it would take us almost a year to fully rid ourselves of these vermin.'[7]

For some, the arrival at their first proper stop in Germany was marked by an ominous greeting – the town's air raid sirens were wailing, and they watched as RAF planes flew overhead and the local population scattered. It served as a warning that as prisoners within Germany they would have to contend both with the violence of their guards and the attentions of the Allied air forces. In time it would become a terrifying combination.

Disembarking from the barges into Germany, many of the veterans of St Valery faced the same treatment that their comrades had faced in Trier. Some recalled how groups of Hitler Youth arrived to goad and beat them. Arriving in Dortmund, where they were sent to a sports stadium, one group recalled the 'devilish torture'[8] by guards who seemed to enjoy every chance to humiliate them. Leslie Shorrock wrote of his first experience of being greeted by German civilians: 'As we approached a village the inhabitants were all lined up ready to receive us, nearly all old men, young and old women and detestable children. As we passed this unhappy crowd they hissed and spat upon us, tried to kick us, unrestrained in their affectionate welcome by the sadistic guards.'[9] As Bill Holmes later admitted, he simply resigned himself to being abused and spat at by civilians. Others were less accepting of the fate. Ronald Holme, of the East Surrey Regiment, recalled the abuse heaped on him by Brownshirts when he disembarked from the barge in Wesel: 'As our morale got lower our hate for the Germans became more intense.'[10] This was a common experience. Jim Charters, who received the same treatment when his barge reached Germany, wrote: 'I would like to have been there in 1944 when the Yankees arrived. I'd like to know if they were trying to kick them!'

One of the groups disembarked from the barges at Emmerich found themselves spat at, washed down with buckets water thrown by locals, and immediately sent on a sixty-mile (100-kilometre) march to Dortmund. The prisoners could hear church bells ringing in the distance and realized it must be Sunday morning. As they marched Tommy Arnott had a stroke of fortune:

As our straggly line of POWs hiked on, we came to a field in which an elderly German lady stood, holding a basket of rye bread. She must have been terrified at the sight of this horrible lot approaching, so she fled as fast as she could, dropping the bread. Now, hunger is a terrible thing. It becomes the survival of the fittest and you do things you never imagined you would. We were starving – there was a basket of bread – so Ned and I ran over and grabbed a loaf. Other POWs were starving as well and they weren't going to stand by and watch us eat it. I was knocked down in the rush and had my loaf grabbed out of my hand. By now the German guards were getting worried and fired over our heads to bring us back into line.[11]

At the sports stadium in Dortmund the prisoners discovered there were groups of wounded British officers who had been transported from France without ever having received treatment. Some were allowed inside the stadium whilst others remained in a field surrounded by barbed wire. The misery of the scene was enhanced by the piles of steel helmets that had been left on the ground outside the fence. French, Belgian and British helmets had been abandoned there since the guards had decreed they were no longer to be worn by the prisoners. As the already dejected prisoners watched, a guard marched around the fence, casually sticking his bayonet into helmet after helmet, piercing them with a deliberate action as if to underline the magnitude of the German victory. Then he reached one particular British helmet. At the first thrust his blade simply slid off the helmet. He tried again and again, until with one almighty thrust steel met steel and his bayonet snapped in two. A great cheer came up from the watching crowds. It was as if this simple act had helped instil some small glimmer of hope for their future.

Following their arrival in the Third Reich, no one bothered to tell the prisoners where they were. All they could do was try to decipher the names they saw on signposts. And nobody told them where they were going.

The final stages of the prisoners' journeys were by rail, crammed again into cattle-trucks, usually with the stencilled words '40 men – 8 horses' on the sides. In place of windows there was a slit running around the top of the wagon that allowed a little daylight to creep in and some air to circulate. Graham King later made light of what was a quite awful experience: 'No horses were travelling on that occasion, so we travelled 80 to a truck.' As many would later recount, in modern Europe there would be angry blockades and boisterous protests if sheep were to be transported in such cramped conditions.

As the first men entered the wagons they had little idea of what lay ahead. Many had already travelled by rail, although on those occasions the army had been careful about how many men were allowed in each truck. Furthermore they had often travelled with the doors open, allowing air to enter as they moved through the French countryside. This was different. When Bob Davies described the experience as 'pretty grim' he was downplaying the reality of what he and his comrades endured. The Germans made no attempt to count how many were going into each wagon. Men who had slumped down onto the floor found themselves trampled on as the space got increasingly crowded and the doors were slammed shut and bolts drawn across to trap them inside. Eric Reeves recalled the experience: 'They kept pushing us in – and pushing us in – you hear various numbers for how many were crammed in, but no one was really counting. All I know is that once we got in, we sat down with our knees up against our chins. Now, if you had to stand up because you'd got cramp, you didn't sit down for a long time – because everybody else had moved to fill your space.'

Within minutes of the doors being bolted, the interior of the wagons became hellish. In the heat of summer it did not take long for the crowded men to feel the temperature rising. It was not too oppressive whilst the trains were moving but as soon as they came to a stop the prisoners began to suffer. Those strong enough to move through the stuffy crowds to gasp with relief beside the vents did so.

Almost as soon as the men crowded into the wagons and jostled for space a new and important question arose – where would they go to the toilet? As Ernie Grainger remembered: 'On the cattle trucks it was a bad time. At least on the barges there was a plank hanging over the rear!' A few discovered a bucket had been put in with them, but most had nothing. Pages were torn from books, bibles and paybooks and used in place of toilet paper. Some tore the pockets from their battledress and defecated into them. Others used their caps. Some even took their boots off, urinated into them, then poured the urine out of the air vents, which was why Gordon Barber had no intention of getting too close to them: 'Heaven forbid if you sat near them. 'Cause if anybody had gone to the toilet they'd throw it out. So if you were near you'd get backdraught and the wind would blow some of it back in.'

Jim Pearce recalled his experiences: 'We were stuck on there – we had to try to pour it out of the window. If not you just went down the side of the truck. Everyone got stomach upsets. We just sat in silence. Everybody was absolutely fed up with life. They didn't care if they lived or died. You thought "If I'm going to die, I'm going to die." I thought my life was finished and that was it. That's how it looked.'

Ironically, Fred Coster, who had earlier warned his comrades about the dangers of drinking dirty water, was not immune to the effects of the deprivations:

There was only standing room and we were in there for about five days – with no food! It was there that I had a bout of diarrhoea. I thought 'Oh God, what do I do now?' You still had a bit of dignity and self-respect. I said to the boys 'Sorry but I've got to do.' So they made a space for me in the corner. I did what I had to do, then threw it out through the window in a handkerchief. It happened two or three times and I felt awful about it. But then it started to happen to the others so I didn't feel so bad. But it was degrading. It was horrible, I can't really describe it. The conditions were inhuman. The Germans were a different breed. They really felt they were the masters of the world. They were the master race and anyone who disagreed with them was to be wiped out.

As the journeys progressed conditions deteriorated. Not all the sick did recover, as Bill Holmes discovered: 'We were on there for three days. We had nothing to eat. Two of our lads died during the journey. We just had to tie up the bodies as best we could. They stayed in the train with us until we reached the POW camp.'

On the first day of his journey, Eric Reeves watched as the doors slid open: 'They pushed in a bucket of water and about three of their big loaves. Well, if you weren't near the door, you didn't get anything. Because you couldn't get over there – too many people were in your way.' Despite being too far from the doors to get any food, there was a positive side to the experience – even if it did mean continuing starvation: 'Through eating this rubbish all the way, these blokes all got diarrhoea.'

Still without food, Graham King and his fellow prisoners found themselves at halt in the German countryside:

Sunday morning and the train stopped about a mile from a country village. In the distance could be heard the tolling of a church bell and we could see the religious people of the Fatherland going to church in their finery, especially those who had minor roles in the administration of the Third and Greater Reich. None spoke to us nor jeered, just looked at us as if we were a new species arriving at the local zoo. Consequently I avoid zoos. To be shut up and stared at by strangers is not pleasant and I wonder if the zoo animals feel as we did.

Their next stop was an altogether more pleasant experience, albeit with unfortunate consequences:

The train moved off and slowly chugged through the outskirts of a big city and eventually pulled into the *hauptbahnhof* of Berlin where the German Red Cross was much in evidence, as were the uniformed civil servants, newsreel crews, shouting officers and grinning master race members. We didn't give a damn. The Red Cross was dishing out extremely thick, hot pea soup, hunks of fresh white bread and lovely, cold water. It didn't last long and we were soon on our way again. The dysentery sufferers, having ignored all advice, had eaten as starving people will and were suffering again and the stench was unbearable – but bear it one must.

As the hours – then days – passed, the POWs became increasingly frustrated. Every yard they travelled jolted them, they felt every vibration as the rails passed endlessly beneath the wheels. Seated on the bare boards, with their knees drawn up to their chest, their bodies became numb both from the constant shuddering of the trains and the cramped conditions within. Every movement of the man leaning against them was irritating, as if it was a personal attack on their space.

Gordon Barber, who considered himself both a survivor and well prepared for the harsh life of a prisoner, finally found it pushed him to the brink of mental tolerance: 'That was the only time I can remember despairing. I fell asleep back to back with another bloke. All you could hear was "boomty-boom, boompty-boom" – for three days! I though it was going to drive me mad. You just had to think, it has to finish. We've got to end up somewhere!'

He was right. Their journeys did eventually have to come to an end. As the trains drew to their final halt, the prisoners were completely unaware of where they might be. Some had seen the names of passing stations as they rolled through towns and villages but the names were meaningless. The small towns and villages of Germany, Poland and East Prussia meant nothing to men whose horizons had been so limited back in civvy street.

As the wagon doors were finally unbolted, the men inside prepared themselves for the next stage of their ordeal. First the light hit them, cutting through the gloom, hurting the eyes of those who had sat in the dimly lit wagons for days on end. One prisoner described them as appearing like cavemen, who would climb nervously from the dark depths of the train, inching into the light with dark-rimmed eyes and wild hair. As their eyes adjusted, Bill Holmes and his companions had one important job to do, unload the corpses of the two men who had died during the journey.

Next came the strain of standing up and jumping – or rather lowering – themselves from the wagons. The men who had fought to guarantee the escape of their comrades from the beaches of Dunkirk were transformed into a ragged army of slaves, stinking and starving, defeated and desperate as they dropped down from the filth-filled railway carriages onto the firm ground of the eastern regions of the Reich.

Arriving at the station outside Stalag 20A, Fred Coster recalled the doors finally opening to allow them out: 'They shouted "*Raus! Raus!*" As we jumped out we all just flopped to the ground. Then we dragged ourselves up to walk into the camp. For me, as I was walking along, it didn't feel like it was me walking – it was as if my spirit was pulling me along.'

One group dismounted from their train only to be greeted by the sound of a loudspeaker broadcasting to the local population. It announced that these were the men who had laid down their arms and refused to fight for Churchill. It was crude propaganda, meaning little to the starving men it was supposed to humiliate. Quite simply, such ludicrous boasts meant nothing to the prisoners. Nothing filled their heads more than the distant hope of filling their bellies. Not the war – not Churchill – not the fall of France. Food and water – even just a mouthful – became the hope and dream of every man who journeyed to the stalags that summer. As Jim Pearce remembered: 'We were all in a terrible state, and it was in this state that we were put into the POW camp.'

CHAPTER TEN

The First Year

Totally exhausted. Starving. Filthy. Covered in lice.

Jim Reed, Seaforth Highlanders,
on life in a POW camp in 1940

All across the Reich the men of the BEF shuffled into captivity. At
some stalags the trains carrying the wretched prisoners pulled up
directly outside the gates. Other prisoners stumbled out of the
trains into fields, then marched towards the barbed wire fences and
watchtowers. Elsewhere, the already weakened men were forced
to march for miles. At Danzig some of the survivors of the
surrender at St Valery dismounted from their cattle-wagons, then
were marched through the city ready for the next stage of the
journey to a POW camp. Gordon Barber remembered the scene:
'There were young Jerry soldiers in the streets flicking their fag ends
to our blokes and some of our blokes were grabbing them. The
Jerries were laughing. Some of them flicked the fags then trod on
them when our blokes went to grab them. I said to my mate "The
bastards, I won't pick 'em up. I'll never let them see they've got the
upper hand." And we were both smokers!'

Just to see a real live city with its crowded streets seemed bizarre.
The bedraggled prisoners shuffled along the cobbled streets like a
dirty brown stain. The neat streets and shops – horses and carts,

trams and buses, people going about their daily business – all were a symbol of a respectable world, one to which the prisoners no longer belonged.

The men on display in the streets of Danzig were representative of the thousands making their way into captivity. Their bodies stank of dried sweat, urine and shit. The wounded also gave off the foetid stench of dried blood and pus. Their filthy clothes hung from their bodies. Soldiers hitched up their trousers, pulling their belts ever tighter around their shrunken waists. Those without belts searched for lengths of string. On the prisoners' buttocks there was no sign of the firm muscles that had been honed on parade grounds and route marches back in Britain. Instead the flesh hung loose and limp where fat and muscle had vanished as their desperate bodies had used up all their reserves of fat to generate the energy to keep them shuffling along.

The Germans were ill-prepared to cope with the size of the influx. The lack of provisions for their journey had seemed like a vicious introduction to life as a prisoner of war. Yet the conditions they faced once within the camps revealed to them that this was to be the limit of their existence for the foreseeable future.

At Schubin, Stalag XXIB was little more than a farmhouse, farmyard and some fields surrounded by a hastily erected barbed wire fence. Yet as the haggard band of prisoners approached the gates an order rang out loud across the field. Eric Reeves remembered the moment:

We staggered out of these flamin' wagons. The Germans were pushing us with their rifle butts. We were all staggering about. Then a voice shouted, 'Pay attention! You are soldiers of the British Army' – he must have been a regular soldier, probably a Warrant Officer – 'You will act like soldiers of the British Army. You will fall in, in three ranks, and we will march into this camp with heads high. Now fall in!' And we did. We marched in. The Germans must have been amazed. Then we got into the camp and straight away we all collapsed again!

During his first days within the camp, Reeves found himself physically unable to react to his new environment. Like so many he was too exhausted to do anything: 'We were out in the open all day. Me and these blokes just found this place and sat there, leaning against a wall. If you wanted to get up it was difficult. You could get up so far then you blacked out and fell down again. So you'd have to get other blokes to help you up. Once you were on your feet it was ok. Malnutrition had hit us.' Elsewhere in the camp Seaforth Highlander Jim Reed was trying to adapt to life as a POW: 'It was shocking. Everyone was a bit low. I wanted to get a shower to get deloused, but we got nothing. It was a stinking hole. We slept on shelves – 100 on the bottom, 100 on the top. It filled the room. The sergeant in charge was as smart as if he was on parade, but he could do nothing for us. It was the worst place. The food was just rotten potatoes, there was no drinking water and we all had dysentery. It was a rough camp – no grass, just one big yard.'

At Thorn the train arrived directly outside the gates of a vast complex of forts that had been constructed in the nineteenth century, following the Franco-Prussian War. One of the arriving prisoners described his first impressions:

My view was dominated by two massive gates made of wood, laced with barbed wire. These gates, I then noticed, were the entrance to a vast flat piece of ground which was surrounded by a double fence of barbed wire. I noticed that each corner of this compound held a raised machine gun post manned by German guards. The two gates were also manned by two guards, one of whom opened the gates on our arrival. We were told to enter whilst the other guard counted us in. It was all so bewildering, especially as I was aware of a commotion inside the compound where there were already many, many POWs settled in.[1]

The forts were mainly underground with prisoners living in two storeys, in fifty dark rooms, each holding around thirty men, that ran along the rear. At the front of the fort were open courtyards below ground level. Graham King later discovered that the moat contained a surprise: 'It was a dry moat, rather overgrown but, surprisingly, teeming with rabbits. In our early days in this fort we had tried to trap some using snares but were told by the Germans that snares were banned in Germany and the punishment was quite severe.'

The prisoners arriving at Thorn were first sent into tented camps where they went through the process of registration as prisoners of war. This included having their heads shaved, being sent for delousing in steaming shower rooms and being photographed holding their POW identification number. Finally they were issued a small rectangular tag – always known as a disc – stamped with their identification number, that they would wear every day for the next five years. Though most prisoners felt dejected as they were processed ready for life in a POW camp, there was one bonus. The shaving of their heads removed the breeding ground for the lice that were already making their lives a misery.

Many of the prisoners were searched and all spare clothing was taken away. The imposed clothing shortages would have a severe effect in the months and years that followed. As well as having their names taken, they were asked to fill in Red Cross forms that were to be used to notify the British authorities of their status as prisoners of war. It was a process every prisoner would eventually go through. Eric Reeves remembered the experience:

> The first morning we were all grouped together. The Germans had a chair and a board. They wrote your number on the board – I was 3479, one of the earliest prisoners – and they took our photographs holding the board. One of our NCOs said 'Show them you're not beat – give them a smile.' So I did. Then they took your thumbprint and wrote down the colour of your eyes and hair. Years later, I got my registration card back from the Ministry of Defence. There's little me sitting there with a sickly grin above this board with my number on it.

During the period of registration some prisoners found themselves washed down with high-pressure hoses, so strong they had to be controlled by two men, and the strength of the spray knocked the weakened prisoners to the floor. Graham King found himself in a group of prisoners who were ushered down into the cellars of the fort to be prepared for POW life. First they had to strip and were then given a small, rough towel and some soap:

> Our clothing was taken away and we lined up, starkers, outside the barbers shop. We entered three by three, carefully explaining how we would like our nearly shoulder length hair cut. Hopes dashed, hand clippers were manoeuvred over the whole body resulting in complete depilation. Then we went into the shower room and stood, three men under each showerhead and the water was turned on, then off! We rubbed the soap over our bodies, leaving a covering of fine pumice and an indescribable body odour. A shouted warning and the water came back on, rinsing the skeletal bodies of the prisoners. Skulls like a phrenologist's dream and the fleshless bodies of the starving – no mother would have recognised her darling. We sat outside the room on a hard wooden bench, wriggling in discomfort, the cushioning fat and muscle of our gluteals having disappeared in the fight for survival.

When his clothing came back from the delouser, King noticed how his freshly washed clothing smelt like a damp dog drying in front of a fire. Others noticed the delousing had done nothing to actually kill the lice, which had survived in the seams. Graham King also noticed that the uniforms they received were not their own, rather they were of far inferior cloth. As he recalled: 'they would not have been accepted by any poverty stricken rag and bone merchant of the thirties, but we were offered no choice.' Dressed in these threadbare clothes, and with his feet soon bleeding from the rough wood of his newly issued clogs, King prepared himself for his first night within the fort – sleeping on the straw-covered floor of a subterranean storeroom. The only light came from a bare bulb at the end of the corridor outside the room.

Once cleaned up, the prisoners were sent to Fort 17, which was not actually one of the main subterranean forts but a series of wooden huts in which prisoners were housed whilst the Germans decided what their fate would be. Living in one of these sheds, that housed 1,000 prisoners, one man recorded: 'So I'm now just gristle and bone, but as hard as iron and in good health, except for diarrhoea which we all suffer from the pumped water . . . we all get the skitters . . . I'm like Gandhi with no hope of getting back any fat on my bones on that diet – I'm always hungry.'[2]

When Jim Pearce entered Fort 17 it seemed life couldn't get much worse. He spent his time shuffling around in straw-filled clogs, thinking of nothing but food and hardly caring whether he lived or died: 'We couldn't care less. We were just wandering around, starving. Nothing mattered. Then a Scottish sergeant-major came along and made us get up and walk around. He made us soldiers again. We became men again. Otherwise we'd have gone under.'

For Bob Davies, who had arrived from Calais, Thorn was a difficult place to describe. Quite simply, he spent his time there in a dream. There was little to see or experience within a camp that was built mostly underground. For men who spent their days sprawled on the cold floor of a dark, damp cellar, memory was a luxury – there was nothing in their day-to-day lives they wanted to remember. All that mattered was raising enough energy to pull themselves up from the straw-covered floor, then to drag themselves along the corridors to collect their next bowl of soup. Ken Willats recalled the first awful days at Thorn: 'You'd see men sitting on the ground with their shirts off cracking lice between their fingernails. A door led out to a path up the hill where the so-called toilet was. It was two trestles and a long plank over a hole. You perched on that and just hoped for the best.'

The dreadful conditions within Thorn only served to further reduce the prisoners to a state of appalling apathy. One of those who became well-acquainted with the stinking latrines was Fred Coster, whose first days in the stalag were spent inside a marquee:

> They said they were going to serve us soup. I thought good – that's the first food we had been given. But, oh my god, I couldn't get up. Luckily there was a tent post by me so I pulled myself up. I was as dizzy as hell. I staggered over and stood in line for hours to get my bit of soup. In mine was a bit of pork fat, floating. I thought 'Lovely!' I polished that off quickly. Then I started being sick. I pulled myself up on the tent post again and tried to stagger off to the latrine. I could feel this saliva flooding into my mouth and I was spitting it out. Then I went back and collapsed again.

Although the very notion of living in subterranean forts appalled even the most exhausted of the incoming prisoners, the alternatives at the other stalags were hardly more appealing. At Stalag 8B in Lamsdorf the prisoners were greeted by a sight that would become common for hundreds of thousands of prisoners in the five years that followed: 'All I can remember is these bloody great five-bar wooden gates,' recalled Norman Barnett. 'They were more than six feet high and covered in barbed wire. Then we could see the barbed wire fence and the machine-gun posts. There were two guards on the outer gates and then a six-foot gap and two more armed guards at the second gate. The Stalag was a massive place, it had previously been a barracks.'

When Stephen Houthakker entered Stalag 8B he was immediately struck by the foul smell that hung over the camp and he could see the condition of men who had arrived before him: 'spiritless men were sprawling about, Poles and British, both so starved, it was difficult for them to get up without reeling.'[3] It was little wonder they were dispirited. Even in the summer, the stone buildings were cold. Bill Holmes could remember how the guards seemed to be certain of a German victory and wanted to make sure the prisoners knew it. On his first day in the camp he had to queue for a whole day to get his first meal. It was just another annoyance for the prisoners who had, in the most, already grown to accept that if they could be made to wait, they would be made to wait.

Cyril Holness remembered the guards at Lamsdorf:

They could be nasty – especially some of the younger Nazi types. They were full of it – they wanted us to learn German because they thought they were going to take over the whole world. But the guard in charge of us was ok, he spoke with an American accent. One day he came along with the commandant, he asked us 'Any complaints, guys?' So we said we wanted more potatoes. He just looked at the commandant, turned to us and said 'The Kommandant does not believe in fat bellies in Germany.' We had to laugh.

Despite the good nature displayed by that guard it did not ease Holness' mind: 'We had no idea what was going to happen. Stalag 8B was tremendously big. When I first saw the place I thought "What is this? What's happened to my life?" That first year was a bad year. When was it all going to end?'

The new huts that were put up to house the prisoners were also unappealing places. Norman Barnett was moved into one of these barrack rooms: 'I was in hut 35A. It was full of wobbly three tier bunks. We just had a straw palliasse on bed boards and one blanket. Bang in the middle of each hut was a washhouse, with cold water and concrete sinks.' Most of these wooden and brick-built barrack blocks had bunk space for nearly 200 men, with little space between the bunks. It was in these overcrowded rooms that Barnett and his fellow prisoners had to adapt to POW life: 'In the first weeks we just sat around. The only time you got up was when a German officer came in. You were supposed to get up quick, but you couldn't. If you were too slow they had these Polish civilians – they were bastards – they had these rubber hoses filled with sand who'd clout you. But when you got up the room used to spin round.'

Arriving at Schubin, Jim Reed was struck by how basic the conditions were. Many prisoners slept on straw mattresses in the attic of what had been a reform school. As the camp began slowly to expand, the prisoners moved into new accommodation, filling each hut as it was constructed. Whilst the construction work continued, the prisoners remained in their attics, tents and barns, all the time hoping their new accommodation would be ready before the start of winter. Reed's first POW camp was also the worst conditions he experienced during five years as a prisoner of war: 'When we first saw the camp there was no barbed wire. We thought it had previously been a nunnery. There was one pump in the yard but the water was unfit to drink. But we were only there for about a month. Then we were marched out and put into bell tents. We stayed there until the winter – when it started snowing. Then we were moved to a foundry where we slept in the sand for about a week.'

The conditions experienced by the prisoners within the stalags varied in everything but awfulness. If one man found himself in an overcrowded, airless room, another found himself sleeping out-doors in tents that barely kept out the wind and rain. For every man living in a draughty wooden hut, there was another living in gloomy subterranean cellars of Polish forts like those at Thorn and Posen. The first year in captivity saw prisoners sleeping in all manner of locations – barns, schoolhouses, stables and cellars. In the fort at Posen, one prisoner decided to record his living accom-modation. He lived in the underground rooms of a moated fort. Their beds were within long, dark, tunnel-shaped chambers, with straw-covered floors, that were lit by a single light bulb. From this chamber, he had to walk twenty-four paces to catch a sight of daylight. It was a total of 107 paces for him to get outside into the fresh air. Fred Coster recalled the effect of living and working underground in rooms untouched by daylight or fresh air:

It was claustrophobic. I used to do tailoring when I was at school, so I knew how to make a pair of trousers out of two worn out

pairs. So I worked in the machining-room. They used to leave
half a dozen of us in there. Then they locked the door. I could
feel the claustrophobia rising in me. I thought 'What's happening to me?' I felt that I was going to go to pieces. But I had to
fight the feeling back. In the end I got used to it – I beat it. But
you can imagine what it would've done to a weaker person – it
would have sent him off his head.

At Thorn, Graham King described the accommodation shared
by thousands of the British prisoners: 'the rooms contained beds,
the same design as those seen in pictures of concentration camps.
Three shelves were against the wall, about six and a half feet wide
with a gap of one metre between the bottom shelf and the middle,
and between the middle and the top. The best position was the top
because there was more light and there was no one tossing and
turning above you, vomiting or suffering loss of bladder control. In
each room there were about thirty men living.' The rooms
themselves: 'they were like semi tunnels; all the ceilings were
arched to give strength. The perpendicular walls were about three
metres high and the height to the arch's top was about five metres.
The width of the room was five metres and the length about
fifteen. Three-tiered wooden bunks provided sleeping spaces and
thirty-two men would sleep, eat, argue, smoke, fart, cough, snore,
groan, moan, play cards, have nightmares and read in each of those
rooms.' Each room had two small windows over which blackout
blinds had to be fitted every night. These allowed no ventilation:
'By the end of the night the air was solid and everyone would have
a headache due to oxygen starvation.'

There were already considerable numbers of British prisoners of
war within the camps. Some were those who had been captured
during the Norwegian campaign. Others had been taken in the
very early days following the German assault. Among these were a
number of senior NCOs, some of whom made a less than
favourable impression upon the incoming men. With the army
having been so heavily defeated, and with a defeatist mentality

having crept into their way of thinking, plenty of the soldiers were not impressed by any idea of military discipline.

The efforts of some to instil discipline met with immediate and vocal resistance. At Thorn, Jim Charters arrived at the camp to find his group confronted by a British Army major dressed in a perfectly pressed uniform, complete with a polished Sam Browne belt. The officer did not care that they had marched hundreds of miles, then travelled in the holds of coal barges and within stinking cattle-wagons. He told them: 'You people are filthy, you get nothing to eat till you get cleaned up.' The reaction of the prisoners was immediate. Some of the senior NCOs told the officer what they would do to him if his threats were carried out.

At Thorn one particular NCO paid the ultimate price for his behaviour, as David Mowatt remembered:

I can't remember entering the camp. All I can remember was a Welsh Sergeant Major. He was trying to get us to march up and down — after all the way we'd walked! I couldn't do it. I collapsed and ended up in hospital. That sergeant eventually wangled his way onto a repatriation ship. On the boat on the way home he vanished. Someone got him and dumped him over the side. It was someone who'd remembered him from Thorn and thought 'I'll have him one day!' The senior NCOs of the King's Royal Rifles were in charge when we arrived at Thorn. They were as fit as fit could be. They'd taken over the POW camp, whilst we'd still been fighting in the rearguard!

During the period following registration and entry into the camps, the prisoners continued to lose weight rapidly. Although they were no longer marching, the deprivations they had suffered, combined with the extreme food shortages, ensured they were fit for little more than collapsing to the ground in exhaustion. Once again they faced the problem of only being able to collect food if they had a receptacle for it. Those with mess tins or the glass jars and discarded tin cans they had found during the march blessed their good fortune. Those without again cursed their luck and once more offered up their filthy, cupped hands to collect whatever was available. So continued the desperate search for anything that could hold food. E. Vernon Mathias, captured at Calais, later described the physical effects of all he had endured: 'It was a near starvation form of diet which dominated our physical health as well as our character. Physically I had lost weight in a rapid and alarming manner and the side effects were weakness, an outbreak of skin sores, loss of some teeth and, worst of all, one's weakness encouraged the infestation of body lice which practically made one's life unbearable.'[4]

What little food the prisoners received made an awful impression upon them – indeed food was their only thought at the time. It was difficult to forget the rancid sauerkraut, thin pea soup, stinking cheese and ersatz coffee that was keeping them alive. Jim Charters remembered mouldy bread and potatoes so black that 'pigs would turn their noses up at them.' For others the rations seemed to be nothing more than a handful of potatoes covered in eyes. If potatoes weren't available they got black bread that seemed to have been bulked up with sawdust. Some prisoners remembered potato bread, in which the bottom of the loaf was thick with what seemed to be rotten potato. As Norman Barnett recalled: 'When you cut it, it stank. But it was edible.' Elsewhere prisoners were fed barley soup mixed with cattle blood. One man recalled receiving a bowl of dirty spinach. Before he could consume it he had to drain off the water and pour away the sand that had settled on the bottom of the bowl. Some of the prisoners made efforts to clean whatever they could before consuming it. Some burnt potatoes in a fire, charring the outsides, before boiling them, in the hope of killing off bacteria. Others toasted all their bread, for fear of infected flour.

The appalling rations meant that those who retained the energy to move still spent all their waking hours dreaming of food. They mustered up what little remained of their strength to drag themselves up to cookhouses just to take in the smell of whatever weak stews were being prepared for them. Graham King recorded his daily rations in the early weeks at Thorn. The day began at 6 a.m. with coffee made from roasted acorns. For lunch they received a litre of vegetable soup, with no meat or fat. At 4 p.m. they received a 1,500-gram loaf of black bread, one between five men. With this they received a little margarine, honey, jam or, very occasionally, liver sausage. He recalled that, after the deprivations of the journey from France, so much food seemed like a feast. That said, it was still not enough to help them recover: 'Each individual collected his own soup from the kitchen, which was downstairs for our group. I found that I did not have the strength to carry my soup upstairs, so sat on the bottom stair and ate it there, every delicious drop, eventually getting enough strength to climb up to the room.'

In the initial months of captivity there were few differences between the treatment of officers and other ranks. The officers lived in segregated camps or in enclosures away from the men. However, like the men, they survived on appalling rations. At Oflag 4D the officers reported they were too weak to take advantage of the exercise facilities in their camp and instead they had to lie down for most of the day. Just like the other ranks, the officers also had had their heads shaved when they entered the camps. Some later commented that their individual personalities disappeared along with their hair, noting that for the first few weeks each officer became a nonentity. Only later did their individual characters re-emerge as their hair began to grow back.

Despite the differences between the POW experience as endured by officers and other ranks, the officers did not live in better conditions. Peter Wagstaff later wrote of an unexpected encounter within a fort at Posen: 'I will never forget one day turning a corner in a passage and being confronted by something sitting up on its hind legs. It was the size of a large rabbit but I knew it could not be. In the next instant I suddenly realised it must be a rat! We managed to kill one later – from head to tail it must have been 24 inches.'[5]

Considering the squalid conditions the prisoners were forced to live in, most were amazed that they seldom saw rats within the main stalags. Looking back, they realize why this was. It was quite simple – there was no food for rats and thus no reason for them to be there. Or as some commented, any rats that did appear would probably have been caught, killed and cooked. As Norman Barnett recalled: 'What were they going to eat? There were no scraps for them to eat. Men were fighting over scraps. I've seen them fighting over potato skins. When they dished out potatoes from these boxes, men would fight over what you could scrape from the inside of the box.' The starving men had learned that to turn down any food was tantamount to suicide. There was no vegetable too rotten, no meat too high, that they did not think it was worth consuming.

As they had begun to realize, it did not take proud men long to adapt to life-threatening conditions. E. Vernon Mathias later wrote: 'This period of physical and mental stagnation was causing great harm to the morale within the camp. Our movements were lethargic and our mental reactions had slowed down. Our self respect suffered and groups of POWs would congregate near the waste bins sifting through the rubbish for potato peelings or anything edible. These were the dark days when we had to adapt our body and mind to a much lower standard of living than we had experienced before.'[6]

Sickness became rife within all the POW camps. Whilst some of the weakest men just gave up and died, hundreds found themselves so weak they could barely move. To do anything was an effort. To stand up, to walk, to talk – all seemed beyond them. One soldier later reported that he had been forced to jump up to salute a German officer. As soon as he did so he immediately collapsed to the ground since the movement had been too sudden. Others reported seeing spots before their eyes whenever they bent over, with one man reporting that he had fainted as he attempted to reach down to tie his bootlaces.

It seemed that life continued to revolve around dreaming of food and then rushing to the stinking latrines as the men were gripped by stomach cramps and diarrhoea. One prisoner later recalled how he had seen a man reading a book. He asked if he might be allowed to borrow it but the man refused. He explained that he was using it page by page as toilet paper and that it was a race between his intellect and his bowels as to to which finished the book first. As Norman Barnett, trying to adapt to life at Stalag 8B, later recalled: 'I don't think anyone did a solid crap the whole time they were prisoners.' At Thorn, Graham King recalled queues of men waiting for the foul latrines, which consisted of just six places for over 1,500 prisoners, large numbers of whom had been struck by dysentery: 'After reaching the head of the queue and performing, it was necessary to go and queue again for the next gut gripping attack.'

Everything seemed to be designed to humiliate the prisoners, and attempts to elevate morale were hard work. Eric Reeves remembered the efforts of one of his fellow POWs: 'His name was Arthur Briton. He was a lay preacher and he got a church service going. That was on about the third day at Schubin. We sat there in the dirt and said our prayers and sang the hymns. He was brave to do that amongst all us hairy, hard old soldiers. He used to complain about our bad language. He was a nice man.'

Despite such efforts, Reeves couldn't help but notice the psychological turmoil within the stalags: 'There were so many of us that we never knew if people were starving to death – blokes were falling sick and disappearing, we never knew what happened to them. But others were dying. One man tried to hang himself, another cut his throat. They got to the point where they couldn't cope.' The depths to which the prisoners sank during that first year at Lamsdorf was recalled by Ernie Grainger: 'The first nine months was my lowest point. I'd dropped from 12 stone to just sixty pounds in weight. We had these big tummies and matchstick legs. The last thing I'd ever expected to be was a prisoner of war. I'd never expected to be in a strange country, surrounded by these evil looking blokes. I thought "What the hell's going on here?" It was awful. Some people went mental. The rest of us thought we'll just do the best we can.'

The mental and physical stagnation within the stalags saw morale collapsing as the prisoners struggled to survive. Prisoners were pitted against one another as the slightest incidents became blown up out of all proportion. Jim Pearce recalled those bitter days:

> The atmosphere was terrible. There were arguments all the time. What little bit of food you got you had to watch it closely otherwise someone would pinch it. Gosh yeah, there were fights over food! I remember one time I got some food and cigarettes from the Red Cross. So I slept on it. I woke up the next morning and the food and cigarettes had gone. They tickled you in your sleep so you'd move, so they could pinch them. They'd pinch everything. We got piles of swedes for food during the week. Once they'd gone we'd get nothing else for the week. So we had to take turns guarding them, so no one pinched them. Chaps lost all respect, they didn't care. It was dog-eat-dog. There was a lot of bitterness, it's not like they show in films and on TV.

Whilst every prisoner was happy to steal from the enemy, only a few were prepared to steal from their comrades. Every former prisoner can recall stories of food being stolen – the most repeated being the tale of men going to sleep with a loaf as their pillow only to awake to find the ends of the loaf cut off. Though such scenes sound comical there was nothing humorous about the loss of rations. Nor was the punishment of thieves anything to laugh about. The punishments for those caught stealing were extreme. Thieves were beaten violently by men who had been their friends. One man was even strapped to a table then whipped for stealing food. The beatings were followed by banishment, leaving the offenders without friends as they struggled to survive. There were even dark rumours, about which few former POWs ever openly talk, of men who were killed for daring to steal food from their comrades. In the overcrowded camps it was easy for men to disappear, as Ernie Grainger remembered: 'There was an unwritten law about stealing. We had this static water tank in the camp and they found a dead prisoner in there one night. No one owned up to it, but everyone knew he'd been stealing.'

The prisoners willing to demean themselves in front of the Germans in exchange for food or cigarettes also got short shrift. At Stalag 20B two men who gave the Nazi salute to German officers in exchange for bread were thrown into a cesspit by their disgusted comrades. Elsewhere a soldier who posed for photographs giving the Nazi salute, receiving cigarettes as a payment, was beaten up by the rest of the prisoners.

Although the prisoners attempted to police themselves, there were some occasions when gangs formed and took over life within the compounds. Descriptions of the gangs vary but most describe them as racketeers, wideboys or 'fly charlies' who had 'nothing to learn from Chicago'.[7] Accounts tend to identify the worst offenders as being from the slums of large industrial cities like Glasgow, London and Liverpool. Many were described as 'cosh boys' or veterans of the razor gangs that had terrorized some inner city areas in the pre-war years. In some camps, Stalag 8B being a particular case, the gangs could dominate by stealing food. By ensuring their own food supply, and thus depriving others, the gangsters provided themselves with enough food to ensure they remained physically stronger than their victims.

Stephen Houthakker at Stalag 8B later wrote of this period:

Fights amongst the starving men were frequent, and thieving rife during those first weeks. However, there sprang up a comrade-ship between the downtrodden or poor of the camp, who were in the majority by far . . . The racketeers somehow or other continued to thrive. The soup queues and the potato queues presented freefights daily. Men reduced to starvation, though weak physically, fought with tremendous zest to prevent the next from obtaining a larger share. Gangs were formed and there was often war between combatant and non-combatant forces.

The prisoners discovered the supply of food was controlled not by the Germans but by elements from within the British Army who had been able to get into positions of authority. The Germans, who

accepted military discipline and the privileges of rank, were prepared to pass power into the hands of senior British NCOs. Whilst
many were dedicated to looking after their men, there were plenty
of others who inspired fury for their efforts to make their own lives
more comfortable. These cliques of senior sergeants and warrant
officers took over the control of food supplies and clothing,
enriching themselves at the expense of the mass of prisoners
who held such behaviour tantamount to treason. In the post-
war period many made official complaints about the behaviour of
NCOs. At Fort 8 in Posen, three 'rotten' Guards NCOs appointed
themselves cooks and kept stocks of food for themselves. At Thorn,
Ken Willats recalled lying on the ground in a state of virtual
starvation whilst being able to smell meat being cooked by the men
in charge of the rations. As Norman Barnett explained: 'The cooks
always used to look healthy. But wouldn't you? If you were in the
cookhouse and you were starving, the first thing you'd do is get a
bit extra. It's human nature.'

In later years many former prisoners noted how the offenders
tended to be long-serving senior NCOs who had a tendency to
band together, just as they had done when the army had begun its
rapid expansion during the late 1930s. Then they had stuck
together to preserve their position and once behind the barbed
wire of the stalags they reverted to type and continued the process.

Considering the threadbare uniforms in which the prisoners had
entered the stalags, there came a desperate need to re-clothe the
men. However, the Germans did not have any stocks of British
uniforms available for 40,000 ragged men. They even made the
prisoners share out the clothing they had. But they did have vast
stocks of captured uniforms from the defeated nations of Europe.
Consequently the new prisoners found their battledress replaced
with all manner of kit. There were trousers, overcoats and tunics
from France, Belgium and Poland, cavalry breeches that were worn
without riding boots, leaving the wearer with ridiculous bare
calves, tall peaked Polish Army ceremonial caps and Great War
overcoats designed to be worn while riding a horse. Arriving at

Lamsdorf, Bill Holmes remembered how the new kit was issued: 'They'd throw you stuff – you had to be quick. You'd either get something that was too big or too small – nothing ever fitted. I got a Polish overcoat – by the time that was on you could only just see my eyes. If you were lucky you got a good coat, if not, that was your bad luck.'

Some of the uniforms had come out of warehouses, smelt of mothballs or were creased and damp with age, yet these were far preferable to the alternatives. Some prisoners found themselves issued with uniforms that had come straight from the battlefields, complete with bullet holes and bloodstains.

As the men pulled on their new uniforms, there was no longer a cohesive look to the remnants of the BEF. Instead they were a motley collection of men clad in the cast-offs of half a dozen European armies. As Dick Taylor later admitted of his early days at Thorn, the British prisoners looked like: 'a real pantomime army'.[8]

If the clothes made the prisoners appear comical, at least they were not uncomfortable. The same could not be said for the footwear they were issued. Those whose boots had worn out were given clogs. As Barnett remembered: 'I had wooden clogs, like Dutch ones. They were just blocks of wood. Christ, it was agony. And you never had socks. We had "*fusslapen*" – just a cloth like a handkerchief that wrapped round your feet. It was easier to walk around in bare feet!' Although clogs and footcloths were common in some areas of Europe, they were totally new to the prisoners. Even those British soldiers who were familiar with clogs had never worn ones like these. They could no longer raise their feet from the ground when they walked. Instead they had to shuffle along, just hoping the cloths would stay wound around their feet and that the clogs would not slip off. R.P. Evans, sent out onto one of the earlier working parties, recorded the effects of wearing clogs: 'My feet became chaffed on the insteps, then one day I developed a sore on the left heel which became progressively worse until I had to limp back to camp using two shovels as crutches.' The following day he reported sick and was sent to a German military doctor: 'He appeared to have no instruments, for he took out his penknife, heated it in a flame and proceeded to make an incision in what proved to be an abscess. He pressed and pressed to no avail until, losing patience, brought his fists sharply together, when it finally burst. I am afraid I passed out and came to to find him inserting metal clips across the incision. I had no dressing on the wound and returned to work the next day.'[9]

In the months immediately following the defeat of the BEF and its allies, there hung an awful question over the fate of the men who had been left behind in France. It would be months before many families discovered whether their loved ones were alive or dead. The scale of the German victory was unprecedented. All in the space of ten months they had defeated and occupied Poland, Norway, Denmark, the Netherlands, Belgium, Luxembourg, France and the Channel Islands. They had also routed the BEF and captured 40,000 of its men. The vast numbers of prisoners absorbed into the stalag system meant their resources were stretched beyond even Hitler's wildest expectations.

If the Germans could not keep up with the numbers that needed to be processed, neither could the Red Cross. All the prisoners needed to fill in registration forms that then had to be sent to Geneva for the information to be transmitted to London. Once the details reached London, they needed to be cross-referenced against both the War Office records and the regimental records to ensure correct information reached the families. Too many already feared the worst for their husbands, fathers and sons. Although it was inevitable mistakes would be made, it was important to keep the errors as few as possible. The situation was not helped by the fact that many of the worst affected regiments had not returned home with any records. Whilst some commanding officers had taken care to entrust their battalion War Diaries to a responsible officer making his way off the Dunkirk beaches, others had taken the expedient measure of burning or burying their records lest they fall into enemy hands. Some units, such as those encircled at Calais and St Valery, had no way of passing any accurate records back to London.

The War Office in London wrote to all the commanding officers, asking for accurate casualty figures but, as they admitted, they were 'up against it'.[10] The returns made for sober reading: 8th Battalion Royal Warwickshire Regiment – 417 men missing, wounded, killed or prisoner; 1st Battalion Cameron Highlanders – 250 POWs; 2/5th Queen's Regiment – 387 men missing; 1st Lothian and Borders Horse – just twenty officers and men returned home; 2nd Field Bakery RASC – fifty-five men lost when the *Lancastria* sank off St Nazaire. And so it went on.

As a result, until September when the first lists of confirmed dead were received from the French Red Cross, it was anybody's guess as to who had succumbed in battle and who had been taken prisoner. With the dead spread so far and wide across France and Belgium, it was a slow process to discover who had fallen in battle. The War Office received news from a variety of sources, often in letters posted from neutral countries by people who had received the news from those living near the battlefields. In the summer of 1940 the names of 123 men whose bodies had washed ashore following the sinking of the *Lancastria* were passed to London. The descriptions of some of the bodies – those with heads and limbs missing – was far more detailed than any family would want to know, but it was all vital information for those recording the fate of the BEF. One Frenchman contacted London with the sad tale of how he had discovered the corpse of a soldier. He had gone in search of his own son and discovered his body side by side with the corpse of a Gunner Harris. He reported that he had paid for the two men to be buried as they had died – side by side. By July 1941 the Belgians had transmitted to London the names of over 3,000 soldiers of the BEF who had fallen in Belgium. Despite the careful efforts of those who cleared the battlefields, there remained plenty for whom no name could ever be found. Some were identified by nothing more than their hair colour or body shape. One sad case of an unidentified soldier was the man described as 1.76 metres tall with black hair, a tattoo of a female head on one arm along with a red rose with the inscription 'mother'. On his other arm was tattooed the word 'father'. They were just two of the many parents who would never discover where their son had fallen.

Once the prisoners were given the opportunity to write home, they found there were serious limits to what they could include. They were allowed to send just four postcards and two specially designed lettercards each month. They could not include news of conditions within the camps or any military details. All writing had to be on the clearly printed lines and the prisoners were denied the opportunity to include any embellishments. As a result, there was little they could do except give the briefest of accounts about their lives and send messages of love back to their families.

Despite these rules, the flow of mail was not regular, especially in the early months of captivity. One prisoner recalled being registered by the Red Cross in July but his family did not receive news of his fate until September. In July the Foreign Office reported that they were still awaiting the names of 14,500 prisoners who had been registered. They had also learned there were a further 9,000 prisoners who had not yet been registered. There were others who waited even longer for news. It took nine months for Fred Gilbert to get news of his survival back to his family. His mother had been told he was dead – hardly surprising considering the fate of his mates and the three bullets that had hit him – and had to wait until his letter, written in September 1940, reached her a few months later. Following his capture at St Valery, David Mowatt's mother heard no news of him for eighteen months. He was the youngest of four sons, all serving in the army, and to all intents and purposes he was lost to her. Somewhere in the confusion of his transfer between Stalags 20A and 20B, the details of his prisoner registration had been lost, thus ensuring the British were unaware he was still alive. It was only when his first letter arrived home in late 1941 that his family finally discovered he was alive.

Many Territorial units had traditionally absorbed recruits from a limited catchment area, meaning there were many close family members, brothers, cousins, fathers and sons, all serving together. Although Jim Pearce and his brother had entered Thorn together, and received consecutive numbers when they were registered, news of their survival was not immediately sent to their family. The authorities alerted them that Jim was alive, but left them believing his brother was still 'missing, presumed dead'. It was only after Pearce received his first letter from home that he was able to set their minds at ease by assuring them their other son had survived.

On 4 July 1940 the *Berwick Journal* reported that one local family had three sons who had been reported missing. The family were the Arnotts, whose three boys, John, Thomas and Peter, had all been called up into the Royal Northumberland Fusiliers on 1 September 1939: 'The last letter received from Thomas was dated 2nd June. And, since the receipt of that letter, their parents have not had news of any kind until the weekend, when they got the official letter. All three brothers were despatch riders in the RNF.'[11] However, against all odds, the brothers had all survived the savage battle for St Valery and had, along with thousands of others, been registered at Stalag XXB in Marienburg.

For one household in the small mining town of Ashington, County Durham the chaos of the defeat in France had an immediate impact. The Charters family had two sons serving as machine-gunners in the 7th Battalion of the Northumberland Fusiliers. Brothers Jim and Jack Charters had both been fortunate to survive the battle at St Valery yet no news of their fate had reached their parents. However, a handful of their regiment had reached home. One of them returned to Ashington with tragic news – a story soon went around the town that the two brothers had been killed at St Valery. What made it worse was that the man did not visit their parents to tell them what he believed had happened. Instead they received the news via friends and neighbours who came to commiserate with them at their loss. It was a terrible blow – to lose one son was bad enough but to lose two was devastating. Then to receive the news indirectly only compounded the emotion blow. The only consolation was that at least they had some notion of their sons' fate – or so they thought.

Whilst so many families were still waiting for any news, the Charters received an unexpected communication. The postman delivered a letter, written in an unfamiliar hand, postmarked Geneva. When Jim Charters had handed over his address to a woman at the roadside during the march into captivity he had no notion of the impact it would have. The woman, Madame Grenier who resided in the town of Wingles, had kept Jim Charters' note and written to his home: 'I've still got the original of the letter she sent to my parents. I handed over the message not expecting the news to get home. But the woman sent a letter to Geneva and that was posted to my parents. The woman had written it in French so my father had to take it to a local schoolteacher to get it translated. It was the first my parents knew that we were still alive.'

That was enough for the family. Their boys were not home but at least they were alive. When the brothers finally returned home they wanted to find out who had so cruelly lied to the town about their supposed fate. Their father seemed to know the identity of the culprit but refused to reveal his name. The local branch of the British Legion even wanted the man to be prosecuted, but Charters senior refused. Instead the people of Ashington took action and drove the man from the town. As for Madame Grenier, she later became a member of the French Resistance and was eventually imprisoned by the Germans. She survived the war, was decorated by the French government and died in 1986.

What with all the delays in passing the details of the captured soldiers to the authorities in London, it took some time for a regular flow of mail to reach the stalags. It was not until autumn 1940 that the prisoners were allowed to receive clothing parcels.

Whilst the vast majority of the 40,000 prisoners were transported via the canals and railways of northern Europe to the stalags of Germany, others remained behind in France. Such was the devastation caused by the blitzkrieg that someone was needed to clear up the mess. German manpower was fully stretched, clearing up the remaining French opposition, occupying the conquered lands, preparing for a possible invasion of Britain and the planned invasion of the Soviet Union. So there were no men available to return France to a semblance of normality. As a result some prisoners were immediately absorbed into a system of 'frontstalags', in which they were put to work.

Initially the organization was haphazard, with local commanders ordering groups of captured soldiers to work for them. In the aftermath of the siege of Calais, whilst some were sent on the march towards Germany, others were forced to help clear up damage in the docks. Elsewhere British prisoners were made to begin the systematic rape of the defeated French nation. They were sent into factories where the produce was immediately packed up and sent back to Germany for sale onto the consumer market. Others found themselves made to clear the roads of the rotting corpses of horses killed during the German advance. Even more humiliating was the experience of three soldiers who were made to clear sewage from blocked drains. As both their guards and a group of French prisoners looked on, the men were forced to remove excrement from the drain and throw it out through a window, with just their hands to use as shovels.

From June to November 1940 British prisoners were employed at Frontstalag 142 in the railway yards of the French town of Besançon. Their work included loading and unloading munitions onto trains to be sent forward to the front. They were also made to load damaged tanks onto wagons ready to be sent back to Germany for repair. Others were taken to Malmedy in Belgium where they were forced to fell trees to make temporary runways for the Luftwaffe. Though their employment in military work of this nature was illegal, there was nobody to whom the prisoners could complain. No Red Cross representatives were able to make contact with them and no news was sent home of their fate.

In the year that followed they became forgotten men. Not until early 1941, nine months after the defeat of the BEF, were the Red Cross able to visit some of the 294 men employed at the front-stalags. Many had remained in the areas where they had been captured. In some areas the prisoners were in small groups, such as

the eight officers and ten other ranks working at Peronne. Elsewhere some unfortunate POWs were held alone, working for the
enemy without the comfort and support of their fellow prisoners.
Slowly, reports trickled back to London, painting a bleak picture.
At Le Mans fifteen British soldiers were held in conditions that
shocked Red Cross inspectors: 'The disorder here is complete. The
huts are falling to pieces. Food is poor and insufficient. The men
sleep on the ground without any blankets. Conditions of hygiene
are deplorable.'[12]

The story was the same across northern France. The fifteen
prisoners at Saveny received just two loaves of bread between them
each day and on just four days a week they shared a small portion of
horsemeat. Prussian guards at Laval were accused of brutalizing
their prisoners who, without even a blanket, slept on a bare
concrete floor. Red Cross inspectors went on to report how the
British in the frontstalags were undernourished, treated most
severely and often shot on the slightest provocation. The threat
of lethal violence was most vividly shown when the 500 British
prisoners at Mulhouse revolted following the outbreak of an
epidemic. As a result of the revolt, twenty prisoners were picked
out at random and executed.

The unfortunate prisoners at the frontstalags' were not the only
men put to work that year. Almost immediately after their arrival at
their designated stalags, the thousands of POWs began to filter out
into workcamps – known as AKs or arbeitskommandos – that
spread rapidly across the Reich. Under the Geneva Convention all
prisoners beneath the rank of sergeant could be put to work. There
were definite rules about their employment that were designed to
protect them from exploitation. They should no be employed in
dangerous jobs, nor in any form of war work. They should be given
rations equal with those allowed for civilian workers and be housed
in clean and heated surroundings. During the following five years,
few of the prisoners were treated according to the rules. Initially
those in London had little idea of the working conditions endured
by the men on working parties. In August 1940 the General

Secretary of the British Red Cross wrote the Foreign Office: 'Several relatives of prisoners of war have been in here during the last few days to enquire about a rumour that is apparently going about, that their husbands, sons etc have been put to work in the salt mines of Poland. I presume we can contradict this.'[13] His presumption was misplaced. As he wrote, hundreds of men were beginning life as enforced salt miners in Upper Silesia.

Initially, and understandably, most prisoners were wary about working for the enemy – after all they had gone to war to stop the Nazi war machine, not become part of it. However, most soon realized there was little choice in the matter – if the Germans told them to work, they would have to work. Furthermore, there was one attractive thing about working parties, it allowed the men out of the stalags and gave them contact with civilians. The first groups of prisoners, who were sent out to work from the stalags each morning, returned in the evening carrying the spoils of illicit deals they were able to conduct. Furtively, the prisoners made contact with civilians and traded whatever they had available. Watches and wedding rings were exchanged for bread and sausage. Desperation led the prisoners to develop an entrepreneurial spirit. If a prisoner knew he could get two loaves for one watch, he would make deals with fellow prisoners, agreeing to take their watches out to sell. He could then offer the seller a portion of what he had received, effectively acting as a broker for those unable to leave the stalag to make their own deals.

With conditions within the camp failing to improve, large numbers of prisoners began to fall sick. There were increasing numbers of TB cases, epidemics of boils, outbreaks of typhoid and a constant array of men suffering from festering sores caused by the constant scratching of insect bites. Despite the dedication of those members of the Royal Army Medical Corps who had been taken prisoner, there was a limit to how much they could do. For Ernie Grainger the desire to help his fellow inmates at Lamsdorf was undermined by one basic problem: 'We had no equipment. There was an awful lot of dry pleurisy. It is not a fatal condition but it's very painful. But we had nothing to treat it with. Bronchitis and asthma were a problem in the winter. Lots of people went down with frostbite and lung diseases. The Germans didn't give us any medicines.'

It was a situation that was painfully obvious to Fred Gilbert. Having been shot three times in his final battle, Gilbert received little in the way of meaningful treatment for his wounds: 'You were just supposed to get better. It slowly started to heal up. But whilst I was in Lamsdorf, I think it was bandaged up a couple of times in three months.'

Remaining at Thorn, Graham King was initially sent to work as an orderly for the dentist looking after the prisoners. He was only able to work two days a week since it was an eight-kilometre round trip to the surgery each day. He was just too weak to contemplate making the trip more than twice a week. Later in the year he began working at the Medical Inspection Room in Fort 15. With medical supplies so limited, their greatest fear was of major outbreaks of disease. Of particular concern was typhoid, since none of the water that arrived in the fort's crumbling underground brick-built water tanks had been treated. Furthermore, water from the cesspits was found to be leaking into the main water tanks. As a result they were forced to carry out mass inoculations, injecting 1,500 men three times over a period of three weeks. In the weeks that followed they had to give a further 3,000 injections to inoculate against diphtheria. The problem was that the hospital had just two syringes and twenty-five needles. As a result, the medics had to regularly sharpen the needles between injections just to keep working.

We worked hard in the MI Room. Following on from the dysentery and malnutrition we now had multiple boils, suppurating wounds from lice and fleabites, respiratory complaints and the threat of diphtheria. All the men had to have throat swabs taken and then inoculations were carried out, compulsorily. The lice and fleabite wounds were most time consuming because there were so many on each patient which took a considerable amount of time to clean and dress. As there was a shortage of dressings, we had to re-use the bandages by giving the slack to the patient to hold and the orderly rewound the bandage. I was dressing the multiple septic lice bite sores of an ancient warrior – claimed to have dropped twenty years off his age to join up, but was a pensioner – when I noticed an army of lice walking up the bandage towards me. A quick shake and they fell to the floor where, with much stamping of booted feet we hoped the majority perished. It took about an hour to dress this guy's wounds so he came every other day.

One of those whose health suffered whilst at Thorn was Seaforth Highlander David Mowatt. Such was his rapidly worsening condition, it seemed he had survived battle and the march into captivity for nothing:

I was in Fort 17. But I got gastroenteritis – twice. My stomach was in a terrible state. The first time I was roped to the bloody bed, for five days. There was no medical attention. I recovered. Then suddenly a week later I had another attack. As I came around the second time I looked into a face of an officer. He had this little tin mug of water and was dabbing my lips. I said to him 'I thought I was in heaven!' He said to me 'No, thank God. You're still in the land of the living.' He told me he was going to get me out of the hospital or else they'd end up carrying me out. He suggested I go on a working party. I said 'Sir. I can't even stand up let alone work!' But he knew he needed to get me out of the camp because the walls were running with water and were green with fungus. So he got me out on a small working party.

Once out at work he began to slowly recover, courtesy of the extra food that he received each day. It was clear to Mowatt that joining a working party had been a small price to pay to escape from the conditions that had reduced him to such an appalling physical state.

Sent initially on a working party to build a road – that was soon washed away during a storm – Dick Taylor was also glad to be working: 'On a working party you were fully employed. You were pretty tired when you came back at night, there was no time for thinking.' His fellow Northumberland Fusilier, Jim Charters, said the same thing: 'It was a relief to go to work. If I hadn't have been working I'd have gone round the bend.'

With time, some workcamps would become well-established, offering a basic standard of living to the prisoners. However, in 1940 this was not the case. Early working parties endured living and working conditions far below the internationally agreed standards for POWs. The food was invariably awful, offering little in the way of sustenance for the working prisoners. One man, who had already lost two front teeth after being beaten by the guards, recorded his daily rations as black bread and coffee for breakfast, a pint of weak broth for lunch and a cup of coffee for his evening meal. He was only saved by the kindness of Polish prisoners who managed to get extra food for him. On an early working party, Bob Davies recalled the daily rations: 'We were weak. We mainly had watery soup with black bread. We shared a ten-inch loaf between five people or, when food was short, it was one between six. It was once a day and that was your lot – no butter, marmalade or jam. We got hungry but the old stomach settles down, shrinks, and eventually you realise you don't need so much food.'

Eric Reeves, who took part in the building work to expand the stalag at Schubin, was soon aware that the food shortages had undermined their ability to carry out even the most menial duties:

> They got loads of bricks and we formed a human chain to move them. One bloke said 'Here, that ain't how you do it. You take two at a time . . .' So someone else shouted 'Oi! We're working for the Germans now. We're not on piecework!' So we passed them slowly from hand to hand. But even at that rate, after an hour or so, we'd had enough – we were shattered. Another time

I was a lumberjack. We were out in the wood cutting trees to make pit props. They gave me a double-headed axe but I couldn't even pick it up. It was too heavy. We were suffering from hunger.

As early as July 1940 some men arrived at Stalag 9C to discover that other prisoners had already been sent to workcamps. The first seventy-six British prisoners sent to work were employed on local building projects. Forty-two of the men slept in a single attic room whilst the remainder slept in a large room above a garage. The kitchen and laundry facilities were insufficient for the numbers living there and all seventy-six of them shared just five toilets. The men worked for nearly twelve hours each day but did not receive any work clothes. As a result their uniforms were soon ruined. It was little wonder the prisoners considered they were being made into slaves.

The story was repeated throughout the system of arbeitskommandos. Sleeping accommodation was always basic, with men sleeping in spartan huts often without even bunks, straw mattresses or blankets. Some of the luckier prisoners found themselves employed as builders and were pleased to discover they were actually constructing huts for themselves to live in. The huts may have been basic but at least knew they would soon be sleeping in purpose-built accommodation rather than living 200 to a room in three-tier bunks contained within a former Polish Army stables.

Toilets at workcamps were seldom more than holes in the ground, which were regularly emptied to spread upon the fields, and washing facilities consisted of a single cold tap – if they were lucky. For Jim Pearce, whose duties that winter included shovelling snow from Luftwaffe runways, there was a tin in the corner of the hut that was used as a toilet during the night: 'I can still remember my mate Bubbles calling out "Mind the toilet tin! Mind the rats!" 'Cause the rats were always in the huts. It was horrible – the rats lived with us. They'd crawl over you in the bunk. No one wanted to sleep in the bottom bunk at night.'

Though the conditions at most of the workcamps left much to be desired, one thing was certain – work meant food, food meant life and thus work meant survival. It was a simple equation.

Despite that, there were some employments that were reviled by the prisoners. Worst of all were the mines of Silesia, into which many of the prisoners from Stalag 8B were sent. There were coal, salt, copper and lignite mines. Conditions within, in particular the unfamiliar sense of claustrophobia, made the mines a place of fear. One of those who soon found himself at a coal mine was Cyril Holness. It was a far cry from his pre-war days at a suburban railway station:

> It was frightening. I had no idea what mines would be like. Before that I'd only read about it – up in Geordie land! We just had these tiny lamps that went out all the time. We didn't have any protective clothing, just rough old clothes. Just an old vest with rags tied around your boots. Going down in the cage was terrible – it was dripping wet, water was running down the walls. I reached a low point in that pit. One time my lamp went out. I was stuck in the pitch black. I was calling out but no one could hear me, because of the noise of the machinery. So I had to crawl along the rock to find my way out. That was the worst time.

For some prisoners the horrors of war seemed to have followed them from the battlefields of France all the way to Poland. Jim Reed recalled his experiences on a working party from Stalag 21B: 'My first work camp was when they sent us to dig up the Jews from the local cemetery. They made 10 different men go on this every day. It was an awful job. But we had no choice. You might not want to go but if you get a few strokes off the guards rifle butt you soon change your mind. It was a terrible job.'

It was little wonder men began to attempt to escape. Some were successful but others were caught and returned to the camp. Reed and his mates heard the punishment handed out to the returning men: 'The guards lived at the end of our hut. We knew someone was getting some stick from the shouting that was going on. We could hear them thumping and banging. They turned us out and the guards were waiting. They lined up and made the escapers run the gauntlet. You wouldn't believe men could be so savage. They beat them all the way – hit them everywhere and kicked them down into the potato store.'

The following day the prisoners were lined up ready for work, but few were in the mood to work for the people they had watched beating their comrades. The sergeant in charge of the prisoners then put on a display of courage that made a lasting impression on Reed:

He said to the Germans 'We want those men out of the cellar to have a look at them. Or we're not going to work today.' The guards came amongst us hitting us with rifle butts. But no one was going to work. The Germans backed Sgt Williams against a wall but he said 'I've told my men they are not working.' The German went mad, he shouted 'They are not your men they are my men!' I've seen one or two brave men – but that was something special. The German pointed his rifle at him and said 'I am going to shoot you.' So Sgt Williams shouted to us 'No one is going out of these gates without my permission!' In the end the Germans backed down. They let the men out of the cellar. I thought we were all going to be shot! So we went to work, but we didn't do a lot that day.

The violence of their guards was not the only issue the prisoners had to deal with. There was also the question of exhausted men attempting to work as they survived on just the most basic rations. The general weakness of the working prisoners resulted in large numbers having accidents or falling sick as a beleaguered medical staff attempted to look after them. By late 1940, Fred Gilbert, barely recovered from the bullet wounds he had sustained during the retreat through Belgium, found himself working at a granite quarry in Poland. It was a far cry from his pre-war days of training to be a commercial artist:

I was on this wagon moving stones and some bright bloke picked up a stone and went to throw it on. I said 'Hold it! Don't let it go!' I was trying to pull it out of the way and the stone dropped and landed on the top of my finger. I was taken to a German doctor who lopped off the top of my finger and stitched it up. So I was sent back to Lamsdorf for the winter. I had to get it dressed most days. This doctor looked at it – it was all wet and soggy – he said 'That wants drying up.' So he cleaned it up and signed me off to go back to work. I could have strangled him!

The working prisoners were lucky if they found any qualified medical staff to treat their wounds. During the early period of captivity large numbers of medics were still preoccupied with caring for those who had been seriously wounded in the battles of May and June. Furthermore, many captured in the fall of France were not initially allowed to work in a medical capacity. Some spent more than a year before being detailed to assist with medical care. Others, like Les Allan, were never recognized as medics and spent the entire war as labourers on working parties. The majority of available medics found themselves remaining behind in the main camps, where they operated hospitals for those suffering from disease or serious injury. As a result, the medics sent to working parties found they had little with which to treat those who suffered day-to-day injuries.

Captured near the Mont des Cats and initially imprisoned in Lamsdorf, Norman Barnett was sent out on an early working party where he attempted to look after the welfare of his fellow prisoners:

There were 125 POWs there. I didn't have any bandages or any medicines. The Germans asked me if everything was in order but I said 'No I need ointment.' We needed it for frostbite. The POWs were cleaning the coal silt from a canal. I did get a few aspirin and quinine tablets and some black tar that came in a tube. When the men got blistered with frostbite we had to use this cream. You had to cut away all the dead skin – when you cut it though, God the stink! Bloody hell! Then rub the cream on it. But you couldn't do much for the blokes. Just help their morale – if you gave them a bit of string to hold their bloody trousers up, it was something good!

As the year progressed, most of the prisoners began slowly to recover their health. It was not that they had suddenly begun to live in luxury but quite simply they were no longer starving. Once they had gone to work, found opportunities to trade, and also to beg, steal or borrow food, they began the slow process of recovery.

More than anything, during 1940 there was just one thing that saved the prisoners from wasting away – Red Cross parcels. As some later commented, it always seemed so strange that a simple cardboard box – no bigger than a shoebox – could bring so much joy to their lives. In the words of Ernie Grainger, struggling to survive at Lamsdorf: 'To be honest, if it wasn't for the Red Cross and the Gold Flake cigarettes they sent us, I wouldn't be alive now. Because those cigarettes were currency. I could buy a loaf for five cigarettes.' Dick Taylor, on working parties from Stalag 20A agreed: 'If we hadn't have got the parcels we wouldn't have survived. That's fairly sure. On the forestry kommando we got what was called "heavy workers rations", but it was only another half ounce of margarine and a bit of sausage – that was all. Not enough to keep us going. In the end the Germans were no better off than we were.'

At first the parcels were shared between large groups of men. In some cases they held lotteries to decide who should get what. Ken Willats celebrated his good fortune when he received a small bar of soap from a Red Cross parcel. Initially he was disappointed not to get any food, but he soon realized he had actually been fortunate. The following day all those who had received food – having consumed it immediately – were just as hungry as ever, whilst he was still able to keep clean. Corporal Allan, who later escaped home via the Soviet Union, reported his share of the first Red

Cross parcels: 'We received one parcel on 28th August, which was divided between 41 men; my portion being 12 cigarettes and half a tin of kippers.'[14]

Graham King later recalled the excitement that accompanied the sharing out of cigarettes and tins of condensed milk: 'We grabbed the tin, raced to our room, punched two opposing holes in the top, lay on our bunks and sucked at one of the holes, a complete reversion to babyhood. Quite soon the tins were emptied and we lay back with full bellies, belching like contented Arabs. Suddenly, there was a mass exodus to the latrines where the sounds of violent vomiting could be heard and sighs of "Never again." Much too rich for our starving guts.' Although the prisoners celebrated the arrival of these parcels, they were not all so lucky. For Eric Reeves, weighing just six stones, the joy of receiving a Red Cross parcel – shared between seven men – did not come until March 1941. As he recalled: 'By that time we were virtually skeletons.'

If their health began to recover, the same could not be said of their emotions. The improvements in health coincided with the arrival of winter. As the days got shorter and the first snows of winter began to bite, it was difficult to maintain morale. Nothing had prepared them for this. The experience of shovelling snow in minus 20° – often without gloves or overcoats – drained the men. Jim Pearce recalled getting 'down in the dumps' since he was living on foul horsemeat stew and working outside in freezing conditions that meant he was unable to do his flies up after urinating.

Though they tried to put a brave face on, beneath the veneer of self-confidence that was displayed for their guards, the reality was that most of the prisoners were sick, tired and frustrated. They were scared for themselves and for the families. They may have been able to switch their minds off as their senses were dulled by long hours of hard labour but, at the end of each day, as they lay to sleep, their thoughts were awash with emotions. As Bill Holmes remembered:

When I thought about things was just before I went to sleep. You were exhausted but you'd think about what had happened that day or about what people had said. It might be a tale about home and you'd wonder if it was true. Then I'd wonder if I was ever going home. On one occasion I had a dream about my parents. And in it my mother was standing beside a grave in our local churchyard. When I woke up I thought about whether it was my grave and the dream was trying to tell me something. It was an emotional time. I kept thinking about that for a long time.

As the year drew to a close, all the prisoners had to cling to was the notion that one day – sometime in the future – they might finally go home. And so, the end of that first year was a landmark. After months of the ceaseless routine of forced labour or the stupefying tedium of stalag life, Christmas and the New Year were a sign that time had not stood still.

Yet as the prisoners made light of their situation and attempted to celebrate the season, there was plenty to remind them that, for those imprisoned by the Nazis, this was not the season of goodwill. On a working party from Stalag 8B, Bill Holmes and his mates did their utmost to wrest some enjoyment from their first Christmas in captivity:

Everybody said 'We'll be home for next Christmas, that's for sure.' There we were, sleeping on hay in an old barn, and we could hear the Germans singing carols – it was 'Silent Night'. Even now, when I hear that it brings a tear to my eye. There we were with nothing – we were full of lice. On Christmas morning we got up and thought we might as well have a laugh. There was this Scots lad with us, he was having a laugh but the guard thought he was laughing at them. So the guard shot him dead. His corpse lay there in the snow for three days. The guard said 'If any of you laugh at us the same will happen to you.' That was my first Christmas in captivity.

Looking out into the snow, all thoughts of the Christmas season were swept away. All they could do was look at the frozen corpse and dream some day they might survive to go home. However, there would be four more Christmases before the men who had escaped via Dunkirk would return as their liberators. It would be a long and arduous wait.

CHAPTER ELEVEN

Five Years

There was no opportunity for individuals to be alone. Everywhere they went, everything they did, was among a group who observed and commented . . . Baths, eating, washing, reading, writing and latrine visits were all carried out in the company of others.

Graham King, RAMC, on his five years in Stalag 20A

All who have been in captivity for a considerable period are more or less abnormal.

War Office report on the psychological impact of life in a POW camp[1]

If the trials and tribulations of 1940 had not been enough, the remnants of the BEF faced five long years of misery in the stalags of Germany. The rosy picture of POW life that emerged in the post-war years was a fantasy, born of the public's reluctance to read stories that did not focus on prisoners spending their days attempting to escape. Though a brilliant piece of film-making, the 1963 film *The Great Escape* helped to create a public image of POWs that was essentially a myth and yet it is one that has survived to the present day. Quite simply, it bore little or no resemblance to the day-to-day lives of the vast masses of prisoners of war, whose lives revolved around forced labour, inadequate food, disease, violence and death.

There were three categories of prisoners. The first were the officers, who lived in separate quarters to the men they had led in battle. The second group were the NCOs, above the rank of corporal, who were excused from work by the conditions of the Geneva Convention. The third group – making up the vast majority of POWs – were the men employed at the workcamps. The lives of men in these different groups were entirely different. The existence of a typical POW lifestyle was the creation of the post-war media, presenting images that revolved around escape committees, wooden horses and tunnel-digging.

At Laufen, home to large numbers of officers captured in 1940, the prisoners were housed in a country palace, formerly the residence of the Archbishops of Salzburg. Others were imprisoned in a former girls' school at Rotenburg, or the hilltop castle at Spangenburg. Most famously, a number of the officers captured in 1940 eventually found themselves housed in the notorious Colditz Castle.

Unlike the men in the main stalags, who had soon discovered the advantages of going out to work and being able to trade with the local workforce, the officer prisoners had no such benefits. In the early years of the war some were allowed to give their parole, taking walks in the countryside on the agreement they would not escape. One Red Cross inspector even arrived at an oflag to be told he would not be able to meet the prisoners since they were out skiing. In most camps where officers were allowed out, there existed an unwritten agreement among the prisoners that they would not breach the conditions of parole. They agreed it was not fair for those who wished to escape to endanger the few freedoms enjoyed by the majority. After all, deep down, most escapers knew they themselves would soon be recaptured and be returning to the stalag.

As well as being able to give their parole and go for walks, the officers benefited from a number of other ranks allotted to each camp to act as batmen – effectively servants – for officer prisoners. Such measures did not meet with everyone's approval. Despite the desperate need for trained medical staff to look after the sick, some were diverted from their duties. In 1941 Fort 15 at Thorn became a camp for officers. Although a medic, Graham King was detailed to act as batman to a group of four senior officers:

> My job was to look after these four, as a general skivvy, tidying up after them and fetching and cleaning. As a medic I took a dim view of this, as there were many sick among the other officers and there were no more medics to spare. Two days later a senior British Medical Officer arrived, Lt. Col. Morris, M.C., RAMC, actually the CO of the unlucky 13th CCS. He was an outspoken man and shortly explained to the Brigadier the rights of protected personnel and I was returned to the sick bay forthwith.

Whilst many working–class men had little more than their work clothes and one suit 'for best', officers tended to have more clothing that could be sent to them from home. Many regular officers requested their best service uniforms be sent from home, allowing them to dress presentably after having lost so much when they were captured. Other privileges were the result of the class differences between officers and their men. Officers usually had bank accounts, something few of the other ranks had access to, and were able to use their savings to continue to spend money at home. They could request purchases from shops and for items to be posted out to them. Or they could arrange to buy presents for their loved ones, with some women recalling how their husbands managed to arrange a weekly delivery of flowers and ensure birthday presents reached their children. Such continuing connections with the outside world allowed officers to remember there was a world outside the barbed wire of a POW camp. However, those officers enjoying these privileges found that, although it made their lives more comfortable, there were certain disadvantages. Having a servant meant they had less to do each day to fill the long, boring hours of captivity. Rather than filling their hours with menial labour they had to find something else to do as they waited between roll-calls and mealtimes.

Despite the supposed glamour shown in the post-war POW films, most officers spent their five years of captivity in stupefying boredom. Their accommodation may have been better than that of the other ranks – having fewer men per room – but it was not a life of luxury. The benefits might have seemed obvious to some, but for others the notion of spending years cooped up in rooms with the same men day after day did not appeal.

Peter Wagstaff explained the effect of prolonged captivity:

I think there is a psychological point – for the prisoner of war – when you come across some extraordinary basis of living – you can't understand it, it's a new form of life. Gradually, as you continue to live that life, the extraordinary becomes ordinary. You think, 'Oh God, how will I pick myself us?' Normally you live a normal life and you compare yourself to that mode of living. But if you lose that way of living, because you are existing in this extraordinary state, you think 'Am I mentally that stable?' A lot of us felt that. We suffered in trying to readjust ourselves.

Stressing how difficult it is fully to explain the changes undergone by a twenty-year-old as a result of the violence of POW surroundings, he went on to discuss his reaction to witnessing deaths:

There was no particular impact. You are used to it. It was part and parcel of your life. Life comes and goes. The Kommandant, a German we called 'The Purple Emperor', told us 'If you look out of the window you are going to be shot.' One officer said he was still going to do it – and he was shot. But you took it, because it was part of life. You accept it. This was happening all the time. But I was not depressed because you were fighting for your physical and mental existence the whole time. You didn't have time to analyse yourself. You are fighting to keep alive.

You've got to keep mentally strong. So you develop a peculiar sense of humour.

The prisoners eventually had the satisfaction of seeing the Purple Emperor tried for war crimes.

The officers shared much of the same mental turmoil and yearning for freedom as was seen within the main stalags. The NCOs and other ranks who passed the years within the barbed wire enclosures were also cut off from the rest of the world, interacting with outsiders solely by letter. As a result, the two groups of men found a commonality of experience that was reflected in much of the behaviour displayed by POWs.

Incarcerated within the main camps were the permanent staffs of senior NCOs who did not have to go out to work. Although out of boredom some chose to go out on working parties, those who remained in camp took on a myriad of duties in support of the working prisoners. They managed the stocks of clothing and Red Cross parcels. There was both incoming and outgoing mail to be sorted and parcels from home to be sent out to men on working parties. The prisoners also ran cobblers' shops where teams of men could use whatever was available to repair boots and clogs. At Thorn, Fred Coster worked in the tailor's shop, using skills he had learned between leaving school and starting in the city. He used worn out clothing to make patches to sew onto threadbare uniforms. Whenever possible they took damaged uniforms to pieces, removing torn sleeves and replacing them with good ones. They even took apart pairs of trousers, using two worn out ones to create one good pair.

With the passing of the years, some of the prisoners who remained within the stalags settled into the life. Men captured later in the war were shocked when they arrived in the camps and witnessed men who had created their own little worlds. Within the forts at Thorn some prisoners curtained off their own areas, as if to construct their own small living rooms. This amazed outsiders, as did the strangely civilized conversations about the latest novels they

had read, plays they had seen back home or records they had heard.
Books and gramophone records were jealously guarded to protect
them within the world they had created. To the outsiders there was
a sense of one-upmanship more expected in the middle-class
drawing rooms of England than the damp bowels of a Polish fort.

Large numbers of those who formed the permanent staff at the
stalags were pre-war regular soldiers – NCOs with many years of
service under their belts. It was easier for them to settle into this life
than it was for many of their fellow prisoners. In many ways the
stalags were not that far removed from army barracks – only they
had even less freedom. As a result, many NCOs found it easier to
settle into stalag life than those men who, until just months before,
had known the freedoms of civilian life.

The senior NCOs had a degree of power and co-operated with
the Germans in maintaining a sense of discipline among the mass of
prisoners. However, maintaining discipline was a fine balancing act.
There were plenty of men who had no desire to be ordered around
by NCOs now that they were prisoners. Instead they felt they had
'done their bit', then been let down by the army. Now they
wanted to be left in peace until they could walk out of the stalag as
free men. For these men, the sight of senior sergeants strutting
around, as if on a parade ground back home, was too much to bear.
So they preferred to be on working parties where at least everyone
seemed to exist at the same level. Such emotions had to be balanced
by an awareness the benefits brought by a measure of order. Many
realized they had been saved in the early months of captivity by
NCOs forcing them to get active, making them wash and shave
rather than to just lazing around the camp doing nothing. The
problem was that the balance was not easy to find, as one NCO
discovered when he was confronted by Gordon Barber: 'They sent
me to a lumber camp. I didn't last three weeks there. I saw too
many blokes with broken arms and legs. I smacked the bloke in
charge – one of our blokes – in the mouth. He was too far up the
Germans' arses. He had a nice billet and we had the shit. One day
he started giving me a lot of mouth so I hit him.'

Although most senior NCOs were scrupulously fair in how they looked after the other prisoners, there were some who abused their positions and whose maintenance of discipline overstepped their responsibility. At Thorn RSM Davidson and Private Puttinger – who wore the rank insignia of a sergeant-major – were both accused of currying favour with the Germans. Prisoners were annoyed to see NCOs handing out punishments to fellow POWs, even getting the German guards to administer the punishment duties for them. Some were accused of collaboration since they were responsible for keeping the best food for themselves and did not provide enough good quality clothing to the men on working parties, keeping it instead for their cronies. Working prisoners felt any man who deprived them of the clothes they desperately needed was as bad as any German guards who made their lives a misery.

Despite the majority of prisoners being employed on arbeits-kommandos, most still spent some periods within the main camps. Bill Holmes recalled why he did not like these return trips to Stalag 8B: 'I didn't like it there. Once you've emptied latrines with a bucket you want to be back at work. There was also a lot of violence between the prisoners. One morning when the frost melted we saw a severed human hand stuck to this metal fire hydrant. It must have been in the ice all winter. It was a prisoner who'd been murdered. They'd cut his hands off. He'd been an informer so our lads hung him. You couldn't blame them for doing it.'

He also witnessed how the experience of captivity had a deadly effect on some prisoners: 'One chap I'll never forget. One night we heard shots go off. He was weary of life in the Stalag and he tried to escape. He hadn't got a hope in hell. They'd riddled him with bullets. We found what was left of him hanging on the barbed wire. He was practically shattered – all his bones were sticking out. It was horrible to see. Then they left him there for three days as a warning to us. Humans can be worse than animals.' In such circumstances, it was unsurprising that many prisoners preferred employment to inactivity. Quite simply, they preferred the arduous toil that seemed to help make captivity pass more swiftly, despite the knowledge that their sweat was aiding the survival of the regime that had enslaved them. Their poor food and living conditions, their lack of freedom, the harsh regime of punishments, the violent behaviour of their guards all served to convince the prisoners that they were slaves. As Jim Pearce remembered: 'We'd go to the villages to be chosen to work on the small farms. The Jerry farmers would come along, look at us, point to men and say "I'll have that one and that one" – it was like a slave market. When you look back that's exactly what it was!'

This state of enforced misery and servitude, under the threat of death, followed the prisoners through their working lives in the Third Reich. Some jobs were better than others, but all working prisoners knew what it was like to toil from dawn until dusk, in all weathers, with little or no concern taken for their welfare. In the summer of 1941 Sapper Thomas Pearson wrote home: 'I am now working at a swine of a place. It is always a hurry and working on nothing but a small bread ration and potatoes. It is nothing to see a man being sick while working because the food is rotten. The guard thinks we are horses although he calls us swine. Working in rain, no parcels, no smokes, threats of shooting now make our lot.'[2]

Les Allan, who should have spent the war years helping the sick and wounded, found himself forced to work in a brewery. One day he found himself face to face with a guard whilst holding a hammer he needed for his work. Seemingly fearing that Allan might attack him, the guard reacted quickly. He swung his rifle at the prisoner, smashing the butt into Allan's jaw. The young British soldier crashed to the ground, his jaw broken. For the second time in his military career he found himself wounded, helpless and reliant on the enemy's mercy for survival.

Such attacks showed how some Germans simply ignored many of the clauses of the Geneva Convention. At Stalag 20B the commandant, Oberst Bollman, forced senior NCOs to go out on working parties, but he sent the Red Cross inspectors and representatives of the protecting powers to specially selected workcamps to ensure any cases of illegal working would not be discovered. During the period in which Oberst Bollman was in command at Marienburg, eighteen prisoners were shot and killed, with a further twelve wounded, at workcamps supplied from his stalag. It seemed the guards had little concern for the men in their charge. At one farm a drunken guard shot a prisoner in the leg, then when the prisoner shouted for assistance the guard fired again, blowing half his head away. Other guards were reported to have lain in wait for soldiers attempting to escape and then opened fire without giving the men a chance to surrender. A Private Mackenzie was even shot and killed for daring to argue about whether a saw was sharp enough to work with. In the case of one of those killed during Bollman's command, it seemed that the guards revelled in the suffering they had inflicted. An announcement was made to the assembled prisoners that Sergeant Fraser had been killed for being the ringleader of a mutiny. The announcer also revealed that the guard who had shot Sergeant Fraser had been promoted for his actions.

Men who had seen the hideous violence and suffering of the battlefield found it difficult to understand why their guards could treat them with such disregard. Bill Holmes was angered to see that some guards seemed to delight in the pain they could cause: 'The brutality was awful. One chap had piles – I'd never seen piles before and I've never seen them since – they were bleeding. It was like a huge bunch of bleeding grapes hanging down. One day he pleaded to be excused from work because of the pain. And the guard came along and kicked him up the backside. There was blood everywhere – the agony must have been terrible.'

It is hardly surprising that many shared one overriding emotion – the desire to be free. Although only a relatively small number of prisoners ever successfully escaped from German POW camps, the exploits of the escapers became fabled during the post-war period. The courageous exploits highlighted in books and films like *The Wooden Horse*, *The Colditz Story* and *The Great Escape* showed a world in which escape was both possible and was the desire of all prisoners. Nothing could have been further from the truth. A vast majority of escape attempts were failures. Prisoners dug tunnels that were discovered or collapsed upon them. They tried cutting through the wire, only to be spotted by the guards or tried sneaking out of camps hidden in sewage trucks or rubbish bins. Legend even has one prisoner attempting to escape by dressing up as the guard dog used by the Germans.

The reality was that escape never entered the minds of most prisoners. Working prisoners couldn't be bothered digging escape tunnels since they had little energy left by the end of their shifts. Prisoners on work details on farms or in forests could have just walked away without anyone noticing, but knew they had little chance of getting away to safety. One group of men simply walked away from a working party on a farm – after all no one watched over them as they worked – and made their way to Danzig in hope of stowing away on board a ship heading to Sweden. When they arrived they found other prisoners working on the docks under guard. Realizing there was no way out, the escapers left Danzig and walked back to their workcamp. When Les Allan escaped from a workcamp he spent three days on the run and soon found himself utterly lost in the Polish countryside. When he was recaptured he discovered that, despite being on the run for three days, he had been going around in circles and was no more than a handful of miles away from the camp.

There was another good reason not to bother escaping. Lance-Corporal Green, who had been captured at La Bassée in May 1940, reported the treatment after he was discovered escaping from a working party: 'Having been escorted back to the camp, I was taken down to the punishment cells, stripped and beaten with a rubber truncheon into insensibility. I was kept there for 26 days with one meal a day of bread and water. For the first twelve days I lost my memory.'[3]

Despite the dangers, and the knowledge that failure was seemingly inevitable, escape activity continued throughout the war. After days, weeks, months then years of seeing the same faces day upon day – sharing the same stale air, the same stale old conversations and trapped in a timewarp in which every day still seemed to be 1940 – it became imperative for some men to escape. Yes, it was their duty to break free but it became increasingly important as a means of mental escape. Many turned to tunnelling or devising plans for getting out of the oflags in the knowledge that they would soon be captured, but admitted that every day outside the wire would be their own personal victory.

Some of the most famous wartime escapers were men who had been captured in France with the BEF. Airey Neave, who later became a Conservative MP and was assassinated by the INLA, was wounded at Calais in May 1940 whilst serving a searchlight battery who had been detailed to help defend the port. Captured when the town fell, Neave was transferred to Germany, where he became a serial escaper. In January 1942 he became the first British soldier to escape from the fabled Colditz Castle via a trap door in the floor of the castle's theatre, then made his way across Germany, through France and Spain, finally arriving in Gibraltar.

Another BEF officer who escaped from Colditz was Captain Patrick Reid, who was captured in France on 27 May 1940. He was initially held at Oflag 7C at Laufen but was transferred to Colditz following an unsuccessful escape attempt. Whilst in the castle he served as the escape officer and himself eventually made a successful escape to Switzerland in October 1942. He later became the most famous of the Colditz escapers after penning the book *The Colditz Story* and acting as an adviser on both film and television adaptations of his work. In the 1970s he even helped design the popular board game Escape From Colditz.

Although the escape routes that became most publicized were to Switzerland or to Gibraltar via France and Spain, some escapers took a different strategy. Despite the massing of German troops in the east in advance of Operation Barbarossa – the invasion of the Soviet Union – some POWs escaped eastwards. In July 1941 Sir Stafford Cripps, the British ambassador to Moscow, reported that fourteen escaped British POWs had been handed over to his care

by the Soviet authorities. One of the reasons that these escape
routes never received great attention was because the British and
the Russians decided that no publicity should be given to the
matter, with Cripps requesting that the censor did not allow any
mention of the subject in the British press.

The passage of troops into the Soviet Union did not always go
smoothly and one Briton was shot and wounded by border guards.
Another Briton spent months in detention in Moscow. Corporal
James Allan was a military policeman who had been taken prisoner
whilst in a military hospital in Boulogne, having been wounded in
the head near Lille on 18 May 1940. He escaped from Thorn after
joining a working party in the company of his mates Gunner Clark
and Lance-Corporal Green. In September 1940 the working party
had been digging up unexploded bombs when the three men made
their escape. After separation from his two comrades, Allan made
his way into the Soviet Union with the assistance of the Polish
underground. Clark and Green were first to cross into Soviet
territory, soon being arrested and sent to a Moscow prison.

James Allan later described his adventures:

I crossed the river Bug in a boat, while Polish scouts kept a watch
for any German patrol. I climbed over the barbed wire fence into
Russia and handed myself over to the authorities within five
minutes of crossing the frontier. I was searched very thoroughly
and everything was taken away from me. I was put in a small cell
for one night. I was then taken to another place and stayed there
for 10 days in company with Polish prisoners. Then I was sent to
Bialystock prison where I stayed for about a month together
with several Polish soldiers. The food was terrible and the
conditions were extremely bad. There was no room to lie down
in the cell at night. I then went to Minsk where conditions were
just as bad.[4]

From Minsk, Corporal Allan was transferred to a prison in
Moscow where conditions were better and he was in the

company of four other British escapers. Although they were all pleased to be together with fellow Britons, they had to go on a hunger strike for five days to win permission to speak to the prison governor about conditions. However, when the others were transferred to an internment camp near Smolensk, Allan was left behind. A group of French escapers who later arrived at the internment camp contacted the British embassy and reported that Allan was still being held in cell 97 at Butirka prison. Whilst there he was beaten up by guards and interrogated on suspicion of being a spy. Although he had no information of use to the Soviets they kept pressing him for information on the British Secret Service. During some interrogations he was forced, at gunpoint, to sign documents which he was unable to read. He remained in solitary confinement for nine weeks, facing more beatings from the guards.

Following the German invasion of the Soviet Union, Allan was transferred to another prison and began to receive improved treatment. He was given cigarettes, was allowed all the food he could eat and his clothes were laundered. Just as he thought life was getting better he was sent back to his original prison and put back into solitary confinement for a further three weeks. Eventually, after more interrogations, he was given a haircut, allowed to bathe, and was told he was free to go. The men who released him simply said he should go to the British embassy. When he told them he had no idea how to find the embassy, the men agreed to give him a lift.

Whilst some prisoners were attempting to continue the war by escaping, there was a handful who turned their attention to assisting the Germans. Some were men who were genuinely politically inspired and believed in the Nazi cause. Others were men who had been compromised by the Germans, agreeing to betray their comrades after being given extra rations. These traitors played a dangerous game, knowing that if they were discovered they would be lucky to survive. Whilst held at Thorn, Fred Coster became aware of the existence of traitors among the prisoners:

The SS raided the camp and they found everything we had hidden – the tunnel, the escape kit. So we knew we had a mole and wanted to find out who. We thought it was someone on the escape committee. So the chaps running the committee gave every man a different piece of information. Then we had another raid and the Germans went to a particular place. So that showed who had given them the information. That bloke didn't survive, he was bumped off. I quite agreed with it. When the latrines were drained they found his body in there. I don't know who actually killed the traitor – and don't want to know – but I'm glad they did it.

The Germans attempted to capitalize on the hopelessness felt by prisoners. Attempts were even made to create an SS unit of British soldiers. Originally called the Legion of St George and later known as the British Free Corps, recruitment to this organization was attempted by sending renegade Englishmen into POW camps to encourage POWs to join the Nazis in their crusade against Bolshevism. Their attempts were largely unsuccessful, as Fred Coster remembered: 'We had one incident where we were told to line up. Out in front came this Englishman, but he was marching like a German. He was wearing a German uniform. He was there to tell us to join the German army. He said if anybody wanted to join they should step forward. I remember one chap stepped forward! I looked round and he was yanked back into line by the blokes around him. I don't think he knew what he was doing – he probably just thought he'd get extra food.'

Those few who did betray their country and join the SS tended to be pre-war members of Oswald Mosley's British Union of Fascists. These included Francis MacLardy, a pharmacist from Liverpool, who was captured at Wormhoudt in Belgium whilst serving with the Royal Army Medical Corps. From there he had spent time in Thorn and also in Stalag 21D where he worked in the camp hospital. Whilst there he volunteered to join the SS. Others were less enthused by the politics of the Nazi regime and were trapped into joining. One of the favoured methods was sexual entrapment, which was used against Private John Welch of the Durham Light Infantry who had been captured in Belgium in 1940. After he was caught having sex with a German woman on a working party at a sawmill, he was told he would have to join the Germans or face execution. Welch agreed and later worked to convert other British soldiers to the Nazi cause. Another convert was Hugh Cowie, a private in the Gordon Highlanders who had been captured at St Valery. He elected to join the Free Corps after being caught with a clandestine radio set whilst at a working party on a Silesian farm. By turning traitor he was able to avoid a court martial.

As the prisoners began to settle down into a life of captivity, not all of the prisoners who befriended Germans were behaving treacherously. The soldiers on arbeitskommandos were inevitably drawn into relationships with German civilians. In the workplace this could involve civilian workers sharing food and cigarettes with the men they worked alongside. However, in the small rural communities where some prisoners were employed, the relationships went much deeper. The remote villages seemed cut off from the rest of the world and consequently many prisoners slipped into village life. Once the guards had accepted they were not planning to run away, many prisoners discovered an unexpected freedom. They used this freedom to do much more than just go walking in the countryside or swimming in rivers. With so many German men away at the front, their wives yearned for the company of young men. In such circumstances it was inevitable that relationships would blossom. Despite the dangers to both prisoners and the women, who could face imprisonment for their actions, after three years of enforced male company the lure of a willing female was difficult to resist. Almost three years after the defeat at St Valery, Gordon Barber was eager to develop his friendship with a local woman:

Some of us used to get our ends away . . . I'd got in with a married woman, Frieda, she was about 35 or 40 . . . You've got to remember we'd been out there for over three years. We were working and we were fit. We were all about 23 or 24 and the young women – in their thirties and forties – liked us. The governor of this big state farm used to make us go and help with their smallholdings. One Sunday I had to take the boar down to her sow. That was a bit funny. I remember watching the boar have a little bit. I could speak quite a lot of German by that time. I said 'Good job we're not like that!' She said 'What are you like?' That was the opening. She wasn't a bad looking woman. But nothing happened that day. But then on my birthday, February 26th 1943, she promised me some cake. I was doing the painting in her bedroom, then she came in and put her arms around my neck. And that was the start of a beautiful friendship.

The Red Cross parcels that began to arrive from late 1940 onwards became the most important thing in stalag life. Every time there was news that parcels had arrived, a buzz would go round a camp. Men who had done little but mope and moan for weeks on end would suddenly start chatting excitedly about the delights that awaited them. Men who had hardly raised themselves from their bunks were discovered playing endless card games, gambling over the precious boiled sweets that came in the parcels. Everything in the parcels was like a treat, whether it was raisins, soap or cigarettes. Even mustard offered the bonus of adding flavour to the dishwater-dull soups. Fruit jam with real pips replaced German jam that seemed to be thickened with sawdust. The smell of bacon emanated from huts where previously only the smell of dirty laundry and old socks had filled the air. Biscuits made a welcome change from the heavy black bread issued each day by the Germans. What a difference it made to consume sticky rich tinned treacle or savour the aroma of real coffee after weeks of surviving on thin vegetable stews and ersatz coffee made from acorns. The rations offered by the Germans were perhaps enough to keep them alive – just – but they were insufficient to offer any quality of life. Quite simply the Red Cross foodstuffs were a mental and physical lifesaver.

As the war progressed, the supply of Red Cross parcels grew to have another importance. With the German war effort faltering, shortages began to appear across the Reich, leaving the guards desperate for commodities such as soap, coffee and cigarettes. Luckily for the prisoners these were three commodities they did have some access to. Those prisoners who received Red Cross parcels were able to trade these items for whatever they desired. Graham King described how the system operated:

Schiller was a staunch member of the Nazi Party and was a Brownshirt. For all that, he was very friendly and I soon had him operating a black-market enterprise with me. He was addicted to English cigarettes (*verboten*). English Red Cross parcels were coming through regularly and certain types of parcels addressed to individuals could be sent. All food was a bulk issue but clothing, books, records, tobacco and cigarette parcels could be sent to individuals, I even had a portable, wind-up gramophone sent out. Cigarettes, tea, chocolate (used to make up weight of 5 Kgms of clothing parcels) were the Euros of the POW camps. German Reichgeld and Lagergeld had very little purchasing power. However, chocolate, coffee, tea and soap were useful items of barter but cigarettes were at the top because they could be used singly or in multiples. The good Doktor could obtain a flash type of cigarette lighter, which became a 'must have' among the POW community. The Herr Doktor swapped one lighter, which cost 7.50Rms for a tin of 50 cigarettes and I sold them on at 50% profit.

Of course, trade was not the only method the prisoners used for improving their lifestyle. Theft from the enemy became an every-day part of stalag life, as Graham King later recalled:

Many of the POWs worked on local smallholdings, many poultry farms. During the egg-laying season the Germans were surprised to experience an immense shortage of fresh eggs. Of

course, they were being smuggled into the camps where we
experienced a glut. Eggs were so plentiful they became an
embarrassment and were used in all kinds of ways. Fresh raw
egg stirred up in tea with sugar and KLIM milk were a guarantee
of erotic dreams and, like Ambrosia cream rice, was much in
demand . . . Eggs were smuggled into the camp by using the
excellent design of the British battledress, which was a baggy
blouse and trousers. The trousers were secured at the ankles by
either gaiters or puttees. The eggs were gently packed into the air
gaps and the smuggler marched into camp. The record number
of eggs smuggled into the camp in this manner by one man, on
one trip, was two hundred.

At Stalag 8B Ernie Grainger saw the effects of the diet on
prisoners: 'The main problem was stomach disorders. People were
so starving, when they got Red Cross parcels they just ate the lot.
Then they got perforated stomachs and duodenal ulcers. It caused
us to get lots of haemorrhage cases.'

The lack of medical care led to all manner of unexpected
infections and strange deaths. At one stalag hospital a post-mortem
was carried out on a soldier who had died of a mysterious
condition. A pus-filled tumour was found on his brain. There
were signs of inflammation leading down from the tumour to the
source of the infection – a decayed tooth. He had been killed by
tooth decay.

While such extremes were fortunately rare, disease still became a
constant companion for the POWs. During the first year of
captivity the medical staff at the stalags had done their utmost
to prevent the spread of disease and infection. Despite their efforts
there was little they could do with the sickest of the prisoners.
During 1940 the Germans put nothing in place for the treatment of
men who contracted tuberculosis. Instead the men just lay in their
beds at the stalag hospitals, hoping to recover. At Stalags 20A and
20B there were deaths among the TB patients, resulting in some
being transferred to Stalag 3A. However, although some treatment

was available, the food was inadequate and men continued to die for lack of care.

Fortunately for the ailing prisoners, someone did care about their fate. In early 1941 the Swiss intervened and insisted that 150 TB patients be transferred to the hospital at Stalag 4A. There they were housed four to a room, had access to hot and cold running water and could stroll in a park. To cope with the numbers of TB patients a second facility was opened for them at Winterberg. Then, when the hospital at Stalag 4A was closed to patients, 130 men from the BEF were transferred to a sanatorium at Königswartha that had previously been a hospital for infectious diseases. Despite its history, the facilities were of a poor standard. Some men were in stone buildings, others in wooden huts, and once again they were sleeping in two-tier bunks with no flushing toilets, just latrines over cesspits. The conditions resulted in the death rate rising again. Treatment of TB only improved in 1942 when mass radiography for suspected cases became available. Even then it could take up to nine months to find a hospital bed for a TB patient.

Quite often, prisoners with TB were offered no treatment at all. Some just continued working, day after day, until they became too sick to continue. On a working detail from Stalag 8B, Bill Holmes witnessed the demise of a fellow prisoner:

We were working at this sawmill and food was tight. There was one chap who had TB. He was only 20 but he was dying. We couldn't do anything with him. We only got a portion of bread – two slices – for the day, but we tried to fill him up to keep him going. But one night he died. The Germans said he'd just have to be buried in the churchyard without a coffin. We argued that we were working in a sawmill so with all the wood, couldn't they spare some. So we had these rough boards and made a coffin. And we got a scrap of tin, hammered it into a cross and put that on the lid. We made a paper wreath. It may seem crazy, but we were just happy he was in a box. What his poor parents would have thought, God only knows.

Stalag hospitals were often depressing places for the patients. Men who had dreamed of getting a break from work were usually desperate to get back to their working parties rather than remain in hospital. One of those who experienced this turmoil was Dick Taylor. A Territorial soldier who had been captured at St Valery, Taylor found himself in hospital after he suffered the swelling of a gland behind his left ear. He needed an operation urgently since the swelling prevented him from eating. As a result he had lost a lot of weight from his already malnourished body. He was sent to a depressing military hospital in Danzig where he witnessed a madman rampaging round the wards waving a cut-throat razor and discovered patients who had lost limbs as a result of scratching insect bites. The bites had got infected and the infection had spread until blood poisoning had set in. For Taylor it was the lowest point of the entire war: 'There were people dying all around me. The bed I got was because a coloured lad had just died of yellow jaundice. There was also a locked ward full of mentally ill Russians. It was a depressing place. The thing was, when someone died, their belongings were put into a small cardboard box. That was all they possessed in the whole world – nothing else. It was pretty depressing to see a man's whole life in one tiny box. It was a sign of a wasted life.'

Physical sickness was not the only burden faced by the POWs. Every prisoner felt the effects of the mental turmoil of captivity. Ken Willats, the chef turned infantryman captured at Abbeville, recalled the impact of knowing how far from home he was:

When you are sitting on a farm in East Prussia and your home is in Elmfield Way, Balham, you cannot possibly see what events could take place to remove you from this little hamlet back to the hustle and bustle of London, SW12. You couldn't imagine how that could come about. It seemed impossible that you would one day be back in normal life. So that was daunting. One realised that if Germany did win the war you'd be there for many, many years – that was a very real thought. But once you'd determined the war was going to be over by Christmas – every Christmas – you were all right. We had no choice, there was no point thinking anything else. It could drive you mad, you'd torture yourself.

Jim Pearce, a Londoner who found himself working on lonely farms in the Polish countryside, took solace in the company of a Bible that had been sent to him by the Red Cross. It also accompanied him on the seemingly endless railway journeys between working parties. Whenever he had the chance he read from it and he prayed every night 'for the Lord to look after me. It really helped me to keep going.' Although he was not alone in turning to religion, others found a more basic use for their Bibles as toilet paper.

For other prisoners the process of retaining morale was nothing more sophisticated than undermining German morale, as Eric Reeves remembered: 'Once we got together we always believed we would win. The guards would say "*England kaput.*" They'd say that the Germans had always won another big battle. But we would say "Yeah, but we're gonna win the last one mate!" We used to needle the guard all the time. That kept morale up.' These were emotions that were shared by another young soldier, Jim Reed: 'I was just a kid, but you soon grow up. Quite a few men went nuts. But I never felt I was wasting my life. I was just waiting for the end of the war to get a bit of justice from them – I wanted to have a go at the Germans. I wasn't afraid of them. We told them we were better soldiers, we were better men and we came from a better country.'

At first the prisoners did anything they could to entertain themselves. They played innumerable games of cards and chess on boards provided via the Red Cross and read whatever books they could find. Some had bizarre competitions, such as seeing who had the most lice on their bodies. At Stalag 20B there was even a contest to see who had the largest penis in the camp. As the camps got increasingly organized more sophisticated methods were found for keeping up morale. They put on plays and concert parties, formed dance bands and orchestras, established educational classes and played sports in whatever space they had available. One of the regular performers at his working party's concerts was Cyril Holness, who had been captured in an aid post in 1940. He could sing and play the accordion but had one other talent that made him in demand. As a small, fresh-faced youngster with good teeth, he was the perfect choice to play female roles. For performances he wore a bra made from a cigarette tin and eventually had a pair of breasts fashioned from rubber by a commercial artist. Whilst in costume he found he received unexpected attention: 'One time I was dolled up in my costume and heading back to my hut. The guard was following me – he was very interested in me! I said to him in German "You're gonna get a shock when I take my trousers off!" He laughed his head off and said "You look so good I wasn't sure." You wouldn't think of those things in a POW camp!'

Certain songs evoked sentimental memories for the prisoners, reminding them of everything they had left behind at home. Cyril Holness remembered the effect of the songs he would sing: 'Every Christmas I'd have the big fellows in tears. All the older men who were married with children would cry when I sang this old song "The Little Boy That Santa Claus Forgot". It's a very sad song about a boy who wants toy soldiers for Christmas but doesn't get them because he hasn't got a father.' As Eric Reeves remembered: 'You'd see all the tears coming when they sang sad songs – that's how you picked out the married men – they cried unashamedly, tears rolling down. Some were blokes who'd got married on their embarkation leaves then been stuck out in Germany for five years. Us single blokes didn't bother, we didn't give a monkey's! But that was when the morale starts to go.'

By March 1945 there were more than 41,000 British POWs who had endured more than four years of captivity, all of whom were thought to be likely to require some from of mental rehabilitation once they were finally released. For some the symptoms were no more than a deep sense of longing for home and family as they lay down to sleep each night. They thought of the parents who were growing older and the children who were growing up. They dreamed of the warm embrace of their wives, were tormented by sexual desire or the thoughts of what their girlfriends might be doing in their absence. They dreamed of walking the streets in freedom or simply watching the sunset from somewhere that wasn't surrounded in barbed wire. However, for the thousands of working prisoners these were brief thoughts that filled their minds before their exhausted bodies slipped into deep sleep.

For other POWs the mental burden was far greater. Those officers and NCOs who remained in the stalags were free from the physical burden of work but carried a far greater mental burden since they had little to do except to ponder their situation – hour upon hour, day after day, year upon year. This mental burden – that probably inspired more escapes than the desire to return to continue the fight against Germany – took its toll on many of the prisoners. One of the most visible signs of mental stagnation was displayed by the men known as 'sack hounds'. These men spent long hours in their beds, hardly bothering to stir for days on end. In November 1944 a Major Higgins wrote from Oflag 7B about the mental state of the 800 officers in the camp who had endured four and a half years of POW life. He was prompted to act after eight officers were removed to mental hospitals: 'I must emphasise that in my opinion it is most important that prompt action is taken if these young officers are to be in a fit condition to render useful service in the future.'[5]

By 1943 the British Army estimated that around 30 per cent of long-term prisoners would be mentally unfit for further service upon their release from captivity. An official report described the individual morale of long-term POWs as 'brittle'. 'It was accepted that after eighteen months of captivity emotional problems became disproportionately severe. This period was remembered by Graham King:

In films the prisoners are always depicted as cheerful but we used to suffer from depression. You'd get annoyed with the person you were living with. Even the way they'd hold a bloody cigarette would get on your nerves – until you could scream. You wouldn't speak to them for about three months – just because they weren't smoking properly! You can't get away from people, you are with them every day. At least civilian prisoners can count the days off as they go through their sentence. We couldn't do that, we didn't know what was happening. Even up to the day of liberation it could all have changed. The International Red Cross referred to these symptoms as 'barbed wire fever' and they recommended that in future wars prisoners should not be held for longer than five years and then sent to a neutral country.

A paper submitted to the War Office by Major Newman of the RAMC set out the psychological impact of captivity:

intense initial depression after capture, the period of recovery of morale with frustrated revenge feelings liable to be misdirected towards the home authorities; the gradual adaptation of the more fortunate PW to his conditions and the storing up of frustration in less fortunate men. Then follows a long boring period which worries the man because unlike a civil criminal there is no period put to his captivity and during this period frets for fear of being forgotten, especially by those from whom he seeks affection.[6]

Major Newman's predictions were echoed by an officer who wrote from a Stalag to the Swiss Legation in Berlin in February 1944: 'More recently, among the older prisoners, the number of mental and nervous cases has been steadily increasing and I see signs now, amongst a number, that they are reaching a breaking point.'[7] The psychological effects of long-term captivity were considered so severe that some in the British military suggested that there should be a straight swap between the British and Germans of healthy

POWs. The suggestion was never put to the Germans since it soon became clear that the Germans would get 3,000 fighting men whilst the British would receive 3,000 men who would most likely be immediately discharged from service.

Desperate not to be forgotten by the outside world, the most important thing in the POW's life became his mail. Over the years of captivity this became a lifeline, the only thing that connected them with the civilian world of their families. Such was the impact of mail that prisoners recalled greeting each other with 'How's your mail?' rather than 'How are you?' It seemed that every prisoner received bad news at some point. Whilst in Thorn, Fred Coster received the devastating news that his brother had been killed in action. He later also heard that his girlfriend had gone off with a Canadian soldier. Yet not all the news was bad, even if it had to be waited for. At working camps from Stalag 8B, Fred Gilbert attempted to keep alive a long-distance relationship with his girlfriend:

> I hadn't known her very long when I was captured. I'd only met her in only 1940. Lads were getting letters off their wives – 'Don't bother to come home – I'm not living there anymore – I'm marrying someone else' – and so on. We heard this time and time again. It destroyed them. It was their only link to the outside world. I thought that was a bit grim. You'd see a bloke with a letter and people would say 'Is it a good one? Is everything alright?' So it wasn't a happy time. However, I wrote home to ask my girlfriend to marry me – I had to wait some months to get the answer. It was the right answer fortunately – I just hoped she'd keep her word.

Others were not so fortunate to receive news they wanted to hear. Peter Wagstaff recalled the impact bad news had upon one of his fellow prisoners: 'He received a letter from his fiancée within a couple of months. She wrote "I don't know how long you are going to be away. I don't think I can wait that long." He climbed the wire and got shot by the guards. That happened to a lot of people.'

Whilst 'Dear John' letters from girlfriends and wives brought devastating news, other letters brought information that just could not be believed. Graham King recalled reading a letter on behalf of an illiterate soldier: 'If men heard their wives were being friendly with Yanks, there was bugger all they could do about it. This one illiterate bloke's wife wrote that she had heard a noise one evening and gone to the back door. When she got there she found a little baby had been left there. She said it looked so much like her husband she had decided to keep it. And this bloke accepted it! I wonder if it had been different if he had been able to read it himself.'

Whilst all the prisoners experienced some form of mental anguish, there were increasing numbers who suffered severe psychological disturbances as a consequence of five years' captivity. For some the trauma was a manifestation of issues that had already plagued them pre-war – in the words of their fellow prisoners they were the type who 'couldn't handle it'. For others the trauma of war had simply devoured their ability to resist the strain of captivity. The most severe cases were later found to be men who were ruminating over the death of friends and comrades or who had experienced a particularly distressing experience in battle.

There was a fine line between misery and madness, and the prisoners all witnessed enough suffering to realize that they were actually among the more fortunate groups detained within the Third Reich. At least they had the nominal protection of the Geneva Convention, something that was not shared by the Russians within the stalags. The British might have been appalled by the treatment handed out to the Russians, but at least they were just witnesses rather than victims. 'Ginger' Barnett, a medic at Stalag 8B remembered: 'The Russians were treated like animals. I saw starving Russian POWs being used like horses to pull carts piled high with their own dead. The poor devils were so cold they fought each other to get the clothes off the dead.'

When prisoners did crack up it was disturbing for the men that witnessed it. Jim Reed recalled watching a man attempting to dig his way through the floor with a spoon: 'I knew him and tried to talk to him but next time I saw him he was barefoot and half way up the barbed wire. The guard started prodding him with a bayonet and made him climb back.' Others were not so fortunate, as Jim Pearce recalled: 'A lot of people got really down in the dumps – they didn't care if they lived or died. They'd pinch anything – they'd commit suicide by climbing the wires. They knew they were going to get shot.' At a working party on a farm at Adlesbruck Ken Willats and Gordon Barber were woken by a fellow prisoner calling out the name of a local girl with whom he had fallen in love. It was clear that the man was losing his mind. Gordon Barber remembered that night:

> It was uncanny, it frightened us. What the fucking hell was going on? All night he stood by the window holding the bars, as he gazed out into the darkness and sang about his lover. My mate Ken went up to him and said 'What's wrong?' He said 'I love her. I don't care what the guards say I'm going to see her tonight.' He'd gone. He'd flipped. All you could see were fag ends burning. None of us could handle it. Next morning he wouldn't go to work. We saw him with his hands through the barbed wire. The guards said they'd shoot him. We said 'You can't shoot him, he's gone crazy.' So 'Dixie' Dean walks over, says 'Fipper, you've got to go.' Then hits him and knocks him straight out. We carried him to the fields, but he was useless. When the sergeant in charge of us came round that month they took him away. He got sent home.

At least this prisoner was protected by his comrades, others had no one there to help them when they needed it most, as Fred Coster recalled: 'I was lined up outside Fort 13 to go on a working party. We heard a clatter in the courtyard. We looked round and one of the chaps had jumped off the roof. He'd gone mad and killed himself. His body was down there on top of this big steel drain cover. We didn't know who it was, we just marched off to work.'

In the summer of 1944 the prisoners were struck by news of a landmark event that helped lift their spirits to new levels. The announcement of the D-Day landings marked a turning point for the men who had been in captivity for four years. After so long waiting, the British Army and its allies were back in France, working hard to advance through the landscape that had seen its defeat back in 1940. Now, it seemed, the soldiers who had escaped at Dunkirk were returning to liberate their comrades who had been left behind.

There was another sign that helped spark the realization that Germany must finally be defeated. From 1944 onwards, those men employed in the factories of the Third Reich, saw an increasing weight of bombs dropped on Germany by the Allied air forces. The very thought that high in the skies above them were their own countrymen, bringing the war to the heart of the Reich, lifted their spirits. However, each pound of high explosive may have helped hasten the end of the war but, for those on the receiving end, it also ushered in a period of mounting danger. Eric Reeves, who had last found himself under bombardment in the fields around Abbeville in 1940, found the industrial complex he was working within was one of the major targets for the bombing campaign. He was unfortunate to be employed at Blechammer, where synthetic fuel was manufactured for the German war machine:

It really got hit! The first time was in June 1944. They hit the place while we were working – but we weren't allowed in air raid shelters. Then they bombed us each month until Christmas. At that time the Germans were so desperate for manpower that we were working every day for four weeks then having a weekend off. We'd just finished our shift and got back to the camp on Saturday afternoon and over the bombers came and hit our camp with five bombs. That's when we lost blokes.

With the commencement of the bombing raids on Blechammer the whole atmosphere changed for the prisoners:

The civilians you used to talk to stopped saying 'good morning'. The offices were all at one end of the camp. They had a line of buses waiting for the air raids. So as soon as the sirens went all the boffins could get in the buses and get away. We were working near there one day and as the sirens went we waited for the buses. When they turned the corner we ran out and climbed up the ladder that took you onto the roof rack. We went about ten miles out while the camp was being bombed – we had a grandstand view of the bombing from this hill. But one time we did it and the bombers actually bombed all round the hill we were on. They were bombing the anti-aircraft sights around us! This German said to us 'You will have to walk back!' I was cheeky, I said to him 'Yeah, and from here we can run away.' So he let us back on the bus to go back to the camp.

Although the air raids helped to reassure the prisoners the Allies were winning the war, they also put them under the psychological pressure of worrying that bombing might turn the guards against them:

You were always in a certain amount of danger that one of the guards was going to run amok. One of the guards went home on leave and previously he'd treated all the blokes well. He'd been fair to them, they'd even given him fags and coffee to take home. But when he came back from leave he was a broken man because his family had been destroyed in a bombing raid. He was a different man after that. He was spiteful to the prisoners. You could see the difference in him. It wouldn't have taken much for them to turn on us.

By 1945 there still remained thousands of POWs – in varying degrees of health – who had been in captivity since the dark days of

1940. Almost to a man, they had developed a 'stalag mentality' in which their prime concern was for their personal survival. They had grown cynical and increasingly accepted anything the world threw at them as long as their own lives were not affected. Les Allan recalled how, in the latter days of the war, long-term prisoners would feel less bitter about violence by the guards, pointing out that the victim had probably brought the violence on himself by his behaviour. Effectively, they had developed a protective shield that helped keep them sane in a world that had grown increasingly mad. As Jim Pearce remembered, as their fifth year of captivity drew to a close: 'Life was getting getting tough and the Jerries were getting tough as well!'

The discovery of just how mad the world had become would include a final trial that was to be faced by the victims of Dunkirk – it was a trial that allowed them the right finally to return home.

CHAPTER TWELVE

Going Home

I met him just after the war and he was a very cynical, very embittered young chap.

Patricia Wagstaff on the effect of five
years' captivity upon her husband

Everything you do in life leaves a scar and those five years left many scars . . . There were about 12 people captured with me and only about six of them came back home.

Peter Wagstaff on the psychological
impact of five years' captivity

As 1944 drew to a close the men left behind at Dunkirk were deep in the midst of their fifth winter in captivity. For six months, since the joyous relief of the D-Day landings, the prisoners had waited for the army that had escaped in 1940 to repay the favour and rescue them. If the summer and autumn of 1944 had been filled with good news, as the Allies advanced on the German frontier, the winter was very different. Every winter had been a miserable experience for the prisoners. Working prisoners spent days out in the bitter cold shovelling snow, cutting ice, digging sugar beet from frozen ground. With no protective clothes they wrapped themselves up as best they could

and prayed to avoid frostbite. Yet this final winter was something
else.

With Germany facing defeat, its economy was slowly collapsing. Rations deteriorated, often falling back to the starvation
levels they had known in the sickening summer of 1940. Back in
their first year of captivity they had been saved by Red Cross
parcels, but by late 1944 the supply of parcels had begun to dry
up. As the Allied advance cut through the supply routes previously used for parcels, the prisoners' future began to look
increasingly bleak. With the icy hand of the war's worst winter
gripping at the prisoners, they once more began to face the awful
realization that if something did not happen soon they might not
live to see liberation.

What did happen was not something any of them would have
hoped for. In early 1945 the stalags and workcamps across the
eastern regions of the Reich – East Prussia and the former Polish
and Czech lands – began to close. For all the prisoners had long
dreamt of camps closing so that they could head home, this was not
the end they had hoped for. Whilst five years previously they had
been crammed into stinking cattle-trucks for the journey east, the
journey west would be different. This time they were heading west
on foot. There was an irony in these circumstances. In 1940 they
had endured the blistering heat of summer as they marched into
captivity. In 1945 they were again sent out onto the roads, this time
on roads deep in ice and snow. Yet, though the weather conditions
were so different, the prisoners soon realized their real enemies
were the same – starvation, exhaustion and the murderous behaviour of some among their guards. It was a journey that drove the
prisoners to the very brink of survival.

Most of the prisoners knew that their camps would have to be
evacuated. Those in the east could hear the guns of the Red Army
as it blasted its way westwards. Those working on the railways had
long seen the trains crammed with wounded Germans heading
home and then watched as increasingly young and nervous soldiers
headed east to face their nemesis. Yet when the word finally came

that the camps were to be evacuated it still came as a shock to the prisoners. At a workcamp in east Prussia Les Allan and his mates were called out in the middle of the night for a roll-call. They lined up in the biting cold – huddling deep into their overcoats – desperate to get back in their bunks. Then the word came they were leaving. No warning, no time to prepare, just line up and march out of the gates. All they had were the clothes they stood up in.

Les Allan cursed his luck. He had been fortunate to survive when the convent at Hazebrouck had collapsed on him back in 1940. Then he had no idea what lay ahead. This time he knew what to expect – only this time it would be colder. He well knew that he would need every ounce of his energy to survive. There was one problem. When they were called outside, Allan had left his boots beside his bunk. When they went outside they only took things they thought would be stolen, as a result Allan had taken his chess set. He knew no one would dare steal his boots since they were marked with his name. To be caught stealing a man's boots would have been far too risky. If caught, it would have resulted in a severe beating – or worse. As a result Les Allan found himself facing a march of hundreds of miles along icy roads wearing just a pair of rough canvas-topped clogs.

As the men left they soon realized they were not alone on the roads. There were thousands of German families who were also heading west – fearful of the revenge they would face from the Poles and Russians once the German Army had retreated. There was also another vast wave of humanity forced out onto the roads alongside the POWs. As Graham King left Thorn he first noticed them:

On the 19th January 1945, we were very rudely awakened by the shouting of our guards. We were to get our things together, food for three days as we were to move out of this camp to another in Germany. We could take only as much as we could carry and rations for three days . . . We fell in outside the compound on the main road, quietly smoking and chattering away. There was a feeling of suppressed excitement as individually we realised that we could be making our first few steps towards Blighty and home. Not far from where we stood was a column of people who appeared to be dressed in striped pyjamas, both sexes. We moved toward them but they retreated and their guards shouted at them to move away. The guards wore Brownshirt uniforms and one kid about sixteen had a whip with which he started beating some of these poor sods, so we took his whip away and threatened him with it. He and his friends shouted to our guards who told them shove off, or words to that effect. We discovered later that they were from a concentration camp. During the next months we were to see many abandoned by the roadside.

The columns of marching men soon discovered the conditions had conspired against them. One night, Graham King was told by a guard that the thermometer on a farmhouse had read −35°C. He later described how, as the moon rose and the temperature dropped he could hear the ominous 'crackling silence of a land freezing under a Polish winter'. Such temperatures would have tested even the best prepared of men, let alone a bunch of men tired after five years of captivity. Many found themselves dressed in nothing more than their battledress and an overcoat. Some had blankets they could wrap around themselves like a shawl. Some had hats, gloves and spare socks, others had nothing. They simply turned up their collars, stuffed their hands deep into their pockets and shuffled along in hope that they would survive.

By night they slept out in the open, unless they were fortunate enough to be herded into a barn. Those with blankets wrapped themselves as best they could, scraped away some snow and curled up, just hoped for the best, as Calais veteran Bob Davies remembered: 'You just stopped in a field, dug a hole in the snow to keep the wind out and − with a bit of luck − you woke up in the morning!' After a day's marching, with snow swirling around them, they dropped to the earth as their desperately exhausted bodies fought a perplexing battle with their minds. What mattered most – rest or food, sleep or protection from the cold? Was it better to take off their boots and risk them freezing or should they keep their boots on and risk frostbite as a result of poor circulation?

Having left his final working party, Jim Pearce joined the march and spent ten weeks on the road. He remembered the conditions:

> I wore two sets of clothes and had a blanket over my head like a shawl – no gloves – it was shocking. My boots soon started to wear out. I remember the first time I took them off – next morning I couldn't get them back on, they were frozen! I fainted – so a bloke rubbed snow on my face to revive me. I never took them off again after that. We slept outside every night, we tried eating raw sugar beet but it was too bitter. I thought I wouldn't survive. People were dying with dysentery. Sometimes they dug latrines but men sometimes fell into the pit – there was nowhere for them to wash! Some men dropped out and they got shot, you'd see bodies by the roadside. Maybe it was better they did shoot them, otherwise they'd have just frozen to death. We despaired – we didn't know what was going to happen to us. Some days we didn't care if we lived or died – life was finished.

One of the men who gave up the will to live was Ken Willats. Always a reluctant soldier, Willats lacked the physical strength to endure the plummeting temperatures of the Polish winter. After his first night sleeping out in the snow he was unable to continue:

> The first night was horrendous. We walked all night and all day. Then we were marched into a field late at night. The temperature must have been 30 degrees below zero. There was no cover . . . When we got up in the morning I was so exhausted I could hear music playing and see houses – I was hallucinating. I

saw these houses that weren't there. It was then I decided I
would sit down and have a sleep . . . My survival instinct was
gone. It was as if I had been anaesthetised. I was at the limit of my
endurance.

Fortunately for Willats he had not been forgotten. He was part
of a group of five, including Gordon Barber, the regular army
gunner who had been captured at St Valery. Though men from
very different backgrounds, the two had become firm friends
during the two years they had spent on a Polish farm. When
Barber noticed Willats was missing he turned back to find him:

He was by the tree. We got hold of him, he was fucking cold.
His teeth were chattering. I said 'You'll die if you stop there.
You won't be tired anymore.' So we put our arms round his
shoulders and off we went and caught the others up. We were
lucky that night we found a barn to sleep in . . . The next
morning it was sunny. I went out and found a horse drawn
wagon the Germans were carrying the sick on. Ken was just
frozen so we got him on this wagon and they went. I never saw
him again until we got home.

As medics, Graham King and his mates knew something about
circulation and survival. To cope with sleeping outdoors they
implemented a rotation system devised by explorers in the Ant-
arctic:

It was essential to clear the snow from the ground, lay down a
covering on which to lie as this would act as a kind of insulation.
The party then lay down in a row like spoons and covered
themselves up. Every 15 minutes, the guy at the right of the row
got up and moved to the other end and everybody moved one
place to the right. In that way every one spent some time being
sheltered by the rest of the group and so kept reasonably warm,
although sleep was at a minimum. To ward off frozen feet, it was

essential to slacken off all fastening so that the blood circulation would not be hindered, in fact it was even better to remove shoes and socks, dry off the feet and wrap loosely in some item of dry clothing. Next morning, of course, the damp socks and boots were frozen solid . . . however, you get frostbite only when feet are frozen. If your boots and socks are damp then the temperature is above freezing and you need not fear frost bitten feet. I explained all this to the group from 16 and, amazingly, they all followed this routine. Of course to thaw out the socks you had to use the warmth of your own feet and gradually ease them over the old tootsies and pull them on, then slowly force on the boots. This took about an hour. Once shod we began to move around to get the circulation going in order to move on the way.

Of course, not all the marching men were aware – or physically capable – of looking after their feet in this manner. As a result, frostbite became a severe problem for them. Graham King helped as far as he could:

At this time another bloke asked me to look at his feet. I asked him what was wrong and he replied he could not feel anything. He took off his boots and socks, displaying a pair of feet as black as ink. I felt them and they were as cold as icicles, frost bitten right through and would be gangrenous very shortly. He needed emergency surgery or he would die. Unfortunately we had no means of carrying out what he needed. I asked his friend if he would let the patient put his feet on his bare body under his jacket in the faint hope that this might get some circulation going. Next day, passing through a small town we left him at a civilian hospital where the nursing sisters of a religious order promised to care for him. Before leaving, I asked him when he had last taken off his boots. Not once since we had left Thorn . . . I never knew what happened to this poor chap; I hope he got home eventually.

Not all were so fortunate. Plenty of men, their feet ravaged by frostbite and unable to march another step, simply collapsed by the roadside. The lucky ones were dragged along by their mates, others were ignored by the men around them, each one of whom was engrossed in his own personal battle for survival. The sound of rifle fire became an increasingly common factor in their lives, as men who had fallen out were executed in cold blood at the roadside. Hardly bothering to look up, the prisoners simply trudged past as the snow covered the corpses of their murdered comrades.

As the marchers moved on, the effects of the shortage of food began to bite just as much as the wind. In 1940 the problem had been thirst, with the Germans refusing to allow them access to pumps and ponds, yet they had survived by stealing whatever was growing in the countryside around them. In the winter of 1944/5 the situation was reversed. They had no shortage of water, since there was endless an amount of snow that could be melted. The difficulty was that there were no vegetables growing in the frozen fields. As Graham King noted: 'Signs of malnutrition were now appearing. Sunken cheeks, haggard looks, baggy clothing and tickling throats all spoke of the lack of essentials in the diet. In effect we were walking ourselves to death and there was little which could be done.'

It was not long before King had his one personal encounter with the dangers of marching week after week on starvation rations. In desperation he picked up a small piece of frozen carrot from the roadside. Knowing that even the smallest piece of food could help ward off hunger, he rapidly consumed the carrot. Minutes later he was gripped by an agonising pain in his stomach. He fell out by the roadside, unable to move any further. One of the guards, accompanied by two English soldiers, soon arrived to hurry him on:

He told me to move on, I refused. He told me again, still I refused. He drew his pistol, cocked it and told me to move or he would shoot me. I blew my top, ripped open my battledress blouse, bared my chest and told him to shoot; I'd had a gutful of Hitler and all the bloody stupid Nazis and didn't care anymore. He looked at me, slowly secured his gun and placed it in the holster. 'The SS will be along soon,' he said 'they'll shoot.' And off the trio went. About ten minutes later, I started to retch and suddenly out popped two small, hard pieces of semi frozen carrot.

Although the prisoners had grown hard during their time in the stalags, some events still made a distinct impression upon them. During the march Fred Coster and his pals encountered a group of Jews marching away from a concentration camp:

We had this Jewish soldier, Freddy Freid, with us. These women came past us, just in their loose fitting dresses. So we were slipping them food, so the guards couldn't see. But Freddy was doing it openly, speaking Yiddish to them. I tried to stop him. The women couldn't believe it. He gave all his food away. The two guards waited with us when the column passed. Then came this very old Jewish woman, she could hardly keep up – she was at the end of her tether, she could hardly walk. This German officer was with her, pushing her along, prodding her in the back with his pistol. As she reached us she stopped. So the officer shot her in the head and she slumped to the floor. We had to hold Freddy back. This bloody officer just marched off, all proud of himself. But we'd seen a lot by then, we were pretty hardened. Even now I feel hardened about death. You are sorry about it, but you can't do anything about it.

Such were the conditions that some of the prisoners decided they would not stay on the march. After nine days Seaforth Highlander David Mowatt decided he would escape with the intention of reaching the Russians:

The wind and snow made it bloody cold and we'd had nothing to eat or drink for nine days. We stopped for the night and there was this big ditch beside the road. One night I was at the back of the column – I thought 'I'm going to die on this march' – so I dived into this big ditch. Within minutes I was covered by snow. In the morning I could hear the guards shouting for us all to get up, but I laid there until everything was clear. I thought I was going to freeze to death. When they'd gone I crawled out. Two other bods crawled up as well. One of them was also a Seaforth.

The three men made the decision to head towards the Russian lines, figuring they would be safer there. They were on the loose in the Polish countryside for two weeks, killing and eating farm animals and sleeping in the beds of German farmers who had fled the area: 'One morning we woke up to the noise of tanks. We thought "Good God! We're in the front line." By the time we got dressed all the doors had been smashed it. We were expecting it to be the Russians, but it was the SS! They put us up against the wall with a firing squad of five men. It's dreadful to think about it even now! Then an ordinary Wehrmacht officer appeared. "Lady Luck" was on our side – he stopped them.' Saved from the firing squad, Mowatt and his mates were taken into the care of the officer, who arranged for them to be sent to Danzig, where they were put into a compound with other POWs.

Despite the extremes of violence shown to some sick marchers, others were offered a measure of care. On some marches horse-drawn carts were available to carry those too sick to continue. Elsewhere, they were able to leave the sick in civilian hospitals. Eventually the marchers began to reach POW camps where medical facilities were available. Graham King reached Stalag 2A at Neubrandenburg where he set to work again. Under the supervision of US Army doctors, his duties focused on treating the feet of the pitiful wretches who had shuffled all the way from East Prussia: 'In this ward most had already lost part of their feet, or all. Gangrene was rife and the sickly smell took some getting used to.

The American surgeon demonstrated cutting off the dead bone with rongeurs. No anaesthetic was necessary, the bone being dead there was no feeling.'

One of the men who understood the depth of suffering endured during the march was Les Allan. Having left his workcamp wearing a pair of clogs he had been ill-equipped to deal with the icy roads. Just a few days after departing, he slipped on the road and fell awkwardly to the ground. Despite the pain there was little he could do but strap up his ankle and carry on. In all he had marched nearly 600 miles by the time he reached Stalag 11A at Fallingbostel, south of Hamburg. It was soon discovered he had fractured his ankle when he fell but had somehow managed to march through the pain to reach his destination.

Jim Reed's war came to an end in a hospital camp in Germany. He was one of the lucky ones who had been taken sick during the march back through Poland and had been allowed to complete his journey by train:

> One of my pals died on the march, he was a Cornishman in his thirties. The conditions were too much for him. He was found dead in the cold. People were just disappearing like that – no one knows how many died. I had a hole in my shoulder, the Germans took me to see a medical orderly. You could have put your finger down into the hole – and they just poured iodine into it! I was calling him all names I could. They sent me to a camp at Schwerin. I was all bandaged up nice and neat. There were half a dozen British in the camp, but there was nothing in that camp – and no food whatsoever. I saw men sitting on the beds cutting gangrene out of their legs with a penknife.

With German resistance collapsing, increasing numbers of POWs found themselves behind the Russian lines. Sometimes they were simply bypassed by the advancing army, elsewhere the Red Army arrived to announce they were free and told them to head off into villages and towns to find their own food. At some camps Red Army officers even asked for volunteers to join them to fight the Germans. Only a few of the most adventurous types accepted the offer. Graham King witnessed the aftermath of the Red Army's advance in the area around the stalag: 'After two days we were out wandering around Neubrandenburg seeing what we could loot. Not much, the Red Army had already been through and taken most of value. We saw lots of bodies lying around, especially later when we wandered around the woods and parks. Signs of rape and suicide. Hanging from a tree branch we found three generations of a family; Granny, wife, three kids about 9, 6 and 3 plus Dad . . . Some had been shot, others bayoneted.'

Despite the violence displayed in some German towns and villages, other prisoners witnessed a disciplined army whose officers and NCOs enforced order with extreme measures – they shot anybody disobeying their orders. Dick Taylor, a veteran of the defeat at St Valery, had an eventful journey to freedom after his liberation by the Red Army. He approached a female tank commander and asked her what they should do. She simply told him, in surprisingly good English, that they should head to the port of Odessa. He was amazed, Odessa was hundreds of miles away and he was given no idea of how to get there:

> I and one or two of the other POWs in the surrounding area got together and organised things. I was able to speak quite good German and make contact with a Russian who could speak German. He got us walking in the right direction. The Russian guards had no idea where they were, until he organised us we went round in circles. But we were on our way home. The Russians treated everyone the same – they were a rough lot. They'd had millions of casualties and they were on their way to Berlin – no one was going to stop them! It didn't matter what anybody said.

On his long journey to freedom he witnessed all the violent madness of modern warfare. One of the first places he passed was a farm whose owners he knew from his time on working parties. On top of the manure heap were the corpses of the seventy-year-old farmer and his wife, having been executed by the advancing Russians. Elsewhere were the corpses of people who, fearing Russian revenge for Germany's crimes in the Soviet Union, had chosen to take their own lives. Everywhere were the bodies of soldiers – either those who had fallen in battle or those executed after they had surrendered. The corpses of German refugees filled the roads where the Red Army had simply obliterated everything that had blocked its way. For the men who had witnessed the German bombing of refugee columns back in 1940 these scenes were wearily familiar. As Dick Taylor remembered: 'You just get used to it. Once you've seen it once, seeing it again doesn't make much difference. It's just one of those things – you have to accept it. It's self-preservation, you're looking after yourself, you're not bothered about anybody else. One more dead person doesn't make any difference. It was the same as the march in 1940, when men broke ranks and got shot – as long as it wasn't me.'

After days of marching east, Taylor and his fellow ex-POWs were sent by train towards Odessa. At least the Russians had taken care to fit stoves inside the wagons to allow the men some heat. Basic as the trucks were, it was still better than any transport the Germans had made them ride in. The journey was an eye-opener for the British soldiers: 'There was nothing left, the whole place was flattened – everything. You'd come to a village and there was hardly one brick on top of another. That's why there was no shelter for us as we went through. Absolutely nothing – we were travelling through a wasteland.'

Arriving in Odessa they were put into a large house surrounded by barbed wire. There was a sense of foreboding for all the ex-POWs to be behind barbed wire again. However this time the ordeal did not last for five years. One morning, without warning, they were told to gather their gear and march to the port. There, waiting for them, was the pre-war liner *Duchess of Bedford*. They were going home.

Whilst the prisoners who had been working in East Prussia headed for northern Germany, the prisoners who had been working in Silesia headed west through Czechoslovakia into southern Germany. Their marches had started later which meant they missed the worst of the weather. They were also fortunate that they did not have quite so far to march. Many took advantage of the hospitality of the local population and escaped from the columns to make their way home under their own steam. Bill Holmes was one of those who escaped, making his way back to the Allied lines via Prague, aided by members of the Czech Resistance.

Also on the run in Czechoslovakia was Eric Reeves. His group had left Blechammer at the end of January and headed through the mountains into Czechoslovakia. It didn't take long for him to decide the conditions were against them. As he marched he had his greatcoat collar up and his hat pulled down. He noticed that not only had his hat frozen against his collar but there was also thick ice on his glasses that had frozen to his head:

> My mates Ted Kane and Flash said to me 'You'll either freeze to death, starve to death or get shot – which is the quicker? So after an hour or two debate I decided to go with them. They said they were only taking me 'cause I could speak German. You could hear the Russians breaking through in Upper Silesia, their barrages sounded like rolling thunder. We rubbed our hands and said 'The Jerries are copping it – good.' That was how we thought. We survived by going to smallholdings – we'd take the food that was hanging under the eaves. The Czechs were helpful. The youngsters could speak German, they told us what they were going to do once the war was over – they were going to hang the German Burgomeister. But we survived by scrounging dripping sandwiches.

The end came differently for each. There were the men liberated by Americans in southern and central Germany, by the Russians in

Poland and eastern Germany or by the British in the north. The final days of war saw the prisoners marching amidst scenes of utter devastation. One scene became imprinted on Fred Coster's memory; the sight of a German sentry box with the bottom half of the sentry's corpse in the box and the top half blown off and lying in the road. Coster thought to himself 'poor sod' as he stepped past the severed torso. Gordon Barber's most vivid memories of the final days of war reflected the desperate situation they found themselves in. Having eaten some pigs they had found dead in a bombed train, Barber became violently ill: 'I can still remember sitting at the latrine they'd dug. The bloke sitting beside me said 'Ain't it terrible. Do you think we'll make it?' I said 'Yeah.' We sat there watching the American bombing raids, knocking the shit out of this town. All we could see going down into the pit was blood. We had dysentery and malnutrition. I said 'I'd wish they'd drop a bomb on us.' . . . I felt so weak and so horrible, every time I moved I shit myself.'

For some, the threat from the air continued to be very real, as Peter Wagstaff soon discovered:

For five years you thought of how – and if – you were going to be liberated. It was most extraordinary. They marched us south from Eichstadt, in a long, tattered, straggling human line. The column was about a mile and a half long. Then we saw a couple of American Thunderbolts. They had spotted a German convoy on the other side of the valley and attacked it. We sat down and roared with laughter. Then they saw us and thought we were Germans – they went up and down, then 'straffed' the life out of us. They killed 12 of us, including one of my best friends. I raced across the road – out of the sun – and found myself cowering with a German guard and an Italian chap. Again, the death of my friend didn't affect me. Things like that happen as a POW. It's difficult to explain. I had become conditioned to seeing death. You don't have time to analyse things and there is nothing you can do about it. The human mind is a most peculiar animal.

For David Mowatt liberation came in the port of Lübeck. He travelled by boat from Danzig, sailing the dangerous waters of the Baltic in the knowledge that Russian submarines were active in the area. The journey was a repeat of the one he had made down the Rhine in 1940. Again he was travelling in the hold of a coal barge, little knowing what his fate might be. This time he was safe in the knowledge that if he survived he would be going home. Arriving at Lübeck, they were held in a cattle barn in the docks. Whilst they were there, the Russian prisoners continued to be held on boats in the port. Unable to leave the ship, the Russians grew so desperate they turned to cannibalism in order to survive.

After an aborted attempt to send the prisoners to Hanover, Mowatt found himself back in the cattle barn: 'We were there a couple of days then the British turned up and liberated us. It was a unit of Seaforth Highlanders! My own mob! I think it was the 10th May – two days after the war had ended.' They were flown home the following day.

Eric Reeves was liberated by a Russian patrol who simply sent him in the direction of the American lines. Effectively he was free but was actually in no man's land between the Russians and Americans – in an area still full of German troops:

It was chaos at that time. We were strolling along – it was May 9th, a lovely day – we thought 'We've won the bloody war!' Then we saw a Hanomag tug – like a big tractor – it was pulling these two trailers full of German troops. Teddy said to me 'Reevo, you stop 'em.' I had an uneasy feeling about it but I stood in the road and shouted 'Halt!' It stopped and a German sergeant major stuck his head out and said 'Who are you?' Ted said 'Tell him we're the bloody British army! We won the war!' So I told him and he started laughing and asked where we we're going. I told him where we were going. When I said we were going to meet the Americans they told us to get on and take them with us!

After a few hours they reached the American lines, where the troops were disarming arriving Germans. As they pulled up a corporal shouted up at them:

> He said 'OK, Krauts, get your asses off the vehicle.' So I translated for the Germans and told them to get off quickly. So they poured off leaving Ted, Flash and me. The Yank looked up and said 'Are you Krauts going to get your asses off or am I gonna come up and get you?' So Ted Kane said 'I'd like to see you try mate!' We expected the Yanks to welcome us with open arms, but they arrested us and locked us in a barn! They didn't know who we were, so they said we'd have to wait till they interrogated us in the morning.

The experience of liberation was very different for those soldiers who were still within the stalags. In many cases their guards had disappeared although, in some locations, the guards were attacked by prisoners celebrating their liberation. Released prisoners went on the rampage within some camps, looting food stores, ransacking the guards' quarters and pinching anything they fancied. Some made straight for stocks of alcohol whilst others quickly armed themselves or re-clothed themselves at the expense of their guards. Whilst some went in search of loot others only wanted basic souvenirs. Jim Charters took nothing more than a comb and his POW registration card, complete with the photograph taken on his first day in the stalag.

Wherever and however their war came to an end, after five years behind barbed wire they were struck by the emotion of the moment. For many it was difficult to put into words. The prisoners were stunned by freedom, it meant everything just to have survived – finally they could return to their families. Jim Pearce remembered his liberation by an American combat unit who were embroiled in battle:

> We marched into a village, where we were stealing and eating seed potatoes. We knew the end was coming because the

Germans didn't try to stop us. At night we were in this big barn.
We could hear tanks but we didn't know if they were American
or German. Everyone was tense. Eventually the American tanks
came. I hid behind this big tractor wheel because they were
firing – I don't know what they were firing at. The crews gave us
cigarettes and food. Men were getting food and wine – men
were flopping down drunk. They couldn't take it! A couple of
the men wanted to take revenge against the Germans. The
Yanks had taken the guards away but some of our chaps wanted
to shoot them. If the Americans hadn't taken them away our
chaps would have set on them. That ten weeks march had done
it for us – they didn't care anymore. But when I got released I
didn't want to kill anybody. But you can't really describe what
goes through your head when you are liberated. It was a
wonderful feeling – it had never seemed possible – 'I'm going
home' – tears were running from my eyes as I stood there
touching the American tanks.

Following liberation most ex-POWs did their best to get home
as swiftly as possible. Some of them 'liberated' vehicles to head west
in the hope of reaching anywhere where they might cadge a flight
to England. Others waited for transport to be arranged. The
majority of British prisoners congregated at airfields around Brussels
and were then flown home in bombers and transport aircraft. It was
an emotional journey for the men who had last seen the UK during
the phoney war. As they flew over the waters of the Channel – the
same waters they had all hoped to escape across back in 1940 – they
were seized by a sense of awe. After five years of uncertainty they
were finally returning to see their loved ones. For many the
highlight of the trip was to look out from the aircraft to see the
fabled white cliffs of Dover. Like the bluebirds of the song they
soared high above the chalk cliffs, a potent symbol of freedom and
the sense of the nation's survival against all the odds.
    Yet this was just the beginning of the emotional impact of
freedom. The realities of life 'beyond the wire' of the stalag had yet

to grip the hearts of the former prisoners. At first they still existed in a state of euphoria that was soon swept away once they were released from the military's care and sent on leave.

Upon arrival at airfields the prisoners were fed, watered, deloused, re-clothed and given a medical examination. Then they were allowed to telephone or send telegrams to their families, although some chose to say nothing, preferring instead to greet their loved ones in person. Once the sick men had been sent for treatment, the rest were allowed home. Eric Reeves remembered his return: 'Getting down from the plane I felt ecstatic – going into the meal I felt wonderful, there was music playing, it was civilised. We were kitted out with uniforms and they sewed on the medal ribbons we were entitled to – which weren't many! Then I phoned the local police station to see if my parents were still at the same address – 'cause I hadn't written home for a year.' Yet despite the obvious elation, Reeves was unprepared for what happened on his first night in England. Due to travel home the next morning, the prisoners were allowed out for the evening: 'The three of us walked into a pub – we stood inside the door and looked at it – I was terrified. We'd had five years of "effing and blinding" – we'd never spoken to women at all – and the pub was full of women. Everybody stopped and looked at us – we turned tail and fled back to camp! I couldn't handle it for weeks.'

Shocked by how captivity had affected him, Eric Reeves made his way home to Reigate where he hoped to be able to settle down to normality. He would soon discover his concept of normality had been swept away by all he had experienced:

It was a strange feeling coming home. A young man met me at the door in the uniform of the Middlesex Regiment. He put his arms round me! I said 'What's going on?' He said 'Blimey, Eric, it's me – your brother!' When I'd left home he was about 15. He'd been over on 'D-Day' – all grown up! Then my mother cried – Dad came home, through the backdoor, then just looked at me and said 'Hello, you had your dinner yet?' Nothing else. I appreciated it – I didn't want anyone falling all over me. That first night I was home my Dad – who was teetotal – took me into a pub. 'Cause I was a local lad word had got around that I was home. I walked in and the landlord said 'I suppose you're going to pay us in Pfennigs?' I grabbed him and pulled him over. I said 'Don't you talk to me about Pfennigs! You're gonna get a punch.' He said 'Oh, I'm sorry – some people are very touchy around here'. I told him 'So would be, if you'd been in a bloody prison camp for five years!' I never liked that landlord after that. It was the smarmy way he said it!

The reaction displayed by Reeves was a common one. Dick Taylor was the first ex-POW to arrive back in Berwick, having travelled from Odessa by ship. He refused the approaches of the local journalists who wanted to interview him. At night he would go out but didn't want to do anything – even if he could bring himself to go to the cinema he couldn't stay more than ten minutes. As he remembered: 'There was no such thing as a joyous home-coming.' Returning to his parents' London home, Jim Pearce was unable to enjoy his six-week leave:

I was very depressed. I used to sit in the front room, which was normally only used for special occasions like funerals. I just sat there – I didn't care. There was no one to look after us. I just kept myself to myself. The depression was bad. These days you'd have counselling, but we had nothing. You'd think you'd be glad to be home but it wasn't like that. My parents realised what I was going through. People came to see me but I didn't want to see anybody. I think it was easier for my brother because he had a wife to come home to. I'd spent all my best years in a POW camp – I had my 21st birthday there!

For some of the prisoners the return home was particularly shocking. Men from the big cities could hardly recognize them when they got back. When Fred Coster had gone to war in 1940, the East End of London had been a thriving area – full of industry, street upon street of terraced houses and mile after mile of warehouses: 'I had leave to go home – so all my relatives went to the various stations I might arrive at. I got off at Aldgate East and my uncle Joe was there. I was very thin but he recognised me. I looked along the Commercial Road at where everything had been bombed and all the buildings had gone. I said "You had a bit of a smacking around here." Joe said how rotten it was. But I told him "Don't worry, the Germans had it a hundred times worse." That helped ease him.'

Coster's fellow gunner, Gordon Barber, had joined the army in 1938 to earn a decent wage and make something of his life. With his first week's army pay he had bought himself a new outfit, then a few weeks later he even got a new suit. When he came home in 1945 he was ready to make use of the suit again. There was one problem, just as she had done all through the 1920s and 1930s, Barber's mother had pawned his only suit. He had to give his mother the money to get it out so that he could go out in something other than uniform.

Efforts were made by the War Office to ensure the mass of returning prisoners could be slowly eased back into civilian life upon discharge from the army. Although the War Office realized that discontent was inevitable, rehabilitation units were established in which the former POWs were given the opportunity to readapt to life in the UK. The camps were named Civil Resettlement Units – CRUs – and courses lasted between four and six weeks. They were not obligatory. However, since they did not count against the soldier's terminal leave, they were an attractive prospect. Part of the reasoning behind the establishment of CRUs was the fear that the ex-prisoners would not return to the army after the initial period of leave given to all men returning from captivity. The hope was that by offering activities that appealed to the soldiers the units might prevent them going AWOL. As one officer described it, the camps were: 'half way between the Army and civil life'.[1] Those who lived close enough were even given 'sleeping out' passes and others were free to go home at weekends. As Jim Reed recalled: 'We had girls feeding us in the morning and officers waiting on us. We were learning how to dance and how to mix with people. We needed it – we didn't know how to mix with women. It was the only good idea the army ever had.'

For men used to the basic facilities of the stalags – or pre-war British Army barracks, for that matter – these camps were a dream come true. There were sheets on the beds and mattresses with springs – no more sleeping on straw. Meals were even served in a dining room. Furthermore, the men only had to wear uniform between 9 a.m. and 5 p.m., for the rest of the day they were free to wear civilian clothing.

These units offered advice on future employment, educational courses, legal advice, medical treatment and assistance with providing clothing. There were visits to factories and visits to Ministry of Labour training centres to discuss courses. Of the activities initially on offer, drill was the least popular. As one man passing through a resettlement unit commented, any regimentation was unlikely to be viewed favourably by former prisoners: 'We know what war is like, don't treat us like recruits.'[2] In the post-war period the only parade the men had to attend was the weekly pay parade. Film shows and sports were the most popular of the activities. Also popular were lectures and discussion groups, as one soldier put it: 'Too many of us didn't think enough before the war.'[3]

Despite the efforts made to ease the former POWs back into society, many complained that it would simply be better to discharge them from the army. The CRU was only available once the man was due to be discharged from the army. Prior to that, the returning prisoners were subject to normal army discipline. As Jim Pearce, who remained in the army for two further years, remembered, it was like being a recruit all over again, being trained on weapons like the PIAT and Sten gun, that had not even been invented when he was captured. However, Pearce found one good thing about returning to the army after leave: 'At the time I cursed going back, but it did me good. It brought me back a bit – otherwise I'd have stayed depressed and remained that way most of my life. Going back into the army I had to do what I was told. Otherwise I'd just have stayed sitting there in my Mum and Dad's house. It was the best thing for me. Of course, I didn't think that at the time!'

Jim Reed also recalled life in an army camp whilst attempts were made to retrain the ex-POWs: 'We'd changed and the army had moved on. At the first camp an NCO said we were going to be disciplined and someone just said "Shut yer gob!" There were about fifty of us. They said to us "There'll be no weekend leave and you will show military discipline!" No one took any notice. Come the weekend, you'd be surprised if there were a dozen blokes in the camp. We cut holes in the fences to get out at night.' As Fred Coster remembered it, the ex-POWs were 'forgotten men' who were told they were being retrained to fight the Japanese: 'Our experiences were ignored – everything we had learned and done. It was against all decency. Thank God for the Atom Bomb! I think the boys would have revolted rather than go and do it all again.'

In the end there were so many complaints about the camp Jim Reed was stationed at – including letters to newspapers – that it was closed down. Reed found himself sent to Scotland, to a holding camp for the Seaforth Highlanders. Once there, his attitude did not change:

After breakfast I used to walk out, get on a train and go into Glasgow for an hour or two. All thoughts of soldiering had gone out of my mind. I didn't take too kindly to being told what to do by someone who didn't know what he was talking about. At Christmas I just got on a train and went home. After I week I thought there was no point going back since I was due for a week's leave at New Year. So I went back after a fortnight but no one ever said anything. I was never missed!

At Fred Gilbert's camp, the former prisoners also took little notice of discipline:

From Plymouth I could get back home to Coventry – with or without a pass. It depended on who was on the gate. If you were on duty, fellas would come towards you and you were supposed to check their pass – but you didn't. It would be a nod and a wink and the lads would go through the gate. You'd get on a train and there were too many people for the guard to be able to check you. So you didn't need a pass. At the station I'd wait until there was a crowd going through the barrier and I'd push past with other soldiers. You'd be gone before the guard could stop you. Other lads would get passes to go home – they'd give their address as towns in the north of Scotland. That meant they could get on a train and go anywhere they wanted to. All they had to do was get on any train – if the guard said they were on the wrong train they'd just get off. So they travelled all over the place. Some even got passes to go as far as Belgium. When you've been locked up for five years, you want to get out a bit.

The behaviour displayed by the former POWs stemmed from the fact that many felt they had 'done their bit' for their country, then wasted five years of life. This sense of disillusionment was recognized by the War Office: 'The suggestion of discharge is undoubtedly related to the apathy and war weariness of men whose morale was damaged beyond complete repair by the general situation at the time of capture – Dunkirk.'[4]

The failings of the British Army during the battles in France seemed to underpin the disenchantment of those who had paid the price of defeat. They had witnessed the effect of pitting a force with the weapons and tactics of 1918 against an army ready for 1940. They had witnessed the superiority, in both numbers and quality, of German tanks and aircraft. They had seen the Allied armies outmanoeuvred by the advancing Germans, then watched as the rift between the British and French grew until the two armies had gone into captivity as virtual enemies. The celebration of Allied unity they witnessed in 1945 was lost on men who had watched French soldiers marching into captivity in full kit, or who had fought Frenchmen for food during the march into Germany. Above all, there was a sense that they had been let down by a government that had sent them to France in 1940 ill-prepared for modern warfare. As one noted: 'the returned POW has lost the respect he had for his senior officers. He has been in tight corners with them and has seen the way they have acted – some were fine but that was a minority.'[5]

There was one group of returning prisoners for whom resettlement into society was a particular burden. Regular soldiers who were due to return to service after their leave faced issues that were of little concern to the wartime soldiers. As one asked: 'How do you think I will stand up to fire when I next go into action?'[6] Yet their concerns went deeper than this. By the time the Dunkirk prisoners returned home the army looked different, carried new weapons, and used tanks and other vehicles that would have appeared fanciful back in 1940. Officers and NCOs who had spent five years behind barbed wire had seen their career opportunities swept aside. Whilst they had been languishing in the stalags a whole new breed of soldiers had taken their place. By 1945, the man who Ernie Grainger had replaced in 1939 had actually reached the rank of brigadier. As Grainger remembered: 'When I came back I was made to feel out of place in the Sergeant's mess. I was virtually thrown out. They'd been there all the war – settled in, they had their wives and girlfriends. They didn't want the likes of me in there, they thought we were after their jobs. They did their best to get rid of us. I was an outsider among those who'd stayed in the UK.'

Men who had never imagined themselves as soldiers were occupying the promotion ladder. War had seen the advancement of officers who had been schoolboys during the Dunkirk evacuation. Now many of the newcomers were senior to men who had spent long years in the army, men who had earned their pips and stripes through years of square-bashing and service throughout the Empire. If that was not galling enough for the old-timers, the newcomers also had a far better understanding of the modern battlefield than men who had been captured in 1940. Whilst they had been enduring German captivity the British Army had been re-learning so much about war.

Despite the general desire to get away from the army as soon as possible, the mental effects of captivity led some men to make the decision to stay on as regulars. The impact of five years of captivity was such that they dared not yet return to civilian life. David Mowatt was among them:

> My mind was all over the place. I was terrible. I'd been to three different rehabilitation camps. Physically, I was alright but not my mind. They put up a notice asking for ex-pows to attend the Nuremburg trials, but you had to sign on for four years. That's it – that was the get out for me – I wasn't looking forward to 'civvy street' at all. So I signed up. It was the best decision I ever made in my whole life. It was five wonderful years. I couldn't handle being a civilian. I couldn't have gone back to the farm. Life was quite different after five years away. When I went home on leave, I couldn't go on a bus, I couldn't go on a train – I couldn't even go into a pub unless I knew one of my mates was going to be in there. I didn't want to meet civilians – people asking me all sorts of questions. Lots of other boys said the same.

As the prisoners returned home there was a general lack of understanding of what they had endured. The world had become obsessed by the eventual victory. Even Dunkirk was turned into a victory, eulogizing the escapers and ignoring the rest of the BEF. Whether it was the soldiers surrounded at St Valery, the men who received disabling wounds during the battles, or the men who had been plucked from the sea following the sinking of the *Lancastria*, the plight of those left behind at Dunkirk seemed like a footnote in history.

When Geoff Griffin returned home he received just a 15 per cent disability rating giving him a pension of 13 shillings a week. His return to civvy street was hampered by the discovery that many vacancies advertised by firms had immediately and mysteriously been filled as soon as he showed his disability card. He remained jobless for some months and was disgusted with the reception he received. He was also unhappy that officials did not intervene to assist him with finding work.

When the repatriates were followed home by the mass of prisoners, the psychological symptoms they displayed were similar to those displayed by the wounded men. The returning men were unable to switch off the 'stalag mentality' that had been essential to their sanity during five long years of captivity. They were found to be restless, irresponsible and irritable. They had a deep disrespect for authority. They displayed a fear of confined spaces and disliked being in the midst of crowds. They were also cynical, embarrassed in polite society and quick tempered. It seemed they suffered a collective crisis of confidence, something summed up by one returning man: 'It's fantastic – me, a Sergeant Major and I can't cross the traffic in Shaftesbury Avenue.'[7]

For some returning prisoners, the five years away from home had an irreversible effect. They had lost their youth and felt out of step with the post-war world. Peter Wagstaff recalled the effect on one of his friends, a very bright man who was tormented by a deep fear of mental illness: 'A very good friend of mine had spent his time as a prisoner writing a long, long novel. He came back and tried to sell it but he found it was completely out of date. He committed suicide within three weeks of coming home. A lot of us did that – or turned to drink.'

Under such pressures to fit back into society, it was little wonder some of the returning prisoners found themselves clashing with the authorities. Around 70 per cent of ex-prisoners reported having problems with the pay owed to them by the army. Some of the protected personnel reported having used the seemingly useless Lagergeld paid to them by the Germans to light cigarettes. They were then upset to discover this money had actually been deducted from their credits upon their return home. These men felt bitter that, having voluntarily stayed behind in France to care for the wounded, they were penalized upon their return to the UK. As one commented: 'I volunteered to stay behind in France because I felt it was my duty. When I came home I find the War Office quibbling about my pay and trying to pay the lowest possible minimum. This makes a man a little bitter.'[8] Another RAMC soldier described the process of attempting to claim the back pay he believed he was owed, it was most easily visualized as: 'a bundle of split hairs wrapped up in miles and miles of red tape'.[9]

For some, the arguments over pay have continued for more than sixty years. For Graham King, the fight for the money he feels he is owed has never finished. Always describing himself as a protected person rather than a POW, King had money deducted from his back pay in lieu of money supposedly paid by the enemy. Yet since he was not receiving these payments he lost out. Furthermore, King felt he had been denied medals. He believed he was entitled to the France and Germany Star for service in north-west Europe between D-Day and VE-Day. He was informed by the Ministry of Defence that he was not entitled to the medal since he had been a POW: 'I pointed out that as a member of the Medical Services I could not be a prisoner of war under the articles of the Geneva Convention. They rebutted this reply so I said I would like the money refunded that had been deducted from my pay. The reply was that was impossible as I was a protected person!'

With these arguments continuing for so many years, it was unsurprising that the men left behind in France in 1940 have always felt their plight has been ignored. There was no campaign medal struck for the BEF, meaning those whose war finished in 1940 have no permanent record of their service and suffering, something that has always caused annoyance to so many of the men left behind. As Les Allan has always pointed out, he can spot a 1940 POW by how bereft his chest is of campaign medals. In recent years the National Ex-Prisoner of War Association has struck its own medal for former POWs, depicting the dove of peace against a background of barbed wire. However, many felt it was not their role to be making the medals, as Jim Pearce noted: 'It would have been nice for the government to do it. Instead we had to pay for the medal – my daughter bought me it for Christmas!' Similarly, Fred Coster noted: 'I think the government should have given us a campaign medal, because we fought behind the lines. I was forever using my ability to speak German to demoralise the Germans. I told my guards "You don't stand a chance. We'll wipe you out! We'll bomb you with 1,000 planes." I made it all up – but in the end it was true! They were so demoralised, I ended up feeling sorry for them.'

The story of the miracle of Dunkirk has always revolved around the plucky amateur sailors ferrying soldiers from the beaches. It is a mythology that ignores the plight of those whose sacrifices meant the escape could take place. The neglected veterans include those who kept fighting – and dying – for weeks after the beaches of Dunkirk had fallen. The forgotten men of 1940 also include those who chose to remain in France to administer medical care to the wounded – giving up their freedom in the name of duty. The true story of Dunkirk must also include those who never gave up the struggle, who hid in France, endured interrogation by the Gestapo and yet somehow still managed to get home via Spain or North Africa. Moreover, it should never be forgotten that for every seven men who were evacuated via Dunkirk one man was left behind as a prisoner of war. All the physical abuse and mental anguish they suffered in the five years that followed are part of the Dunkirk story.

Ever since the world's press first celebrated the miraculous evacuation from the beaches, the story has been a one-sided affair. The pain that has been omitted from it has always angered the veterans. When Graham King was contacted by the BBC for a programme about Dunkirk he was appalled that they knew little about the rearguard and were once again focused on what happened on the beaches. The subject of the post-war films about POWs also always raised a laugh with the former prisoners. 'A load of crap,' thought Norman Barnett. 'They just looked too well fed, they needed to get some skinny blokes in there.'

For Fred Coster the sacrifices of the rearguard need to be more widely known: 'You'd think they'd mention the rest of us. Dunkirk was a great success, but it wouldn't have been a success if it wasn't for the rearguard. Every time the rearguard held up the Germans another 1,000 men got away. It wasn't a willing sacrifice but we did our duty.' As Dick Taylor remembered: 'They've forgotten all about us. There were 8,000 prisoners from my Division. We were still fighting whilst those who get all the credit were getting away. We didn't get any recognition. The 51st Highland Division gets forgotten. People think everybody got away at Dunkirk.' Another of the Highlanders, Jim Reed, put it even more bluntly: 'I still believe Churchill sold us down the river, he said "stay behind to stiffen French resistance". It was a load of bullshit.'

One of those left behind in 1940 found his version of events questioned by government officials. Corporal Hosington, who escaped from one of the columns of prisoners marching into Germany, found staff at the Treasury Solicitors Office did not believe his story. They could not accept that the Germans had inflicted so much suffering on their captives. In July 1943 they questioned his account: 'The only thing I don't like about it is the length of time you were either without or with a wholly inadequate amount of food. It is difficult to conceive how a column could have remained on the march for six days under these conditions.'[10] The corporal could not accept their protestations, writing back to them that: 'As far as I am concerned it is quite in order and none of the contents are exaggerated.' He later wrote to reinforce what he had told them: 'You will find out when our men return from German prison camps that my statement has not been exaggerated. If life itself is at stake men will, and can, carry on even though conditions seem to make it impossible to do so.'[11]

With these words Corporal Hosington had unwittingly provided a fitting epitaph to all the men who – whether wounded, a prisoner or an evader – had been left behind in France in June 1940.

Epilogue

And so the 40,000 men left behind at Dunkirk came home to a strange, new world – one far removed from that they had left back in 1939. After five years nothing had prepared them for this. They had been on rehabilitation courses, retrained, enjoyed leaves, found employment, re-acquainted themselves with their families, picked up relationships with wives and tried to rekindle affection with girlfriends. But there was always something missing.

Beneath the smiles of rejoicing for their survival were emotions that would remain hidden for many years. Parents found themselves with sons who had outgrown their childhood bedrooms. Wives hardly knew the men who returned. Girlfriends remembered the youths who had left home five years before, full of enthusiasm, eager for 'a crack at the Hun'. Instead they got tired, prematurely aged men, often nervous, painfully malnourished and bitter about wasting five years of what should have been the prime of their lives.

Perhaps we should finish where we started – Dunkirk. Like so many of those men who fought in the BEF, Bill Holmes finally made the return trip to the beaches from which so many of his comrades had escaped and where his own war had come to an abrupt end as a German soldier pointed a machine-gun towards him. Returning to that fateful location, it was difficult for him to suppress the memories of all those years before:

The first time I went back to Dunkirk, I looked out to sea as a military band was playing 'Abide With Me', that took some stomaching, I can tell you. Everywhere was peaceful but I looked back to remember what it had been like in 1940. You think of everybody who's died. The last time I saw my mates from the village was when they were going to the cinema and I was going to Chichester barracks to start my training. They said 'Cheerio, Bill' but only one of them survived the war. The rest were killed. I was lucky to survive and stay healthy. The only thing I have are three or four marks across my back – where the skin grows scaly – I will never lose them. It was when we were made to 'run the gauntlet' we all got beaten across the back by the guards with their rifle butts.

I'll never forgive the Germans. I can't trust them, but I don't hate them. But when you see things that bad – to see someone shot for no reason – and the guard laughs about it – well, how low can you get? There was a railway near our camp. Twice a day a train would go up to Auschwitz carrying the Jews. You knew they were going to the furnace – it went on day after day, month after month. I don't think you can forgive people like that.

When I came back home from Germany, I only weighed nine stone. I got out at the railway station and I was quite frightened. I'd left the lads at Victoria Station and I was suddenly on my own. I'd not been alone for five years. So I was a different character when I came home. I sat in the room and just flung my cigarette butt on the floor. Mum said 'What are you doing? You'll burn the house down!' Then I realised I had to get rid of my POW behaviour. Words would slip out, POW language wasn't what you should use in front of your mum!

It took ages to get over the war. I spent three years on valium. I used to shout and scream out in the night. Even now I sometimes still do it, so my wife clouts me. The effect on the mind of having to kill – you have to do it. It's not your own choice. If I had a choice I would never have done it. You can only put up with so much. I never spoke about my experiences, I thought people wouldn't believe me. People would be horrified if they realised what we had to go through. I look back and think 'Did that really happen?' So I stayed silent. It wasn't until I joined the Dunkirk Veterans Association that any of it came out.

Finally able to meet up with other men who had shared his experiences – men who would understand why he had stayed silent for so many years – Bill Holmes knew he had to return to the town where he had been captured. From the view of the town's skyline, no longer swirling with flames, to the mournful sounds of the brass band playing 'Abide With Me', every moment was drenched in emotion. Yet whilst he remembered the five years he had lost after he was marched away from the beaches into captivity, a visit to the cemetery helped to put everything into perspective: 'When I was back in Dunkirk for the 60th anniversary, I looked at all the graves of the soldiers who'd died there. A whole generation of men had been wiped out.' Bill Holmes realized he was one of the lucky ones, he may have been left behind at Dunkirk, but those men had stayed behind forever.

Appendix

Les Allan

Formerly an apprentice toolmaker, Les Allan returned home to Slough with six months of his apprenticeship remaining. On completing his training, Allan realized he could not continue with the work since the damage sustained to his feet and ankles during the long march out of Poland meant he was unable to stand for long periods. As a result he established his own engineering and engraving firm where he worked until retirement. Initially Allan was reluctant to talk about his wartime experiences and even failed to reveal to his future wife Doris that he had been a prisoner of war. Instead he told her he had spent the war in North Africa. Eventually he began to open up about his experiences, revealing the truth that he had concealed for so long. Finally happy that he had comes to terms with the past, Allan established the National Ex-Prisoner of War Association in the late 1970s. This allows former POWs to come together to discuss their experiences, with Allan and his fellow members continuing to promote a greater understanding and awareness of the sufferings of POWs.

Gordon Barber

Gordon 'Nobby' Barber (on the right of the left-hand picture above) returned home from the war in such poor health that his mother failed to recognize him when she visited him in hospital. He later discovered that she had spent much of the back pay he had hoped to use to settle down post-war. Barber later went to work as a bus driver on the routes around South-East London. He remains a close friend of Ken Willats (see pages 389–90) whose life he saved during the long march out of Poland in 1945.

Norman Barnett

Norman Barnett was one of the first of the POWs to return to the UK, coming home in the first repatriation scheme in late 1943. Although no longer allowed to serve overseas, he remained in the army throughout the war. He returned to live in Croydon where he settled down to marry his pre-war girlfriend and raise a family. He continues to attend reunions of the surviving members of 133 Field Ambulance and still has the collection of photographs he smuggled home from Germany hidden inside his accordion.

Fred Coster

Fred Coster returned home to find the East End of London very different to the area he had known when he was growing up. Determined to break free of the poverty of his youth, he returned to the City of London to work as a stockbroker. He later went to work for the *Sunday Times* newspaper. Following retirement he took up part-time employment as a lunchtime assistant at the school where his daughter is head teacher. He retired from the school in 2007, having enjoyed the opportunity to encourage children to profit from education in the same way that he had.

Fred Gilbert

Fred Gilbert was training to be a commercial artist when he was called up in 1939. Following his return home, now minus the fingertip he had lost in a POW camp accident, he completed his training. He then worked as a commercial artist, eventually building up a successful business in the East Midlands. Fred passed away in early 2007.

Fred Goddard

Fred Goddard had worked in a number of jobs before the war, including as a shop-boy, a cinema projectionist, a shoe repairer, a stable-yard hand and as an assistant to a surveyor. He joined the army to escape a miserable family life that had blighted his youth. After serving in France in 1940, and successfully escaping to England, he returned to his regiment and saw service in North Africa. In 1941 he was badly wounded in the leg and captured by the Italians. He received minimal treatment for his wounds – an Australian doctor used a penknife heated over a cigarette lighter to remove a bullet from his leg. Eventually Goddard was transferred to a POW camp in Italy from where he was eventually repatriated to England in 1943, since his leg wounds meant he was no longer fit for service. Goddard then faced long battles with the British authorities to receive the correct disablement pension. Post-war he trained as a plumber and set up his own business, which his son still runs as a family firm.

Bill Holmes

Bill Holmes returned home from Germany to the same East Sussex village that he had lived in as a child. He also returned to his job on his father's small farm until, realizing that there were greater opportunities elsewhere, he took up employment raising plants for a local firm. Following the loss of both parents and his brother in the years immediately following the war, he moved into the family cottage. He and his wife remain there to this day.

David Mowatt

David Mowatt, born and raised in the Highlands of Scotland, never returned to live in his native land. Uncomfortable in company and finding it difficult to adjust to life after five years of captivity, Mowatt 'signed on' as a regular soldier and remained in the army for a number of years. Eventually he found himself in Hertfordshire, working in a camp for officers who were being discharged from the army. There he met a local girl and he settled down, remaining in the area after leaving the army. Despite never returning to live in Scotland, he retains close links with his regiment, the Seaforth Highlanders, returning each year to attend reunions.

Jim Pearce

Jim Pearce was among the many POWs who returned home from war only to find it difficult to settle down. It was only after his leave was complete and he returned to army discipline that he began to come to terms with no longer being in captivity. Pre-war, Pearce had been a porter in a block of flats in London's Maida Vale, however post-war he moved into the catering industry, eventually working as a catering manager for a large oil company in Essex. His experience during the war years had heightened his faith in God, a faith he still retains.

Eric Reeves

Eric Reeves, the pre-war Territorial who never reached the minimum height for an infantryman, returned home to Reigate. In later years he joined the Dunkirk Veterans Association and acted as a 'company commander', leading parades during the Association's annual pilgrimages to the town. He is also the Vice-Chairman of the National Ex-Prisoner of War Association, working closely with Les Allan to promote a greater understanding of life in a POW camp.

Peter Wagstaff

Despite his bad experience of war and captivity, Second-Lieutenant Peter Wagstaff returned home from Germany and decided to remain in the army. He took a commission in the Royal Scots Regiment and served throughout the world, seeing action in many regions including Malaya and Korea. He retired with the rank of major and later joked that he and his family had moved from one country to another as the British Empire contracted around them. Ever thankful to have survived the war, and grateful to have been spared the psychological damage that affected so many of his fellow POWs, he continues to enjoy life in a quiet Oxfordshire village.

Notes

See Bibliography: unpublished sources for an explanation of the National Archives abbreviations used below.

Prologue
1 Nigel Nicolson, *Alex: the Life of Field Marshal Earl Alexander of Tunis*, Weidenfeld & Nicolson, 1973

Introduction: Victory or Defeat
1 Frederick Foster. Imperial War Museum 01/4/1

Chapter 1: Missing the Boat
1 Major R.L. Barclay. Imperial War Museum pp/mcr/373
2 National Archives CAB106/260
3 National Archives WO32/4610
6 Major W.W. Wagstaff. Imperial War Museum 93/11/1. (Walton Wynter Wagstaff adopted the name Peter to avoid being known as Walt or Waldo.)
7 National Archives CAB106/248
8 National Archives CAB106/292
9 National Archives CAB106/292
10 Major W.W. Wagstaff. Imperial War Museum 93/11/1
11 National Archives WO197/99
12 National Archives CAB106/248
13 National Archives WO167/807
14 L.B. Shorrock. Imperial War Museum 80/12/1

Chapter 2: The Round Up

1 John Lawrence, *A POW's Story*, Woodfield Publishing, 1991
2 Captain Munby. Imperial War Museum 87/25/1
3 Sergeant Stephen Houthakker. Imperial War Museum 98/5/1
4 National Archives WO167/804
5 National Archives WO167/804
6 National Archives WO167/804
7 National Archives WO167/804
8 National Archives WO167/804
9 National Archives WO167/804
10 National Archives TS26/65b
11 National Archives TS26/205
12 National Archives TS26/400
13 National Archives TS26/224

Chapter 3: The Fight Goes On

1 National Archives WO167/710
2 National Archives WO167/710
3 National Archives WO167/818
4 National Archives WO167/455
5 National Archives WO167/710
6 Captain Peter Royle. Imperial War Museum 99/72/1
7 National Archives WO167/455
8 Captain Peter Royle. Imperial War Museum 99/72/1
9 National Archives WO167/455
10 John Forbes Christie. Imperial War Museum 88/47/1
11 National Archives WO167/818
12 National Archives WO167/818
13 National Archives WO167/455
14 National Archives WO167/704
15 National Archives WO167/455
16 National Archives WO167/455
17 National Archives WO167/455
18 National Archives WO167/473
19 Captain Peter Royle. Imperial War Museum 99/72/1
20 National Archives WO167/705
21 National Archives WO167/705

Chapter 4: The Death of a Division

1 H. Watt. Imperial War Museum 03/10/01
2 H. Watt. Imperial War Museum 03/10/01
3 H. Watt. Imperial War Museum 03/10/01
4 John Forbes Christie. Imperial War Museum 88/47/1
5 John Forbes Christie. Imperial War Museum 88/47/1

Chapter 5: The Wounded

1 National Archives WO32/10746
2 Geoff Griffin. Imperial War Museum 92/10/1
3 Geoff Griffin. Imperial War Museum 92/10/1
4 John Forbes Christie. Imperial War Museum 88/47/1
5 L.B. Shorrock. Imperial War Museum 80/2/1
6 L.B. Shorrock. Imperial War Museum 80/2/1
7 L.B. Shorrock. Imperial War Museum 80/2/1
8 W. Simpson. Imperial War Museum 96/41/1
9 W. Simpson. Imperial War Museum 96/41/1
10 W. Simpson. Imperial War Museum 96/41/1
11 Major W.W. Wagstaff. Imperial War Museum 93/11/1
12 Geoff Griffin. Imperial War Museum 92/10/1
13 National Archives FO916/2591
14 National Archives FO916/133
15 National Archives WO309/857
16 National Archives TS26/222
17 National Archives TS26/222
18 National Archives TS26/223
19 W. Simpson. Imperial War Museum 96/41/1

Chapter 6: The First Men Home

1 J.F. Sweeney. Imperial War Museum 85/18/1
2 Don Clark, *Cede Nullis: a Personal History of the 1940 Normandy Campaign*, Pentland Press, 2000
3 National Archives WO167/818
4 National Archives WO167/473
5 Fred Goddard, *Battlefields of Life*, Finial Publishing, 2004
6 V. Tatton. Imperial War Museum 01/57/1
7 S.D. Coates. Imperial War Museum 06/42/1
8 S.D. Coates. Imperial War Museum 06/42/1
9 Sergeant Wally Hewitt. Imperial War Museum 67/378/1

10 Corporal Charles Raybould. Imperial War Museum 75/12/1
11 Corporal Charles Raybould. Imperial War Museum 75/12/1
12 J.F. Sweeney. Imperial War Museum 85/18/1
13 J.F. Sweeney. Imperial War Museum 85/18/1
14 Corporal Charles Raybould. Imperial War Museum 75/12/1
15 J.F. Sweeney. Imperial War Museum 85/18/1
16 J.F. Sweeney. Imperial War Museum 85/18/1

Chapter 7: The Long Way Home

 1 National Archives FO371/24507
 2 National Archives FO371/24507
 3 John Forbes Christie. Imperial War Museum 88/47/1
 4 Major G.S. Lowden. Imperial War Museum 80/6/1
 5 Major G.S. Lowden. Imperial War Museum 80/6/1
 6 D.N. Peterson. Imperial War Museum 90/4/1
 7 John Forbes Christie. Imperial War Museum 88/47/1
 8 John Forbes Christie. Imperial War Museum 88/47/1
 9 John Forbes Christie. Imperial War Museum 88/47/1
10 National Archives FO371/24326
11 National Archives FO371/31908
12 National Archives FO371/24507
13 John Forbes Christie. Imperial War Museum 88/47/1
14 National Archives FO371/24326
15 National Archives WO222/16
16 National Archives FO371/24507
17 National Archives FO371/24507
18 National Archives FO371/24507
19 National Archives FO371/24507
20 John Forbes Christie. Imperial War Museum 88/47/1
21 John Forbes Christie. Imperial War Museum 88/47/1
22 National Archives FO371/31908
23 National Archives WO222/245
24 National Archives FO916/47
25 National Archives FO916/48
26 Geoff Griffin. Imperial War Museum 92/10/1
27 Geoff Griffin. Imperial War Museum 92/10/1
28 Geoff Griffin. Imperial War Museum 92/10/1
29 National Archives FO916/540
30 Geoff Griffin. Imperial War Museum 92/10/1
31 National Archives FO916/539

32 National Archives WO32/10757
33 National Archives WO32/10757
34 National Archives WO32/10757

Chapter 8: The Journey East

1 National Archives TS26/207
2 National Archives TS26/204 – United Nations War Crimes Commission
3 National Archives WO32/18489
4 National Archives TS26/214
5 National Archives FO916/2591
6 National Archives FO916/2591
7 H. Watt. Imperial War Museum 03/10/01
8 National Archives TS26/211
9 National Archives TS26/207
10 R.P. Evans. Imperial War Museum 90/18/1
11 R.P. Evans. Imperial War Museum 90/18/1
12 National Archives WO32/18489
13 W. Bampton. Imperial War Museum 94/49/1
14 W. Bampton. Imperial War Museum 94/49/1
15 Sergeant H.S. Houthakker. Imperial War Museum 98/5/1
16 Sergeant H.S. Houthakker. Imperial War Museum 98/5/1
17 John Forbes Christie. Imperial War Museum 88/47/1
18 National Archives TS26/207
19 National Archives TS26/211
20 W. Kite. Imperial War Museum 94/26/1
21 National Archives TS26/65A
22 National Archives TS26/207
23 National Archives TS26/221
24 R.A. Wilson. Imperial War Museum 83/41/1
25 John Forbes Christie. Imperial War Museum 88/47/1
26 W. Bampton. Imperial War Museum 94/49/1

Chapter 9: The Journey Continues

1 National Archives CAB106/260
2 W. Bampton. Imperial War Museum 94/49/1
3 Fred Kennington, *No Cheese After Dinner*, privately published, 2004
4 National Archives TS26/207
5 National Archives TS26/207
6 Tommy Arnott, *A Long Walk to the Garden*, privately published, 2005

7 L.B. Shorrock. Imperial War Museum 80/2/1

8 W. Bampton. Imperial War Museum 94/49/1

9 L.B. Shorrock. Imperial War Museum 80/2/1

10 Ronald Holme, *Adventures of a Brown Job*, Imperial War Museum 19/82/1

11 Tommy Arnott, *A Long Walk to the Garden*, privately published, 2005

Chapter 10: The First Year

1 E. Vernon Mathias. Imperial War Museum 85/8/1

2 National Archives WO32/18489

3 Sergeant H.S. Houthakker. Imperial War Museum 98/5/1

4 E. Vernon Mathias. Imperial War Museum 85/8/1

5 Major W.W. Wagstaff. Imperial War Museum 93/11/1

6 E. Vernon Mathias. Imperial War Museum 85/8/1

7 Sergeant H.S. Houthakker. Imperial War Museum 98/5/1

8 Fred Kennington, *No Cheese After Dinner*, privately published, 2004

9 R.P. Evans. Imperial War Museum 90/18/1

10 National Archives CAB106/214

11 Tommy Arnott, *A Long Walk to the Garden*, privately published, 2005

12 National Archives FO916/133

13 National Archives FO916/2574

14 National Archives FO371/2607

Chapter 11: Five Years

1 National Archives WO32/10757

2 National Archives WO311/146

3 National Archives FO371/29607

4 National Archives FO371/29607

5 National Archives WO32/10746

6 National Archives WO32/10757

7 National Archives WO32/10757

8 National Archives WO32/10757

Chapter 12: Going Home

1 National Archives WO32/10757

2 National Archives WO32/10757

3 National Archives WO32/10757

4 National Archives WO32/10757

5 National Archives WO32/10757

 6 National Archives WO32/10757
 7 National Archives WO32/10757
 8 National Archives WO32/10757
 9 National Archives WO32/10757
10 National Archives TS26/63
11 National Archives TS26/63

Bibliography

Published sources

Leslie Aitken, *Massacre on the Road to Dunkirk*, William Kimber, 1977
Anon, *The Diary of a Staff Officer*, Methuen, 1941
Anon, *Infantry Officer*, Batsford Books, 1943
Tommy Arnott, *A Long Walk to the Garden*, privately published, 2005
W.H. Aston, *Nor Iron Bars a Cage*, Macmillan, 1946
Earl of Cardigan, *I Walked Alone*, Routledge & Kegan Paul, 1952
Field Marshal Lord Carver, *Britain's Army in the Twentieth Century*, Macmillan, 1998
John Castle, *The Password is Courage*, Souvenir Press, 1954
Don Clarke, *Cede Nullis: a Personal History of the 1940 Normandy Campaign* Pentland Press, 2000
Richard Collier, *The Sands of Dunkirk*, William Collins, 1961
Saul David, *Churchill's Sacrifice of the Highland Division, France 1940*, Brassey, 1994
John Elwyn, *At the Fifth Attempt*, Leo Cooper, 1987
C. Denis Freeman and Douglas Cooper, *The Road to Bordeaux*, Cresset Press, 1942
Fred Goddard, *Battlefields of Life*, Finial Publishing, 2004
Alistair Horne, *To Lose a Battle*, Macmillan, 1969
Nicholas Harman, *Dunkirk, the Necessary Myth*, Hodder & Stoughton, 1980
Gordon Instone, MM, *Freedom the Spur*, Burke Publishing Company, 1973
Fred Kennington, *No Cheese After Dinner*, privately published, 2004
Sam Kyd, *For You the War Is Over*, Bachman & Turner, 1973
John Lawrence, *A POW's Story*, Woodfield Publishing, 1991
Walter Lord, *The Miracle of Dunkirk*, Viking Press, 1982
Mac MacIntosh, *The Bolo Boys*, Victoria Press, 1989
William Moore, *The Long Way Round*, Secker & Warburg, 1986
Airey Neave, *The Flames of Calais*, Hodder & Stoughton, 1972
Nigel Nicolson, *Alex: the Life of Field Marshal Earl Alexander of Tunis*, Weidenfeld & Nicolson, 1973
Keith Panter Brick, *Years Not Wasted*, The Book Guild, 1999

Anthony Rhodes, *Sword of Bone*, Faber & Faber, 1942
David Rolf, *Prisoners of the Reich*, Leo Cooper, 1988
Warren Tute, *Escape Route Green*, J.M. Dent, 1971
Adrian Vincent, *The Long Road*, Allen & Unwin, 1956
Adrian Weale, *Renegades: Hitler's Englismen*, Weidenfeld & Nicolson, 1994

Unpublished sources

National Archives

CAB21/513	Cabinet Committee on Army Recruiting.
CAB21/515	Relations between Germany and UK, September 1938 to August 1939
CAB21/516	Mobilization of the Territorial Army
CAB21/1264	Conscription: National Service Act 1939
CAB21/2546	Colonial armies
CAB106/214	Casualties May/June 1940
CAB106/215	Casualties May/June 1940
CAB106/216	Despatches on BEF
CAB106/217	Artillery reports
CAB106/219	Equipment losses
CAB106/220	Lessons of operations in Flanders 1940
CAB106/225	Lecture notes on campaign
CAB106/228	2nd Welsh Guards at Boulogne
CAB106/229	657 Company, Royal Engineers
CAB106/230	20th Guards Brigade at Bolougne
CAB106/232	Personal account of withdrawal
CAB106/233	3RTR
CAB106/238	Summary of Flanders campaign
CAB106/240	12th Lancers
CAB106/241	QVR at Calais
CAB106/242	Royal Scots
CAB106/243	HQ retreat
CAB106/244	BEF operations
CAB106/245	Irish Fusiliers
CAB106/248	131 Brigade Diary
CAB106/250	Northumberland Fusiliers
CAB106/251	Bedfordshire and Hertfordshire
CAB106/252	2 Corps withdrawal
CAB106/252	'Crowded House' personal report
CAB106/254	Diary of POW Brigadier-General Davidson
CAB106/260	Report by Lord Gort on the state of the army
CAB106/254	Report by Brigadier-General Davidson
CAB106/292	Notes on the 61st in France
CAB121/294	POWs in Europe: repatriation and exchanges
FO371/28277	Internees and POWs in France 1941
FO371/28285	Welfare of POWs in France and Belgium

FO371/31908	Welfare of POWs in France and Belgium
FO916/123	Welfare of British prisoners in Belgium
FO916/133	Welfare of POWs in Belgium and France
FO916/2574	POW welfare
FO916/2579	POWs 1940
FO916/2591	Welfare of POWs and internees in France and Belgium
FO916/2599	POWs in France 1940/41
HO213/1745	Repatriation and exchange: specified German nationals in UK and British subjects in Gemany; POWs in UK and Germany
LAB25/33	Ministry of Labour War Book – conscription
LAB25/110	Position of reservists upon mobilization
PREM1/312	Mobilization of the Territorial Army
PREM1/385	Prime Minister's statement on conscription
PREM 3/364/8	Repatriation of long-term British and German prisoners, and of Russians captured on Western Front
TS26/63	War crimes reports
TS26/64	War crimes general file
TS26/65a	War crimes general papers
TS26/65b	War crimes general notes
TS26/66	UNWCC General File
TS26/108	War crimes prior to D-Day
TS26/137	War crimes, German cases in suspense
TS26/189	United Nations War Crimes Commission UK/G/12
TS26/202	United Nations War Crimes Commission 124/UK/G/24
TS26/203	United Nations War Crimes Commission 125/UK/G/25
TS26/204	United Nations War Crimes Commission UK/G/26
TS26/205	United Nations War Crimes Commission UK/G/27
TS26/207	United Nations War Crimes Commission UK/G/29
TS26/208	United Nations War Crimes Commission UK/G/30
TS26/209	United Nations War Crimes Commission UK/G/31
TS26/210	United Nations War Crimes Commission UK/G/32
TS26/211	United Nations War Crimes Commission UK/G/33
TS26/212	United Nations War Crimes Commission UK/G/34
TS26/213	United Nations War Crimes Commission UK/G/35
TS26/214	United Nations War Crimes Commission UK/G/36
TS26/215	United Nations War Crimes Commission UK/G/37
TS26/216	United Nations War Crimes Commission UK/G/38
TS26/217	United Nations War Crimes Commission UK/G/39
TS26/218	United Nations War Crimes Commission UK/G/40
TS26/219	United Nations War Crimes Commission UK/G/41
TS26/220	United Nations War Crimes Commission UK/G/42
TS26/221	United Nations War Crimes Commission UK/G/43
TS26/222	United Nations War Crimes Commission UK/G/44
TS26/223	United Nations War Crimes Commission UK/G/45
TS26/224	United Nations War Crimes Commission UK/G/46
TS26/225	United Nations War Crimes Commission UK/G/47
TS26/226	United Nations War Crimes Commission UK/G/48

TS26/227	United Nations War Crimes Commission UK/G/49
TS26/228	United Nations War Crimes Commission UK/G/50
TS26/247	United Nations War Crimes Commission UK/G/69
TS26/400	United Nations War Crimes Commission UK/G/223
WO32/2982	Recruiting after mobilization
WO32/4447	Requisitioning of road transport vehicles
WO32/4496	Provision of officers on mobilization
WO32/4610	Criticism of organization and training of TA
WO32/4643	Physical standards for recruits
WO32/4645	Recruiting organization under National Service Act
WO32/4726	Committee on the examination of recruits by civilian medical boards under Armed Forces Act
WO32/9376	Repatriation of personnel protected by Red Cross Convention
WO32/9915	Applications for repatriation
WO32/9977	Enrolment of personnel called up for military training (Militia)
WO32/10742	Repatriation negotiations with the German Government: administration questions
WO32/10746	Repatriation of long-term POWs
WO32/10757	Rehabilitation of repatriated POWs
WO32/10950	Psychological aspects of rehabilitation of repatriated POWs
WO32/11129	Rehabilitation of British ex-POWs
WO32/11135	Negotiations with the German Government for repatriation of prisoners: third operation
WO32/11136	Second repatriation operation with Germany
WO32/11138	Negotiations with the German Government for the repatriation of POWs: fourth operation
WO 32/11692	Fourth repatriation operation with Germany. Reception and disposal of British POWs
WO32/13474	Enlistment of boys for general duties
WO32/16617	Territorial Army expansion
WO32/18489	Evacuation of POWs 1941
WO33/1558	War Office Reserve – mobilization appointments July 1939
WO33/1639	Mobilization, secret instructions – August 1939
WO33/1641	Mobilization of the Territorial Army
WO81/167	JAG letter books 1939
WO106/1727	Casualty figures for BEF
WO163/591	Repatriation Committee No. 1 (Policy): minutes of meetings and memoranda
WO163/592	Repatriation Committee No. 2 (Administration and Operations): minutes of meetings
WO163/593	Combined Repatriation Committee: minutes of meetings
WO166/4597	War Diary 4th Bn Royal Sussex Regiment
WO167/179	Casualty returns
WO167/448	War Diary 2nd Royal Tank Regiment 1940
WO167/762	War Diaries 4th Bn Royal West Kent Regiment 1940

WO167/804	War Diaries Buckinghamshire Battalion, Ox & Bucks Light Infantry
WO167/807	War Diaries 1/5th Queen's Regiment, 1940
WO167/808	War Diaries 2/5th Queen's Regiment, 1940
WO167/834	War Diary 4th Bn Royal Sussex Regiment
WO167/835	War Diary 5th Bn Royal Sussex Regiment
WO197/11	Visits to BEF – questionnaires
WO197/20	War Office visits
WO197/35	Deployment of BEF
WO197/37 to 39	Composition of BEF
WO197/58	Plan D instructions
WO197/74	Admin situation May 1940
WO197/87	1 Corps reports and notes
WO197/88	Evacuation progress reports
WO197/91	Diary of Major Finlayson
WO197/95	Bridge demolition reports
WO197/97	Reports and notes on Flanders campaign
WO197/98	Summary of 12th Division
WO197/99	Diary of Major General E.A. Osborne
WO197/111	Observations on operations
WO197/112	QM reports on BEF
WO197/116	Belgium operation reports
WO197/118	Reports by force commanders
WO197/124	Movements of 51st Highland Division, April to June 1940
WO197/125	Summary of events in Flanders
WO197/127	Summary of first year of the war
WO197/128	Experiences of 10th Field Regiment Royal Artillery
WO197/136	Lord Gort manuscript
WO197/137	Order of battle
WO197/138	Despatches on operations
WO199/1834	Mobilization plans in an emergency 1938/39
WO204/10264	Repatriation of POWs: Allied and Enemy
WO204/12899	Secret policy files: repatriation and handling of PoWs etc
WO222/18	TB among POWs
WO222/245	Account of 500 British wounded POWs
WO222/551	No. 133 Field Ambulance 1940
WO222/1382	Repatriation of seriously wounded POWs
WO222/1577	Reorganization of the TA 1939
WO229/61/2	Repatriation (exchange) of sick and wounded POWs and civilians with Germany: volume 1
WO229/61/1	Repatriation (exchange) of sick and wounded POWs and civilians with Germany: volume 2
WO258/22	Repatriation of POWs
WO309/28	Wormhoudt and Le Paradis massacres
WO309/857	Mistreatment of POWs at College of St Augustine, Enghien, Belgium
WO311/146	Murder of POWs at XXB
WO311/243	Murder of Ptes Johnson and Marsh

Index